The Weidenfeld and Nicolson Universal History

16: Central Asia

Central Asia

Gavin Hambly

with Alexandre Bennigsen, David
Bivar, Hélène Carrère d'Encausse,
Mahin Hajianpur, Alastair Lamb,
Chantal Lemercier-Quelquejay and
Richard Pierce

Weidenfeld and Nicolson
5 Winsley Street W1

DS
786
.H313

SBN 297 76314 8

Printed in Great Britain by
Morrison and Gibb Ltd, London and Edinburgh

Contents

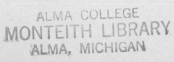

CONTENTS

Contributors to this volume:

Dr Gavin Hambly (Yale University), Introduction, Chapters 5–9, 12–13, 17–19

Prof. Alexandre Bennigsen (Ecole Pratique des Hautes Etudes, Paris), Chapter 14

Dr David Bivar (School of Oriental and African Studies, London), Chapters 1–4

Mme Hélène Carrère d'Encausse (Fondation Nationale des Sciences Politiques, Paris), Chapter 16

Mme Mahin Hajianpur (New Haven, Connecticut), Chapter 11.

Dr Alastair Lamb (University of Leeds), Chapter 20

Mme Chantal Lemercier-Quelquejay (Ecole Pratique des Hautes Etudes, Paris), Chapter 10

Prof. Richard Pierce (Queen's University, Kingston, Ontario), Chapter 15

Chapter 16 translated by Anne Carter

List of Illustrations

[*between pages* 212 *and* 213]

Acknowledgements

The publishers wish to thank the following for providing illustrations for this volume:

Paul Popper Ltd, plate 1; Karl Flinker and Thames & Hudson Ltd, plates 2, 3; Professor Charles Bawden, plate 4; The Oriental Institute, University of Chicago, plate 5; Hermitage Museum, Leningrad, plates 6, 18; Dr David Bivar, plates 7, 8, 9, 14; Archaeological Survey of India, plate 10; British Museum, plates 11, 12, 17, 22, 30, 32, 34; Staatliche Museen, Berlin, plates 13, 20; Délégation Archéologique Française en Afghanistan and Librairie C. Klincksieck, plate 15; Derek Hill and Faber & Faber Ltd, plates 16, 21, 25, 27, 28; Musée de l'Histoire de France, plate 19; Metropolitan Museum of Art, New York, plates 23, 31; B. A. Seaby Ltd, plate 24; Edition B. Arthaud, plate 26; J. A. P. Watson and Bernard Quaritch Ltd, plate 29 (also appearing on jacket); Paul Hamlyn Ltd, plate 33; John Freeman Ltd, plates 35, 38, 40, 41, 42; American Museum of Natural History, plate 36; National Museum of Ethnology, Leyden, Holland, plate 37; National Museum Copenhagen, plate 39; Ernst Wasmuth Verlag, plate 43.

Maps

[between pages 356 *and* 371]

Foreword

As a geographical expression the term 'Central Asia' tends to elude precise definition. In the pages which follow it is used primarily to describe the area comprising the Kazakh, Kirghiz, Tajik, Turkmen and Uzbek Soviet Socialist Republics of the USSR, the Mongolian People's Republic, and the three dependencies of China known today as the Inner Mongolian Autonomous Region, the Sinkiang-Uighur Autonomous Region and the Tibet Autonomous Region. Since, however, the peoples of Central Asia have been for many centuries in almost uninterrupted communication with their neighbours living beyond the fringes of the Eurasian steppe-zone the contributors to this volume have found it necessary to refer on many occasions to events and movements occurring beyond the borderlands of Central Asia proper.

Hitherto few attempts have been made to provide a general account of the history of this area and in preparing this book for publication the editor has felt keenly the lack of any previous survey of similar dimension to serve as a model. From the outset, however, it was realised that in a volume of this size it would not be possible to include a comprehensive narrative of events covering two thousand five hundred years of recorded history. The aim, therefore, has been to write a selective account which would concentrate upon those aspects of Central Asia's past which the contributors feel to be of particular significance. Of necessity, much of interest has had to be omitted and those who wish to investigate the history of the area in greater detail should consult the bibliographical references in the notes and the bibliography itself, both of which have been put together with this requirement primarily in mind.

Readers should note that the general discussion on pastoral nomadism which appears in the Introduction has been deliberately written in the past tense and is mainly concerned with conditions in pre-colonial and pre-industrial Central Asia. It should also be noted that no attempt has been made to enforce conformity in the transliteration of Central Asian names into English upon contributors working with source-material in a number of largely unrelated languages.

GAVIN HAMBLY,
Yale University

Introduction

The first and most striking geographical feature of Central Asia is its complete isolation from oceanic influences, resulting in a lack of precipitation which in turn produces conditions of extreme aridity over the greater part of the area. Geographical isolation from oceanic influences has its historical counterpart in the exclusion of the peoples of Central Asia from any role in the movements of maritime exploration, trade or political expansion which have played a major part in human history since at least the eighteenth century. Although Central Asia has always been in intimate contact with the regions which border it the fact remains that no other area in the Old World north of the Sahara has been so impervious to external pressures – at least until the eighteenth century when Russia and China began to advance their frontiers into the steppes.

The romantic equation of Central Asia with a vast expanse of desert and steppe is by no means inaccurate although it requires some modification and, as a general proposition, it may be fairly said that where the steppe and desert give way to a different landscape there Central Asia ends – as in the north where the steppes meet the southern limits of the *taïga*, the Siberian forest-zone. The southern boundary of Central Asia is marked by an almost unbroken chain of mountain ranges, nearly four thousand miles long, which run from China to the Black Sea and which restrict access in the direction of South-East Asia, the Indian sub-continent and the Middle East. From east to west these ranges are the Nan Shan, the Altyn Tagh, the Kun Lun, the

1

Karakorum, the Hindu Kush, the Paropamisus, the Elburz and the Caucasus. Only certain sections of this chain present insuperable barriers to human penetration although the Kun Lun are virtually impassable and the passes of the Karakorum were probably little used before the nineteenth century; the Hindu Kush, the Paropamisus and the Elburz have never restricted the movements of peoples in either direction. South of this chain are two plateaux whose history has been inextricably linked with that of Central Asia proper: Tibet, enclosed on the south by the Himalayas, and the Iranian plateau, flanked on the south-east by the Kirthar and Sulaiman ranges and on the south-west by the Zagros.

The eastern and western limits of Central Asia are less easily defined. In the east an approximate line can be drawn along the Great Wall of China and then extended northwards from Jehol following the edge of the Manchurian forest-zone; in the west, however, the grasslands of the Ukraine, extending as far as Rumania and Hungary, constitute both a geographical and historical extension of the Central Asian steppe-zone.

Despite the predominance of steppe and desert Central Asia possesses physical features ranging from some of the highest mountain ranges in the world to depressions such as those to be found north-east of the Caspian and around Turfan in Sinkiang, and there are comparable extremes of temperature. Lying approximately between latitude 35° and 55°, Central Asia can be divided for convenience into a northern and a southern zone by drawing an imaginary line along the Syr-Darya and the Tien Shan. Although arid in parts, much of the northern zone enjoys sufficient moisture to provide the extensive grazing which is a prerequisite for pastoral nomadism – the way of life of the Turkish and Mongol tribes which dominated the area until the appearance of large numbers of Russian and Chinese peasant colonists in the late nineteenth and twentieth centuries.

The southern zone, having very little precipitation, is extremely arid and consists mainly of desert so that prior to the massive irrigation projects initiated by the Soviet Government most of the population was confined to the oases and to the riverine tracts where, by means of the skilful application of hydraulic techniques, intensive cultivation of the land has been practised since very early times. Here too the civilizing influences of Iranian culture and of Islam have long been characteristic features of urban and oasis society. Apart from the lure of its wealthy cities this southern zone possessed few attractions for the pastoral nomads so that although, for example, nomad raiders from north of the Tien Shan from time to time plundered and occupied the oases of the Tarim basin they never remained in large numbers where the pastures were poor and where shortage of water necessitated laborious irrigation-works.

In striking contrast to the steppes and deserts are the great mountain ranges which bestraddle the area from the southern end of the Caspian to the shores of Lake Baikal. Highest of these are the Pamirs, stretching northwards from the knot where the Himalayas, the Karakorum and the Hindu Kush meet and not inappropriately styled the Roof of the World, with Muztagh Ata rising to 24,388 feet and some of the Qungur peaks exceeding 25,000 feet. Separating the Tarim basin from the basins of the Amu-Darya and Syr-Darya, the Pamirs are approached from the north and west by a series of lesser ranges which enclose the valleys through which the Amu-Darya and the Syr-Darya descend to the plains – Badakhshan, famous among mediaeval travellers for its turquoise and ruby mines, and fertile Farghana, home of the 'celestial horses' so highly prized in T'ang China. North-east of the Pamirs and stretching far to the east towards the Gobi are the Tien Shan which separate the fertile valley of the Ili and Jungaria to the north from the arid Tarim basin (Kashgaria) to the south. The Tien Shan, the Pamirs and Kun Lun enclose the latter region on every side except towards the east. Unlike the forbidding Kun Lun, the Tien Shan have never prevented intercourse between the areas to the north and south of them and in this respect they resemble the loftier Pamirs. Known to the Chinese as the Heavenly Mountains, the Tien Shan are one of the grandest ranges of Asia, with Khan Tengri reaching a height of 23,600 feet.

To the north-east of the Tien Shan and rising to a height of some 10,000 feet are the Altai, traditional home of the Turkish peoples and linked with the Tien Shan by a series of low ranges

– the Jungarian Ala Tau and the Khrebet Tarbagatai – pierced by long valleys through which nomadic peoples have so often made their way from Jungaria and the Gobi region into what is now Kazakhstan. Further to the north and east of the Altai lie the eastern and western Sayan ranges, the mountains of Outer Mongolia, and these extend almost as far as Lake Baikal. Thus it may be said that Central Asia is divided into two halves by an uneven chain of mountain ranges running from south-west to north-east, starting near Herat in western Afghanistan and ending in the neighbourhood of Irkutsk in Siberia. With the exception of the Uighurs of Sinkiang and the Chinese Dungans, Muslim influences have tended to be restricted to the western side of this chain while the eastern side has been strongly influenced by Tibetan Buddhist and Chinese civilization.

The configuration of the mountain ranges has exercised a profound effect upon the movements of the peoples of Central Asia. At least equally decisive has been the influence of the deserts – the Ust Urt between the Caspian and the Aral Sea, the Kara Kum between the Kopet Dagh (the northern escarpment of the eastern Elburz) and the Amu-Darya, the Kizil Kum dividing the lower reaches of the Amu-Darya from those of the Syr-Darya, the semi-desert of the Betpak Dala (known as the Hungry Steppe) between the Syr-Darya and Lake Balkhash, the immense Gobi dividing Inner and Outer Mongolia, and the Takla Makan south of the Tien Shan which Aurel Stein considered 'probably the most formidable of all the dune-covered wastes of this globe'. East of the wind-eroded loess of the Takla Makan lies the Lop-Nor (the salt crust of the old Lop Sea which originally extended some 160 miles south-west to north-east with a maximum width of about 90 miles) and beyond that again lies the Pei Shan. It was the utter desolation of these three deserts – the basins of the Tarim, the Sulu Ho and the Etsin Gol – which led the American geographer Ellsworth Huntington to assume that Central Asia was a region characterized by major desiccation and cyclical climatic changes. Huntington's theories, however, were far from confirmed by the archaeological discoveries of Stein who concluded

that climatic conditions quite as arid as the present ones prevailed

4

INTRODUCTION

within the big trough of the Tarim basin as far back as ancient
remains and available records can take us. The other conclusion is
that the amount of water carried by its rivers has greatly diminished
during the same historical period.[1]

Central Asia has fulfilled two distinct and in some ways contradictory functions in the history of mankind. On the one hand,
as a result of its enormous extent, prevailing aridity and the
absence of natural means of communications (most of its major
river-systems flow north into the Arctic Ocean) its principal
function has been to keep apart from each other the civilizations
which lies on its peripheries – Chinese, Indian, Iranian, Russian,
etc. On the other hand, its ancient caravan-routes provided a
slender but almost unbroken thread by means of which those
same peripheral civilizations acquired a limited knowledge of
their neighbours in addition to valuable commodities which
might otherwise have been inaccessible or at least more difficult
to obtain.

In terms of commerce, manufacture and cultural achievement
probably the most important part of Central Asia has always
been the area bordering the Amu-Darya and the Syr-Darya –
known to the Greeks as the Oxus and the Jaxartes and to the
Arabs as the Jayhun and the Sayhun.[2] South of the Amu-Darya
and extending south-west as far as the Iranian Dasht-i Kavir lay
the country known to the Arabs as Khurasan (a far more extensive area than the modern Iranian province of that name) and in
mediaeval times its principal cities – Nishapur, Tus (later super-
seded by Mashhad), Marv, Herat and Balkh – were famous for
their commercial activity and fine craftsmanship, especially in
metal-work. Between the middle reaches of the Amu-Darya and
the Syr-Darya lay the country known to the Greeks as Transoxania and to the Arabs as Mawarannahr, with Bukhara and
Samarqand as its most important urban centres during the
Muslim period. Khwarazm lay on the lower reaches of the
Amu-Darya due south of the Aral Sea with Urganj as its early
mediaeval capital, later to be replaced by Khiva which by the
nineteenth century had given its name to the surrounding
countryside. North-east from Mawarannahr beyond the Syr-
Darya was Shash, the country around Tashkent, and the cities

5

of Shash, like those of neighbouring Farghana, were celebrated in mediaeval times for their manufacture of armour, weapons and saddles although not one of them equalled in size or importance the major cities of Mawarannahr or Khurasan. Moreover, their location made them more vulnerable to periodic upheavals among their nomadic neighbours. This whole area, in addition to producing a disproportionately large number of Muslim scholars, artists and craftsmen of a very high calibre, occupied a key-position in the organization of transcontinental commerce between the Far East, the Middle East and the Mediterranean world. Its role in this traffic, coupled with its inhabitants' possession of high-quality manufacturing skills, accounts for the prominent place of Mawarannahr and the adjacent territory in the history of Central Asia during the early mediaeval period.

Over many centuries the Central Asian caravan-trade followed a number of different routes but the most important were always those which linked China with the West. Before the establishment of the Mongol Empire in the thirteenth century the most frequented routes seem to have passed through Kashgaria, starting at the Tun-huang oasis in Kansu and then following either a route south of the Takla Makan running north of the Altyn Tagh to Khotan and Yarkand before commencing the crossing of the Pamirs or, alternatively, skirting the Lop-Nor to Hami and Turfan[3] and then passing on through Kucha and Aqsu to Kashgar and the approaches to the Pamirs. There was also a third alternative for caravans reaching Turfan which could then turn north-west into Jungaria and the Semirechie, leaving the Tien Shan to the south, and come down to the north bank of the Syr-Darya.

From the Syr-Darya caravans could either travel across the steppes north of the Aral Sea and the Caspian towards the Black Sea ports or, alternatively, cross the river (generally at Otrar) and enter Mawarannahr, heading either for Urganj in Khwarazm or for Samarqand and Bukhara where they would meet the traffic coming down from the Pamirs through the Farghana valley (the southern crossing of the Pamirs came down into Badakhshan and led towards Balkh south of the Amu-Darya). From Bukhara the Amu-Darya was usually crossed at Charjui

6

on the road to Marv although caravans bound for Kabul and the Indus crossed higher up stream in the direction of Balkh and the passes over the Hindu Kush. From Marv the caravans either converged on Herat or took the direct route to Nishapur and thence to Ray (close to modern Tehran) where they had a choice of roads: south to Isfahan, south-west to Hamadan and Baghdad, or due west to Tabriz and Byzantium.

Political circumstances naturally affected the importance, security and popularity of any one route at any given time. Under the thirteenth-century *Pax Mongolica*, for example, the routes north of the Tien Shan through the Semirechie and Jungaria appear to have been preferred to the ancient routes through Kashgaria. In the seventeenth and eighteenth centuries, after the Russians had penetrated as far as the Lake Baikal region, many traders chose to travel through the far northern fringes of the steppe-zone where they could enjoy Russian protection for at least part of the way.

Even apart from the dangers of warfare and banditry the physical discomforts likely to be met with on the road were forbidding and the distances to be traversed immense. Transport depended upon beasts of burden which were slower than ships and not necessarily safer: the horse, the mule and the ass, the one-humped camel in the south-west and the Bactrian camel in colder climates, the yak and the hainag (a cross between a bull-yak and a domestic cow) at high altitudes, and carts drawn by horses, oxen and camels. Messengers on post-horses and cavalry accompanied by re-mounts undoubtedly travelled fast but for ordinary travellers – merchants, pilgrims or mere adventurers – the enormous distances were made worse by the tedious pace of their beasts. The camel, the most important beast of burden in the arid zones of the world, generally set the pace, travelling four miles per hour unloaded or two and a half to three miles per hour loaded, and probably covering thirty miles a day with an average load of three hundred pounds.[4] The Russian explorer Przhevalsky noted that in the Khalkha country the huge Mongolian camel, which could carry a load of five hundred pounds, covered twenty-eight miles a day compared to Mongolian horses which covered forty to forty-seven miles. The camels of the Koko-Nor region covered no more than twenty miles a day.[5]

The fourteenth-century Florentine merchant Pegolotti left a description of the northern route from the Black Sea to China which vividly illustrates the way in which the mediaeval traveller made his painful way across Central Asia.[6] Starting from the mouth of the Don the merchant whose ultimate destination was China had an initial journey of twenty-five days by ox-wagon or ten or twelve by horse-wagon to the Volga close to the site of Astrakhan from which point he would probably make a detour up river to Saray, residence of the Khans of the Golden Horde. From Saray he would sail down the Volga into the Caspian and then ascend the Ural River to Saraychik, the principal settlement of the Noghay Tatars, a voyage of eight days which was four days shorter than the same journey by land. After Saraychik there was insufficient fodder for horses and since Europeans were unaccustomed to the motion of camel-riding they usually travelled in camel-drawn wagons. In this manner the journey from Saraychik to Urganj took twenty days (Ibn Battuta in the same period reckoned thirty to forty) and from Urganj to Otrar another thirty-five to forty days, still in wagons. Most traders followed this route in order to transact business in Urganj but it was quicker to travel from Saraychik to Otrar direct in around fifty days. From Otrar through the Semirechie to Almaliq in the valley of the Ili was reckoned to take forty-five days with pack-asses, and from Almaliq it was a further seventy days with pack-asses through Jungaria to Kanchow (modern Changyeh) in the Kansu Corridor. From here the traveller still had ahead of him at least a further forty-five days on horseback to Hangchow (Marco Polo's Quinsai) and thirty more to Peking. The whole journey would have taken at least nine months yet Pegolotti probably erred on the optimistic side and made no allowance for the almost inevitable delays to which most travellers at some stage or another were exposed. In comparison, it is interesting to note that in the nineteenth and early twentieth centuries under Manchu rule caravans from Peking to Urumchi in Sinkiang were estimated to take eight to twelve months on the road.[7]

It was in the regular contacts of commercial life rather than

8

through the spasmodic impact of war that the sedentary societies on its fringes became familiar with the peoples of Central Asia, a region so long exposed to the ebb and flow of races that it has inevitably produced racial and linguistic patterns of great diversity and complexity although down to at least the end of the eighteenth century the general trend has been for Turkish peoples and languages to supersede or overwhelm their predecessors. Even the thirteenth-century Mongol conquests did little to modify this trend, the Turkish tribal aristocracies thereafter claiming descent from Chingiz Khan or his paladins with as much pride as did the true Mongols.

There can be little doubt that, outside the oases and the cities, Central Asia has always been an area of low population density due partly to climatic conditions, prevailing aridity and lack of precipitation but also to the requirements of a pastoral nomadic economy which demands vast areas of grazing-land in place of the man-power essential for hydraulic agriculture, the extensive animal husbandry of Central Asia being the complete antithesis of the intensive cultivation characteristic of, for example, northern China. It may also be, as some have suggested, that extreme cold (as on the Tibetan plateau) and a continuous life in the saddle reduce sexual potency.[8]

The study of Central Asian demography is bedevilled by sharply conflicting evidence and interpretations of that evidence so that the subject will probably long remain one of acute controversy. The following figures, therefore, aim to provide the reader with no more than a very rough framework based upon the present situation.[9] Chinese and Slav colonists, as well as the smaller minorities, have been excluded.

Uzbeks	Over 6 million	Muslim Turks
Uighurs	Around 4 million	Muslim Turks
Dungans	Around 4 million[10]	Muslim Chinese
Kazakhs	Less than 4 million	Muslim Turks
Mongols	Around 3 million[11]	Buddhists
Tibetans	Less than 3 million	Buddhists
Tajiks	1½ million[12]	Muslim Iranians
Turkomans	1½ million	Muslim Turks
Kirghiz	1 million	Muslim Turks
Karakalpaks	Less than 200,000	Muslim Turks

Prior to the establishment of industry in the region and the introduction of mechanized transport, neither of which were much in evidence before 1917, the peoples of Central Asia had evolved over many centuries two entirely distinctive and highly specialized ways of life which to some extent were complementary to each other but in certain respects were mutually antagonistic. The first of these consisted of sedentary agricultural communities to be found on the banks of rivers such as the Zarafshan and the Tarim or in the oases where the construction of elaborate irrigation-works permitted intensive cultivation of the land. Such settlements (perhaps best exemplified by the Marv oasis in the Kara Kum) formed little islands of cultivation surrounded by desert or steppe and although they were often isolated from each other they were comparatively self-sufficient for most every-day needs. It was in such oases or at river-crossings that there grew up the towns which were to play an essential part in the operation of the transcontinental caravan traffic, in addition to developing as manufacturing or distributing centres for some valuable local product. Inevitably, the location of these towns tended to produce among their inhabitants a recognizable 'oasis-mentality' characterized by an absence of intellectual curiosity only partly offset by the comings and goings of those employed in the caravan trade. As for the urban elites, their culture was generally an extension of that of contemporary China or Iran and at least in the southwest it was the urban centres which acted as spearheads for the penetration of Muslim civilization into Central Asia. Almost down to the twentieth century the cities of Mawarannahr and the western part of Kashgaria remained cultural offshoots of Iran so that the traveller leaving Isfahan or Mashhad for Bukhara or Yarkand would find upon reaching his destination a way of life not altogether unfamiliar.

The other and more characteristic way of life in Central Asia was that of the nomadic tribes on the steppes where conditions favoured a pastoral economy which enabled men to dispense with the toil of cultivating the land and even permanent settlement in one location. From their livestock – reindeer, horses, camels, sheep, cattle, yaks, etc. – the nomads obtained food, clothing, shelter, fuel and transport as well as a surplus of products with which to barter with their sedentary neighbours for such necessities as grain and metalware which a nomadic life could not provide.[13] Not only, therefore, were the nomads almost self-sufficient economically. Their mode of life allowed them enough mobility to give them an overwhelming advantage in warfare against agricultural communities, especially if they happened to be hunters and horse-breeders since such occupations presuppose a skill in archery and horsemanship impossible for farmers or oasis-dwellers enlisted as soldiers for short campaigns to acquire without long practice.

Yet the dependence of the nomads upon their animals is worth stressing. Loss of their flocks and herds meant starvation and this factor firmly restricted the extent of their mobility since they would never willingly take their beasts where there was insufficient water or grazing. They themselves might live hard and in small numbers even penetrate the most inhospitable desert-regions when out raiding or eluding pursuit but they could not expect comparable feats of endurance from their animals without serious loss of life. Thus their mobility – so striking in comparison with the immobility of the riparian or oasis cultivator – was nevertheless restricted, except in times of extreme crisis, by the distance and terrain over which cattle, sheep or horses could be driven with safety and they would certainly not want to tax their beasts' strength more than necessary. The notion of nomadic hordes sweeping across Asia accompanied by apparently untiring flocks and herds beyond count is a fanciful exaggeration of the physical potentialities of pastoral nomadic life. In fact, the migration from winter to summer pastures often covered a comparatively short distance which might nevertheless represent a marked change in altitude or climate as with the Kirghiz of the Tien Shan who passed the winter months in sheltered valleys only a few miles below their exposed summer feeding-grounds several thousand feet above them. Pastoral nomadism has shown a tendency to develop in different directions both from one region to another and from one period to another so that it is unwise to attempt generalizations or to draw conclusions about, for example, thirteenth-

11

century Mongol society from observations made in eighteenth-
or nineteenth-century Mongolia or, even more, Kazakhstan.
Moulded by factors absent from sedentary societies Central
Asian nomadism has had its own history of change and transformation reflecting not only the internal tensions of pastoral
nomadic life but also the impact upon the steppe peoples of the
civilizations which bordered their territory.

It is perhaps worth stressing that the nomad was not only a
member of a family but also of a clan or sub-clan, a tribe and
sometimes even a tribal confederation and with each of these
units he shared a well-defined relationship based upon long-
established traditions of mutual loyalty and obligation. Whether
at the level of family, clan or tribe, leadership was a crucial
factor since without it flocks and herds could not be protected,
pastures and water-holes defended, aggressive neighbours
repelled and marauding expeditions undertaken. Hence there
was a tendency for pastoral nomadism in a Central Asian setting
to encourage the development of hierarchical relationships
between families and groups which has been described, not
inaccurately, as 'nomad feudalism'. Leadership was, of course,
determined by a combination of factors in addition to the
obvious qualities of physical prowess and a dominant personality: wealth in livestock, a large following of retainers, a
favourable distribution of traditional tribal and clan loyalties,
and distinguished ancestry. After the thirteenth century it
became almost a pre-requisite over much of Central Asia for a
tribal leader to be able to claim that the blood of Chingiz Khan
flowed in his veins and throughout the Chinese borderlands the
princely title of *khungtayji* eventually came to mean a descendant
of Chingiz Khan.

Nomadic life demanded a more robust physique than that
needed by the sedentary oasis-dweller. It also demanded a more
independent mind which might, in times of crisis, be called upon
to make swift judgements and take the initiative in a way
scarcely conceivable to the cultivator bound to the ceaseless
routine of the farming calendar. In the struggle for pastures, in
inter-tribal warfare and in pursuance of the blood-feud the
nomad naturally developed aggressive instincts which, taken

12

with his need for the products of sedentary society, often led him to prey upon his settled neighbours. These predatory habits and the destructiveness which accompanied them won for the nomad a reputation for innate savagery yet although he might prove himself reckless in the taking of human life he rarely indulged in the sophisticated cruelties of Imperial Peking or Byzantium. He invariably held in contempt the settled population of the oases and although the Mongols, for example, always sought the gold and silver, silks and cereals of China, at times even serving as auxiliaries for Chinese women or titles, they always despised the Chinese just as the nomadic Turkoman or Kazakh despised the farmer and townsman of Mawarannahr, whether Tajik or settled Uzbek. The historian who regards pastoral nomadism as an inferior activity to agriculture is likely to be misled in his reading of the Central Asian past since he will certainly fail to appreciate the immense prestige (based primarily upon superior military prowess) which the nomad has usually enjoyed among the oasis-dwellers. While it has been more common for nomads to be converted into cultivators than for cultivators to be converted into nomads (even when allowance is made for an element of compulsion, as in the case of the decline of pastoral nomadism in twentieth-century Inner Mongolia) there are also recorded cases of individual cultivators as well as cultivating communities opting for the more aristocratic life of the saddle.[14]

Unlike the oasis-dweller in whom isolation not infrequently bred fanaticism the nomad tended to be latitudinarian in religious matters. Before the advent of Islam and Buddhism in Central Asia he relied for spiritual comfort upon the supernatural powers of the shamans who could communicate with dead ancestors and act as intermediaries with the spirit-world which resided in all natural phenomena – in earth, wind and water, on the mountain peaks and in the trees of the forest, in the sudden storm made more frightening by the solitude of the steppes and in the sky stretching endlessly away beyond an unknown horizon. It was only by adopting the ways of the shamans and their lore that the Muslim dervish or the Buddhist lama could gain any lasting ascendancy over the nomad's mind. By the nineteenth century the majority of Central Asian nomads were Muslims but orthodoxy rested lightly upon many of them, especially in the case of the Kazakhs and the Kirghiz who lived so far from the heartlands of Islam. Ignoring the injunctions of the Quran the nomad drank his *kumis* (an alcoholic beverage made from fomented mare's milk) and sometimes blood, and consumed carrion and animals which had died a natural death.

Relations between the sexes among the Central Asian nomads were also in striking contrast to the sexual *mores* of Arabia and the older Islamic lands where men and women were strictly segregated and where female virginity before marriage was sacrosanct and its pre-marital loss (like adultery after marriage) punishable by death. Even among the Central Asian nomads who became Muslims the sexes tended to fraternize relatively freely, there was mixed dancing on festive occasions and sexual matters were often alluded to with less reserve in conversations between men and women. Neither loss of pre-marital virginity nor female infidelity after marriage incurred the full rigour of Muslim law and all this, in part at least, reflected the very different role played by women in Central Asian nomadic society from that played in purely sedentary societies. The women were an important element in the pastoral nomadic household not only managing the home and weaving but also assisting with the animals, especially in the breeding and sharing seasons, milking the beasts and weaning their young, guarding and handling them when the male members of the household were away, and (since they were necessarily as skilful on horseback as their menfolk) helping when the flocks and herds were on the move. Obviously the status of women among the nomads of Central Asia has shown marked variations from one area to another and from one tribe to another so that the subject remains a matter of controversy, some emphasizing that the nomadic woman's life has generally been one of unremitting drudgery, with few rights worth the name and almost always subject to the institution of the *qalym* (bride-price), while others have favourably compared the liberty she enjoyed with the secluded lives and veiled faces of the women of the Middle East whose relatively passive role in the annals of Islam (even among

14

ruling dynasties) is in sharp contrast with the authority and influence exercised publicly by the wives, widows and sisters of the Chingizkhanids and even the Muslim Timurids in Mawarannahr.

The nomadic life was generally monotonous and allowed little scope for artistic expression so that the tribesman's creative potentialities were restricted to a narrow range of activities – the weaving of carpets and rugs, saddle-bags and simple tent-furniture – in the making of which he nevertheless could demonstrate a subtle sense of colour and design. Since most nomadic peoples were illiterate (the Mongol and Tibetan nomads of the Lamaistic period were, to some extent, exceptional) nomadic literature was generally an oral one consisting largely of poetry and legends built around ancestral deeds of valour and the traditions of the tribe. The proudest possessions of chieftains and the richer families were luxury goods acquired from the peoples of the oases or from the peoples living beyond the borders of the steppes – sometimes by means of war but more often by legitimate trade. The commercial history of Central Asia has yet to be attempted but the general pattern is tolerably clear: nomadic rulers patronized commerce because by taxing the caravans instead of plundering them they assured themselves of a regular revenue with which to purchase necessities such as weapons and metalware as well as the luxuries for which they and their women craved. In return, they assumed the responsibility of ensuring the safety of the goods passing through their territories, thus providing additional employment for their followers as caravan-guards and guides.

The nomads themselves supplied their neighbours with a number of useful commodities – horses and cattle, hides, felt, wool, hair, slaves (such as the Turkish slaves who made up the *mamluk* armies of mediaeval Baghdad, Cairo, and Delhi), hunting eagles and falcons – as well as passing on the products of the far north such as furs, iron, amber, and walrus and mammoth ivory. In return they obtained such necessities as cereals, domestic utensils, weapons and horse-accoutrements as well as luxuries for the ruling elite and, after the seventeenth century, for the Buddhist monasteries in Mongolia such as silks, precious

15

metals and jewellery, elaborately finished arms, armour and saddles, and tea.

Before the advance of Russia into Central Asia in the eighteenth and nineteenth centuries the most important neighbours of the nomads in terms of both cultural contacts and commerce were the Chinese and the Iranians. Over many centuries Chinese contacts with the nomads fluctuated between a policy of active diplomacy, reinforced from time to time by punitive expeditions, and a policy of static defence based upon a system of walls and watch-towers such as the elaborate *limes* which Stein uncovered in the Kansu Corridor. Iranian regimes, despite the surviving remains of defensive works east of the Caspian in Gurgan, rarely operated a closed frontier system – perhaps because the intermediate zone between the Amu-Darya and the Syr-Darya with its mixed population of nomads and oasis-dwellers acted as a sort of buffer between Iran and the steppe-region proper. Not that this prevented the invasion of Iran by successive waves of nomads or semi-nomads although the fact that these invaders often acquired a veneer of Iranian and Muslim culture during their initial penetration of Mawarannahr did ensure that the impact of their arrival in Iran itself was not so disastrous as it might otherwise have been. On the whole, however, China's traditional awareness of the need for a frontier policy, whether aggressive or defensive according to the period, enabled her to maintain a more positive relationship than Iran with her nomadic neighbours. This relationship has frequently been described in terms of a tribal zone lying outside the Great Wall where nomadic hordes perpetually hovered, waiting until some indication of weakness inside China or some powerful impulse among the tribes themselves (such as the emergence of a leader capable of binding them into a temporarily cohesive confederacy) launched them into action. Generalizations of this sort are not wholly false but they certainly need to be kept in proper perspective since for long periods the relations between China and the frontier tribes were relatively stable and mutually fruitful. It needs to be emphasized that the economic system of northern China and that of the nomads were complementary to each other: the Chinese farming communities required livestock, hides and wool from the nomads almost as much as the latter wanted Chinese cereals and metalware.

Until the advent of artillery in Central Asia the nomads were usually victorious when they fought their sedentary neighbours although their numerical inferiority rarely permitted them to press home their advantage. Since protracted warfare which could dislocate agricultural life and interfere with the regular maintenance of elaborate irrigation-works was less harmful to a pastoral economy the nomads were better able to face a war of attrition than were armies of peasants anxious to return to the cultivation of their fields although nomad military superiority was due primarily to a combination of mobility and skill in the use of the bow which made the mounted archer almost invincible prior to the invention of gunpowder. If discipline could be added to this combination – as it was by Chingiz Khan and his lieutenants – the feigned retreat and the ambush which followed it hardly ever failed.

The most useful weapons in steppe warfare were the bow and the long lance, the latter sometimes equipped with a hook for hauling enemy riders out of the saddle, and these were supplemented by a battle-axe or mace, a sword or scimitar, a lasso and a dagger. One weapon which was perhaps indigenous to the steppes and was originally used by horsemen attacking Chinese infantry was a flail consisting of a wooden cudgel to which was attached a chain ending in another piece of wood bound with iron. This was subsequently adopted by the Chinese themselves and used down to the reign of Ch'ien-lung (1735–1796).[15] The use of armour in Central Asia must date from very early times. Hide treated in various ways was probably the first protective material to be extensively adopted and it was described in the thirteenth century by William of Rubruck. The possession of stronger, more elaborate and costlier armour such as chain, ring or scale mail implied some degree of wealth although, as in mediaeval Europe, the wearing of armour by horse and rider greatly reduced mobility – as the Timurids of the late fifteenth and early sixteenth century found to their cost when fighting the more lightly-armed Uzbeks. Throughout the Muslim period the cities of Iran and Mawarannahr were important manufacturing centres of arms and armour for the peoples of Central Asia, even for the distant Tibetans who were still fighting in protective mail as late as the Younghusband expedition of 1904.

Artillery and firearms made their appearance in Central Asia from the sixteenth century onwards and once these became part of the standard military equipment of the Russian and Chinese armies which blazed the trail for the subsequent establishment of permanent garrisons and colonies in the steppes the nomad lost for ever both his former military superiority over his neighbours and also his ability to determine his own destiny, bringing to an end the role of Central Asia as a dynamic element in world history.

1

The Achaemenids and the Macedonians: Stability and Turbulence

In the seventh century BC when history opens in the steppes east of the Caspian Sea, a large-scale nomad migration was already in progress. The powerful tribal confederacy known as the Massagetae had driven westwards across the Volga the peoples who later became celebrated as the Scythians. These Scythians arriving in the Ukraine in turn displaced the Cimmerians, its earlier inhabitants, whom they pursued headlong across the Caucasus into Anatolia. The triumphant Scythians, reaching the neighbourhood of Lake Urmia, encountered and overcame Cyaxares, the Median ruler of Iran. Thus for twenty-eight years, under their prince Madyes, the son of Protothyes, they were able to enjoy the suzerainty of Asia. It was only after Cyaxares had contrived the massacre of their chiefs at a banquet – so tradition records – that the surviving Scythians were driven back from Asia into the Ukraine. Having secured his flank by this success, the Median king was free to turn south, and prepare his attack on Nineveh. There followed in 612 BC the sack of the capital city and the extinction of the empire and civilization of Assyria.

Commentators have expended much labour to elucidate Herodotus' narrative of these events.[1] A variant tradition held – with less probability – that it was the Issedones, not the Massagetae who expelled the Scythians from Central Asia. Yet a variety of fabulous details scarcely impairs the charm of the old historian's survey of the steppe peoples. East of the mountains (it may be either the Pamirs or the Urals that are meant) lived the Argippaei,[2] a bald-headed race with flat noses and large chins, feeding on the juice of wild cherries. Their religious sanctity protected them from attack, enabling them to arbitrate in the disputes of their neighbours. Further east dwelt the Issedones, who seem to be rightly identified with the Wusun known from Chinese sources.[3] Discoveries in the tumuli of Pazyryk appear to confirm the Herodotean account of the practice of ceremonial cannibalism by this people. Further east, beyond the Issedones was the home of the 'one-eyed' Arimaspians.

The peoples named are not all so easily identifiable, either in Chinese or Old Persian sources, or from archaeological finds. Another clue to their locations is the statement, in another context, that the habitat of the Massagetae lay 'opposite' to that of the Issedones.[4] The latter seem to have frequented the Altai; subsequent narrative makes clear that the Massagetae were regarded as occupying the steppe north of the River Jaxartes (Syr-Darya), where they reappear during the career of Cyrus the Great of Persia (559–530 BC).

In 550 BC Cyrus had overthrown the empire of the Medes, and extended Persian rule eastwards from Iran into Central Asia. The story of his conquests is not preserved in detail, but a tribe along the River Helmand were accounted royal benefactors for their services in supplying his army,[5] and Cyrus is said to have demolished the city of Capisa,[6] metropolis of the fertile Koh-i Daman Valley north of Kabul. Another tradition held that Cyrus had led an army through the deserts of Gedrosia (Baluchistan). On the Jaxartes the city of Cyropolis is evidence of his activity in that region.[7]

The fatal moment came in about 530 BC when Cyrus attempted to extend his power north of the River 'Araxes',[8] and to subdue the Massagetae. After their queen, Tomyris, had allowed the Persians to cross the river unopposed, Cyrus by a stratagem won a short-lived success, and captured Spargapises, son of Tomyris, who quickly put an end to his own life. Then the main force of the Massagetae met the Persians in bitter contest. The Persians were defeated, and Cyrus, founder of the Achaemenid Empire, was slain.

The seriousness of this disaster seems none the less to be over-stated in our sources. For the body of Cyrus was apparently recovered for interment in his homeland at Pasargadae,[9] and Achaemenid rule endured between the Jaxartes and the Indus. Any disturbances, indeed, were due not to invaders from the steppe – if we except an uncertain reference to the Pointed-Cap Sacae in the Behistun inscription[10] – but to internal conflicts within the Persian empire. After the death of Cyrus' son, Cambyses, and the usurpation of the Magian pretender Gaumata in 522 BC, Darius the Great (522–486 BC) seized power with the help of six fellow-conspirators. In many parts of the empire disturbances followed. East of the Caspian, in Parthia and Hyrcania, the governor was Hystaspes (Old Persian Vištaspa), the father of Darius. He was abandoned by the provincials, who declared their support for a Median rebel Fravartish. Hystaspes defeated them in battle, and when reinforcements arrived from Darius at Raga (Ray) he won a second, decisive, victory. In Margiana, a rebel named Frada was overthrown by Dadarshi, satrap of Bactria loyal to Darius. In Arachosia, partisans of the Persian rebel Vahyazdata were suppressed by the satrap Vivana after battle at Kapishakani.[11] With Hystaspes, father of Darius and hero of the insurrection in Parthia, some authorities are inclined to identify the traditional patron of the Iranian prophet Zoroaster, who was also called Vištaspa (New Persian Gushtasp). It is true that the dialect of the Avestan scriptures associated with Zoroaster belongs to the north-east of Iran, which was the scene of Hystaspes' activity. The identification may even be compatible with Zoroaster's traditional date, '258 years before Alexander', which if related to the Seleucid Era of 311 BC[12] would place the prophet's date (perhaps his birth) in 569 BC. Yet in view of the conflicting interpretations of the prophet's chronology which scholars have put forward, and which were wittily reviewed by Henning in his Oxford lectures,[13] it should probably be admitted that the career of the prophet cannot yet be discussed in strictly historical terms.

Whether or not they therefore involved Zoroaster, these dis-turbances in the provinces of Central Asia were of short duration. The Old Persian inscriptions regularly list these provinces,[14] and Herodotus (III, 91 ff.) could even quote their annual assessments of tribute to the Persian treasury.

Province		Tribute in Talents[15]
Parthia	⎫	
Aria	⎪	
Chorasmia	⎬	300
Sogdia	⎭	
Bactria (with adjoining tribes)		360
Drangiana (with the Sagartians, Thamanaei, Utii and Myci)[16]		600
Gandara (with the Dadicae and Aparytae)	⎫	
Sattagydia	⎬	170
Sacae	⎫	
Caspians	⎬	250

The assessments give an indication of the relative economic importance of each province, but the figure for Drangiana (the Sistan basin), even allowing for the great decline of the area in modern times, appears unduly high. There is some confusion in the list, since Arachosia is omitted – it was perhaps consolidated with Drangiana – and Pactyica on the Upper Indus erroneously grouped with Armenia, the true position being clear from Herodotus III, 102. On the whole, however, the list is very informative.

Achaemenid control of these provinces was no doubt fully effective during the reign of Darius I. His Susa building-inscription records that gold for the work on the palace was obtained from Bactria, lapis-lazuli and carnelian from Sogdiana, and turquoise from Chorasmia. Ivory came, naturally, from India and Ethiopia, but also from the province of Arachosia.[17] This region of modern Afghanistan, around the city of Kandahar, supports no elephants today. If the ancient province extended as far east as the Indus Valley[18] it may have harboured a few; if not, it is merely a question of Indian ivory re-exported.

It is clear that the Persian empire imported gold across its eastern frontiers, and exported it to the west. Silver, however, came as tribute from the Aegaean and Balkan areas, and tended to travel eastwards. Evidence of this trend is the Chaman

Huzuri hoard of Greek silver, buried near Kabul c. 380 BC and discovered in 1933.[19] Such bullion movements were a natural consequence of the strict bimetallism maintained by the Achaemenids.[20]

Its impact on agriculture was however the most far-reaching economic consequence of Achaemenid rule in Central Asia. Xenophon, who knew the Persians well, lays stress on their active agricultural policy,[21] which was no doubt partly motivated by a wish to increase the land-revenue. Herodotus (III, 117) gives a rather confused anecdote of irrigation works carried out in Central Asia. It is obvious that no single barrage, however opportunely placed, could have at once commanded the water-supplies of Chorasmia, Hyrcania, Drangiana and the unlocated Thamanaei, as he seems to have supposed, but he may have conflated accounts of numerous engineering works. His cynical informant implies that the purpose of the scheme was to extort dues from the cultivators by holding back the water-supply. It is a fact that irrigation works can in time of stress assist a centralized regime to impose its will on the countryside, and that a minority may occasionally suffer from such works; yet this interpretation is obviously malicious. In actual fact we ought to understand the story as an echo of a great plan to expand the food supplies of Central Asia.

It is therefore strange that Soviet writers, when they discuss the mighty irrigation works of Chorasmia, have tended to minimize the Achaemenid contribution, and carry back their beginnings to the unknown early first millenium BC.[22] Canals are indeed the most difficult of ancient constructions to date by field methods, but the celebrated examples of such works by Darius I at Suez,[23] and of Xerxes I at Athos[24] leave no doubt as to Persian skill in these matters. The Achaemenids may well prove to be the intermediaries who transmitted the irrigation techniques of Babylonian civilization to Central Asia.

The famous Persian underground water-systems, nowadays known as *karez* or *qanat*, which extract water from limestone formations where none is present on the surface, were already known in late Assyrian times.[25] Their transmission as far afield as Cyrenaica, the Kharga Oasis in Egypt,[26] and the Quetta-

Kandahar region, would only have been possible under the Achaemenids. Another development was the diffusion of exotic food-plants. Our informant is silent as to what trees were planted by Cyrus the Younger in the garden on which he worked with his own hands while satrap at Sardis between 406 and 400 BC.[27] Darius the Great was also interested in the propagation of food-plants, as a Greek inscription from Magnesia records,[28] but again the specific crops are not named. The peach (*Persicum*) and the apricot (*Armeniacum*) come at once to mind. Though they are not described in the west until Columella in the first century AD, and the use by Theophrastus[29] of the names *Persicum* and *Medicum* is rather obscure, these trees may have completed the first stage of their long journey from China during the reign of Darius.[30] If silk was indeed available to the Persians by the second half of the fifth century BC,[31] this would strengthen the possibility that the Achaemenids had established communication, perhaps indirect, with China. In any case, the fabric is unequivocally described by Aristotle at the end of the fourth century.[32]

So far as Indian products are concerned, rice, which was a novelty to the companions of Alexander, was found by them growing in Bactria, as well as in Susiana, Babylonia and parts of Syria.[33] Presumably it had been introduced there by the Achaemenids. The question of sugar-cane and of the orange (though *Medicum* in fact may actually designate the citron) is not so clear. Yet these too could have reached Iran from India under the Achaemenids.

During the reign of Xerxes (486–465 BC) the adherence of the Central Asian provinces to the empire is confirmed by the presence of their contingents in the army which invaded Greece in 480 BC. The Bactrians and Amyrgian Sacae (Old Persian *Saka Haumavarga*) were under the command of Hystaspes, a son of King Darius and Queen Atossa. The Arians were under Sisamnes, son of Hydarnes; the Parthians and Chorasmians under Artabazus, son of Pharnaces; and the Sogdians under Azanes, son of Artaeus. The Gandarians followed Artyphius and the Caspians Ariomardus, both sons of Artabanus. Pherendates, son of Megabazus, led the men of Drangiana, and

Artayntes, son of Ithamitres, the Pactyes.[34] These commanders were all members of the high Persian nobility, and many must have held office in time of peace amongst the subject peoples whom they led to war.

For the nomadic tribes who lived beyond the Achaemenid northern frontier, the evidence of the sources is more scanty. For example the Massagetae who figure so prominently with the Greek writers are never explicitly mentioned in the Old Persian inscriptions. It may be that this confederacy preserved its independence, but that amongst the Sacae who entered into relations with the Achaemenids were a few of its constituent tribes. Thus the inscriptions name the Saka Tigrakhauda 'Pointed-Cap Sacae', who are vividly represented on the Persepolis sculptures (Pl. 5), and the Saka Haumavarga, who correspond to the 'Amyrgians' of Herodotus. In Darius's Suez inscription the hieroglyphic text renders the first as 'Sacae of the marshes' (presumably those on the shore of the Aral Sea) and the second as 'Sacae of the plains'.[35] In the post-Achaemenid period the Sacaraucae (*Saka rawaka*) were to play an important part. Yet the sparseness of the literary evidence enhances the value of the Soviet finds from Pazyryk in the Altai, which offer a glimpse of conditions amongst the tribes beyond the Achaemenid frontiers. The finds show that the nomad chiefs were luxuriously equipped, and enjoyed trade contacts with lands as distant as Iran and China.[36] One of the princely burial-mounds at this site has been dated as early as the fifth century BC, and thanks to the accumulated ice in their vaults, ancient textiles have been preserved in excellent condition. These include the world's oldest pile carpet, decorated with a central square field filled with rosettes, and borders enclosing processions of elks, horsemen and griffins (Pl. 6). This, like another fabric with a border of marching lions, is strongly reminiscent of the art of the Achaemenids, and both may therefore be imports from Iran. Locally made felt cutouts were also present, showing animal combats in the full vigour of the Siberian 'Animal Style'. Moreover, a tapestry with an exotic rendering of flying cranes may be one of the earliest specimens of Chinese textile art.

Also preserved by ice was the body of a chief, his arms, back

25

and legs also tattooed with 'Animal Style' patterns. Yet with all these sensational finds, lack of real evidence to identify the occupants of the tumuli is very tantalizing. The likeliest hypothesis may be that they represent the Issedones of Herodotus, a view which is further reinforced if hints of ceremonial cannibalism are taken seriously.[37] Similar in many ways to the Pazyryk finds but of later date are those from the tumuli at Noin-Ula in Mongolia.[38] The latter burials are attributable to a branch of the Hsiung-Nu (Huns). Here finds included a woollen carpet decorated with fighting animals, imported Hellenistic textiles, and Chinese lacquer bowls, one dated to the year 2 BC.

It was not until 330 BC, when Alexander the Great passed through the Caspian Gates, that Central Asia took on a more significant role. During his pursuit by Alexander the fugitive Achaemenid king, Darius III, was fatally wounded by his own officers, and from that moment the conqueror found himself in an ambiguous position. As King of Macedon, he depended on the military strength of his Macedonian troops, to whom he owed his success, and it was essential for him to retain their loyalty and affection. At the same time he was now acknowledged King of Persia, head of all that remained of the Achaemenid system of government. Dwindling man-power and enormous lines of communication obliged him to conciliate his newly-won subjects. He tried to gain their respect and co-operation in the work of administering the territory.

It is therefore natural that whilst in Central Asia Alexander came to adopt Persian dress, in which he is picturesquely represented on the famous 'Porus medallion'.[39] The etiquette of the Persian court was increasingly observed. Prostration before the king (the notorious *proskynesis*) had long been customary for the Persians. The introduction of the custom amongst themselves was resisted by the Macedonians and Greeks, who thought such honours were appropriate only for a god. In fact, divine honours were enthusiastically granted to Alexander after his death. Had he desired, or achieved, such recognition in 330 BC a standardized court ceremonial might have been established for all classes of his subjects. At this stage, however, the innovation aroused too much resentment amongst his Greek followers, as is clear from the telling passage in which Arrian makes the sophist Callisthenes the mouthpiece for their feelings.[40]

With Darius III now dead, the immediate task was the pursuit of Bessus, the murderer of the king, who had assumed royal honours. Soon disturbances further south diverted Alexander to Artacoana (modern Herat?) and to Drangiana. He expelled Satibarzanes from his satrapy of Aria and Barsaentes from Drangiana. In the latter province he seized and put to death a prominent Macedonian officer, Philotas, on suspicion of conspiracy, giving to the scene of the event the name of Prophthasia, 'Anticipation'. Then swinging north in a great encircling movement, he traversed Arachosia, founded the city of Alexandria-of-the-Caucasus at the foot of the Hindu Kush,[41] and burst into Bactria from the south-east, throwing the hapless Bessus into confusion. In a few weeks the Macedonians were across the Oxus and Bessus was taken prisoner, to be sent eventually to Ecbatana for execution. Meanwhile Alexander pressed on to the Jaxartes, crushing local opposition with drastic severity.

Resistance in the Trans-Oxus province of Sogdiana was still by no means at an end. A new leader, Spitamenes, now came to the fore, and began to harass the Macedonian garrison at Maracanda by cavalry raids. He was re-inforced by some six hundred Sacae from the steppe, and when the Macedonians attempted a sortie, he inflicted a serious defeat on them. Only by a forced march of 185 miles in three days was Alexander able to support his garrison. He drove Spitamenes once more back onto the steppe, before crossing the Oxus to Zariaspa (Bactra), where he passed the winter (329–8 BC). During this halt another conspiracy was suspected, this time amongst the royal pages, a number of whom were stoned to death. Callisthenes the sophist was also put to death for complicity in the supposed plot. Then after receiving a state visit from Pharasmanes, the King of Chorasmia – a kingdom now apparently autonomous – Alexander recrossed the Oxus into Sogdiana towards the close of winter, and divided his army into five columns in order to deal with local disaffection.

Meanwhile Spitamenes, drawing further re-inforcements from

'the branch of the Sacae known as the Massagetae', crossed to the south bank of the Oxus, and began to inflict losses on the Macedonian garrisons there, venturing even to attack Zariaspa. He was drawn away when the Macedonian captain Craterus made a feint against the homeland of the Massagetae; then colliding with another column commanded by Coenus, he was heavily defeated, and driven back onto the steppe. There Spitamenes was put to death by his Sacae auxiliaries, or, according to Quintus Curtius, by his resentful wife, and his head sent to Alexander. His daughter, Apama, was later to become the wife of the Macedonian general Seleucus.

Opposition to Alexander in Bactria and Sogdiana was thus virtually at an end. But Oxyartes the Bactrian still kept the field, having entrusted his family to a formidable mountain stronghold called the Rock of Sogdiana.[42] The garrison jested that if Alexander was to take the Rock, his soldiers would need wings; but three hundred Greek cragsmen scaled the cliffs by the use of pitons, and forced the garrison to surrender.

Amongst the prisoners was the daughter of Oxyartes, Roxana, a woman of unusual beauty. It is said that Alexander fell in love with her at sight. Their marriage soon effected a reconciliation with Oxyartes. Amongst modern writers, Tarn represents the marriage as an act of policy, intended to reconcile the Macedonians with the East Iranian peoples, Bactrians, Sogdians, and Sacae;[43] and to secure for the depleted Macedonians East Iranian allies, especially re-inforcements of cavalry, in the forthcoming invasion of India. That in the end the marriage had this effect is evident enough. Indeed, the long-term consequence of Alexander's march was the destruction of Persian overlordship in Central Asia, and the strengthening of local East Iranian elements in traditional concord with the Macedonian rulers. Persian government was not restored in the area until the third century AD. Yet it is hard to disbelieve the ancient authorities when they stress that it was not diplomacy but spontaneous desire which was the inspiration of Alexander's marriage.

Prominent in the story of these campaigns is Alexander's 'foundation' of cities, many of which became famous in subsequent history. Amongst those named were Alexandria in

Ariana, the modern Herat; Alexandria Prophthasia in Drangiana, which has not been exactly located; Alexandria in
Arachosia;[44] Alexandria-of-the-Caucasus, probably located on
the site of the mediaeval city of Parvan, at Jebel Suraj on the
Salang; and the short-lived Alexandria Eschata on the Jaxartes.
The conqueror's real work need have been little more than to re-
furbish and garrison old-established strongpoints. Yet his
practised strategic eye enabled him to choose sites which would
remain key-points in Asia for centuries. With these points
strongly garrisoned, the Macedonian rulers had a firm grip of
the land routes across the continent.

In 327 BC Alexander moved on to his conquest of the Punjab.
His armies marched down through Bajaur and Malakand, and
overwhelmed all opposition.[45] Unrest soon followed amongst
the garrisons left behind, many of which contained former
mercenaries of Darius III. In only the next year, three thousand
Greek settlers mutinied in Bactria and Sogdiana, abandoned
their posts, and set out on the long march back to Europe.
Accounts of their fate differ.[46] After Alexander's death in
Babylon during 323 BC a more serious dissension broke out. In
the 'Upper Satrapies'[47] some 23,000 men mutinied,[48] and set out
for Greece. Perdiccas, regent of Alexander's empire, sent a force
under Peithon to oppose them. This unscrupulous commander
applied a combination of diplomacy and force, in the secret
hope of winning the mutineers to his personal following. In a
battle, some deserted to his side and others were defeated. But
Peithon's troops, acting on the strict order of Perdiccas that the
mutineers were to be punished, massacred the survivors now
sharing their camp, and looted their property.

Disappointed, Peithon retired to Babylon, and in 322 BC took
a leading part in the assassination of Perdiccas during an attack
on Egypt. In Antipater's partition of the empire he was restored
to Media, at once replacing his neighbour Phrataphernes,
satrap of Parthia, by his own brother Eudamus. This aggression
forced the other Central Asian satraps to make common cause
with Peucestas – Alexander's bodyguard who was now satrap of
Persis – in a league against Peithon. Prominent amongst them was
the father of Roxana, Oxyartes, now satrap of the Paropamis-

adae. Some authorities have been inclined to see Oxyartes as the owner of the celebrated Oxus Treasure, now in the British Museum, but the identification of his name with that on one of the rings in the treasure is far from certain. In any event, Oxyartes in 322 BC was sadly separated from his daughter, who, having borne Alexander's posthumous heir, Alexander IV Aegus, accompanied Antipater on his return to Macedon in the same year. After the death of Antipater she took refuge with Alexander's mother Olympias, after whose fall in 316 BC she was imprisoned by Cassander at Amphipolis with her child, and four years later done to death. How Roxana came to leave at Athens offerings as a memento of her stay in Europe is something of a mystery.[49]

Also leagued against Peithon were Stasanor, satrap of Aria and Drangiana, and Sibyrtius, satrap of Arachosia. The confederate satraps joined Alexander's former secretary, Eumenes of Cardia, when he arrived in Persis after a great march from Asia Minor during his war on behalf of Alexander's heirs against Antigonus the One-Eyed. Antigonus overthrew the confederates in a battle near Isfahan. But he returned to the west, leaving the eastern satrapies undisturbed under the existing governors.

It was Seleucus, after his re-occupation of Babylon in 312 BC, who first attempted the re-unification of Alexander's eastern provinces. Liquidating Nicanor, governor of Media for Antigonus, he re-conquered Bactria, and passed the Hindu Kush to attack the newly established Maurya Empire in India. However, its founder, the redoubtable Chandragupta, who had been inspired as a youth by the sight of Alexander, and later conquered Northern India with an army of 600,000 men,[50] was more than his match. Peace was at last made towards 304 BC, the ambassador of Seleucus being Megasthenes, the former secretary of Sibyrtius, and later famous for his book on the wonders of India. Seleucus agreed to cede to the Maurya the Paropamisadae, Arachosia and Gedrosia.[51] A matrimonial alliance was concluded between the dynasties, and Seleucus received the gift of five hundred elephants,[52] which after his return to Asia Minor, won him the day at Ipsus in 301 BC.

Several recent discoveries have proved that Maurya rule of

the ceded provinces was effective. In modern Afghanistan no less than three inscriptions of Chandragupta's grandson, the great Asoka, have come to light. A fragmentary text in Aramaic was discovered at Laghman, north-west of modern Jalalabad.[53] Two other inscriptions have been found in the old city of Kandahar: one, bilingual in Greek and Aramaic, tells of Asoka's conversion to Buddhism, and its benefit to his people;[54] the other, in Greek alone, is a striking rendering of parts of the Twelfth and Thirteenth Rock Edicts of Asoka.[55] So it appears that Asoka introduced the Buddhist religion into the newly acquired provinces. This extension of Buddhism was to have far-reaching consequences in the centuries that followed.

After Alexander's return to Susa in 324 BC Seleucus, like many of the Macedonian chiefs, had taken an Iranian wife. This was Apama, daughter of the redoubtable Spitamenes. By 293 BC their son Antiochus, well qualified by ancestry and up-bringing for the task, was ruling as his father's joint-king in eastern Iran. His task was to repel Saca incursions from the steppe and strengthen Seleucid control of their remaining territories in Aria and Bactria. Marv was fortified and re-named Antiochia.[56] At Bactra itself a Seleucid mint was in operation, issuing coins with the names of Seleucus and Antiochus juxtaposed.[57] But when Antiochus inherited the sole rule in 280 BC, his attention was diverted to Asia Minor, and the Seleucid hold in Central Asia weakened.

A newly found inscription confirms that before Antiochus' death in 261 BC, a certain Andragoras was governing as satrap Parthia and Hyrcania.[58] At some time during the next reign, that of Antiochus II (261–246 BC), he asserted his autonomy by issuing coins in gold and silver, still without the royal title. But within a few years he was crushed by a new leader, Arsaces, founder of the Parthian Empire, who overran the province at the head of his nomadic followers, the Parni. The original language of these tribesmen must have contained East Iranian elements,[59] but it was quickly assimilated to the North Iranian dialect of the settled population of Parthia. The overthrow of Andragoras in 247 BC was followed by the accession of Arsaces, thus beginning the Arsacid era.[60] An important early capital of the new dynasty

31

was at Nisa, near the present-day Ashkhabad in Soviet Turkmenistan. Half a century later the site received the Parthian
dynastic name of Mithradatkert. Here Soviet excavations
brought to light important finds, including more than forty
ivory drinking-horns in Hellenistic style.[61] Many potsherds
with ink inscriptions (ostraca) were also found. These constitute
the archives of a great wine-store, and serve to illustrate
economic and agricultural life. With regard to their language,
the view now seems to prevail that this is not Parthian written
with Aramaic ideograms,[62] but a form of stylized Aramaic with
many Iranian loan-words.[63]

In later centuries the Parthians pressed on towards Mesopotamia. Thus their centre of gravity was removed from the
Turkoman steppe. Meanwhile on their eastern border another
state was forming. During the rise of Arsaces, Diodotus the
Seleucid satrap of Bactria also gained his independence. Its first,
partial, manifestation is the appearance of his portrait on coins
still carrying the name and reverse type of Antiochus II. Soon
appears the name of Diodotus as king, and his punning device,
the figure of a thundering Zeus. Diodotus' kingdom of Bactria
was to show surprising vitality, and in later reigns to extend its
boundaries across the Indian sub-continent. One extraneous
factor which rendered the separation of Bactria, as of Parthia,
from the Seleucid state final was the invasion of the empire on
the death of Antiochus II (246 BC) by the king of Egypt,
Ptolemy III Euergetes. In the words of a remarkable inscription
seen centuries later at Adulis on the Red Sea by the Christian
monk Cosmas Indicopleustes, '(Ptolemy) crossed the river
Euphrates, and subjected to himself Mesopotamia, Babylonia,
Susiana, Persis, Media, and the rest (of the empire), as far as
(the borders of) Bactriana'.[64] With the Seleucid heartlands in
the grip of this invader, the eastern provinces were left to fend
for themselves.

In Bactria the rise of Diodotus is followed by some decades of
uncertainty. Understanding of his coinage has been complicated
as his son and successor had apparently the same name.[65] The
second Diodotus is said to have reversed his father's policy of
hostility to Parthia. But full illumination returns only with

Polybius' account of the eastern expedition made by the Seleucid king Antiochus III the Great.

Marching from Ecbatana in 208 BC Antiochus brushed aside Parthian resistance south of the Elburz range; he crossed into Hyrcania, capturing the palace at Tambrax, and storming the entrenched city of Sirynx. Later, at the River Arius (Hari Rud) he drove off the cavalry of the Bactrians, who were now under the rule of Euthydemus, a Greek from Magnesia. He laid siege to their capital at Bactra, but in vain. After two years fighting before the huge mud-brick ramparts[66] and surrounding marshes, unnerved by his opponent's threat to admit the menacing Saca tribesmen of the steppe, Antiochus granted terms. Euthydemus – who claimed he was no rebel, but the slayer of the children of rebels (i.e. of Diodotus) – was allowed to retain his kingdom. He surrendered his elephants to Antiochus, concluding a treaty of alliance; and the kingly bearing of his son Demetrius so impressed the Seleucid that he offered the prince a daughter in marriage – a contract that seems not to have been fulfilled. Then Antiochus crossed the Hindu Kush into the Paropamisadae, made terms with its Indian prince Sophagasenus, and returned to his capital by the long road through Carmania. At Bactra Euthydemus was left alone as the ruler of the Greeks and Macedonians of Central Asia.[67]

No ancient narrative preserves the tale of the Greek kingdoms of Bactria. Their history has been reconstructed from scattered literary references, and the remarkable surviving coinage. Tarn's monumental study[68] marks an epoch in the subject, but its defect is the over-theoretical approach, which forces numismatic evidence into conformity with thinly-based historical deductions. Salutary criticisms were advanced by Narain,[69] whose treatment of Tarn's mature judgements is nevertheless occasionally captious. Knowledge of the later Graeco-Bactrian invasion of the Indian North-West depends mainly on coin evidence, which must therefore be interpreted critically.[70]

When the Maurya empire declined after Asoka, a vacuum was left in Gandhara. The Bactrian Greeks, disturbed by the Saca menace on the Jaxartes, must have coveted a retreat beyond the Paropamisus. It seems that Demetrius played a role

33

in their occupation of this area, for he assumed the elephant-scalp headdress once associated with Alexander, and the conqueror's title *Anikētos* 'The Invincible'. Narain[71] also rightly stresses the activity of Antimachus Theus in the invasion of the southern watersheds. The date of this movement must have been between 190 and 170 BC. Yet the Graeco-Bactrians were disunited, and behind Demetrius a rival had arisen, the formidable Eucratides, who soon overthrew him, and advanced to Pushkalavati. The various kings of Bactria and the Punjab can be seen as divided between the two rival dynasties, and their affiliations are most easily shown in tabular form:

	DIODOTUS I	c. 247 BC
	DIODOTUS II	
House of Euthydemus	*House of Eucratides*	
EUTHYDEMUS I		208 BC
DEMETRIUS I	EUCRATIDES I	
EUTHYDEMUS II	PLATO	
DEMETRIUS II	EUCRATIDES II	
	SOTER	
PANTALEON	HELIOCLES	
AGATHOCLES		
ANTIMACHUS THEUS		

The discovery during 1948 in Afghanistan of an important find of Graeco-Bactrian silver coins, which has since come to be known as the Qunduz Treasure, adds to our knowledge of these earlier Bactrian rulers. The find, previously known only from the brief preliminary publication,[72] has been described in detail in a recent memoir of the Délégation archéologique française en Afghanistan.[73] Besides many issues of the normal tetradrachm denomination, this find was remarkable for containing five medallic pieces of the double-decadrachm size, issued by the later ruler Amyntas, and each weighing a little over 84 grammes (Pl. 7). It is to the complex period of these later Indo-Bactrian rulers that we turn in the following chapter.

2

The Nomad Empires and the Expansion of Buddhism

After the rise of Eucratides, the Bactrian territories north of the Hindu Kush passed under the rule of his dynasty. Meanwhile south of the mountains were formed the Indo-Bactrian kingdoms, in which the two dynasties, those of Eucratides and of Euthydemus, continued to compete with one another and with obscure usurpers.

Each of the four decades following the death of Demetrius (c. 170 BC) was dominated by a great personality. During the first, from c. 170–160 BC Apollodotus I,[1] who is briefly mentioned by Trogus,[2] issued a copious coinage. Menander I Soter, principal figure of the next ten years, won a greater claim to the affection of posterity. His genial treatment of the Buddhist communities led to his characterization in a Buddhist canonical work, the *Milindapañha* ('The Questions of Menander'), a religio-philosophical dialogue in almost the Platonic manner.[3] The Buddhist tradition places Menander's capital at Sagala, often identified with Sialkot in the Punjab. Yet though this may, indeed, have been his occasional cold-season residence, numismatic evidence is strong that the focus of his kingdom was at Pushkalavati, the modern Charsada near Peshawar. Several modern authorities attribute to Menander the era by which a number of early Indian inscriptions are dated, and which may in fact, have been a Greek era. This era commenced in 155 BC and may have marked the general acknowledgement of Menander's rule. Other evidence for his reign is scanty, but

35

Menander was evidently the most distinguished of the Greek kings in India.

In the following decade, perhaps c. 145–135 BC, must be placed the emergence of Antialcidas. As were the kings previously named, Antialcidas is noted for a numerous issue of coins. He is also mentioned in the famous Brahmi inscription of the Besnagar pillar, a dedication to the Hindu god Vishnu set up by the king's ambassador Heliodorus in an adjoining realm.[4] This Heliodorus was a citizen of Taxila, but Antialcidas may have had his headquarters at Gardiz in Afghanistan, before his occupation of Pushkalavati and the rest of the Indo-Bactrian territory on the demise of Menander.

For the last generation of Graeco-Macedonian rulers in the Indo-Bactrian kingdoms, literary and epigraphic indications are lacking, the only evidence being that of the coins. In this period the dominant figure is Strato I (c. 135–125 BC), who appears to have commenced his reign at Pushkalavati, but after years of varying fortunes, and some periods of exile, to have transferred his activity to Taxila and Gardiz. An analysis of the coinage produces helpful results for this confused period, and is shown in fig. (a), but its full reasoning cannot be detailed here.

It will be seen that though the full monogram-sequence of the rulers earlier than Strato cannot yet be demonstrated, the general trend of events is reasonably clear. After a first accession of Strato (his 'Phase I'), a certain Heliocles, who may, or may not, be identical with the Heliocles of the Bactrian area, but who is distinguished by numismatists with the designation of 'Heliocles II', for a short time gained control of the four major mints. Later Strato returns to Pushkalavati, where he is subjected to the incursions of several rulers. When finally displaced here, he re-appears at Taxila, Gardiz, and Alexandria-of-the-Caucasus, at the first and last of which he appears as the successor of Amyntas, the ruler celebrated for his double-decadrachms. Finally, Strato is succeeded at all mints by Archebius, except at Pushkalavati, where the position remains obscure. The story of the fourth generation of Indo-Bactrian princes is one of obscure campaigns, marches, and counter-marches, with striking reversals of fortune. Further east, in the

PUSHKALAVATI	TAXILA	GARDIZ	ALEXANDRIA-OF-THE-CAUCASUS
		Apollodotus I	
Eucratides Menander I Soter ? Zoilus I Dikaios		Menander I Sōtēr	
{ Theophilus { Nicias Lysias (drachms only)		Lysias (drachms)	
Philoxenus (a) Antialcidas Strato (Phase I) ? Hermaeus (a)		Philoxenus (a) Antialcidas	
'Heliocles II' Strato (Phase IIa) Strato & Agathocleia Philoxenus (b) + Σ Hermaeus & Calliope Hermaeus (b) Strato (Phase II b) Strato (Phase III)	{ 'Heliocles II' { Menander II Dikaios	'Heliocles II' (drachms)	'Heliocles II'
			Hermaeus & Calliope Hermaeus (b)
			Strato (Phase II b)
	Amyntas Strato (Phase IV) Polyxenus Archebius	Strato (Phase IV) Polyxenus Archebius	Amyntas Strato (Phase IV)
			Archebius
Strato (Phase III)	Maues		(Attic tetradrachm and examples with double monograms
		Archebius	

Summary of Indo-Bactrian mint activity.

Punjab, a group of lesser rulers maintained themselves, the most notable being Zoilus II Soter and Apollophanes, who issued base coins of the small *drachma* module.

Whilst the Bactrians and the Indo-Bactrians were thus involved in intestine struggles, storm clouds were gathering along their Central Asian frontier of the Jaxartes. Even in the time of Euthydemus (c. 208 BC), the threat from the nomad Sacae had been contained with difficulty. In the years which followed, new pressures were to be felt in the Jaxartes steppe which quite overpowered the defensive capacity of the Bactrian Greeks. The origins of these pressures were far away to the east on the frontiers of China; and it is to these origins that we must now direct our view.

On the Mongolian frontier of China there existed a powerful pastoral nation known as the Hsiung-nu. The view will be taken in this account, though it is often contested, that this tribe was identical with that known centuries later in the history of Europe as the Huns. Nothing is known with certainty as to the linguistic and ethnic affinities of this people, but there is a tendency to regard them as in some ways related to the Turks. The outstanding commonplace both in the Eastern and in the Western sources is their extreme ferocity in war. It is true that writers were inclined to dramatize the sufferings inflicted on their compatriots by the Huns, and some exaggeration may be suspected. Yet descriptions of this kind are so universal and spontaneous that they must contain some basis of fact. Thus in later centuries Ammianus Marcellinus, though he had no notion of the relation between the European Huns and the Central Asian Chionites, describes both groups in similar terms of opprobrium.[5] Throughout their eight centuries of history, the Hsiung-nu/Huns were obviously devastating opponents.

It was during the third century BC that the Hsiung-nu reached the height of their power in Mongolia. Soon they were constituting a major threat to the rulers of northern China. The Great Wall, best-known of all Chinese monuments, was built to ward off their attacks; but with the passing of the Chin dynasty (221–206 BC) the defensive power of China declined. At the same time, the strength of the Hsiung-nu increased under their *Shan-*

yü ('paramount chief'), T'ou-man. It reached its zenith under his son, the great Mao-tun (c. 209–174 BC), who subdued the neighbouring tribes, the Hsien-pi, Khitans, and the Tungus, to become the emperor of the steppes.

In Kansu province, westwards of the site which later became famous as Tun-huang (The Thousand Buddhas), there pastured another tribal confederacy of rather mixed character known as the Yüeh-chih. These were defeated by Mao-tun whilst further to the north he impinged on the Wu-sun and drove them to the west. After the death of Mao-tun, his son Lao-shang again attacked the Yüeh-chih routing them and killing their king in battle. This final reverse caused the harassed Yüeh-chih, pastoral nomads like the Hsiung-nu, to trek away to the west, passing, so it seems, down the Ili valley and along the southern shore of Lake Issyk Kul. From this area they expelled a group of Saca tribes, to which the *Chi'en-Han Shu* applies the label of 'Sai-Wang' (Saca Kings), and drove them south-westwards; but on their march the Yüeh-chih had collided with the Wu-sun, who now returned to attack them in the rear, and drive them pell-mell into Farghana on the heels of the Sacae. Thus, soon after 160 BC, two powerful hordes, the Sacae and the Yüeh-chih, hung poised over the Graeco-Bactrian frontier of the Jaxartes.

It is at this point that the western sources take up the story of the nomad conquest of Bactria. Scholars today seem agreed, even if formal proof is lacking, that the Yüeh-chih of the Chinese sources are effectively identical with the tribe named as the Tochari in the western texts. Subsequent events are described in a celebrated passage of the *Geography* of Strabo:[6]

The nomads who became the most famous were those who took away Bactriana from the Greeks–the Asii or Asiani, the Tochari, and the Sacaraucae, who set out from the far bank of the Jaxartes, adjoining the Sacae and Sogdiani, which the Sacae had occupied.

Here the Asii or Asiani make their first appearance in the narrative. Their part in events is illustrated by two notices in the *Prologues* of Pompeius Trogus – for his Prologues survive though the full text of his narrative is lost. *Prologue* XLI contains the statement: 'The Scythian tribes of the Saraucae (read: Sacaraucae) and the Asiani seized Bactra and Sogdiana.' Whilst *Prologue* XLII, referring to later events, includes the sentence: 'The Asiani became kings of the Tochari and the Saraucae (read: Sacaraucae) were destroyed.'

From these texts, summary though they be, it can be concluded that the displaced nomad groups soon afterwards overran the Graeco-Bactrian kingdom. Tarn's deduction that the invasion took place at a date after 141 BC[7] now finds confirmation; in the Qunduz Treasure (surely buried at the time of this very invasion) there is a single tetradrachm of the Seleucid Alexander Balas (150–145 BC). Allowing five years for the travel of this coin from Syria to Bactria, one arrives at an almost identical upper limit. In 129 BC a wave of nomad invaders burst into Parthia,[8] so that by this date, if not before, the invasion of Bactria must have been well advanced.

Direct evidence is lacking for the subsequent movements of the nomad tribes; but some inferences are possible from the occurrence of relevant place-names. It was about this time that the region of the Helmand Lake (now called the Hamun) ceased to be known as Drangiana, and acquired the name which developed from Sakastan (Segistan) into the modern form Seistan (Sistan). The Kharoshthi inscription of the Mathura Lion-Capital[9] actually suggests that at the height of Saca power in the first century BC the name of Sakastan may have had a wider meaning, to include all the lands which the Sacae conquered in India, the Indo-Scythia of the Roman authors.[10] Yet its strictest application is to the land of the Lower Helmand; even in the mediaeval period the people of this region were known as Sagzi (from an earlier Sagčik), a name which emphasizes their Saca origin. It seems safe to conclude that the Saca tribes passed south through the Herat gap, and established themselves in the former Drangiana. During the first century BC they must have continued north-eastwards into Arachosia, and reached the Indus, which they followed both upstream and down. Thus they penetrated on the one hand to Taxila and the North Indian plain, and on the other to Saurastra and Ujjain.

The first century BC is thus the epoch of the Saca empire in India and Arachosia. The history has to be reconstructed almost entirely from inscriptions and coins, the best recent attempt being that of Sir John Marshall.[11] Yet though the mass of the Saca tribesmen may have passed by the route described, it is remarkable that the first Saca emperor attested on coins is Maues, who appears at Taxila in the heart of the Indo-Bactrian kingdoms. This paradox influenced Narain[12] to revive an old theory that Maues led a separate Saca group directly to Taxila from the north, passing from Khotan over the Pamirs and through Indus Kohistan – an arduous route called that of the 'Hanging Pass' by Chinese chroniclers. So fantastic a feat is scarcely credible. A more acceptable explanation would be to assume that Maues began his career as a commander of Saca mercenaries in the service of the late Indo-Greek kings, in particular Archebius. With the Indo-Greek princes divided, and Saca invaders at the gates, such a personage would be well placed to assume sovereign power.

By an analysis of the coins, Jenkins has shown that the Greeks under Apollodotus II eventually succeeded in ousting Maues (97–c. 77 BC) from Taxila,[13] whilst the Kabul Valley and Gandhara seem to have remained in Greek hands. In Arachosia is found a parallel Saca dynasty, perhaps the newly arrived invaders, whose coins can be distinguished. The sequence of rulers which emerges here is the following: Vonones, Spalyris, Spalagdames, Spalirises, Azes I and Azilises. Maus himself was killed in battle at Mathura, where the Lion-Capital was set up as his monument (Pl. 8). Soon, however, Azes I set about the restoration of the Saca cause at Taxila also. The fortunes of war fluctuated, but eventually Azes I put an end to the Greek dynasties and asserted his paramount rule. No doubt this is the event commemorated by the establishment of a new era, 'The Era of Azes',[14] which commenced in 57 BC. Though the Parthians encroached on Saca territory in Drangiana and Arachosia, the Saca empire was firmly established in the Punjab until the close of the century. There is no further evidence for exact dating, but Azilises was succeeded by Azes II.

The extreme mobility of the Saca forces must have been an important factor in enabling them to overrun so wide a territory. As equestrian nomads they had great advantages in open country, though they never penetrated the broken terrain of the Hindu Kush. The decisive factor was probably their introduction of a new method of fighting – the charge of massed cavalry wielding the two-handed lance, and protected by the full-length laminated armour well illustrated on their coins (Pl. 9). A precious fragment from Trogus preserved in a mediaeval text aptly describes their equipment:[15]

> The fierce tribe of the Scythians, very swift in battle on the level ground, their bodies encased in armour, protect their legs with iron, and wear golden helmets upon their heads.

At the moment of the Saca thrust through the Herat gap into Arachosia and the Punjab plain, we left the other participants of this migration, the Tochari and the Asiani, camped on the north bank of the Oxus, and to the east of the Saca line of advance. The identity of the Asiani presents some problems. Their historical role is however clear, for we have seen that they were the group who 'became kings of the Tochari'. In this respect, though the identity of the names is unlikely, their activity co-incides with that of a clan-group later celebrated, the Kushans. They were regarded as historically equivalent by Tarn,[16] and his hypothesis is more satisfying than that of Haloun,[17] lately endorsed by Sinor,[18] that the Asiani were identical with the Wu-sun. At any rate, the first occurrence of the Kushan name in history is during the first half of the first century BC on coins of the Transoxine chief Heraus, which are inspired by the Graeco-Bactrian tetradrachms of Heliocles, and bear a legend in Greek script 'Under the rule of Heraus, Kushan Chief (?)'.[19] The legend is interesting as the first use of Greek script in Bactria for the writing of local names; it attests the introduction of the extra Greek letter *san* to represent the *š* sibilant common in Iranian languages.[20]

Meanwhile the advance of the Tochari is indicated by the attachment of their name to the district of Tukharistan, which centres round Qunduz and Baghlan close to the Upper Oxus. Here they were reported, a 'great tribe', in the *Geography* of Ptolemy.[21] Early in the first century BC their advance-guards must have been pressing southwards towards the passes of the

Hindu Kush. Yet it was not until the opening decades of the Christian Era that they achieved final unity under the leadership of the Kushan clan, secured the Kabul Valley, and under their king Kujula Kadphises broke out of the mountains onto the Punjab plain. These events are summed up in a well-known passage of the Chinese *Hou-Han shu*:[22]

Formerly the Yüe-chi were conquered by the Hiung-nu; they transferred themselves to the Ta-hia (i.e. Bactria), and divided that kingdom between five *hi-hou* (subordinate chiefs), viz. those of Hiu-mi, Shuang-mi, Kuei-shang Hi-tun, and Tu-mi. More than a hundred years after this the *hi-hou* of Kuei-shang, called K'iu-tsiu-k'io, attacked the other four *hi-hou*; he styled himself king; the name of his kingdom was Kuei-shang. He invaded An-si (i.e. Parthia) and seized the territory of Kao-fu (Kabul); moreover he triumphed over Pu-ta and Ki-pin, and entirely possessed these kingdoms. K'iu-tsiu-k'io died more than eighty years old. His son Yen-kao-chen became king in his stead.

At the start of the Christian Era the Saca empire in Arachosia and the Punjab was in decline under Azes II, a state of affairs marked by the drastic debasement of its silver coinage. Meanwhile a dynasty of provincial Parthian rulers were pressing eastwards along the Helmand Valley. Their chronological sequence is debatable, but the list of names includes Pacores, Orthagnes, Gondophares, Abdagases, and Sasas (Sasan), besides a certain Arsaces Theos whose affiliations are uncertain. There is also evidence of one Sanabares towards the western end of this region. Of all this dynasty, Gondophares is by far the best known, his dates at Taxila being firmly fixed by the Takht-i Bahi inscription of the year 103, which is dated to the twenty-sixth year of his reign. The first date must be reckoned by the 'Era of Azes' commencing in 57 BC, and thus corresponds to AD 46. It emerges that the reign of Gondophares extended to at least that year from AD 20. This reckoning tallies with the only notice of Gondophares known before the discovery of ancient Indian coins and inscriptions. This is his appearance in the tale of the voyage of the Apostle Thomas to India. If tradition is believed, Thomas set out immediately after the Crucifixion (i.e. in AD 29 or 33).[23] Another traveller from the Roman world who saw the

Indo-Parthian kingdom about a decade later was Apollonius of Tyana. He was at Babylon in the third year of the Parthian king Vardanes (AD 43–44) and appears to have reached Taxila about AD 46.[24]

The Takht-i Bahi inscription is often thought to contain a mention of the Kushan prince Kujula Kadphises, whose rule over the Yüeh-chih horde is thought to have begun early in the Christian Era. The Kushan Empire which he founded was soon to expand on both sides of the Hindu Kush and to become the most influential civilizing power in Central Asia. Not only did the Kushans thrust forward to dominate the north Indian plains, but conscious of their nomad origins they sought to restore contact with the Chinese borderlands where their wanderings had begun. No doubt their resources in animal transport gave them the means to stimulate Chinese trade and to form a bridge between the civilizations of India and China. As for the race and language of the Kushans, the complexity of their migration raises many problems. Impressed by the bulbous features and the drooping moustaches of the ruling clan, commentators of several centuries have found it hard to consider them Indo-Europeans. The mediaeval Arab writer al-Biruni called them Tibetans,[25] a notion perhaps supported by their matriarchal tendencies reported by the Syrian Bardesanes.[26] Nor can the idea that they were of Turkish origin be completely disregarded. Yet they wore the typical costume of the Iranians of the steppe, with the buckled cloak, long shirt, and baggy trousers of the horseman, an outfit well depicted in the statue of the Emperor Kanishka from Mathura (Pl. 10). In battle they wore laminated armour like the Sacae, and amongst their weapons was a straight sword over three feet long.

If the Kushans themselves once spoke a special language of their own, it is now unknown. Beneath them in the tribal hierarchy came the Tochari, with whom earlier scholars connected the two Indo-European dialects of the *centum* type found in manuscript fragments from Kucha and Qarashahr. At the present day, these dialects are usually designated Kuchaean and Agnaean. Some authorities however continue to refer to them as 'Tocharian A' and 'B', thus specifically ascribing them to the historical Tochari. This view is no doubt a possible one, though it has been disputed, for example by W. B. Henning, who went so far as to say: 'As to the so-called "Tocharian" languages, the odds are heavily on that they are U-sun dialects and not forms of Uë-Tsi speech.'[27] More recently, further indications have come to light which seem to connect these dialects with the Tochari, but the whole question must still be regarded as unsettled.

Lower perhaps in tribal standing than the Tochari in the expanding Kushan empire were the Sacaraucae, whom the Kushans had found as the ruling group in much of Northern India, and whom they had partly displaced, but partly absorbed in their own administration. There is no doubt that the Sacaraucae spoke an East Iranian dialect, and it seems possible that they are the only one of the three tribes whose language has left living descendants. The exact identity of the Sacarauca dialect is rather uncertain, but there are three relevant points of reference. Thus a group of Iranian loan-words in the Kharoshthi and Brahmi inscriptions of the sub-continent are comparable with words occurring in the Khotanese manuscripts: e.g. *horaka-*, *horamurta* 'supervisor of donations'; *bakanapati-*, 'priest';[28] and the personal name Ysamotika.[29] The Khotanese and related dialects of the Tarim Basin are sometimes described by the embracing term 'Saka', but Bailey has observed that 'The name "Saka" applied to the language of these documents is not directly attested in the texts themselves.'[30]

It is also argued that the Pashtu language of Afghanistan and Pakistan derives from the speech of the Saca invaders.[31] Once more the link is strengthened by a coincidence with the Brahmi inscriptions, the satrapal name Castana being compared with the Pashtu word *tsax̌tan* 'master'. An integrated view of the problem must take into account all three languages, 'Indo-Scythian', Khotanese, and Pashtu – but the last two are not closely related, and if both are 'Saka', it is in some different sense. Meanwhile the discovery at Surkh Kotal in Afghanistan of a 25-line inscription in an East Iranian language written in Greek script introduces a fourth factor. The new language is the same as that known from coins of the Kushan dynasty, and is now shown to be the local dialect of Bactria.[32] Once more, words occur in common with the Khotanese texts: e.g. Bactrian *xšono*, Khot. *kṣuna-*, 'regnal year'[33] but it is hard to say in which East Iranian dialect this word originated.

A well-known subject of historical controversy is the chronology of the Kushan kings. Yet it may be that the difficulties of the problem have been overstated. The sequence of the rulers, as deduced from their coins, is in general agreed upon. Starting in the first decades of the Christian Era, there were Kujula Kadphises, then a 'Nameless King' known by his title Soter Megas ('The Great Saviour'), and Vima Kadphises; the next series included several better-known personalities, Kanishka, Huvishka and Vasudeva. It may be noted that Vima Kadphises substituted for the debased currency of Indo-Parthian times a splendid gold coinage regulated on the Roman weight-standard, and perhaps struck from bullion received in Roman trade-payments. The absolute chronology of these rulers depends on the many dated inscriptions in Kharoshthi and Brahmi script from various parts of the sub-continent, but complications result from the fact that several different eras are found. The best hypothesis assumes the existence of three different eras, on the following scheme:

a) An Indo-Bactrian Era of c. 155 BC. (Often called the 'Old Saka' Era.)
b) The Era of Azes in 57 BC.
c) The Era of Kanishka c. AD 128.

It is the last dating which is the most keenly disputed, but the solution accepted here is the traditional one.[34] It has been little impaired by numerous counter-arguments, and was recently reinforced by an inscription discovered at Surkh Kotal in Afghanistan.[35] The table of dates in the Era of Kanishka corresponding to the principal Kushan rulers is thus as follows:

Years	Name of Ruler
2 – 23	Kanishka I
24 – 28	Vasishka
28 – 60	Huvishka
74 – 98	Vasudeva
99	No name of ruler

46

The name Kanishka is also found in an inscription of the year 41, which is generally referred to a second ruler of that name, Kanishka II. It is thus clear that the duration of the dynasty after the accession of the first Kanishka was almost exactly 100 years, which on the reckoning adopted here would bring it to an end c. AD 227.

It thus appears that the epoch of Kanishka and his successors corresponds with that of Hadrian and the later Antonines at Rome. It was a period of great prosperity in the ancient world, in which the empire of the Kushans took its share. The first and second centuries AD were the time of greatest activity for the overland silk trade between China and Rome. Whenever Parthian hostility intervened, the Kushans could divert the caravans southwards from Balkh to the Indus Delta, whence the goods could complete their journey by sea. In return for this staple import of silk, Rome sent manufactured goods of many kinds – woollen tapestries[36] engraved gems and camei, figurines and metalware; and perhaps most important of all, the magnificent glassware of Alexandria – China had not yet developed the manufacture of glass.[37] At the same time the Indian territories of the Kushans (whose conquests by AD 75 extended to the Ganges Valley) sent exquisite ivories. For all this trade the French excavations at Begram in Afghanistan are the most revealing source,[38] but minor finds are known from many sites.

At the same time, the prosperity of the Kushans was not uninterrupted. Hints of a civil war in the time of Huvishka are hard to substantiate in detail, but another event has left more concrete traces. The frequent appearance in sculpture of the Gandhara School, of votive figures of Hariti, the goddess of smallpox, seems significant. In the main this art was concerned with scenes from Buddhist scripture, but these particular figures could well have a topical relevance. It is well known that when the Roman armies under Avidius Cassius entered Ctesiphon during their Parthian campaign of AD 165, they were struck by a devastating epidemic.[39] Recent research indicates signs in Southern Arabia at the same period of 'un fleau qui ne pouvait être qu'une épidemie foudroyante'.[40] The epidemic is likely to have been smallpox which began in the Kushan empire and spread along the trade-routes to the rest of the ancient world. If confirmed, this synchronism will support the traditional dating.

Religious problems in the Kushan empire are of considerable interest, for the coins of Kanishka and Huvishka illustrate a remarkable variety of deities. Many of these are Zoroastrian, and the Kushans must have adhered to some extent to this religion[41] though they were probably not orthodox in the Sasanian sense. Other coin-types, such as Heracles and Roma suggest classical influence but Serapis, who is also present, had long been acclimatized in Central Asia.[42] Of Hindu deities, Siva is the most prominent, whilst Skanda and others appear. The most far-reaching question is still that of the Kushan attitude to Buddhism. The Buddha is depicted on a rare coin of Kanishka, whose kindly attitude to the faith is well known from the Buddhist sources. The emperor was also the founder of the great *stupa* at Peshawar, where the celebrated Kanishka casket was excavated in 1908. Its Kharoshthi inscription, recently re-interpreted,[43] describes the casket as the gift of the Emperor Kanishka to his monastery in Kanishkapura, the latter evidently a dynastic name given to the city of Peshawar. Also linked to the memory of Kanishka was the Third Buddhist Council, convened in Kashmir (or according to another version of the story at Jalandhara) to prepare commentaries on the canonical Buddhist texts.[44] One of these commentaries was the *Mahavibhasa*, compiled jointly by Parsva and Vasumitra, leading personalities of the Council, and still extant in Chinese. Though assertions of the Emperor's personal conversion to Buddhism may be doubted, this religion made swift progress under the Kushan rulers. Soon it spread across the Hindu Kush along the trade-route to China, and to this epoch is usually attributed the shaping of the giant clay Buddhas at Bamiyan, Surkh Kotal,[45] and at Adzhina-Tepe in Tajikistan.[46] Meanwhile similar currents of travel were carrying along the road to China the knowledge of the Indian Kharoshthi script, found in the documents from Niya, not far from Khotan, and such Buddhist scriptures as the Gandhari *Dharmapada*.[47] It was during the reign of Kanishka, if not before, that the extension of Buddhism to Central Asia and to China began.

3

Sasanians and Turks in Central Asia

The route along which the Buddhist religion spread across the Hindu Kush from Gandhara to Bactria, the Tarim Basin, and China is marked by the find-spots of the sculptures and paintings of the Gandhara School. The best-known products of this art are the sculptures and reliefs carved in green schist which were first made at Taxila and in the Peshawar Vale soon after the middle of the first century AD. However, the most important epoch in the development of the style is marked by the appearance of the Buddha image. The earlier schools of Buddhist art in India had never ventured to depict the sacred person of the Buddha. But in Gandhara, under the influence of such iconic traditions as those of the Graeco-Roman world, and perhaps simultaneously at Mathura, the decisive innovation was produced. Although it is not yet possible to determine the exact date at which the Buddha was first represented in Gandhara, figures on the coins of Kanishka prove that by the middle of the second century AD the image of the Buddha had become familiar. Perhaps the earliest example which can be quoted is that which appears on the famous gold casket from Bimaran, now in the British Museum, which may have been made around AD 75 (Pl. 11).

Besides the representation of the Buddha himself, Gandhara art reproduced many scenes from his life, both during his period on earth, and during his presumed former existences. It is these scenes of narrative sculpture which, after the free-standing image of the Buddha alone, form the most characteristic subjects of Gandhara art. The Kanishka and Bimaran caskets show us the achievements of the school in metalware. Yet among its most remarkable products, surely datable to the lifetime of Kanishka in view of the close identity in style and subject-matter with the Kanishka casket, are the painted frescoes of Miran in the Tarim Basin, discovered during the expeditions of Sir Aurel Stein. The existence of such early Gandhara frescoes so far from the main centres of Kushan power helps to confirm a persistent tradition that Kanishka extended his rule far along the route to China.[1] This penetration along the silk-route could only have been short-lived, and Chinese authority soon afterwards replaced that of the Kushans in the area. Yet the influence of Gandhara art continued in those regions and even after the destruction of the Kushan empire it appears that painting in a derived style was still being executed, for example at Qizil in the area of Kucha. As already noticed, the foundation of the cave monasteries at Bamiyan, with their enormous Buddha figures, can also be attributed to the period of the Kushans. But here the earliest of the surviving paintings, those in the vault of the 35-metre Buddha, are once again of the period subsequent to the fall of the last of the Great Kushan emperors, Vasudeva, in about AD 227. Some may indeed be as late as the fourth century AD, to judge by the ornate crowns of Kushano-Sasanian type which they depict.

There is now a fair measure of agreement between historians that the downfall of the Kushan Empire was due in the main to the conquest of its north-western territories by the Sasanian Persians. It was in AD 224 that the founder of the Sasanian dynasty, Ardashir I, defeated and slew the Parthian emperor, Ardavan V, and made himself paramount ruler of Iran. He also overthrew many of the minor local rulers who had flourished under the Parthian dispensation, replacing them with governors of the Sasanian royal family. If credence is to be accorded to the well-known statement of al-Tabari,[2] Ardashir even waged a campaign in the east of Iran, occupying Sistan, Abarshahr (the modern Nishapur), Marv, Balkh and Khwarazm and receiving a surrender mission from the King of the Kushans. AD 227, the last attested year of Vasudeva I, would be a suitable date for these events. There are, indeed, indications that eastwards of the river Indus a branch of the Kushan house continued to reign for some decades. To this branch the designation of 'Murundas' may be given. One of them may be a third Kanishka, whose existence is attested by his coins. However, there is other evidence that the heartlands of the Kushan empire in Bactria and the Kabul valley now passed into Sasanian hands.

The confirmation comes from the inscription of the Sasanian Emperor Shapur I (AD 240–72), at Naqsh-i Rustam near Persepolis. This document, drafted in three languages, Pahlavi, Parthian and Greek, lists the provinces of the Sasanian Empire as it was in about AD 260. The Greek text is reproduced by Honigmann and Maricq in their commentary on the inscription, though a definitive edition of all three versions is still awaited.[3] The provinces listed include 'The Kushan empire as far as Peshawar'. The inscription thereby shows that by the time of Shapur I, only a fragment of the original Kushan state can have existed as an independent kingdom. The date at which this annexation took place is not specified. Nor is there any description of the arrangements which existed in the time of Shapur for the administration of the Kushan lands under the Sasanians. However, since Herzfeld has shown that one of the earliest Sasanian governors known from the coins of the Kushano-Sasanian series was named Shapur, it may be deduced that the first governor of the province was the future emperor Shapur I before his accession to the imperial throne of Iran.

For the next hundred years after AD 260 the area of Bactria, Sogdiana and Gandhara remained under governors of the Sasanian royal house. Their coins have been described by Herzfeld,[4] and further analysed in a study by the present writer.[5] The list of the governors whom they record is as follows:

Shapur (subsequently Shapur I of Iran, AD 240–72)
Ardashir I Kushanshah
Ardashir II Kushanshah
Firuz I Kushanshah
Hormizd I Kushanshah (c. 277–86, rebel against Bahram II of Iran)
Firuz II Kushanshah

51

Hormizd II Kushanshah (subsequently Hormizd II of Iran, AD 302–9)

Varahran I Kushanshah

Varahran II Kushanshah (reigning AD 360)

References to these governors in the literary histories are extremely scanty but a passage in the Latin *Historia Augusta* appears to refer to the rebellion of the Kushanshah Hormizd I against his brother the Sasanian Bahram II (AD 276–93),[6] and Marquart also called attention to a mention of the same events in a late Latin panegyric.[7] It seems that when the Roman emperor Carus occupied Ctesiphon in AD 283, the Sasanian Bahram II was locked in war with his rival in eastern Iran and thus forced to leave his capital unguarded before the Roman invader. There is the evidence of coins to show that Hormizd I Kushanshah occupied both Marv (where he coined gold) and Herat (where silver was issued). In the end Hormizd was evidently defeated, though the connexions of his successor Firuz II Kushanshah are far from clear.

All the Kushano-Sasanian governors are to be distinguished on the coins by their characteristic, and individual, head-dresses. In the case of Varahran II, this has the form of a ram's horns. It is therefore plausible to identify him with a personage seen by Ammianus Marcellinus (xix, i, 1–2) wearing a diadem of similar form at the siege of Amida in AD 360, and taken by the historian for the Sasanian emperor Shapur II. If the identification with Varahran is correct, this fixes his date, for he must have been still reigning in AD 360. It may be noted that some of the gold coins of the Kushanshahs bear a mint-name, *Baxlo* (for Balkh). The greater number, however, lack any mint-designation and must be assumed to be the issues of the area-headquarters of the Sasanian governors, which would have been either at Kabul or Capisa. It is noticeable, however, that the mint-name of Balkh is not found on the issues of Varahran II Kushanshah. Presumably by the time of his accession the Sasanians had lost control of the Bactrian plain to a fresh wave of invaders coming from the steppe and they retained only the Kabul Valley. It is the story of this new onslaught which now commands our attention.

By the fourth century AD the nomad empire of the Hsiung-nu in Mongolia had long been divided into two separate parts, the northern and the southern respectively. Both groups had led a turbulent career and in AD 311 the southern section of the Hsiung-nu had captured and burnt the capital of Northern China at Lo-yang.[8] This was the city which had been celebrated amongst the Romans as Sera Metropolis, the terminus of the overland Silk Route. The ensuing disturbances along the land routes further west are reflected in the Sogdian Ancient Letters.[9] Subsequently at Lo-yang the southern Hsiung-nu set up a dynasty which survived until massacred by a renegade of their own race in AD 350.

Meanwhile the northern section of the same people had been driven westwards from the vicinity of Lake Baikal by the growing power of their rivals, the Hsien-pi. For more than a century their movements, apparently to the north of the Tien Shan range, were unnoticed by the historians of the major civilizations. Ultimately, however, they emerged upon the Jaxartes steppe to the north of Sogdiana. From AD 350 onwards, various sections of these Hsiung-nu invaded the eastern provinces of the Sasanian Empire, where they became known as the Chionites; and subsequently others appeared among the Alans and the Goths of the South Russian plain to the west of the Volga, to be known as the European Huns.

It was in AD 350 that Shapur II of Iran (AD 309–79) was besieging the fortress of Nisibis in Roman Mesopotamia. Suddenly news reached him of an attack by nomadic invaders upon his eastern frontiers. He at once raised the siege and marched to the threatened area. Whether it was under the shadow of these events that Seleucus (*Slwky*), the Sasanian judge of Kabul, made his journey to the court of the Sasanian king, has recently been called into question.[10] But it was apparently at this time that Shapur II made his headquarters at the city now named Nishapur 'the good deed of Shapur', a designation which it received in honour of this occasion. For nearly ten years Shapur II was obliged to wage war against the Chionites with the purpose of stabilizing his eastern frontier. For the time being he was indeed successful and when in AD 360 he returned to resume the war with Rome, the Chionite forces under their king Grumbates followed him as his allies. Yet in the long run all his efforts were in vain. Within a few decades of the year AD 360 it is sufficiently clear that the former Kushan provinces were no longer under the control of the Sasanian governors, but were subject to the chiefs of the new invaders from the steppe. A new power had arisen in eastern Iran, that of the Chionites and of their successors, the Kidarites and the Hephthalites (or Ephthalites).

It thus seems that the first Huns to appear in Khurasan (some twenty-five years earlier than the arrival of the Huns in Europe), were the Chionites mentioned by Ammianus Marcellinus.[11] Their name seems to consist of the Middle Persian *xiyōn*, 'Hun', plus a Greek tribal ending -ῖται. Henning, however, considered the termination of the name Ephthalitae as a Sogdian plural form.[12] After the Chionites had finally allied themselves with Shapur II they joined in his campaign against the Romans in Mesopotamia. There, at the siege of Amida (Diyarbakr), the son of their king Grumbates was killed. Ammianus Marcellinus describes how the prince's body was cremated, an event of some significance, since the Sasanian army which the Chionites accompanied was Zoroastrian, and to them cremation was anathema. However, the detail tallies with the archaeological data for the European Huns.[13] There are similar reports from the Bishkent Valley in Tajikistan,[14] whilst the *Chou shu* attributes the same customs to the perhaps related people of Qarashahr during this period.[15]

Not long afterwards, we learn of the rise of the Hunnish chief Kidara, who was the dominant figure amongst the tribes of Bactria during the last decades of the fourth century AD. His coins – for it is to him that they are best attributed – were found with those of Shapur II (AD 309–79), Ardashir II (AD 379–83) and Shapur III (AD 383–8) in the treasure of Tepe Maranjan, near Kabul.[16] No doubt his reign overlapped, and perhaps succeeded, those of the three Sasanian rulers. Priscus, the Greek historian of the Huns, often has occasion to speak of the 'Kidarite Huns'. This seems sufficient reason for acknowledging that the followers of Kidara were indeed Huns, and not, as certain writers maintain, Kushans, despite the fact that Kidara continued to place upon his coins the old territorial title Kushanshah 'King of the Kushans', which had also been used by his Sasanian predecessors. It is true that the use by Priscus of the expression 'Kidarite Huns' with reference to the fifth century AD may in turn involve some element of anachronism. For by that time a new horde had appeared on the scene. It seems that towards the end of the lifetime of Kidara, and during the reign of his son (who must, as the coins indicate, have borne the same name, and was thus Kidara II), a fresh wave of Hunnish invaders, the Hephthalites entered Bactria, and drove the Kidarites into the Punjab. In the latter region the name of Kidara is found on many gold coins of which the mints and exact attributions are uncertain.

In the opinion of Ghirshman the Chionites (a term which he understood to include the Kidarites) were not distinct from the Hephthalites who play a prominent part in the history of the fifth century AD. However, in the preceding paragraph the view of sinologists such as McGovern[17] and Enoki[18] is followed. These authorities maintained that the Hephthalites were fresh arrivals, who descended on Bactria early in the fifth century AD, and drove the Kidarites southwards. Thus the eastern invaders repulsed from Iran by Bahram IV in AD 427 may have belonged to either group. But this upheaval was in any case probably the result of disturbances arising from the appearance of the Hephthalites. It was indeed specifically to the latter that the Sasanian prince Firuz resorted in AD 457 for aid to gain the throne of Iran from his brother Hormizd III. Later Firuz turned against his Hephthalite allies; but he was defeated and captured by their king, called Akhšunwar by al-Tabari, or, by Firdausi, Khušnavaz. On this occasion, Firuz obtained his release by leaving his son Qubad as a hostage. Later he ransomed Qubad and returned to the attack, but charged his cavalry into a hidden ditch and perished with all his men. It is interesting, in view of the foregoing discussion of the funeral customs of the Chionites, that according to al-Tabari, Khušnavaz had the bodies of the Persians interred in tumuli.

In this context of their burial practices, and the defeat of

Firuz by the Hephthalites, the classic description is by Procopius,[19] who claims that though they were Huns by name and race, they did not live as nomads; that they were of fair complexion and regular features; and that they practised inhumation of the dead, burying up to twenty of his boon companions with each of their chiefs. Here therefore we find for the Hephthalites a point of contrast with the cremation practised by the Chionites.

In AD 488 or 489 the Sasanian king Qubad, who had lived as a hostage amongst the Hephthalites during his youth, achieved his restoration to the Persian throne through Hephthalite support. None the less the tribe continued to threaten the security of Iran. The next Sasanian emperor, Khosrau Anoshirvan (AD 531–79) built fortifications against them in the Gurgan plain. Finally, with the appearance on the scene of the Turks, he allied himself with the Turkish Khan, called in the western sources Sinjibu or Silzibul,[20] to crush the Hephthalites. In a fierce battle soon after AD 557 the latter were dispersed, and their lands partitioned along the line of the Oxus between the Sasanians, who took the southern part, and the Turks, who took all that lay to the north.

It was during the later part of the Hephthalite predominance in Bactria, during the fifth and early sixth centuries AD, that Indian sources record a series of incursions into the Punjab and Western India by a people known as the Hunas. These were evidently Huns but it is not clear which branch of the nation they represented. The sept most prominent in these invasions appears to have been that of the Zabulites. As early as AD 458 the Gupta prince Skandagupta had been called upon to resist the onslaughts of invaders who appear to have been Hunas. During his lifetime he held them at bay but by the end of the century the Gupta Empire was in dissolution and by AD 510 the Huna chief Toramana had established his rule over a large part of India. The son and successor of Toramana was the notorious Mihirakula who, after ruling much of the Punjab in about AD 525, was repulsed from the Indian plains but continued to maintain himself in Kashmir. The tale is told of Mihirakula that he delighted in having elephants rolled over the precipices of Kashmir for the pleasure he derived from their squeals as they fell on the rocks below. Toramana and Mihirakula were succeeded by other Huna kings. Amongst these were Lakhana and Khingila, whose reigns fell in the second part of the sixth century, but whose exact dates are not known. These kings must have reigned at Kabul or at Gardiz, and the reign of Khingila lasted for at least eight years, as a recently discovered inscription proves.[21]

Unless it survives in the dialect of Khalji Turkish reported by Minorsky,[22] the language of the Asiatic Huns, like that of their European cousins, is entirely unknown. There have been two main hypotheses to explain the linguistic and ethnic affinities of this people. However, the 'Iranian' hypothesis argued by Ghirshman[23] and Enoki,[24] and based mainly on the coin legends in cursive Greek script, has now been overtaken by the discovery that these legends are actually in the local East Iranian dialect of Bactria. The discovery of the Bactrian inscription at Surkh Kotal has made this conclusion certain. No doubt this Iranian language was occasionally used by Hunnish groups for administrative purposes; but as to the actual speech of the Huns, Minorsky's 'Turkish' hypothesis now holds the field. Puzzling, none the less, is the statement of the *Chou shu*[25] that the Hephthalites practised polyandry. This would no doubt weigh against the theory that their origin was Indo-European, but suggests Tibetan rather than Turkish affinities. The military equipment of the Eastern Huns (in this case, apparently, that of the Kidarites), represented on a silver dish in the British Museum (Pl. 12),[26] has also some relevance to the question of their racial origin. It included a straight, two-handed sword and a compound bow, but no stirrups. The first feature and the last clearly set them apart from their successors the Avars, of whom curved swords and stirrups were the characteristic equipment, and who are thought to have been Mongols. Minorsky argued that both the Turkish-speaking Khalaj of Iran, and the Pashtu-speaking Ghilzai of Afghanistan (who seem to have been identical with the people known to mediaeval records as the Khaljis) represent descendants of the Hephthalites. This view seems paradoxical at first sight, but it finds support in a number of small pieces of evidence which suggest the earlier presence in

57

the area of Afghanistan now occupied by the Ghilzais of a Turkish-speaking element. It could well be that a Turkish group related to the Khalaj of Iran and bearing the same name, was once dominant amongst the Hephthalites in this area. Subsequently they must have been absorbed by the more numerous Pashtu-speaking tribes of East Iranian origin, but bequeathed the name of Khalji to the resulting tribal amalgam. That an invading tribe should ultimately lose its own language, and adopt that of the previous substratum people is not unparalleled in Afghanistan. The Mongolian Hazaras of Central Afghanistan are today almost entirely Persian-speaking, though conscious of their own Mongolian origins. Minorsky's theory is thus decidedly attractive, though it has to be admitted that the evidence for the racial and linguistic affinities of the Hephthalites is extremely fragmentary, and therefore by no means conclusive.

Whilst the various groups of the Eastern Huns were ruling in Bactria, and other parts of present-day Afghanistan, major dynastic changes were taking place amongst the steppe-peoples in Mongolia. These changes in fact eventually brought about the downfall of the Hephthalite empire. After the Huns had been driven away from the Orkhon and Minusinsk regions into Bactria, the Hsien-pi for a time dominated the steppes of Mongolia. However, by the sixth century AD a group known as the Juan-juan were in the ascendant there. These Juan-juan appear to have been identical with the tribe which later appeared in Europe under the name of Avars, and who, soon after AD 560, were lording it over the Hungarian plain. Though very little is known of the dynastic history of the Avars, either in their Mongolian or in their Hungarian habitat, this nation is of some interest to the historian, as it appears that they communicated to Europe two important devices for cavalry warfare, the stirrup and the sabre.[27] Both the stirrup and the curved cavalry sword seem to have been invented on the frontier between China and the steppe during the fifth century AD. After their transmission by the Avars to Europe, they were soon adopted by the Byzantines.[28] It is indeed a striking fact that so elementary a device as the stirrup remained unknown not only to all the peoples of Classical Antiquity, but even to such practised horsemen as the Sasanian Persians. Yet this appears to have been the case.

The expulsion of the Juan-juan dynasty from the Mongolian steppe was the result of the rise of the Turks, who thus make their first appearance in history. By AD 552 the downfall of the Juan-juan was complete. The founder of the Turkish empire was the chief called in the Chinese sources Tu-men (Bumin in the Turkish inscriptions). The residence of the Turkish khan was established in the Aq Dagh, to the north of Kucha. However, the western extensions of the Turkish realm reached as far as the Oxus and the Caspian Sea, and were, as we have seen, under the virtually independent rule of Istemi, the brother of Tu-men, the same personage as is called in the western sources Sinjibu (Silzibul). It was he who formed the alliance with Khosrau I Anoshirvan of Iran which resulted in the destruction of the Hephthalite kingdom and established for the Turkish Empire a common frontier with Sasanian Iran. In AD 576 Istemi died but Turkish influence remained strong in Sogdiana, even though both parts of the Turkish Empire made nominal submission to the T'ang dynasty of China, the Eastern Turks in AD 630, and the Western Turks in AD 659.

It was not until AD 682 that there was established in Mongolia a new empire of the Eastern ('Blue') Turks. This was the Turkish state which produced the Runic inscriptions of the Orkhon.[29] A bibliography of these inscriptions has been prepared by Sinor.[30] These texts recount how Elterish (AD 681–91) overwhelmed the Oghuz at Inigek Kol, and raided across China to the Pacific Coast. His successor Qapghan subjugated the Kirghiz and Türgesh in the West, and reached the Iron Gates in Sogdiana. Under the third emperor, Bilge (AD 716–34), the defection of the Oghuz, and their flight to China, heralded the decline of the 'Blue' Turks, in spite of a series of desperate battles. Between AD 699 and 711 the khanate of the Eastern Turks included that of the Western Turks. Eventually amongst the latter the Türgesh clan attained the ascendancy. With the campaigns of the Türgesh chief Su-lu against the successors of the Arab general Qutayba we come to the period of the Arab conquest of Sogdiana, which will henceforth be known under its

59

Arabic name of Mawarannahr. Already in AD 651 the Arab armies had overrun the whole of Iran and had pursued the fugitive Sasanian king Yazdagird III (AD 632–51) to Marv where he met his death at the hands of an assassin. Before many years had passed, the Arab armies were to find themselves poised on the banks of the Oxus, ready to dispute with the Turks the possession of the provinces to the north of the river.

Meanwhile, at the eastern extremity of the Turkish world in Mongolia, there was formed at this time a Turkish state of outstanding cultural interest, that of the Uighurs (Pl. 13). In concert with other Turkish groups such as the Qarluq and the Bismïl, the Uighurs overthrew the empire of the Eastern Turks, and in AD 744 established their own, with its capital at Ordu-Baligh on the River Orkhon. This site was still known in recent times as Qara Balgasun, and famous for its trilingual inscription to which we shall return. Hamilton's study[31] gives the dynastic table of the Uighur emperors, but this is rather complex since most of the rulers' names are known from Chinese transcriptions; and where the Turkish designations are known, or can be reconstructed, they are merely titles of a rather stereotyped form. Thus the first of the new line, in Chinese transcription Kou-li P'ei-lo, was in Turkish designated *Qutlug bilgä kül qaghan* 'Majestic, wise and glorious emperor'.

The most influential cultural event in the history of the Uighur Kaghanate was the conversion of the rulers to the Manichaean religion under the third Kaghan in AD 762. This is the event recorded in the trilingual inscription of Qara Balgasun.[32] The texts are in Chinese, Sogdian and Turkish, of which, however, only the first is satisfactorily preserved. Apparently it was as a result of the Uighur occupation of the Chinese silk-route terminus of Lo-yang that the Kaghan was brought into contact with Manichaean missionaries who had been established in China since AD 694. Their syncretistic religion, including elements of Zoroastrian, Christian and Buddhist origin, had been founded in Mesopotamia by its prophet Mani soon after the rise of the Sasanian Empire in Iran, which took place in AD 224. The new creed penetrated early into Khurasan and Sogdiana under the leadership of the apostle Mar

Ammo, and when the community came under increasing persecution in Sasanian territory (as it did again later under the Caliphate), its devotees, many no doubt of Sogdian nationality and by tradition traders, tended to drift increasingly towards the East along the routes to China.

For future generations the main importance of the Manichaean community was to lie in their preservation of their canonical scriptures in such otherwise little-known languages as Parthian, Sogdian and Middle Persian. These works included fragments of the Middle Persian book *Shaburagan* '(The book) of Shapur', in which Mani expounded his belief to the Sasanian emperor Shapur I. Besides the surviving Middle Persian fragments, the opening sentences of this work are preserved by the Arabic chronographer al-Biruni:[33]

Wisdom and deeds have always from time to time been brought to mankind by the messengers of God. So in one age they have been brought by the messenger called Buddha to India, in another by Zaradusht to Persia, in another by Jesus to the West. Thereupon this revelation has come down, this prophecy in this last age through me, Mani, the messenger of the God of Truth to Babylonia.

Of Mani's other works, there were also preserved amongst the Uighurs significant fragments of the *Kavan* or *Book of Giants*.[34] The emphasis placed by Manichaean thought on calligraphy was naturally important in assisting the transmission of such works, as also, amongst the arts, was their interest in manuscript illumination and painting.

With the conversion of the third Uighur Kaghan, who adopted the Persian title *zahag-i Mani* 'the (spiritual) child of Mani', this faith, once that of a persecuted minority, became for the first time the state religion of a powerful empire. It gained correspondingly in influence and prosperity. The Uighur tribes, hitherto devotees of a somewhat ferocious Shamanism, through the new religion acquired a measure of access to the gentler cultures of Transoxania and Iran. Thus in the words of the inscription:[35]

Que [le pays] aux moeurs barbares où fumait le sang se change en une contrée où on se nourrit de légumes; que l'État où on se tuait se transforme en un royaume où on exhorte au bien.

61

The first Uighur empire lasted until AD 840, when a sudden rising of the Kirghiz tribes along the River Yenisei led to the destruction of its capital, and the dispersal of the thirteen principal Uighur tribes. However, certain groups of survivors migrated to the south-westwards, establishing themselves in the oases of the Tarim basin (Sinkiang). Here they tended to supersede the previous Indo-European populations, in particular the speakers of the so-called 'Tokharian' dialects. Particular centres of this later Uighur settlement were at Kan-Tcheou, to the east of Tun-huang, and at Qočo in the oasis of Turfan. It was at the latter site, in particular, that a large proportion of the important manuscript finds were made, containing examples written in the Uighur, Manichaean and Syriac scripts, and representative of the Manichaean, Christian and Buddhist communities. From these texts, published for the most part in widely scattered articles in the periodical literature, our knowledge of the complex cultural life of the later Uighur kingdoms is derived. These kingdoms survived until the period of the rise of the Mongol Empire, in which the Uighurs were finally incorporated, and to which they bequeathed their characteristic script, adapted from the Sogdian, and their scribal tradition. Thus it was that traditions of the Uighurs and their former empire, of their supreme ruler known latterly by the title of Idiqut, and even of the impressive inscriptions of Qara Balgasun, were available (occasionally perhaps in a slightly distorted form) to Juwaini when he wrote his history of Chingiz Khan, the *Tarīkh-i Jahān Gushā*.[36]

4

The Ascendancy of Islam

One of the causes both of the military effectiveness and of the strategic complexity of the Arab invasion of Central Asia lay in the fact that the advance was conducted simultaneously along two separate, but converging, lines of communication. The destruction by the Arabs of the Persian royal army at the battle of Nihavend in 21/642 put an end to centrally-organized Persian resistance, and the last Sasanian king, Yazdagird III, became a fugitive. Sporadic opposition was offered by local authorities but this was seldom very effective. In 29/649 the forces of the governor of Kufa, Sa'id b. al-'As, were pressing forward along the northern road from Hamadan and Ray towards Jurjan and Khurasan. At the same time, the Arab governor of Basra, 'Abdullah b. 'Amir, had begun his advance through Fars and Kirman to the oasis of Tabas, and on to Nishapur and Marv. The historian al-Baladhuri, whose history of the Islamic conquests provides the most concise account of these events,[1] reports a story that the Persian *marzban* of Tus had sent a letter to each of these governors, offering to surrender the province to whichever arrived first. Though 'Abdullah b. 'Amir had the less hospitable route to travel, the rapidity of his movements enabled him to win the race, and gain control of the province. Of the major cities of Khurasan, Nishapur, Sarakhs, Tus, Herat and Marv all quickly came to terms with the invaders. In the operations against Sarakhs, 'Abdullah b. Khazim, a future governor, distinguished himself. From Kirman a detachment had been sent to conquer Sistan under al-Rabi' b. Ziyad and this mission was successful. However, the advance-guard sent out to the north-east of Herat under al-Ahnaf b. Qais ran into heavy opposition near the Murghab river and only after severe fighting succeeded in occupying the local towns and pressing forward to Balkh.

Disturbances in the Arab empire occurring during the Caliphate of 'Ali (35/656 to 40/661) led to the withdrawal from Khurasan of 'Abdullah b. 'Amir, and to a slackening of Arab control over the province. However, after the accession of Mu'awiya to the Caliphate, 'Abdullah returned to the governorship of Basra; yet though his lieutenants regained control of Khurasan, he was dismissed in 44/664 for undue leniency. His successor at Basra, Ziyad b. Abi Sufiyan, initiated the division of the province of Khurasan into four 'quarters', those of Nishapur, Balkh, Marv al-Rud (on the Murghab river) and Herat respectively. But it was only with the appointment of this governor's son, 'Ubaydullah b. Ziyad, to the governorship of Khurasan in 54/674 that the Arab advance was restarted, and Arab troops crossed the Oxus (Amu-Darya) to defeat the ruler of Bukhara.

Some of the sources attribute a prominent role in the defence of Bukhara against the Arabs to a Turkish empress designated by the title of 'the Khatun' but this version is usually regarded as legendary. In any event, the subsequent governors of Khurasan continued to raid north of the Oxus; in particular Salm, another son of Ziyad, who was appointed in 61/681 and waged a successful campaign against the people of Khwarazm. Later he advanced to Samarqand where his wife, the first Arab woman to accompany an expedition north of the Oxus, gave birth to a son who was afterwards surnamed al-Sughdi (the Sogdian).

The position of the Arab governors on the eastern frontier of Islam was none the less gravely prejudiced by disturbances which broke out in the heart of the Caliphate as a result of the rising of the anti-Caliph, 'Abdullah ibn al-Zubayr, between 64/683 and 73/692. The Arab tribes which had moved into Khurasan were in consequence torn by factional disputes, so that Salm was unable to maintain his position and was forced to hand over the government to 'Abdullah b. Khazim, who now came forward as a supporter of Ibn al-Zubayr. Ibn Khazim continued to govern Khurasan as a virtually independent ruler until he was killed in an affray in 72/691. Moreover, his son, Musa b. 'Abdullah b. Khazim succeeded in getting possession of the fortress of Termez (Tirmiz) on the north bank of the Oxus where he continued to maintain himself in open rebellion against both the Umaiyad governors, and the Turkish and Sogdian chiefs, until his death in battle in 85/704.

Meanwhile in Iraq the great viceroy al-Hajjaj had assumed the government on behalf of the Umaiyad caliph 'Abd al-Malik. He sent a noted general, al-Muhallab b. Abi Sufra, to Khurasan as governor in 78/697. Al-Muhallab sought to divert the energies of the feuding tribes by renewing the Arab campaigns across the Oxus and he raided Kishsh (Shahrisabz) and Nasaf (Nakhshab); but on his return he contracted pleurisy, and died in 82/701. His successor was his son, Yazid b. al-Muhallab, a flamboyant personality of lavish generosity but ruthless cruelty. A recently discovered Arab-Sasanian coin records his levying of the poll-tax in the district of Juzjan, and apparently preserves his portrait.[2] Later Yazid intervened further south on behalf of his superior al-Hajjaj against a dangerous rebel; this was 'Abd al-Rahman b. Muhammad b. al-Ash'ath who had been sent out by al-Hajjaj from Basra to Sistan at the head of the splendidly equipped army called 'the Army of Peacocks', but who had subsequently turned against his overlord al-Hajjaj, and waged war against him.

Nevertheless in 85/704 al-Hajjaj relieved Yazid of the governorship, replacing him first by his brother al-Mufaddal b. al-Muhallab, and subsequently, after a few months, by the celebrated Qutayba b. Muslim. Qutayba was in fact the general responsible, in a series of energetic campaigns, for the definitive annexation by the Arabs of the lands north of the River Oxus. After conquering both Bukhara and Samarqand, he established a base north of the Jaxartes at Shash (Tashkent), and pressed forward to the north as far as Isfijab. At the same time, Qutayba's brother 'Abd al-Rahman reduced the kingdom of Khwarazm (Chorasmia) to submission. Qutayba was still campaigning in Farghana in 96/715 when news came of the accession to the Caliphate of his bitter personal enemy Sulayman. When Qutayba refused allegiance to the new sovereign his army mutinied and attacked the general's tent. Only his bodyguard of Sogdian hostages remained loyal, and Qutayba and many of his household were slain.

The period following the death of Qutayba was marked by considerable setbacks to the power of the Arabs in Mawarannahr. Qutayba had enjoyed a unique advantage in having the wholehearted support of his overlord al-Hajjaj. His successors were less well-supported and no doubt also less competent. Factional disturbances were rife amongst the Arab tribes in Khurasan, and to these were soon added the clandestine propaganda of the 'Abbasid emissaries, who were working to effect the overthrow of the Umaiyad Caliphate. But the most powerful factor was probably the rise of the Türgesh Turks to the north of the Jaxartes. The Türgesh responded quickly to the appeals of the local Sogdian chiefs, by whom they were called in as a counterpoise to the power of the Arabs. In 106/724 a Muslim expedition into Farghana was heavily defeated by the Turks and only escaped to recross the Jaxartes after a bitter action known, from the suffering of the troops, as the 'Day of Thirst'.[3] Henceforth, for over a decade, the Arabs were forced onto the defensive. It is noteworthy, too, that during this period both the Arabs and the local princes of Sogdiana and Tukharistan sent many embassies to the Chinese court – no doubt in the hope of persuading the Chinese emperor to influence the Türgesh in their interest.

From this period of disturbances after the death of Qutayba a remarkable cache of documents has been preserved, the majority of which are in Sogdian script and language. These constitute the archives of the Sogdian prince Divastich, the ruler of Pyanjikent on the upper Zarafshan river. Divastich took refuge from an Arab punitive expedition in his mountain castle at Mount Mugh, which was eventually taken and sacked by the Arabs. Here in recent years the archives were discovered;[4] Pyanjikent itself has also been the scene of a successful excavation in which a remarkable series of wall-paintings were discovered by Soviet archaeologists[5] and dated to the immediately pre-Muslim period.

During these campaigns the Arabs lost control of practically all their territories north of the Oxus, and the Türgesh *khaqan*, Su-lu, was even able to make incursions south of the river. He was, however, defeated by the Arab governor, Asad b. 'Abdullah al-Qasri, and soon afterwards assassinated by one of his own officers. This event was the signal for the disintegration of the Türgesh kingdom and the removal of the threat to Arab rule so that the next governor, Nasr b. Saiyar, who succeeded on the death of Asad in 120/737, was able to undertake the pacification and re-organization of the province with considerable success.

Nasr was a wise and mature officer who did much to restore the prosperity of Khurasan, despite the bitter factional strife among the Arabs under his command. His memory has been tarnished by the part which he played in bringing about the death of Yahya b. Zayd, one of the 'Alid claimants to the Caliphate, who was the centre of an active propaganda campaign. When Yahya appeared at Balkh, Nasr had him taken into custody and ordered him to proceed to the capital at Damascus. But Yahya broke away near Nishapur and after engaging in a number of skirmishes with the local governors, gathered a small force and made his way to Anbir (modern Sar-i Pul, in Afghanistan). Nasr sent against him a detachment of cavalry and in the ensuing battle Yahya was killed. His body was exposed on the wall of the town, to be buried eventually by the followers of Abu Muslim. The burial-place is greatly revered to the present day and is the site of an exquisitely decorated Seljuqid shrine (Pl. 14).

It was in 129/747–8 that the 'Abbasid missionary Abu Muslim (his official name was 'Abd al-Rahman b. Muslim) arrived in Khurasan, and his recruiting campaign immediately scored a notable success. He won the whole-hearted support of the *dehqans* (Iranian landowners), and all the elements hostile to the Umaiyad government joined forces with him. With the Arab garrisons still deeply divided by faction, the position of Nasr b. Saiyar soon became untenable. He had no alternative but to withdraw to the west, and died in the course of his retreat.

This triumph of Abu Muslim was the prelude to the downfall of the Umaiyad dynasty and the establishment of that of the 'Abbasids. But while these momentous events were taking place in the west a new danger to the Arab province was appearing in the east. A powerful Chinese expedition had entered the valley of the upper Jaxartes and even went to the lengths of putting to death the ruler of Shash for disobedience. They were opposed, in 134/751 by Ziyad b. Salih, the general of Abu Muslim, and heavily defeated in a battle which put an end to Chinese pretensions to rule in Mawarannahr. But the battle had an interesting consequence since it was from Chinese prisoners captured on this occasion that the people of Samarqand learnt how to manufacture paper, a commodity which was eventually to supersede parchment and papyrus as a writing-material in the west.

In 138/755 Abu Muslim was decoyed to Iraq by his 'Abbasid overlord, the Caliph al-Mansur, and put to death. But the great influence which he had exercised in the province made a lasting impression on the people of Khurasan and his memory was constantly being revived in connexion with the aberrant religious cults which made their appearance in later years. These cults sometimes took the form of movements of open revolt against the 'Abbasid government. The most dangerous of these movements was that of 160/776, which was led by a certain Hashim b. Hakim, known as al-Muqanna' 'the Veiled One', who claimed to be an incarnation of the deity, previously manifested in Adam, Noah, Abraham, Moses, Jesus, Muhammad and Abu Muslim.[6] The sectaries were besieged by the government forces in a fortress near Kishsh, where they ultimately took their own lives.

Meanwhile the Kharijite dissidents, who had separated themselves from orthodox Islam in the Caliphate of 'Ali (35/656 to 40/661), continued to maintain themselves in a state of rebellion against the central authority, 'Abbasid no less than Umaiyad. They were especially numerous in the provinces of Sistan and Kirman, and though repeatedly suppressed, they as often re-asserted themselves. One of the Kharijite anti-Caliphs, Hamza b. 'Abdullah (also called Hamza b. Atrak or Hamza b.

68

Adhrak), became prominent in 181/797 and even dared to defy the 'Abbasid Caliph, Harun al-Rashid. The Arab historians take little note of the doings of Hamza, but the Persian *Tarikh-i Sistan*[7] greatly elaborates the tale of his adventures and quotes in full an eloquent exchange of letters between the Caliph and the Kharijite. Though himself little more than a bandit chief, Hamza appears to have given expression to a widely-felt desire for independence of the Baghdad Caliphate and the saga of his deeds was evidently a popular one in Sistan. He was credited with the foundation of the city of Gardiz in Afghanistan but he failed by a narrow margin to capture the city of Zaranj, the capital of Sistan. According to the *Tarikh-i Sistan*, the Caliph Harun al-Rashid was on his way to suppress Hamza when he died near Tus in 193/809. Another purpose of the caliph's expedition was no doubt to bring to an end the rebellion of Rafi' b. Layth, the grandson of the former governor Nasr b. Saiyar, in Samarqand. However, it was not until the reign of al-Ma'mun, in 195/810, that Rafi' was induced to make his submission, and the ultimate fate of Hamza is not recorded.

When at his death Harun al-Rashid divided his empire between his two sons, al-Amin (who received Iraq and the west), and al-Ma'mun (who was to reside in Khurasan), the arrangement paved the way for the break-up of the Caliphate. There followed the formation of local and national states in the eastern provinces. Al-Ma'mun eventually dethroned his brother and rewarded his Persian general, Tahir 'the Ambidextrous', with the governorship of the province of Khurasan. When Tahir omitted the name of the caliph from the Friday prayers, al-Ma'mun had him secretly poisoned, but the governorship remained in the same family, passing first to Tahir's eldest son, Talha, and then to a second son, 'Abdullah, so that the province evolved into a hereditary and effectively independent kingdom, with its centre at Nishapur.

The Tahirids were content to limit their rule to the boundaries of their original province, and to maintain the forms of government which had prevailed under the caliphate. However, an innovation which has been credited to this period is the use of the Persian language written in Arabic script for literary purposes.[8] For all literary work under the Caliphate had been in the Arabic language and it seems probable that Persian was previously written only in the cumbrous Pahlavi script.

Very different from the kingdom of the Tahirids was the state set up in Sistan by Ya'qub b. al-Layth al-Saffar 'the Copper-smith', from which title his dynasty takes the name of the Saffarids. Ya'qub was not an officer of the 'Abbasid caliphs but a formidable ruffian who had enlisted in a group of levies serving under Salih b. Nasr, the governor of Bust. When Salih marched to Zaranj to expel the Tahirid governor, Ibrahim al-Qawsi, Ya'qub accompanied him and exploited the confused fighting which ensued to displace both Salih and another possible rival, and to secure his own election as Amir in 247/861. A redoubtable soldier, Ya'qub went on to seize the fortress of Bust and to fight a difficult battle with the garrison, who were supported by the Turkish chief Zunbil, ruler of the hill-country to the north-east. In the battle, Ya'qub was hard pressed but by a brilliant charge with fifty horsemen he slew Zunbil and put the enemy to flight, seizing booty sufficient to fill two hundred river-barges.

After this victory Ya'qub continued to gain rapidly in strength. He slew the Kharijite chief 'Ammar and dispersed his army, before advancing on Herat to take the city from its Tahirid governor. Then he turned west to the conquest of Kirman and Fars, and finally advanced on Nishapur, taking the town and imprisoning the Tahirid Amir Muhammad. He subsequently occupied Jurjan and invaded Tabaristan, putting to flight the 'Alid ruler of that province, al-Hasan b. Zayd. The increasing power of Ya'qub aroused the apprehension of the Caliph al-Mu'tamid who denounced the Saffarid as a usurper. Ya'qub consequently resolved to march against the Caliph himself and in 263/876 advanced upon Baghdad. Near the capital he sustained his first defeat at Dayr al-'Aqul and retired to Jundai Shapur, where he died in 265/879.

His brother and successor was 'Amr b. al-Layth, who though lacking the iron resolution of Ya'qub, ruled effectively over the Saffarid empire of Sistan, Fars, and Khurasan for twenty-one years, and displayed considerable military ambition. One of his

70

officers named Fardaghan, on appointment as governor of Ghazni, took and pillaged the Hindu temples of Sakavand in the Logar Valley near Kabul. This provoked a strong reaction from Kamalu, the Hindushahiya king of Ohind on the Indus, in whose territories the desecrated shrines lay.[9] In 287/900 'Amr, led on by the deceitful encouragement of the Caliph, attempted to make good a claim to rule over the trans-Oxus provinces. He advanced to Balkh but meanwhile a new power, that of the Samanid dynasty, was forming in the territories coveted by 'Amr. At Balkh the Saffarid army was met and surrounded by the forces of the Samanid Amir, Isma'il b. Ahmad. When 'Amr sought to escape by flight, he was captured and sent as a prisoner to Baghdad, where he eventually died in captivity. The Muslim historians are fond of contrasting the pomp of 'Amr before this disaster with his subsequent wretchedness.

In Sistan survivors of the Saffarid dynasty continued to maintain themselves for several decades and the lineage persisted for centuries.[10] But the Samanid dynasty of Mawarannahr was now established, under the largely nominal suzerainty of the Caliphs, as the paramount power in Islamic Central Asia and as the overlord of Sistan. On their western border from the time of Isma'il the Samanids attempted with varying success to establish their control over Jurjan and Tabaristan. To the north of the Syr-Darya, Shash (Tashkent) was an important Samanid commercial centre and their frontier extended as far as Isfijab near Chimkant. Authority over Khurasan was exercised by governors residing at Nishapur whilst the capital of the Samanid Amirs themselves was at Bukhara.

Whilst in its heyday the Samanid state played a substantial military role in protecting the Muslim world from the incursions of the pagan Turks of Central Asia, it also exercised an important cultural influence. It was thanks to the Samanids – despite allegations that the Amir Nasr b. Ahmad (301/913 to 331/943) had been secretly converted by an Isma'ili missionary[11] – that Sunni Islam of strict orthodoxy was firmly established in Mawarannahr. Law and order and the rights of property were strongly upheld and the Islamic judges and religious leaders enjoyed great prestige. Literary activities were also strongly

71

encouraged by the Samanid rulers. Though Arabic was the language of administration and of much scientific writing it was during this period that Persian literature began its full development. The poet Rudaki lived at the court of Nasr b. Ahmad and in a brilliant Persian ode describes the scene at a royal banquet.[12] Persian prose was also coming into fashion, an example being the Wazir Bal'ami's translation of the Arabic Annals of al-Tabari.

Samanid campaigns against the pagan Turks of the steppe produced little in the way of booty but they were the source of a plentiful supply of slaves. Some of these were traded with the metropolitan lands of Islam where they provided recruits for the slave-bodyguards of the 'Abbasid Caliphs. The Samanids themselves also made extensive use of Turkish slave-soldiers, who became an important element in their armies, and thanks to the well-known military virtues of the Turk, often rose to positions of high authority in the Samanid service. One such promoted slave-officer was the celebrated Alptigin, who rose to the rank of commander-in-chief of the troops in Khurasan under the Amir 'Abd al-Malik b. Nuh (343/954 to 350/961). Fearing his successor, Mansur I b. Nuh, against whom he had been intriguing, Alptigin resolved to withdraw towards the south-eastern frontier of the Samanid state. There he could hope to set himself up as a semi-independent ruler on the border of India where there were good opportunities to support himself by conducting a 'Holy War'. There was precedent for such an expedition in the career of the Samanid general Qaratigin (c. 317/929) at Bust. There Qaratigin was later succeeded by his own slave-officers.

On his arrival at Ghazni Alptigin was refused entry by the local ruler Abu Bakr Lawik (or Anuk) but succeeded in capturing the town in 351/962. In the following year Alptigin died[13] and was succeeded by his son Ishaq (or Abu Ishaq) who secured recognition by the Samanid government and who, when expelled from Ghazni by Lawik, induced the Samanid authorities to effect his restoration. Ishaq died in 355/966, being succeeded by another slave-officer, Bilgetigin, who in turn was killed by an arrow whilst besieging the Kharijite Amir of Gardiz in 364/975.

Another officer, Piri, was deposed after two years and Sebük-tigin, also of slave origin and the real founder of the Ghaznavid empire, came to the throne.

In 367/977 Sebüktigin attacked the Hindushahiya kingdom of Ohind, taking prisoner its king, Jaypal, who was released on payment of tribute. Yet at the same time Sebüktigin always regarded himself as the faithful vassal of the Samanid Amir. Thus in 383/993 when the Amir Nuh II b. Mansur was faced with the rebellion of his generals Fa'iq and Abu 'Ali Simjuri, he called in Sebüktigin to intervene in Khurasan and redress the balance. After his victory in 384/994 Sebüktigin was rewarded with the additional governorships of Balkh, Tukharistan, Bamiyan, Ghur and Gharchistan, whilst his son Mahmud (the future Sultan Mahmud of Ghazni) was invested with the post of commander-in-chief of Khurasan, with headquarters at Nishapur. Consequently when Sebüktigin died in 387/997 Mahmud found himself strong enough to become sole ruler over his father's former territories and to consolidate his possession of the lands south of the Oxus. Meanwhile the Samanid empire had fallen into a state of great confusion. A new power, that of the Turkish Qarakhanids, had been advancing from the north, and was soon to divide the territory of the Samanids with Mahmud.

The question of the tribal origin – amongst the various Turkish groups – of the Qarakhanid dynasty has been much discussed.[14] The disagreement between the modern authorities is to some extent a matter of terminology, but the view now pre-vailing is that the rulers represented a branch of the Qarluq tribe. This people before their conversion to Islam seem to have lived to the north-east of the Samanid frontier round the centres of Balasaghun (on the Chu river) and Taraz (Talas). Writing in Arabic during the reign of the Caliph al-Muqtadi (d. 487/1094), the author Mahmud al-Kashghari gives a detailed account of the Turkish tribes and dialects of the Qarakhanid period in his work entitled *Dīwān lughāt al-Turk*.[15] He lists the tribes of his day in two zones running from West to East, giving the names as: Pečeneg (on the Byzantine frontier), Qipcaq, Oghuz, Yemek, Bashghird, Basmil, Qai, Yabaqu, Tatar and Qirqiz (Kirghiz).

And in the second zone: Čigil, Tukhsi, Yaghmā, Ighraq, Čaruq, Čumul, Uighur and Tangut. No doubt he occasionally includes amongst his supposedly Turkish tribes subject peoples of different origin, whom he admits to be bilingual, and to speak also indigenous non-Turkish languages. Amongst Turkish dialects, he distinguished 'Khaqani Turkish', evidently the dialect of the Qarakhanid court, as the 'most elegant'; whilst the speech of the Yaghmā and the Tukhsi is said to be the 'most correct', and that of the Ghuzz is also differentiated. At the same time, it is not always clear which dialect al-Kashghari regards as his standard of comparison.

The Qarakhanid territories quickly extended eastwards to include Kashghar. The first of their rulers to adopt Islam is said to have been a certain 'Abd al-Karim Satuq, who died in 344/955. There are grounds for thinking that a Muslim religious leader from Bishapur in Persia, Abu'l-Hasan Muhammad b. Sufyan al-Kalamati, who died at the court of their Khan in 350/961, played a part in bringing about the conversion.[16] It was thus as a Muslim ruler that the Qarakhanid Bughra Khan Harun took advantage of the disturbances in the Samanid empire to cross its northern borders in 382/992, and to occupy Bukhara. Shortly after his arrival in the Samanid capital, however, Harun was taken ill. He consequently withdrew, and died on the march soon afterwards.

However, the respite for the Samanids was not to be of long duration. For in 389/999 a new Qarakhanid army marched on Bukhara, this time led by the *Ilek* Nasr. The city was occupied without resistance and the Samanid Amir 'Abd al-Malik b. Nuh was imprisoned with his brothers and deported to Uzkand. Though one of the Samanid princes named Isma'il succeeded in escaping from captivity and continuing the struggle for a few months, this was only a forlorn hope. Meanwhile, in the same month that the *Ilek* entered Bukhara, Mahmud of Ghazni, the son of Sebüktigin, acceded to the throne. He sent ambassadors to the *Ilek* Nasr and a pact was concluded making the Oxus the boundary between the two kingdoms but the Qarakhanids quickly infringed this agreement by sending expeditions across the river. However, Mahmud was easily able to defeat these invaders so that the boundary between the two states was stabilized on the lines of the treaty, though Mahmud was later able to extend his authority to include Khwarazm.

It was during the confused fighting which occupied the closing years of the Samanid dynasty that a new tribal group appeared upon the historical scene. These were the Seljuq Turks, a branch of the Oghuz tribe who were moving south from pastures near the mouth of the Syr-Darya at Jand. Their leader Seljuq had accepted Islam and in 382/992 his son Isra'il had assisted the Samanids in their campaign against the Qarakhanid Bughra Khan Harun. Later, Mahmud of Ghazni, during one of his campaigns north of the Oxus, became apprehensive of Isra'il's power, seized him, and confined him in India until his death. But at the same time, Mahmud granted permission for the tribe to cross the Oxus and settle in his own territory near Nasa and Abivard. The leaders of the immigrants were Chaghri Beg and Tughril Beg who rapidly increased their power until in 429/1037 they were enthroned as Amirs, Chaghri Beg at Marv and Tughril Beg at Nishapur. In 432/1040–1 Mahmud's successor, Mas'ud of Ghazni, gave battle to the Seljuqs at Dandanqan, near Marv, but was completely defeated. He fled to Ghazni and thereafter relinquished Khurasan to the Seljuqs. This event marked the beginning of the decline of the Ghaznavids. Henceforth their main centre was transferred to Lahore and their chief preoccupation was with the affairs of their Indian territories.

The century which followed saw the rise of the dynasty of Ghur which took its name from the mountainous, almost inaccessible region in central Afghanistan approximately half-way between Herat and Kabul. During the Muslim conquest this difficult area had been to a large extent passed by, though the author of the *Hudud al-'Alam* (written 372/983) claimed that in his day the majority of the inhabitants were Muslims,[17] an assertion which is rather doubtful. Mahmud of Ghazni had conquered the rulers of this country by force of arms and established his suzerainty there. The first Ghurid prince to achieve substantial power was 'Izz al-din Husain, contemporary and vassal of the Seljuq Sultan Sanjar (511/1117 to 552/1157), to whom he sent tribute of the characteristic products of Ghur,

75

weapons, coats of mail, and steel helmets – for the work of the blacksmiths of the region was celebrated. Later, when the Ghaznavid Sultan Bahram Shah (512/1118 to 547/1152) put to death a member of the Ghurid family, Qutb al-din Muhammad, the murdered man's brother, Sayf al-din Suri, marched on Ghazni, drove out Bahram, and took possession of the town. Returning unexpectedly however, Bahram surprised and seized Suri, and put him also to death in 544/1149. A third brother, 'Ala al-din Husain, then acceded to the principality of Ghur. Seeking vengeance he marched against Ghazni, took the city, and burnt it to the ground. For this ferocious deed 'Ala al-din received the surname of Jahansuz, 'the Burner of the World'.

Qutb al-din Muhammad had already commenced the construction of the new capital of the Ghurid empire at Firuzkuh on the Hari Rud but the major monument of the site was the work of a later ruler, the great Ghiyath al-din Muhammad (558/1162 to 599/1202). This is the magnificent minaret of the cathedral mosque, discovered by André Maricq in 1957 (Pl. 15).[38] Towards the end of his reign, in 596/1200, Ghiyath al-din embarked on a campaign to extend his rule over the whole of Khurasan. He already held Herat and now his forces advanced to capture Nishapur, Sarakhs and Marv, and to push westwards as far as the town of Bistam. The opponents from whom these territories were briefly won were the Khwarazmshahs, governors of the Seljuq Sultans in the land of Khwarazm. It is to an account of the rise of these Khwarazmshahs that we now turn.

The founder of this dynasty was a Turkish slave called Anushtigin, who rose to the office of cupbearer to the Seljuq Sultan Malikshah (465/1072 to 485/1092). Under a subsequent Sultan, Barkyaruq, the sun of Anushtigin was appointed governor of Khwarazm, The third of the line, the Khwarazmshah Atsiz, displayed much independence under the Seljuq Sultan Sanjar who reduced him to obedience only after three strenuous campaigns. With the subsequent decline of the Seljuq Sultanate, the Khwarazmshahs became the most powerful rulers of the Muslim world and extended their influence over Khurasan. The sixth of the dynasty, Takash, owed his accession to support from the pagan Qara-Khitay, survivors of the nomadic

Liao dynasty of China, who had been driven out of China by rival tribes and had crossed Central Asia to win control of the declining empire of the Qarakhanids.[19] Whilst paying tribute to the Qara-Khitay, Takash overran not only Khurasan but also entered Iraq, thereby causing friction with the government of the 'Abbasid Caliph. Takash died in 596/1200 and it was at this moment that Ghiyath al-din Muhammad of Ghur seized the opportunity to occupy Khurasan but he too died in 599/1202.

His successor, Shihab al-din Muhammad of Ghur (who later became known as Mu'izz al-din) was opposed by the new Khwarazmshah 'Ala al-din Muhammad b. Takash, and worsted in the encounter. In 602/1206 Mu'izz al-din was himself assassinated and none of the surviving Ghurid princes possessed the capacity to hold their empire together. At Ghazni and Delhi the Ghurid slave generals, Yildiz and Aybak, proclaimed their independence. The Khwarazmshah recaptured Herat, reduced Ghur to vassalage, and in 607/1210, conscious of his strength, he at last refused tribute to his overlords, the Qara-Khitay. Soon he was able to lead an army against them and at the same time the Qara-Khitay were weakened by the rebellion on their eastern frontier of Küchlüg, ruler of the Naimans. Thus on the eve of the invasion of Chingiz Khan, the empire of the Qara-Khitay was breaking up and the Khwarazmshah was exercising sole rule over all the Central Asian territories of Islam.

5

The Foundations of Tibetan Civilization

The Tibetans, a Mongoloid people with a language akin to Burmese, have inhabited the Tibetan plateau for as long as records have existed of that remote region and they have also been present in smaller numbers in areas outside the present frontiers of Tibet.[1] But the mountain ranges which prevent easy access to the plateau have tended to isolate Tibetan society from its neighbours, and even the great Turkish and Mongol conquerors of the Central Asian steppe-lands avoided campaigning over such uninviting terrain. The Tibetan countryside has never been able to support more than a small and sparsely distributed population which even today is probably less than three million. Most of this population has always been concentrated in agricultural settlements in the southern region, where the Indus, Sutlej and Tsang-po (Brahmaputra) rise, and where the towns of Lhasa, Shigatse and Gyantse as well as most of the larger monasteries are situated. In the north-east, however, in Tsaidam and Amdo around the Koko-Nor lake there is adequate pasture for a nomad economy.[2]

The early history of Tibet is unknown because of the absence of archaeological evidence but the earliest Tibetans were probably nomads whose way of life differed little from that of the tribesmen who still inhabit the bleak Chang Tang. Those examples of Tibetan nomad art which have so far been recovered reveal a close similarity to objects found on the Eurasian steppes and suggest that contacts with the north may have been more frequent in earlier times.[3] Tibetan literature preserves the memory of legendary rulers preceding the historic kingdom of the seventh century AD, but the Tibetans never developed a strong historical sense and their records are more concerned with accounts of spiritual enlightenment rather than with the narration of political events. Thus virtually nothing is known about Tibet before the seventh century, except for the fact that the indigenous Bon religion, a Shamanist faith similar to that which was once prevalent over the greater part of continental Asia, must have been firmly entrenched in the minds of the Tibetans at a very early stage in their history.[4] Tibetan history therefore begins in the early seventh century with the emergence of a strong and aggressive monarchy based on Lhasa, and it was the impetus provided by monarchical institutions in a predominantly tribal and aristocratic society which explains the achievements of the two succeeding centuries. The monarchy provided the necessary leadership during a unique period of expansionism when the Tibetans were brought into conflict with most of their neighbours, particularly with China under the T'ang dynasty (618–907). It also encouraged and directed the introduction into Tibet of Indian Buddhism which first challenged and then assimilated the Bon religion, thereby bringing about the synthesis known as Lamaism. In this way was established the traditional relationship between Tibet and the neighbouring civilizations of India and China. From India came the spiritual values and the literature which were to imprint an indelible mark upon Tibetan life though political contacts always remained insignificant. From China came material benefits – paper and ink, silk and other luxury commodities, tea, butter and barley-beer – as well as Chinese manners, arts and crafts, and also some of the intangible attitudes of mind with which China has always beguiled her less sophisticated neighbours. Thus the period of the first Tibetan monarchy (seventh–ninth century) was the most formative period in Tibetan history, a fact unconsciously recognized by the Tibetans themselves who have always regarded with peculiar nostalgia the heroic age of Song-tsen Gampo, Tri-song De-tsen and Tri-tsug De-tsen, warrior-kings who were also, paradoxically, the founders of Tibetan Buddhism.

Many years of unrecorded consolidation must have preceded

the achievements of Song-tsen Gampo's reign (c. 620–c. 649). His father had already given some sort of unity to the southern part of the country and had embarked upon a policy of expansion which Song-tsen Gampo continued, perhaps partly with a view to compensating the aristocracy for the loss of its independence under a strong monarchy by providing it with extensive opportunities for plunder. At all events, during his reign Tibetan armies were sent into western China and upper Burma, and Tibetan suzerainty was probably asserted over Nepal. So great was Song-tsen Gampo's prestige that the T'ang emperor, T'ai-tsung, sent him an imperial princess, Wên-Ch'eng, for a wife, while the ruler of Nepal sent his own daughter, Bribsun. Both of these women were devout Buddhists who brought with them into Tibet Buddhist monks and sacred writings as well as some of the more mundane amenities of their respective countries.[5] Partly under their influence and perhaps partly through political motives Song-tsen Gampo became a staunch supporter of Buddhist missionary activities in Tibet, and under his direction a priesthood was established and temples were constructed. The king himself founded two famous temples in Lhasa, the Ra-mo-che and the Jo-khang, as well as a palace on the site of the present Potala while his chief minister, Thon-mi Sambhota, was sent to Kashmir, then a major centre of Buddhist learning, to acquire a script which could be adapted to the hitherto unwritten Tibetan language.[6]

Song-tsen Gampo's death resulted in a lull both in Tibetan expansion and in the spread of Buddhism in Tibet itself, but under Tri-song De-tsen (c.754–c.797) both trends vigorously reasserted themselves. Tibetan authority was acknowledged in Nepal and Kashmir; in the north, Tibetan outposts came into contact with the Uighurs and the Tiu-Kiu, and on the Chinese frontier Tibetan armies occupied the Kansu Corridor. The emperor Su-tsung was compelled to ransom his capital Ch'ang-an (modern Sian in Shensi) and when his successor Tai-tsung refused to pay what must have amounted to tribute the Tibetans retaliated by capturing Ch'ang-an itself in 763.[7] One significant feature of this expansionist phase was the apparent indifference of the Tibetan royal house to the attraction of the rich Gangetic plain. Whether this was due to dread of the Indian climate, reverence for the Buddha's homeland or the difficulties of a state centred on the Tsang-po valley in assimilating the nomad tribes of the north-east, the fact remains that Tibetan energies during this period were mainly directed against the frontiers of China.

Tri-song De-tsen's military triumphs were not, however, his most enduring achievement. More important for the future was his enthusiastic patronage of Buddhism which further consolidated its position during his reign, following a century in which it had won little more than a tentative foothold. The Mahayana Buddhism which was brought to Tibet during the seventh and eighth centuries was already overladen with a luxuriant growth of Tantric occultism. Once established in Tibet it soon absorbed elements of the Bon faith and produced a synthesis in which lofty metaphysical speculation flourished side by side with gross superstition. Characteristic of this process was the career of the celebrated missionary and sorcerer Padmasambhava who became the principal object of veneration of the Nying-ma-pa or 'Red Hat' sect. Padmasambhava spent his early life in Udyana (modern Swat) which was an ancient centre of Buddhism and syncretism. Famous as a necromancer, he was summoned from Nalanda to Tibet by Tri-song De-tsen to fight the demons who were reputed to be opposing the introduction of Buddhism (presumably the Bon adherents). Having overthrown the demons by his miraculous powers he founded the monastery of Samye, oldest of Tibetan lamaseries, around 779 and thereafter left a permanent mark upon the religious history of Tibet as the founder of the Nying-ma-pa sect, giving to Tibetan Buddhism its distinctly Tantric character.[8]

From the time of Padmasambhava the increasing activity of Buddhist missionaries, reinforced by the circulation of Buddhist texts, provoked a violent reaction from the Bon faith. This was headed by the aristocracy who probably recognized that the monarchy was trying to use the new religion as an instrument for reinforcing royal authority.[9] It is indicative of the strength of this reaction, even in the lifetime of Tri-song De-tsen, that the king's principal wife (presumably a member of one of the leading aristocratic families) was counted as the leader of the anti-

Buddhist party, and that the king's ministers (recruited from the same class) tried to persuade the king to prevent the entry into Tibet of so many Indian and Nepalese missionaries on the ground that they were sorcerers. All this seems to suggest that the Tibetan monarchy, intent upon establishing its authority at the expense of the aristocracy, saw in Buddhism a suitable weapon for its centralizing aims and this would explain the steady opposition of the aristocracy to the work of conversion. This struggle came to a head during the first half of the ninth century leading to the extinction of the ruling dynasty, the temporary submergence of Buddhism and apparent victory for the aristocracy. The latter's triumph, however, was to prove illusory. In destroying the monarchy it had dismantled the most elaborate institution in the simple Tibetan polity but despite a lengthy interlude of freedom from restraint the aristocracy itself succumbed to an even more elaborate institution than the monarchy, the complex ecclesiastical hierarchy which was to evolve from the persecuted Buddhist sects and into which the rejuvenated Bon faith would finally be absorbed.

These developments were not, however, predictable at the time of Tri-song De-tsen's death in the last years of the eighth century and during the first two decades of the ninth century the monarchy and its protégés, the Buddhist monks, probably seemed stronger than ever. The change came with the accession of Tri-tsug De-tsen or Ral-pa-chen (815–38) whose memory is still revered throughout Tibet as one of the greatest protectors of Buddhism. Whatever the motives which had led his predecessors to patronize the new faith Tri-tsug De-tsen was a devout adherent of Buddhism who took every available opportunity to win converts. His superstitious veneration of the Buddhist clergy made him a pliable instrument in their hands and, in consequence, an object of dislike to his subjects, the majority of whom probably still followed the old religion. Buddhist influence in the country's affairs was now flaunted more openly than ever before and a Buddhist monk was even elevated to the rank of chief minister. The result of this tactless acceleration of what should have been a gradual transformation was a well-organized conspiracy resulting in the king's assassination. The throne passed to a certain Lang Darma (838–42), a nominee of the Bon party, and a ferocious persecution of Buddhists was initiated until the new king in his turn was murdered by a Buddhist hermit and both parties embarked upon a period of bitter religious strife. The major casualty in the ensuing anarchy was the monarchy, and with its dissolution Tibet's reputation as a military power was finally shattered. Even as late as the reign of Tri-tsug De-tsen Tibetan armies had raided Kansu but these conquests had now to be abandoned, and a Sino-Tibetan treaty negotiated in the last days of the kingdom confirmed the frontier of Tibet in the Koko-Nor region.

It was from these north-eastern marches that most of the important families in Tibetan history claimed to have come, implying that in the distant past aristocratic nomad clans had emigrated from Amdo to the south where they had mastered the indigenous inhabitants.[10] But after the fall of the kingdom and the consequent decline in political importance of the south the Tibetan tribes of the north-east struck out on their own and in the eleventh and twelfth centuries established the Tangut empire of Hsi-Hsia, which extended north and east from the Nan Shan mountains and the Etsin Gol through the Ala Shan range in Ninghsia to Ordos and the great bend of the Yellow River. Until its destruction by Chingiz Khan in 1227, this state was based upon a mixed pastoral and agricultural economy, but its importance lay in its control of the caravan-route through the Kansu corridor.

In the south, meanwhile, decay set in and the fall of the monarchy threatened to bring about the total extirpation of the Buddhist faith. Temples were destroyed, rituals were forgotten or perverted for necromantic use, and the monks were slaughtered or expelled from the country. Almost everywhere the Bon religion reasserted itself, and where it did not wholly destroy the remains of the new religion it absorbed Buddhist practices into its own traditional ways. Yet it was in these unfavourable circumstances that the great Buddhist renaissance of the eleventh and twelfth centuries began. During the last years of the kingdom Buddhist civilization had been spreading rapidly. New temples had been built. The ecclesiastical organization had been expanded. Numerous missionaries had been entering the country not only from India and Nepal but also from China. Most important of all for the future development of Tibetan civilization, a commission of scholars sitting during the reign of Tri-tsug De-tsen had formulated a literary language into which the Buddhist scriptures were translated from Sanskrit, Pali, Khotanese and Chinese. Thus on the eve of Tibet's 'Dark Ages' there was a great age of literary synthesis, translation and exegesis which ensured the preservation of the work of previous generations until there should emerge new concepts and institutions for the expression of Buddhism in a distinctly Tibetan form which would synthesize the heritage of the old kingdom with fresh accretions from outside.

Then came the anarchy of the second half of the ninth century and the duration of the tenth century, a period when the Tibetan state disintegrated into feudal principalities such as must have existed before the reign of Song-tsen Gampo. Yet it was in these unfavourable circumstances that the Buddhist revival began early in the eleventh century, originating in two districts remote from Lhasa and at opposite ends of the country. In Kham, in the eastern part of Tibet, a nucleus of Buddhist monks had survived who were dedicated to the restoration of their faith to its former pre-eminence, and these eventually made their way to Samye which they used as their base for what was to be the re-conversion of central Tibet. At the same period a ruler of Guge in the Ladakh region, which has often served as a cultural corridor between Tibet and India, became a Buddhist monk under the name of Ye shes-od, and renewed the former contacts between India and Tibetan Buddhism by sending carefully selected young men to study in the Buddhist centres of Kashmir. Among these was the man known in Tibetan history as 'The Great Translator', Rin-chen Zang-po (958–1055) who by the renewed impetus which he gave to the movement for translating the Buddhist scriptures into Tibetan and by the foundation of a number of temples and monasteries in the western region played a major part in restoring the steady stream of Indian spiritual experience into Tibet which had been interrupted during the period of the Bon reaction.[11] His work, important in itself, was strongly reinforced in 1042 when the famous Bengali scholar and mystic, Atisha, came to Guge from Vikramashila in Magadha, and so great was the reputation which preceded him that the eighty-five-year-old Rin-chen Zang-po offered himself as the Bengali's disciple. In Guge Atisha continued Rin-chen Zang-po's mission of rejuvenation and purification, consolidating his predecessor's work and assisting in the task of translation. He then moved into central Tibet to strengthen the mission at Samye where he remained until his death in 1054. The impact of his ministry can scarcely be exaggerated. With his coming to Samye the two widely separated revivals in Guge and Kham joined forces to ensure the effective conversion of the rest of the country and it is difficult to visualize the course of Buddhism in Tibet without the example of Atisha's luminous personality to inspire it. His exertions gave to Tibetan Buddhism a spiritual and literary distinction which had hitherto been lacking and throughout the twelfth and thirteenth centuries the example of his work was to inspire teachers and sages such as Mar-pa (1012–97) and the gentle poet-hermit Milarepa (1040–1123).[12] The final triumph of reformed Buddhism was exemplified by the collection, during the thirteenth century, of all the known Tibetan translations of the Buddhist scriptures in the monastery of Nartang near Shigatse. It was during this age of encyclopaedic writing that the historian of Tibetan Buddhism, Bu-ston (1290–1364), gave the final form to the two canons of the Tibetan faith, the *Kanjur* and the *Tanjur*.

Yet if the twelfth and thirteenth centuries saw the final triumph of Buddhism in Tibet they also witnessed the beginning of its ossification, due partly to the character of the ecclesiastical institutions which emerged in that age, and partly to the isolation of Tibet from India, where the final destruction of Buddhism in the north-west severed Tibet from the source of much of her civilization, thereby ending many centuries of profitable contact. Henceforward, the religious (and political) life of Tibet would be diverted towards China and Mongolia, a change which had its origins in the religious predilections of the family of Chingiz Khan.

6

The Career of Chingiz Khan

The Mongols made no obvious impact upon Central Asia before the twelfth century and the name 'Mongol' was applied before the time of Chingiz Khan only to members of one small tribe living south-east of Lake Baikal. At the beginning of the twelfth century three important tribes dominated the area now known as Mongolia. In the extreme east around the Buir-Nor and the Kulun-Nor were the Tatars. West of them in the country watered by the Tola, Orkhon, upper Onon and Kerulen rivers were the Karaits. Further to the west, between the Selenga river and the Altai were the Naimans. The Mongols themselves grazed their flocks and herds beside the Onon and Kerulen rivers between the pastures of the Karaits and the Tatars. North of the Karaits and the Naimans were other tribes of which the most important were the Oirots and the Merkits. Today all these tribes would be collectively designated 'Mongols'. Ethnically and linguistically related to each other, they were also distantly related to the Turks and Tunguses. Except for the tribes of the northern forest-zone who lived by hunting, reindeer-herding and fur-trading, they were all part of that fluid nomad world on the marches of China whose threatening presence, exemplifying maximum military mobility in a pre-mechanized age, provided a major theme in Chinese history – frontier-defence. The influence of China on these tribes, whether direct or indirect, depended partly upon their respective military strength at a particular time and partly upon the receptivity of different tribes to the blandishments of Chinese civilization.

Significant for relations between China and the nomads in the second half of the twelfth century (the lifetime of Chingiz Khan) was the fact that, for the previous three centuries, northern China had been ruled by dynasties of nomadic origin – the Khitans or Liao dynasty (947–1125) and the Jürchids or Kin dynasty (1122–1234)–from whom the Mongolian tribes probably acquired more knowledge of Chinese civilization than from the Chinese direct. In general, it was the tribes in closest proximity to the Chinese frontier who were most affected by Chinese culture, their chieftains proudly accepting such Chinese titles as *Wang* and *T'ai-tsi*.

Most of the inhabitants of Mongolia were Shamanists, although it was only among the forest-dwellers that the shaman (*böge*) exercised a dominant influence over tribal affairs. On the steppes leadership was invested in tribal and clan chieftains whose status and functions gave society a distinctly secular and aristocratic character. Tribal chieftains were called *khans* and the ruler of a tribal confederacy took the title of *khaqan*. Away from the forests economic life was pastoral nomadic, the prosperity and capacity for survival of a tribe depending upon the quality and extent of the pastures to which it had access. Among the more advanced tribes trade played a subsidiary but not unimportant part in the economy.

Early in the twelfth century there appears to have developed a trend towards the disintegration of large clans into smaller units, thereby expanding numerically the ruling elite, the steppe aristocracy. Why or when this change began is far from clear, but it may have been connected with an intensified division in function between those engaged in rearing sheep and cattle and those engaged in horse-breeding, the latter occupation being considered more aristocratic since the possession of horses conferred military superiority. Whatever the reasons for this development, however, it seems clear that throughout the twelfth century a new pattern of social relationships was emerging – a sort of nomadic feudalism. It provided the social and military basis for Chingiz Khan's conquests but was also greatly strengthened, in turn, by them. Precise definition of this phenomenon is not yet possible, but some of its features distantly resembled those of contemporary European feudalism. There was, for instance, the *quriltai* or assembly of princes and chieftains which, despite different functions, might be compared to the Great Council of an Angevin or Capetian king. Society was divided into classes with a military aristocracy immediately beneath the ruler and his family (the complete antithesis of the bureaucratic hierarchy of Confucian China), and with serfdom and slavery at the base of a well-defined social pyramid. The nomad aristocracy was elevated above the rest of the community by its wealth in livestock, and it was bound together by intimate ties of birth and marriage as well as by the exclusive outlook and heroic code of morality of a warrior caste. In comparison with western Europe, however, there was probably far greater social mobility. The subject of Mongol serfdom remains obscure, but there certainly existed a class of persons to whom the name of serf may be applied, and who were usually prisoners-of-war or their descendants. These enjoyed a certain amount of personal liberty, owned property and gave to their superiors only a proportion of the fruits of their labours but apart from service with the army they performed only such menial functions as erecting tents, working as herdsmen and acting as beaters in the *battues* organized for the benefit of the ruler and his entourage. Such rights as they possessed must have been exercised on sufferance.

Continuing the comparison with twelfth-century Europe, Mongol khans granted fiefs to their supporters and maintained their authority through a military retinue bound to the ruler by common ideals and loyalties, mutual interests and—commonly—by kinship. This retinue or bodyguard was probably the most characteristically 'feudal' institution of the Mongols and during the period of their empire was outside the military organization established by Chingiz Khan, although in wartime it might serve as a *corps d'élite* and provide commanders for other units. In peacetime trusted members might serve as local governors. The origin of this body seems to have been the personal following whom Chingiz Khan gathered around him at the outset of his career, and who assisted him in asserting his supremacy over neighbouring rivals. Membership was almost wholly restricted to men of illustrious birth, and it is significant that the Mongol word for retinue – *nököd* – is the plural form of *nökör* (a companion), a word with distinct feudal and heroic overtones. These personal followers of a ruler could, in theory, voluntarily transfer themselves from the service of one lord to another, and whether (as is still in doubt) they took any kind of oath of allegiance, they certainly lived in great intimacy with their lord as friends and advisers. There are echoes here of the Anglo-Saxon *house-carl*, the Angevin *comitatus* and the *druzhennik* of early Kiev.

Yet the parallels with contemporary Europe must not be stretched too far. The differences are obvious. Nomadic society, always preoccupied with grazing-rights, was not concerned with those problems of land-tenure and occupancy-right which are so important in an agricultural society. There were no political units comparable to the mediaeval European barony or county. Nomadic society was little troubled by those disputes over sovereignty, jurisdiction and property-right which played so large a part in mediaeval Christian or Islamic history. The *Yasa*, the law of Chingiz Khan, was not a code of mutual obligations or rights. It was a collection of mandatory injunctions to be obeyed without question by his subjects and successors alike.[1] In theory there was no limitation to the exercise of unrestrained tyranny by the ruler, but in practice tyranny might be curbed by custom and the strength of clan feeling which cut across gradations in the social hierarchy – as well as by fear of revolt.

The society into which Chingiz Khan (his original name was Temüjin) was born, somewhere around 1155–6, was thoroughly permeated with feudal values, and throughout his life he behaved as the born aristocrat he was, displaying unmistakable preference for the interests of the Mongol aristocracy as against those of the tribal rank and file. Born a member of the distinguished Borjigin clan, his father Yesügei-Baghatur was a grandson of a certain Qabul Khan who had at the height of his career harried the frontiers of Jürchid China and even assumed the lofty title of *khaqan*. This short-lived phase of Mongol aggrandisement had ended when the Jürchids persuaded the Tatars to crush their aspiring neighbours, but the memory of Qabul Khan and his sons probably provided a stimulus to Temüjin's youthful ambitions. Yesügei-Baghatur was a characteristic product of nomadic feudalism, a lord possessing his own herds and serfs, who could muster a strong following of kinsmen and retainers to assist him in the endemic tribal warfare of the age. Temüjin was therefore not an obscure barbarian of genius; he was, despite a youth passed amidst great hardship, the heir to an aristocratic tradition and to dreams of ancestral glory.

Yesügei-Baghatur died around 1165 and for many years thereafter Temüjin and his brothers barely managed to provide for themselves and their few animals with the disintegration of their father's household, struggling against destitution and the hostility of rival clans. At times their poverty was so great that they lived by hunting and fishing. Yet participation in minor feuds stimulated martial instincts and the capacity for survival, so that Temüjin gradually gathered around him a small following of men of equal rank and desperation, drawn to him on account of his powers of leadership, his intelligence and his caution as much as by any display of physical prowess. He also enjoyed the protection of Toghrïl the khan of the Karaits and a former ally of his father. Toghrïl's support gave Temüjin status as a minor chieftain, and when his wife Börte was abducted by Merkit tribesmen, he was able to call upon Toghrïl for help, although he was careful to ensure that Toghrïl did not increase his already considerable strength at the expense of the Merkits. Meanwhile, Temüjin was beginning to organize his own followers more effectively than was usual; he established a personal bodyguard, arranged a system of re-mounts for his men, and employed couriers to do his bidding.

Towards the close of the twelfth century the Tatars, whom the Jürchids had once employed to crush incipient Mongol ambitions, had grown dangerously powerful and the Jürchids therefore turned to the Karaits for allies against this new threat. Like the Tatars and the Mongols, the Karaits were nomads, but they were more civilized than the other Mongolian tribes as a result of their contacts with China and the Tangut empire of Hsi-Hsia. Many of them had been converted to Nestorian Christianity at the beginning of the eleventh century, and Toghrïl himself was identified with the legendary Prester John by the crusaders in the Levant.[2] Toghrïl, with Temüjin's support, attacked the Tatars from the west while the Jürchids attacked from the south; the Tatars were defeated and ceased to exist as an independent tribe and the Jürchids rewarded their barbarian allies in the appropriate manner, both Toghrïl and Temüjin receiving Chinese titles. Temüjin, however, was still Toghrïl's subordinate and the relationship allowed ample room for mutual misunderstanding and recrimination. Tradition has preserved for Toghrïl a reputation for treachery, and he certainly seems to have plotted with Temüjin's enemies, but the latter easily overcame his former patron and after a brief struggle Toghrïl was defeated and killed.[3]

Temüjin had risen to prominence as an ally of the Karaits with whom he had assisted in the destruction of the Tatars. Now both peoples were his subjects and with these successive additions of man-power he attacked the Naimans, whose territories had once been part of the old Uighur realm, who were the first Mongols to use Uighur script, and whose contacts with the lands to the south-west exposed them to influences unknown elsewhere in Mongolia. The conquest of the Naimans was followed by that of the Merkits and the absorption of all the tribes of Mongolia into a single confederacy with Temüjin as its undisputed leader.

The establishment of this confederacy was marked in 1206 by a *quriltai* held near the source of the Onon, at which, despite some obscurity as to exactly what happened, Temüjin assumed the title of *khaqan* and the name of Chingiz Khan. It appears that thereafter the conquered and confederate tribes collectively assumed the name of Mongol. One of the architects of these events was an influential shaman, Kökchü or Teb-Tengri, who seems to have spread the idea (thereafter firmly held by Chingiz Khan's descendants) that Chingiz Khan's conquests fulfilled a pre-ordained destiny.

It is tempting to see the *quriltai* of 1206 as the turning-point in Chingiz Khan's career, yet nothing hitherto had indicated that Chingiz Khan was about to become the greatest conqueror in history. Turned fifty and no youthful Alexander, he was merely the ruler of a nomadic tribal confederacy on the northern

91

marches of China, a role played by many nomadic chieftains before him. But already his genius as a strategist and organizer was beginning to emerge. To the advantages of mobility and manoeuvrability inherent in steppe-warfare he had added the ruthless enforcement of discipline. His forces were divided into units of ten, a hundred, a thousand and ten thousand, with a clear-cut chain of command from top to bottom. Absolute obedience was imposed upon all ranks, and notwithstanding Chingiz Khan's aristocratic prejudices, ability and energy were rewarded wherever they were to be found.

The structure of the tribal confederacy established by Chingiz Khan was distinctly feudal – a pyramid of power at the summit of which stood the *khaqan's* family. Chingiz Khan probably saw himself not as the leader of the Mongol people but as the head of the Mongol aristocracy, and the latter, whenever possible, were employed in preference to men of humble birth. In this way Chingiz Khan retained the loyalty of the clan chieftains not only of his own tribe, but also of the confederate and conquered tribes, and the granting of large appanages served a similar purpose without weakening Chingiz Khan's personal control over his possessions. It is possible that the origins of Chingiz Khan's laws for the government of his growing empire can be traced back to the time of the 1206 *quriltai*. These laws consti-tuted the *Yasa*, unchanging rules which were ruthlessly en-forced, and which sanctioned a social code of conduct and re-inforced a conception of society in which the aristocrat and his ideals reigned supreme.

Between 1206 and 1209 the Oirots and Kirghiz of north-western Mongolia were subdued, and the Uighurs, former vassals of the Qara-Khitans south-west of the Altai, prudently made their submission. Chingiz Khan then turned to attack his more powerful sedentary neighbours. It is unnecessary to explain the movement which followed in terms of a population-explosion in thirteenth-century Mongolia or to attribute it to the dessication of former grazing-grounds. Large tribal con-federacies could only be held together by leaders who could convince the nomad aristocracy that a confederacy was to its advantage because it offered increased opportunities for plunder and wealth, for the blackmail of weaker neighbours and for collecting revenue along the caravan-routes. Chingiz Khan offered his followers all this and, in addition, the oldest and greatest temptation of all to the impoverished nomads of inner Asia – the conquest of China with its immense wealth, its countless luxuries and its reservoirs of man-power for enslavement.

South of Mongolia lay four kingdoms ripe for a potential aggressor: northern China, ruled by the Jürchids; China south of the Yangtze, ruled by the Sungs; the Tangut state of Hsi-Hsia based on Kansu; and south of that, Tibet. Chingiz Khan first attacked Hsi-Hsia, whose population consisted of a mixture of sedentary agriculturists and pastoral nomads. Having acquired the necessary information about Hsi-Hsia from the Karaits, Naimans and Uighurs who had direct dealings with the Tanguts, Chingiz Khan invaded the country in 1209 and penetrated as far as its capital, Chung-hsiang, on the Huang Ho although he failed to capture it. The Tangut ruler capitulated, however, and became a Mongol vassal. With the prestige accruing from this triumph and with new experience of campaigning against fortified cities and among a sedentary population, Chingiz Khan now turned against northern China. As usual, he collected as much information as possible beforehand – in this case from the Öngüts who, like the Karaits, included among their numbers many Nestorian Christians and who lived close to the Chinese frontier, and from Muslim merchants who traded with China and who welcomed the unification of the steppes under one master, since this ensured relative stability along the trade-routes by restraining brigandage and tribal warfare. In 1211, accompanied by his best commanders and his four sons Jöchi, Chaghatai, Ögetei and Tolui, Chingiz Khan crossed the Jürchid frontiers and swept through northern China, demonstrating superior tactical skill over a powerful adversary whose forces were very far from contemptible. These triumphs continued into 1212 when the Khitans of southern Manchuria rebelled against the Jürchids and became Mongol vassals. By 1214, Chingiz Khan was outside the walls of Peking but since he was laden with valuable booty which he was determined to transport in safety to Mongolia he did not attempt to storm the heavily fortified capital which was guarded by the finest troops of the Kin empire, and peace was therefore concluded, Chingiz Khan receiving an imperial princess with a suitable dowry of slaves, horses and precious stones. But the war was soon renewed, and Mongol armies again entered China, this time commanded by the generals Jebe and Muqali. In 1215 Peking was taken, and with it the treasury of the Kin dynasty. Yet Jürchid rule still survived in China, desultory negotiations and skirmishes continuing for the remainder of Chingiz Khan's lifetime. Chingiz Khan's campaigns against the Jürchids were probably the hardest-fought campaigns of his career and in them he displayed the greatest skill in combining broad strategic concepts with detailed tactical movements, commanding troops over vast areas of unknown country where the Mongol detachments were often miles apart from each other.

Meanwhile the Mongols were acquiring direct experience of the Chinese and their civilization. Among the captives brought to Chingiz Khan after the fall of Peking was a descendant of the former Liao dynasty, Yeh-lü Ch'u-ts'ai, a scholar-poet whose family had served the Jürchids for three generations. Taking him into his service, Chingiz Khan was soon impressed by his administrative ability as well as by his skill as an astrologer. This representative of Chinese culture and the Chinese bureaucratic tradition rapidly gained great influence with the conqueror and became the principal adminstrative officer of the Mongol empire. China's conquest of the Mongols had begun.

The Mongol campaigns against the Jürchids brought splendid victories, but it is probable that practical experience of warfare in China taught Chingiz Khan caution in dealing with a country of such size and with so vast and intelligent a population. He may have foreseen that further penetration into China would place an enormous strain upon his newly created Mongol army, and he refrained from embarking upon such a hazardous undertaking so long as there remained unconquered nomadic peoples as mobile as his own Mongols on his flanks who might be tempted to attack him while he was engaged in a final struggle with the Jürchids. He therefore withdrew from China to deal with his western frontier.

In the Altai pockets of Naiman and Merkit resistance still survived and these dangers were now eliminated by Sübetei. Meanwhile Jebe attacked the Naiman chieftain Küchlüg who had recently usurped the throne of the *gür-khan* of the Qara-Khitans, a branch of the Khitans who had formerly ruled northern China and who had migrated westwards into the Semirechie in the early twelfth century to escape the Jürchids. In 1218, Jebe occupied the Qara-Khitan realm and identified himself with Muslim grievances against Küchlüg, who fled into Kashgaria where he was overtaken and killed.

The conquest of the Qara-Khitan realm gave the Mongols a common frontier with the principal Muslim state of the thirteenth century, that of the Khwarazmshah, 'Ala al-din Muhammad (1200–1220), whose north-eastern frontier was the Syr-Darya and who ruled in addition to Khwarazm and Mawarannahr the greater part of present-day Iran and Afghanistan, thereby controlling the trade-routes between China and the Middle East. Chingiz Khan was intent upon securing the un-hampered movement of merchants across the steppes, and perhaps initially at least he planned no aggression against so formidable a neighbour as 'Ala al-din Muhammad. Then in 1218 a band of some four hundred and fifty Muslim merchants (mostly from Khiva and Bukhara) returning from Mongolia to Mawarannahr were massacred by the Khwarazmshah's governor at Otrar and their property looted. When an envoy was sent from Chingiz Khan to demand retribution for an act of barbarity which was contrary to Chingiz Khan's policy of protecting the commercial classes, 'Ala al-din Muhammad had him executed. This was a challenge to Chingiz Khan's prestige which was bound to be taken up.

Chingiz Khan planned his attack upon the Khwarazmshah even more carefully than his campaigns against the Jürchids, relying on information supplied by Muslim merchants whose interests he was, in fact, defending. Leaving one of his best generals, Muqali, in command in northern China, he marched westwards with the bulk of his troops, his principal generals and his sons, and by the summer of 1219 had reached the Irtysh, moving slowly and organizing great *battues* and manoeuvres to ensure maximum fitness for men and horses. His army probably numbered between 150,000 and 200,000.[4] The Khwarazmshah's forces were much larger but lacked discipline, cohesion or leadership. Between the two protagonists Chingiz Khan's mobility and sense of strategy gave him every advantage. Accompanied by his youngest son Tolui he struck first at Otrar and then advanced to Bukhara which surrendered almost immediately (March 1220), an example followed by Samarqand. Meanwhile two other Mongol forces had crossed the Syr-Darya: Jöchi's division had gone down stream to Jand and thence to Urganj while a third had crossed up stream and made for Banakat and Khojand. Resistance to the Mongols was feeble, due partly to the conduct of 'Ala al-din Muhammad who soon abandoned the struggle and fled to an island in the Caspian, where he died shortly afterwards.

After the capture of Bukhara and Samarqand, Chingiz Khan approached the Amu-Darya where he spent the winter of 1220–1 while Jöchi and his brothers were capturing Urganj. Then in the spring of 1221 he captured Balkh, while Tolui raided Khurasan, sacking Herat, Marv and Nishapur. At Ghazni, however, the Khwarazmshah's son, Jalal al-din, rallied his father's forces and defeated one of the Mongol generals in a hard-fought engagement at Parwan between Ghazni and Bamiyan. This was the most serious reverse the Mongols suffered in the west, and Chingiz Khan avenged it in person by crossing the Hindu Kush and confronting Jalal al-din on the Indus where he was decisively beaten. Chingiz Khan spent the summer of 1221 in the Hindu Kush region near Balkh; his return from the Amu-Darya to Mongolia proved leisurely, and it was not until 1225 that he reached the valley of the Tola.

He was now at least seventy, but his zest for war remained undiminished. During the campaign against the Khwarazmshah the vassal-ruler of Hsi-Hsia had refused to send troops to aid his Mongol overlord, and had subsequently rebelled while Chingiz Khan's long absence in the west (1219–25) had encouraged the Jürchids to reassert their authority over much of north China. Both prestige and strategic considerations relating to the Chinese frontier now demanded the extinction of Hsi-Hsia, and in 1226 Chingiz Khan set out on his last campaign. After an obstinate resistance the Tanguts were finally crushed but not before Chingiz Khan had died in 1227.

Much has been written about the personality of Chingiz Khan; the evidence is contradictory and points to a personality of considerable complexity. Possessing iron will-power and self-control he could be by turns courteous and magnanimous, treacherous and vengeful. His cruelty was perhaps no worse in kind than that of contemporaries such as the Jürchids, the Khwarazmshahs or the leaders of the Albigensian crusades in Europe. He was in this respect very much a man of his age but his reputation was never stained by acts of senseless sadism. To Chingiz Khan terror was a psychological weapon of war, a form of propaganda designed to ensure instant submission and obedience. A shrewd judge of men, admiring courage, frankness and loyalty in others, his own career reveals the politician's caution and cunning as much as the traditional virtues of the warrior, and in his early life, especially, he displayed the greatest skill in manipulating the conflicting forces and tensions of tribal politics. Addicted to alcohol, like most of his family, and possessing a strongly sensual temperament, he revelled in warfare, hunting and skilful horsemanship. While love of power must have been the dominant motive for his conquests, love of material possessions must have been an additional incentive.

Contact with higher civilizations little affected his way of life, and in this respect he differed greatly from his grandsons who easily assimilated Chinese or Iranian culture without recognizing its utter incompatibility with the nomadic life upon which the Mongols' military superiority over their neighbours was largely based. He seems scarcely to have modified the nomad chieftain's inherent assumption that the accumulation of material possessions was the main incentive for action, believing that Destiny had given the whole world to him and his family to enjoy as they pleased. Chingiz Khan was probably illiterate and knew no language other than his own so that he communicated with his Chinese, Turkish and Iranian subjects through interpreters. Yet despite his lack of education, one of his most impressive qualities was his ability to learn from experience, so that his understanding seems to have broadened with the horizons of his empire. During the early years of tribal conflict he can have known little of the world outside Mongolia, but as his circumstances changed he became receptive to any new ideas or influences from which he could derive advantage.

Certain factors which contributed to Chingiz Khan's extraordinary achievement as an empire-builder deserve special mention. First, conditions in Central Asia and on its fringes during his lifetime were peculiarly favourable for a conqueror emerging from the steppe-zone: China was divided between two dynasties, the Sung and the Kin, both of which were past their prime while the latter was itself alien; neither Hsi-Hsia nor the Qara-Khitan realm were any longer formidable military powers; while the still-expanding empire of the Khwarazmshahs was to prove itself little more than a cardboard façade when called upon to withstand an invader.

Secondly, there was the Mongol army itself, the personal achievement of Chingiz Khan and his commanders. The discipline of the Mongols (unique at that time) and their formation in units of ten have already been mentioned. Of almost equal importance was the establishment of a commissariat for provisioning the troops, supplying re-mounts and transporting siege-equipment superior to anything possessed by their opponents. The Mongols also enjoyed tactical superiority over their enemies, and there can be no doubt that the speed, mobility and secrecy with which Chingiz Khan employed the forces at his disposal were major factors contributing to his success. Moreover, the way in which he obtained information about opponents and the topography of the regions he invaded was unique in the thirteenth century – information being provided by merchants among whom Chingiz Khan and his family were regarded as protectors.[5] The Mongols' most obvious weakness at the beginning was their ignorance of siegecraft, and this was soon rectified by the enrolment of skilled Chinese and Muslim artisans.

Thirdly, as a commander in the field and as a politician who could foster the rivalries and misunderstandings among his enemies, Chingiz Khan was outstanding. His strategic thinking was invariably far-sighted and illustrates his intelligence better than any other aspect of his career. His ultimate objective (not achieved until the reign of his grandson, Qubilai) was undoubtedly the conquest of China. Yet as soon as he had established his authority in eastern Mongolia he did not, contrary to expectations, attack the Jürchids, since even if he had been initially successful, he would have exposed himself to attack from the Karaits and Naimans of central and western Mongolia in his rear. He therefore resisted the temptation of leading a direct assault upon northern China, and concentrated upon making himself undisputed master of all the tribes in Mongolia. Even then he was still not prepared to attempt the conquest of the whole of China, and his campaigns against the Tanguts and the Jürchids (with whom he was quite willing to negotiate) were partly defensive measures taken before he turned back to attack the Qara-Khitans and the Turkish tribes west of the Altai. Their mobility and methods of warfare were similar to those of the Mongols, and they might easily have crushed the newly-established Mongol confederacy once the latter became seriously embroiled in a major conflict with China. Only after the western nomads and their restless neighbour, the Khwarazmshah, had been overthrown was Chingiz Khan ready to undertake the destruction of the Tanguts and the Jürchids, and it was then that his death left his successors to complete his unfinished task.[5]

Finally, certain psychological factors made the task of empire-building progressively less formidable. Success breeds success and the desire for plunder among the Mongol troops was reinforced by a courage and determination derived from confidence in their commanders and not only in Chingiz Khan himself. Several sons and grandsons, as well as such favourite paladins as Muqali, Sübetei and Jebe, inspired equal trust and remained remarkably loyal to the ideal of imperial unity, while Chingiz Khan himself, with his unerring eye for situations, never attempted more than he felt he could achieve. The opponents of the Mongols, divided among themselves, ignorant of their adversaries, demoralized by deceit, bribery and a deliberate policy of terror, were rarely capable of prolonged resistance.

7

The Mongol Empire at its Zenith

The death of Chingiz Khan in 1227 hardly affected the course of Mongol expansion, and the momentum of his initial conquests was sustained for more than half a century afterwards by his sons and grandsons. His career had pointed the way to a nomadic empire embracing the greater part of the Eurasian land-mass, and his descendants came near to achieving this when they overthrew the Kin and Sung dynasties in China, liquidated the 'Abbasid Caliphate and launched armies into South-East Asia, the Punjab, Syria, Anatolia and Slav Europe. The Mongol empire had three distinct phases. The first covered the career of Chingiz Khan and the creation of the military machine which made possible the subsequent conquests. The second lasted from 1229 to 1259 (the reigns of Ögetei, Güyük and Möngke), and was marked by further territorial expansion as well as by the consolidation of what had already been won. The third phase began in 1264 when Qubilai won his brother Möngke's heritage, and lasted until the fragmentation of the empire in the early fourteenth century.

Before his death, Chingiz Khan had divided his conquests among his four sons – Jöchi, the eldest, being allotted as his *ulus* (fief) the Mongol conquests west of the Irtysh. As Jöchi predeceased his father, however, this immense area passed to his son Batu, who enlarged it at the expense of his western neighbours, founding what became known as the Golden Horde. Chingiz Khan's second son, Chaghatai, was allotted Mawarannahr, Kashgaria, Semirechie and western Jungaria, while the third, Ögetei, received eastern Jungaria, Mongolia and the Chinese provinces already conquered. In accordance with Mongol custom, the fourth son, Tolui, took charge of his father's household, the treasury and the ancestral pastures, together with the crack-troops of the empire. It was by means of the latter that two of his sons, Möngke and Qubilai, made themselves masters of the empire and completed the conquest of China, while another son, Hülegü, employed these troops in the destruction of the Caliphate and the establishment of the Il-Khanate of Iran.[1] These arrangements did not imply that Chingiz Khan envisaged the dismemberment of his empire; on the contrary, this territorial division, a traditional Mongol family arrangement, aimed at perpetuating the unity of the empire on the basis of family co-operation. To this end Chingiz Khan nominated Ögetei as his successor. Jöchi was already dead and Chaghatai was considered too harsh and inflexible to retain the loyalty of the tribal chieftains. Ögetei, however, could be both tactful and conciliatory, so that his succession was accepted unanimously and Chaghatai gave him loyal support. Following his formal elevation to the throne at the *quriltai* which assembled after his father's death, Ögetei reigned from 1229 to 1241. During these twelve years civil administration began to evolve in the hands of Uighur, Chinese, Iranian and Arab officials and a sense of stability was achieved. Ögetei himself, although severe when severity was demanded, was a courteous, magnanimous and relatively humane ruler, and his court at Qaraqorum (the former Karait capital) soon acquired trappings of splendour which accorded with Ögetei's exalted conception of imperial sovereignty. The new *khaqan* even founded several cities in the Semirechie; presumably this was to stimulate trade, and probably also the same motive lay behind the favour he showed to his Muslim subjects.

The early part of his reign also saw a great expansion of the empire's frontiers. Prior to Chingiz Khan's death, Mongol troops had been recalled from their advanced positions in Iran, while in northern China a series of uprisings had followed the death of Muqali in 1223. In 1230, however, Ögetei appointed as commander in Iran Chormaghun Noyan who finally defeated

101

the Khwarazmshah's son Jalal al-din and his Turkoman followers while in 1231 Korea was invaded and in 1234 the Kin dynasty was extinguished and the Mongols became masters of China north of the Yangtze. Following another *quriltai* in 1235 Korea, still defiant, was again invaded;[2] desultory and indecisive warfare broke out with the Sungs which continued for the rest of the reign; Batu invaded Russia, Poland and Hungary, and Chormaghun Noyan conquered northern Iran, Azarbayjan, Armenia and Georgia, advancing as far as the frontiers of Seljuqid Anatolia. The momentum for this expansion, however, was shifting from the centre and becoming located among the field-commanders, so that Ögetei's death in 1241 produced the first signs of strain in the unity of the empire. Chingiz Khan's sons were now all dead, and on the assumption that Chingiz Khan intended the succession to pass to Ögetei's descendants, the latter's son, Güyük, became *khaqan*, following the regency of Ögetei's widow, Töregene Khatun. In his father's lifetime Güyük, who was not particularly able, had quarrelled with Batu on the Russian campaign and had returned to Qaraqorum in disgrace. Batu was now the senior Chingizkhanid and he promptly formed an alliance with Tolui's eldest son, Möngke, against the family of Ögetei.

Töregene Khatun's regency (1241–6) and the reign of Güyük (1246–8) marked a pause in the course of Mongol expansion while the *khaqan's* authority was probably weakened by the feuds inside the imperial family and by the rapid elevation of a succession of favourite ministers. In 1242, however, Baichu (the successor of Chormaghun Noyan as commander in Iran) defeated the Seljuqs at Kuzadag, captured Erzurum, Tokat and Kayseri, and forced the Seljuqs to become Mongol vassals. The Mongol victories in Anatolia and Batu's advance into Hungary greatly increased European awareness of the new Great Power in the east, which was half-believed to be Christian (the result of contacts with Central Asian Nestorians) and became linked with the indestructible legend of Prester John, the Christian ruler whose realm lay somewhere beyond the Islamic world. It was from the middle of the thirteenth century that missions from Popes, kings and crusaders were sent to the

Mongols, Friar John of Plano Carpini, the envoy of Innocent IV and the author of the *Historia Mongolorum*, reaching Qaraqorum in time for Güyük's enthronement in 1246.

During his short reign Güyük alienated the most powerful members of his family and at the time of his death (reputedly poisoned by agents of Batu or Tolui's widow) he and Batu were a week's march away from confrontation. His widow, Oghul-Ghaimish, became regent and it was she who, in 1250, received envoys from Louis IX of France. The Chingizkhanids were now divided into two factions, Batu and Möngke (representing the lines of Jöchi and Tolui) combining against the descendants of Ögetei and Chaghatai. A *quriltai* assembled in 1250 near the Issyk Kul to settle these differences, but the result was inconclusive. A second *quriltai* held a year later near the Kerulen was dominated by Batu's brother, Berke, who engineered the elevation of Möngke as *khaqan*, Batu having declined the throne. Möngke's first act upon ascending the throne was to order the execution of his and Batu's opponents, so that for the remainder of his reign (1251–9) he was able to concentrate upon further expansion. In 1253 two major expeditionary forces were assembled in Mongolia. The first, commanded by Möngke's younger brother, Qubilai, was to attack the Sung empire in southern China. The objective of the other, commanded by another brother, Hülegü, was the destruction of the Batinid sect in northern Iran (known to Europeans as the Assassins) and the 'Abbasid Caliphate. In 1257 Hülegü captured Alamut and most of the other Batinid fortresses in the Elburz, and in February 1258 Baghdad fell to a Mongol assault, the last 'Abbasid Caliph, Musta'sim, being murdered in the ensuing holocaust. Meanwhile, Qubilai's advance into southern China had proved so successful that by 1257 Möngke's jealousy was aroused and Qubilai was recalled. Thereafter, the two brothers campaigned together in China with Qubilai in a subordinate position, Möngke dying of dysentery in Szechwan two years later.

Möngke's reign marked the zenith of the Mongol empire prior to its rapid sinification under Qubilai. The description of Qaraqorum left by Friar William of Rubruck who visited

Möngke's court on behalf of Louis IX in 1253–4 shows how this city of tents had already developed into a cosmopolitan capital. Yet cosmopolitanism was hardly compatible with the continuing mastery of a vast subject population by a relatively small number of Mongols and their allies. As the imperial administration passed into the hands of officials recruited from the subject and sedentary races, the higher culture of these races proved increasingly seductive to the Chingizkhanids, and the empire ceased to be specifically *Mongol*, and ceased to exist for the sole benefit of the nomadic tribes who had won it for Chingiz Khan. Given the numerical weakness of the Mongols in relation to the peoples whom they had conquered assimilation with their Turkish, Iranian or Chinese subjects meant their extinction as a ruling race. In the struggle for the throne which followed Möngke's death, the ambitions of the rival candidates exemplified the choice with which the Mongols were confronted.

Qubilai, as the eldest of Tolui's three surviving sons, was the obvious choice as Möngke's successor but before he could return from China to Mongolia, his younger brother, Arïgh Böke, convened a *quriltai* and arranged his own elevation to the vacant throne. This act seems to have had the support of those Mongol chieftains who hated Qubilai's tendency to subordinate Mongol interests to those of the Chinese provinces of the empire. Qubilai then convened a rival *quriltai* at which he assumed the title of *khaqan* and advanced into Mongolia to attack Arïgh Böke, compelling him to capitulate without much difficulty. Arïgh Böke died shortly afterwards, presumably from foul play, and by 1264 Qubilai controlled the greater part of Möngke's realm – though the struggle with Arïgh Böke had revealed the fragile nature of the empire's unity. Hülegü, who had been campaigning in Syria at the time of Möngke's death, played no part in the contest between his brothers. He gave his allegiance to Qubilai but his major pre-occupation was the consolidation of his conquests in the Middle East which became the Il-Khanate of Iran.

Qubilai ruled more in accordance with Chinese than with Mongol traditions: in 1264 Khan-baliq (Peking) replaced

Qaraqorum as the imperial capital; in 1271 the dynasty assumed the Chinese name of 'Yüan'; and when the Sung dynasty was finally extinguished in 1279 Qubilai found himself the first 'barbarian' ruler to have taken possession of the whole country. Having thus made it clear that he considered China the centre of his empire he embarked upon an expansionist policy more characteristic of Chinese than of nomadic traditions. During the 1280s Mongol armies were sent into Annam, Champa, Cambodia and Burma, but although in 1288 a number of Indo-Chinese rulers acknowledged Qubilai's suzerainty, the Mongols soon withdrew, probably as a result of climatic conditions. Qubilai's naval expeditions against Japan in 1274 and 1281 and against Java in 1293 were large-scale disasters which stressed the limitations of Mongol military skill away from the steppe-zone where Mongol superiority was strongest, and which ought to have served as warnings against further departure from Mongol traditions. It was during Qubilai's reign that the Venetians, Maffio and Niccolo Polo, first visited China in 1262, and between 1275 and 1292 Niccolo's nephew, Marco, served in Qubilai's administration. Marco Polo's famous account of his adventures captures much of the pomp and splendour of Qubilai's court, but it is only necessary to compare Marco Polo's book with the accounts of the Mongols by John of Plano Carpini and William of Rubruck to appreciate how far and how fast the process of sinification had moved with Qubilai's support. Although ruling largely in accordance with Chinese traditions Qubilai himself probably possessed only an indifferent knowledge of Chinese, communicated with Chinese *savants* through interpreters, and may not have been sufficiently literate to read the Uighur script. But by his patronage of Chinese scholarship and by providing a Chinese literary education for the imperial princes he ensured that his descendants would draw closer to Chinese than to Mongol culture.[3]

Yet China had proved to be the most formidable opponent of the Mongols, possessing far more resilience than the Muslim or Christian states of the west. Chingiz Khan had first fought on Chinese soil in 1211 and half a century later his grandsons were still faced with stubborn Chinese resistance. It was the Chinese campaigns which sapped the strength of the Mongol army just as the attractions of Chinese civilization sapped Mongol vigour and initiative. The impact of Mongol rule upon China is outside the scope of the present work, although it should be noted in passing that the expansion of commercial life under the Yüans owed much to Mongol patronage. The newly enriched Mongol aristocracy lent its gold, silver and jewellery at high rates of interest as the working capital of merchants, especially associations of Muslim merchants (*ortaq*) with trans-continental interests, to whom the imperial revenues were frequently farmed and who often acted as business agents of the khans. The result was a rapid growth of credit facilities in which paper currency played an essential part.[4] Of all China's conquerors, however, the Mongols proved to be the least assimilable. Mongol 'feudalism' was utterly incompatible with China's bureaucratic traditions and the incompatibility was accentuated by the differences in numbers and in level of culture between conquerors and conquered.

If, in retrospect, Qubilai appears as one of the greatest of Chingizkhanid rulers, his authority, even after the death of Arïgh Böke, remained precarious in Mongolia where for the greater part of his reign he was confronted by a formidable rival in Qaydu, a grandson of Ögetei. Qaydu had survived the execution of Möngke's opponents in 1251, and by 1269 was undisputed leader among Ögetei's and Chaghatai's surviving descendants. Basing his power upon Jungaria and the Semirechie, he had expelled Qubilai's representatives from Kashgar, Yarkand and Khotan by 1273, and in 1276 was threatening the Turfan-Kucha region. Recognizing the gravity of the situation, Qubilai soon reasserted his authority in the Tarim basin but in 1277 Qaydu captured Qaraqorum, supported by Mongol chieftains who resented Qubilai's policy of sinification. In 1278 Qubilai's best general, Bayan (Marco Polo's 'Bayan of the Hundred Eyes'), invaded Mongolia and recaptured Qaraqorum, but Qaydu retained control of Jungaria and continued to raid Mongolia with impunity, severing the empire's lines of communication – which was why Marco Polo travelled by sea when he conducted an imperial princess from China to Iran in the late 1280s. Qubilai's preoccupation with his Indo-Chinese and naval expeditions prevented him from launching a decisive attack upon Qaydu, who enjoyed the strategic advantage of control over the Chinese marches where he could recruit followers from among the same warlike tribes which had won Chingiz Khan's empire for him. It was not until the reign of Qubilai's successor that Qaydu met with a major reversal. His career was proof of Qubilai's lack of foresight in withdrawing the court and government from Mongolia, thereby severing his family's personal links with the Mongol and Turkish tribes upon whose loyalty the survival of the empire depended. Qaydu's death (c. 1301–3) removed the most formidable threat to the Yüan dynasty until its expulsion from China by the Mings over sixty years later.

Qubilai's death in 1294 led to no immediate decline in imperial power. His grandson and successor, Temür (1294–1307), supported by the veteran Bayan, resolutely upheld his position as *khaqan*, checked Qaydu's ambitions, and reasserted his primacy over the western khanates by vigorous diplomacy while, at the same time, he consolidated Qubilai's administrative measures inside China itself. His successors, however, had little influence over the course of events in Central Asia. Between 1307 and the end of the dynasty in 1369, nine Yüan emperors became more and more sinified while the increasing feebleness of the regime made it comparatively easy for the Mings to sweep away whatever remained of Mongol domination inside China itself.

At some stage between the death of Qubilai in 1294 and that of the Il-Khan Abu Sa'id in 1335, the empire founded by Chingiz Khan ceased to exist. So long as the Yüan dynasty in China and the separate khanates maintained some show of diplomatic, cultural and commercial relations among themselves, the idea of an ecumenical empire survived. So long as the khanates retained enough power to protect and promote the trans-continental caravan-trade, which had been an important factor in the initial establishment of the empire, the separate units would have common economic interests to hold them together. By the middle of the fourteenth century both idea and

107

reality had vanished. At the close of the century in Mawarannahr a Barlas Turkish conqueror, Timur, attempted to reproduce a similar relationship between Central Asia and its peripheries, but without success. The principal *raison d'être* of Central Asian imperialism – control of the caravan-trade – finally ended with the development of oceanic trade-routes and the consequent decay of the caravan traffic.

From its inception the Mongol empire contained internal contradictions and tensions from which it could never free itself. The Mongol imperial system, an attempt to combine nomadic military power with an administrative system derived from the example of sedentary societies, was founded upon two mutually antagonistic elements – the centrifugal, conservative and feudal traditions of Mongolia, and the concept of a Mongol world-order which originated with Chingiz Khan and which was strongly reinforced by the employment of non-Mongol officials – Uighurs, Arabs, Iranians and Chinese – many of whom belonged to societies with long-established traditions of centralized, bureaucratic government such as the Mongols had never known. The sheer size of the empire, especially under Möngke and Qubilai, was a further disadvantage, since thirteenth-century communications and administrative techniques were wholly inadequate for coping with such distances. Above all, the division of the empire into fiefs for the sons and grandsons of Chingiz Khan (which conformed to Mongol custom and was probably inevitable if the empire was to be properly administered) meant, in practice, fragmentation. Mongol civil government was always inferior to its military counterpart, and since there was no organic relationship between the centre of the empire and its outlying provinces, the development of these fiefs was determined not by the needs of imperial policy, but by each khanate's local circumstances, including its ruler's personal ambitions and predicaments. Feuds among the reigning princes and the proliferation of descendants of Chingiz Khan, most of whom aspired to independent sovereignty, destroyed what remained of the empire's unity, since conflicting interests, undefined frontiers and disputed pastures provided endless pretexts for friction. The successful assertion of purely local over wider imperial interests was accentuated year by year through the gradual assimilation of the khans and their followers to the higher culture of their own particular region. Just as the Yüan dynasty felt the magnetic attraction of Chinese civilization, so the Il-Khans in Iran (largely Buddhists until the conversion of Ghazan to Islam at the close of the thirteenth century[5]) were steadily drawn to Irano-Islamic civilization. By the middle of the fourteenth century China had either absorbed her Mongol conquerors or was about to expel them. About the same time Iran, with her similarly tenacious capacity for absorbing invaders, was doing the same. More remote from the centres of civilization, the Chaghatai khans and the khans of the Golden Horde retained their nomadic customs and the ways of the *Yasa* far longer, but even they were not immune from similar alien influences.

Yet the Mongols' achievement as empire-builders should not pass unrecognized. During the campaigns in which they made themselves masters of the greater part of the Eurasian land-mass, the loss of life, the destruction of cities and the utter disregard for civilized values were undoubtedly appalling – even by thirteenth-century standards – yet the horrors of Mongol warfare should not be allowed to obscure the positive contribution of the Mongol empire to human development. As a united empire under Ögetei, Güyük and Möngke (1227–59) and then as a sort of imperial federation under Qubilai and Temür (1264–1307), the territories conquered by the Mongols experienced three-quarters of a century of relative stability and there is a good deal of truth in the assertion of a contemporary Arab historian:

Historians do not record, nor biographies make mention of any dynasty blessed with as much obedience on the part of its citizenry and soldiery as this victorious Mongol dynasty. In fact, the obedience, civil and military alike, with which it has been blessed is such as no other dynasty in the world has ever enjoyed.[6]

The *Pax Mongolica* was a reality which enabled men to travel in comparative safety from the Crimea to Korea, permitting ideas and inventions as well as merchandise to pass from one end of the known world to the other. Venetian merchants in

Peking, Mongol emissaries in Bordeaux and Northampton, Genoese consuls in Tabriz, French craftsmen in Qaraqorum, Uighur and Chinese *motifs* in Iranian painting, Arab revenue officials in China and Mongol law in Egypt are proof that the world of the thirteenth century was contracting. In this sense Marco Polo's famous book was more than a catalogue of wonders; it symbolized the dawning of a new age. The East-West contacts of the thirteenth century certainly contributed to widening the horizon of later mediaeval and early Renaissance Europe while the Portuguese and Spanish voyages of the fifteenth and sixteenth centuries were the direct result of the spread of knowledge of the Far East contained in the writings of Marco Polo and other European travellers of the Mongol period.

In Asia, Chingiz Khan's career gave birth to a new concept of *imperium* which certainly captured men's imaginations, although at first the predominant emotion was one of terror. But thereafter the memory of his empire was to be as pervasive and as challenging for later generations as the memory of Charlemagne's *reich* was to be for mediaeval Europe. It is surely more than a coincidence that the major Muslim states of post-Mongol times – the Timurids in Central Asia and India, the Safavids, the Ottomans, the Uzbeks, and the Mamluks in Egypt all seemed to acquire an institutional stability and a capacity for survival greater than the Muslim regimes of pre-Mongol times. Did they owe something to Mongol example? Certainly after the fall of the Mongol empire every princeling in Central Asia sought, if he could, to legitimize his rule by claiming descent from Chingiz Khan and even the 'Great Mughuls' in India stressed their descent from Chaghatai as much as from Timur. The testament of Asaf Jah I, first Nizam of the Deccan in the middle of the eighteenth century, contains the injunction that the ruler should live under canvas – a direct link, surely, with the men who first administered the *Yasa*. Yet among Muslims, in particular, memory of Mongol domination evokes a peculiar feeling of revulsion, derived partly from accounts of Mongol savagery and sacrilege, and partly from the fact that, prior to the European colonial empires of the eighteenth and nineteenth centuries, the Mongol empire was the only important example of Muslims and Muslim civilization being subjected to infidel rule. In contrast, the Chinese, far above the Mongols in civilized values, but comparatively familiar with the tribal world beyond their frontiers, seem to have accepted Mongol rule as less of a humiliation, perhaps because in the north at least, it followed the rule of two other alien peoples, the Khitans and the Jürchids. The account by a disciple of the Taoist hermit, Ch'ang-chun, of a journey made from Shantung to Chingiz Khan's camp near Balkh, suggests that to these members of an ancient and sophisticated civilization, the Mongols were objects of genuine interest and respect, in the way that the Romans of the late empire might have regarded the Goths.

They have no writing. Contracts are either verbal or recorded by tokens carved out of wood. Whatever food they get is shared among them, and if any one is in trouble the others hasten to his assistance. They are obedient to orders and unfailing in their performance of a promise. They have indeed preserved the simplicity of primeval times.[7]

Once the initial Mongol conquests were over, and it became clear that the world of Chingiz Khan was not simply a passing cataclysm but a total reconstruction of the relations between Central Asia and its peripheries, the empire began to draw to its service officials and administrators of high calibre from among the conquered peoples – first Uighurs, Naimans, Khitans and Muslims from Mawarannahr, then Chinese, Iranians, Jews and many others. In China Qubilai employed Arab fiscal officers, and it was he who enrolled Marco Polo in his service. In this way the imperial administration became increasingly cosmopolitan and the Il-Khans, in particular, were remarkably catholic in the way in which they employed men in their service. In consequence the Iranian official classes (with that remarkable tenacity which has ensured their survival through centuries of upheaval) soon found ways of making themselves useful to their unsophisticated but dangerously unreliable masters although few Iranians who occupied high office under the Il-Khans died a natural death.

111

The Il-Khanate of Iran, at first stretching from Kashmir to the Lebanon,[8] remained a formidable power in the Middle East for three-quarters of a century and, despite protracted wars with the Chaghatai khans, the Golden Horde and the Mamluks of Egypt, the period of Mongol rule was a brilliant one for Iranian civilization. The restoration of orderly government was followed by a rapid revival of learning and literature while in the arts, and especially architecture, Il-Khanid patronage was particularly generous,[9] Iranian architects and master-builders being commissioned to build larger and more ambitious structures than anything seen in Iran since the Arab conquests.

The high level of Iranian culture in the Il-Khanid period was due to the relative stability of internal government between 1258 and 1335, notwithstanding disputes over the succession and frequent conflicts with neighbouring states. Several factors contributed to this stability: the military establishment of the Il-Khans which was equal to, if not superior to that of the Golden Horde and the Chaghatai khanate; the efficient organization of the revenue system under skilled Iranian officials; and the Il-Khanate's favourable position on the major trade-routes of the Middle East. As soon as the Mongol empire was firmly established, commerce and urban life began to revive, partly as a result of the demand for luxury goods by the new Mongol ruling class. Nowhere was this revival of economic activity more obvious than in Iran where the Mongols based their rule upon Azarbayjan, partly for strategic reasons but mainly because that province offered suitable climatic conditions for the Mongol way of live and excellent grazing for their horses. In consequence Tabriz rapidly developed as one of the most prosperous and cosmopolitan entrepôts of the late mediaeval world, benefiting from its proximity to the Il-Khans' encampments, the destruction of Baghdad in 1258, and from the Mongol-Mamluk conflict in Syria which diverted trade-routes north of the Fertile Crescent.

Prospering trade implies effective government protection for the merchant and in this respect it was the greatest of the Il-Khans, Ghazan (1295–1304) who exemplified Mongol kingship at its best. During his reign weights and measures were standardized, post-horses stationed on the imperial highways, banditry ruthlessly suppressed, and villages held responsible for the security of roads in their vicinity. In Ghazaniyeh, a newly built suburb of Tabriz, caravansarays, workshops and bazaars were built to encourage foreign merchants, and at the customs-posts were erected stone-pillars inscribed with current rates of dues to prevent ignorant travellers being exploited by corrupt officials. The strength of the Mongol empire partly lay in the quality of leadership provided by rulers like Ghazan, and their disappearance led inevitably to decay. If the Il-Khanate under Ghazan exemplified Mongol rule at its best, its end, three decades later, exemplified the weaknesses to which the system was exposed. The foremost weakness of Mongol government was its feeble institutional basis. The civil and military framework was highly personal, resting upon effective leadership at the top, and upon the obedience and restraint of subordinates who often possessed extensive local influence and resources. Once the quality of leadership deteriorated at the centre, local military commanders would challenge the central authority, and in the ensuing conflict they or local leaders would assert their independence. This was what happened in the Il-Khanate. The last effective Il-Khan, Abu Sa'id (1316–35), was a minor at his accession, and his reign witnessed the beginning of the struggle for power between the Mongol clans of Jalayarids and Chupanids, in whose hands his feeble successors became mere pawns. Ultimately, the Jalayarids triumphed over their opponents and established the principal successor-state to the Il-Khanate in Azarbayjan and Iraq.[10] In the east, the Kart dynasty ruled over an extensive area from Herat. Western Khurasan and Gurgan fell to the Sarbardarids, and in the south the Muzaffarid dynasty, former protégés of the Il-Khans, established themselves in Shiraz, Yazd, Isfahan and Kirman. Within fifty years of the death of Abu Sa'id these successor-states had been swept aside by the conquests of Timur.

8

The Golden Horde

Chingiz Khan's eldest son, Jöchi, received as his share of his father's empire the lands west of the Irtysh (modern Kazakhstan and western Siberia), together with Khwarazm. His fief therefore contained, in addition to extensive and rich grazing-grounds, the important commercial entrepôt of Urganj which had been devastated by the Mongols in 1221 but which had rapidly recovered its former prosperity. West of Jöchi's *ulus* and north of the Caspian and the Black Sea lay the still unconquered Dasht-i Qipchaq, inhabited by Turkish peoples such as the Cumans, and to the north of that lay the Bulgar khanate of the upper Volga and the Russian principalities. During the lifetime of Jöchi (whose death in 1227 preceded that of Chingiz Khan) the Mongols took little interest in these peoples, although in 1223 the two generals Jebe and Sübetei penetrated the steppes north of the Black Sea via the Caucasus, and defeated a combined force of Cumans and Russians in a skirmish beside the river Kalka. This was of little significance to the Mongols but to the Russians it was a foretaste of the main onslaught which would come fifteen years later. This raid, which was also a reconnaissance, was not followed up by any further probing westwards during the lifetime of Chingiz Khan, but the reign of Ögetei saw further expansion in that direction. Between 1237 and 1242 Jöchi's second son, Batu, assisted by the veteran Sübetei, extinguished the Bulgar khanate, subdued the tribes of the Dasht-i Qipchaq and the Russians (Kiev was sacked in 1240), and penetrated deep into Poland and Hungary. The

114

overwhelming Mongol victories at Liegnitz in Silesia and Mohi in Hungary (April 1241) exposed the vulnerability of thirteenth-century European armies when confronted by more mobile and better disciplined opponents, so that it was probably nothing more than a purely fortuitous circumstance which saved western Europe from a Mongol invasion. In December 1241 Ögetei died, and Batu's presence in Qaraqorum became essential if, as one of the senior Chingizkhanids, he was to influence the *quriltai* assembled to choose the next *khaqan*. Leaving garrisons behind him, Batu therefore withdrew eastwards towards Mongolia but he never reached his destination. During his campaigns in the Dasht-i Qipchaq he had quarrelled with his cousin, Güyük, Ögetei's eldest son, and sent him back to his father in disgrace. Following Ögetei's death Güyük's supporters quickly gained control of the imperial administration and it was clearly dangerous for Batu to place himself in the hands of his old enemy. He therefore established himself at Saray on the Volga, sixty-five miles up stream from Astrakhan, and busied himself in the government of his immense *ulus*. This contained almost limitless grazing-grounds, numerous warlike tribes from whom recruits could be taken for the army, and several valuable trade-routes which guaranteed a stable revenue. These circumstances probably explain why Batu took only a peripheral interest in the politics of the empire as a whole, although it was his intervention in the *quriltai* of 1251 which resulted in the elevation of Möngke as Güyük's successor, despite the hostility of Ögetei's and Chaghatai's descendants. Hence Batu's *ulus* rapidly developed as an independent khanate relatively isolated from the rest of the empire, although at a personal level Batu's relations with his suzerain appear to have been cordial. The latter, recognizing that he shared a sort of condominium with his cousin, told Friar William of Rubruck that 'just as the sun spreads its rays in all directions, so my power and the power of Batu is spread everywhere'.[1]

Whether at Saray or encamped beside the Volga Batu maintained a court which combined nomad informality with some of the trappings of sedentary kingship. According to the eye-witness accounts of the two friars, John of Plano Carpini and

115

William of Rubruck, Batu conducted his daily business in a large tent of fine linen in which a rigid silence was maintained. No one was permitted to enter the tent without permission and those who were summoned to the khan's presence knelt on the ground when speaking to him while an amanuensis recorded the conversation. Batu himself sat with a favourite wife upon a golden throne placed upon a dais in the centre of the tent. His other wives sat on benches on the left while his brothers, sons and principal retainers sat on the right. Near the entrance was a table upon which stood gold and silver drinking-vessels and bowls of *kumis*. For the khan to extend his hospitality to a particular visitor by offering him *kumis* was a mark of very special favour. When the khan and his nobles drank it was to the accompaniment of singing and guitar-playing. When he rode out of his encampment the *chatr* (sunshade), ancient symbol of royalty in the Middle East, was carried above his head. Among his subjects Batu was known as *Sayin Khan*, an epithet which probably implied the wisdom and sense of justice traditionally associated with great Oriental rulers rather than moral goodness.[2] Unlike his son, Sartaq, who became a Christian or his brother, Berke, who became a Muslim, Batu remained a Shamanist, like his father and grandfather, all his life although the Iranian historian Juzjani mentions a rumour that both Batu and his uncle, Ögetei, were secret Muslims. Yet if Batu remained all his life an infidel he acquired a reputation for princely magnificence among the Muslim historians of Iran who, as subjects of the Il-Khans, were under no necessity to praise him. Juvayni, for instance, writes of him:

His bounty was beyond calculation and his liberality immeasurable. The kings of every land and the monarchs of the horizons and everyone else came to visit him; and before their offerings, which were the accumulation of ages, could be taken away to the treasury, he had bestowed them all upon Mongol and Muslim and all that were present, and heeded not whether it was much or little. And merchants from every side brought him all manners of wares, and he took everything and doubled the price of it several times over.[3]

Batu's *ulus* is known in history as the Golden Horde. The origin of the name is obscure, but it may have been connected

116

with the Mongol idea that gold was an imperial colour, or with the fact that the khans possessed a tent of gilded silver such as Ibn Battuta described in the fourteenth century. Characteristic of Mongol practice, Batu apportioned various regions of his *ulus* to his brothers and their families for their support, retaining for his immediate needs the heart of the Dasht-i Qipchaq. After his initial conquests he was preoccupied for the rest of his life with the consolidation of the new territories west of the Volga, which meant first and foremost the establishment of an effective fiscal system, and the enforcement of the submission exacted from the conquered peoples during the 1237–41 campaigns. In Russia this was achieved with the co-operation of leading Slav rulers such as Iaroslav of Vladimir, his son Alexander Nevsky, and Daniel of Galich, who recognized the hopelessness of trying to resist the Mongols and in this way was inaugurated a system of 'indirect rule' whereby the Russians were able to retain intact their religious and cultural identity by the payment of regular heavily-assessed tribute and by maintaining a façade of loyalty to their Mongol overlords.

Batu died in 1255, and except for the reign of his brother, Berke, the Golden Horde was ruled for over a century by his direct descendants, until 1359 when the throne passed to descendants of other sons of Jöchi. During that period, and apparently with less stress than in the other khanates, the Mongol ruling class and its Turkish troops gradually assimilated themselves with the original inhabitants of the Dasht-i Qipchaq to become the Tatars of later times, Islam became the dominant religion, and the Tatar language began to evolve as a *lingua franca*. Batu's death was followed with suspicious rapidity by the deaths of his sons, and by 1258 Berke was undisputed ruler. A man of restless ambition, energy and great ability, he was one of the most outstanding Mongol rulers of the thirteenth century and the first to become an avowed Muslim. Juzjani (although he had no first-hand knowledge of the Golden Horde) describes Berke as being surrounded by Muslim theologians and a Muslim bodyguard of 30,000 men, all of whom carried prayer-rugs with them and abstained from all forms of alcohol.[4] Berke founded a rival residence to Saray some miles further up the Volga. Known as Saray-Berke or New Saray, it did not become the seat of government until the reign of Uzbek in the first half of the fourteenth century. Excavations at both Saray and New Saray have uncovered evidence of a remarkable urban civilization in which the dominant cultural influences appear to have been Egyptian and Syrian, not Iranian.[5] The reason for this was almost certainly the foreign policy pursued by Berke and his immediate successors. Berke's reign (1258–67) was dominated by his conflict with his cousin Hülegü and the latter's son Abaqa, for control of the Caucasus, which became during the second half of the thirteenth century the fiercely disputed barrier between the Golden Horde and Il-Khanid Iran. Berke's feud with Hülegü was partly due to his conversion to Islam, which led him to oppose Hülegü's policy towards the Caliphate, but it also sprang from resentment at Möngke's transfer of the Caucasus region (formerly belonging to the Golden Horde) to his own brother, Hülegü. Berke began military operations against the Il-Khan in 1261 and won a notable victory on the Terek in 1263, but by the time of his death, campaigning near Shirvan, he was no nearer achieving his final objective. As a result of his feud with the Il-Khans, Berke cultivated the friendship of their enemies, the Egyptian Mamluks, over whom he exercised some sort of nominal suzerainty since his name was read in the *khutba* (the Friday homily) in the mosques of Cairo, Damascus and Mecca. Indeed one historian has gone so far as to see the relationship between the Golden Horde and Egypt as a colonial one, based upon the Mamluks' need for constant Turkish recruits from the steppes north of the Black Sea.[6] Political alliance with the Mamluks unquestionably enriched the cultural life of the Golden Horde, bringing from Egypt to centres such as Saray and New Saray artists, craftsmen, scholars and theologians, but it also marked the end of that phase of Mongol expansion which took for granted Chingizkhanid family unity as the basis for world-conquest.

Berke's successor, Möngke-Temür (1267–80), a grandson of Batu, inherited from Berke the Mamluk alliance, the struggle for the Caucasus and a tenuous friendship with the Chaghatai khans based upon mutual hostility towards their relatives in Iran and China. These factors further intensified the isolation of the Golden Horde from the rest of the Mongol world, and drew it closer to the commerce and culture of the shores of the Black Sea and the eastern Mediterranean. During Möngke-Temür's reign there arose to prominence a former favourite of Berke called Noghay whose ambition may well have been stimulated by his marriage with an illegitimate daughter of the Byzantine emperor, Michael VIII Palaeologus, who had married off another daughter to the Il-Khan Abaqa. Noghay's reputation as an outstanding commander made him a natural contender for the throne, but it was apparently still not possible for a usurper to supplant descendants of Chingiz Khan and Noghay remained therefore as a sort of co-ruler during the short reigns of Möngke-Temür's brother, Tuda-Möngke (1280–87), and of his nephew, Tulabugha (1287–90), his victories enhancing his own prestige as well as that of the Golden Horde. The accession to the throne of Möngke-Temür's son Tukhtu (1291–1313), a strong and energetic ruler, led inevitably to open warfare between Noghay and his sovereign. Noghay was killed in 1299, but his memory was preserved by the Tatar tribes north of the Caspian who thereafter were known as the Noghay Horde. Freed from Noghay's dangerous rivalry, Tukhtu resumed an aggressive policy in the Caucasus, tempted by the wealth of Tabriz and encouraged by the ruler of Georgia. Yet despite the fact that the Il-Khans were forced to protect their south-western frontiers from the Mamluks, and guard the line of the Amu-Darya from Chaghatai incursions, neither Tukhtu nor his nephew Uzbek, whose long reign marked the zenith of the Golden Horde, achieved any permanent advantage in the Caucasus against Ghazan or Uljaytu (1304–16). This is a significant indication of the relative strength of the two khanates at this period.

During the reign of Uzbek (1313–40), and his son Janibek (1342–57), the Golden Horde became a fully-fledged Islamic state (despite its numerous non-Muslim subjects), and the *Yasa* gradually began to be replaced by the *Shari'at*. The conversion of the Golden Horde to Islam was an event of crucial importance

119

in the history of both the Tatars (as the Muslims of the Golden Horde will henceforth be called) and the Russians, since thereafter the two peoples were divided from each other by religion and culture, making future assimilation impossible. Ibn Battuta, greatest of mediaeval travellers, twice visited Uzbek's court between 1332 and 1334, and was much impressed by the wealth and power of the khan, the ceremony and magnificence of his household, and the respect which the khan and the Tatars in general paid to their womenfolk. Travelling through the Dasht-i Qipchaq, he was also struck by the immense herds of horses to be seen there, many of which were exported annually to as far away as India.[7] This was ideal nomad country and the tribesmen were able to herd their horses, cattle and camels on fertile grasslands where there was no pressure of population for either man or beast.

The cities ruled by the Golden Horde – Saray, New Saray and Astrakhan on the Volga, Urganj in Khwarazm, Machar on the Kuma, Azaq at the mouth of the Don, and Kaffa, Qiram and Surdaq in the Crimea – were thriving centres of craftsmanship and commerce, protected by the khans as major sources of revenue as well as of luxury goods. Ibn Battuta was much struck by the size and prosperity of New Saray and Urganj, especially the former with its crowded bazaars and cosmopolitan populace, but he was also impressed by Kaffa, a Genoese colony of great prosperity with an almost wholly Christian population, a fine bazaar and a spacious harbour in which he counted two hundred vessels.[8] The wealth of these cities was due to their location close to the trans-continental caravan-route, which starting at Azaq, passed east across the Volga and over the steppes to Mongolia and China, or turned south-east to Khwarazm, Mawarannahr and even India. The Black Sea ports, linked with the markets of eastern Asia by the *Pax Mongolica* of the thirteenth and early fourteenth centuries, shipped to Byzantium, Egypt, Syria and Italy luxuries of Chinese or Central Asian origin as well as grain, cattle, horses, slaves, fur, wood and fish from the steppes or the northern forest-zone. They received in return textiles, including Flemish cloth, jewellery and precious metals, perfume, fruit and exotic animals from Africa.

120

Ibn Battuta was an eye-witness to the splendour of the Golden Horde in the reign of Uzbek, a splendour which survived the succession of Jani Bek who was destined to enjoy a triumph denied to all his predecessors. For nearly a hundred years the khans of the Golden Horde had fought their Mongol kinsmen in Iran without gaining any obvious advantage. The death of the last effective Mongol ruler of Iran, Abu Sa'id, in 1335 had seemed to offer Uzbek a unique opportunity to intervene south of the Caucasus, but even he had failed to achieve anything of note. In 1357, however, when the Il-Khanate had completely disintegrated and Azarbayjan was held by Malik Ashraf, a son of Ghazan's general, Amir Chupan, Janibek crossed the Caucasus with a force which may have numbered 300,000 men, captured Tabriz with its great treasure and executed Malik Ashraf. The triumph proved a barren one. Possibly fearing the plague, Jani Bek did not remain long in Azarbayjan but soon returned to the Dasht-i Qipchaq, leaving his son Birdi Bek as governor in Tabriz. Jani Bek's death shortly afterwards demanded Birdi Bek's immediate presence in the north and Tabriz was evacuated, to be occupied almost immediately by the Jalayarid, Shaykh Uwais.[9]

The capture of Tabriz was an isolated triumph which preceded a period of steady decline. In 1348–9 the Black Death struck the Crimea, reputedly killing 85,000 people, before passing along the trade-routes with the caravans leaving desolation wherever it went. Not long afterwards the dynastic stability which the Golden Horde had enjoyed for almost a century ended with the extinction of Batu's line. Following the short reigns of Birdi Bek (1357–9) and two other, probably spurious sons of Jani Bek, a period of twenty years' anarchy ensued while various descendants of Jöchi struggled for the throne. These conflicts affected the relations of the Golden Horde with its neighbours and especially with the Russian princes, vassals of the khans, whose squabbles and intrigues constituted a serious threat to stable government. In 1332 Uzbek had granted the title of Grand Duke to Ivan I of Moscow, who was thereafter expected to impose order upon his quarrelsome neighbours. Unfortunately for the Tatars, this step of Uzbek's was to have

121

disastrous consequences since it enabled the Grand Dukes to consolidate their power with the khan's sanction, resulting in the permanent aggrandisement of Moscow over its Russian rivals. A warning of the danger which threatened from this unobtrusive but voracious neighbour came in 1380 when Mamay, a Tatar general who aspired to rule the Golden Horde, attacked the Grand Duke Dmitri at Kulikovo Polye and was soundly beaten. The engagement was not of much immediate significance, but the fact that the Tatars had been defeated by their own vassals proclaimed a decline in their former military prowess. Kulikovo Polye shattered the ambitions of Mamay, thereby paving the way for the rise of Tuqtamish, a descendant of Batu's eldest brother, Hordu, who by 1381 had made himself undisputed ruler of the Golden Horde. He swiftly restored its fading prestige by attacking Moscow in person in 1382 and enforcing the restoration of the annual tribute to the Horde, which had been temporarily discontinued after Kulikovo Polye. Tuqtamish probably perceived the potential threat to Tatar rule which the growth of Muscovy implied, and he may have planned to crush this potential rival once and for all but Moscow was spared, just as the capture of Constantinople by the Ottomans was postponed for half a century, by the advent of Timur as a *deus ex machina*.

Before Tuqtamish had gained control of the Golden Horde he had fought a bitter struggle for leadership with his kinsmen of the White Horde (the original *ulus* of Hordu) in modern Kazakhstan. In this contest he had received assistance from Timur, a nominal vassal of the Chaghatai khan of Mawarannahr who was rapidly carving out a kingdom for himself at his overlord's expense. Once Tuqtamish became ruler of the Golden Horde he seems to have appreciated the fact that Timur's ambitions constituted a threat to his own, and that even the vast expanse of Central Asia was insufficient for two such men to share. The immediate pretext for a clash came when Tuqtamish, reviving his predecessors' aggressive policy towards the Caucasus region, re-established friendly relations with the Mamluks of Egypt (as Berke had done in order to obtain support against Hülegü) and then crossed the mountains in 1385–6 and sacked

Tabriz. Timur retaliated by ravaging the Caucasus in 1386-7, but meanwhile Tuqtamish struck at Mawarannahr itself, raiding to within sight of the walls of Bukhara. Timur hurriedly returned eastwards to the Amu-Darya and restored his prestige by sacking Urganj, a major source of revenue to the khans of the Golden Horde. In 1389 Tuqtamish took the initiative again, leading a huge army to the Syr-Darya but withdrawing again to the Dasht-i Qipchaq after an indecisive engagement. In 1391 Timur counter-attacked, leading an expedition across Kazakhstan to the middle Volga where he defeated Tuqtamish in a bloody encounter on the Kondurcha river but failed to consolidate his victory by pursuing his enemy across the Volga. Tuqtamish proved to have formidable powers of recuperation and by 1394 had once more returned to the offensive, crossing the Caucasus a second time from north to south. In 1395 Timur himself marched through the Caucasus from Azarbayjan and crushed Tuqtamish decisively beside the Terek. Tuqtamish, one of the greatest rulers of the Golden Horde, whose one fatal mistake had been to underestimate his erstwhile patron, never recovered from this defeat and passed the remainder of his life a fugitive in search of allies who would restore him to his lost throne. From the Terek Timur advanced deep into the realm of the Golden Horde, penetrating as far north as the Russian city of Ryazan (but not Moscow, as is often asserted) and devastating Azaq, New Saray and Astrakhan (presumably as a means of weakening the commercial prosperity of the khanate) before returning to Samarqand to plan the invasion of India.

The collapse of Tuqtamish after 1395 cleared the way for the emergence of the last major figure in the history of the Golden Horde, Idiku, a Noghay Tatar of the Mangit clan who in 1399 defeated Grand Duke Vitold of Lithuania (1377-1430), who was planning to expand his frontiers at the khanate's expense. By thus temporarily repelling Lithuanian aggression Idiku restored the prestige of the Golden Horde with its western neighbours and with the Russian princes while in the east he recaptured Khwarazm from the Timurids in 1405-6 and penetrated as far as the neighbourhood of Bukhara. In 1408 he attacked Moscow and exacted a heavy tribute as the price of his withdrawal. Not being a Chingizkhanid, Idiku was unable to assume full sovereignty but was content to exercise authority in the name of puppet-khans descended from Chingiz Khan. Unfortunately, his death in 1419 and the inevitable struggle which followed among the Tatar chieftains who aspired to take his place gave Vitold (whose ambitions had been forcibly held in check during Idiku's lifetime) the opportunity for which he had waited so long, and from then until his death in 1430 the khanate was steadily weakened by his constant interference in its internal affairs.

During the fifteenth century the Golden Horde disintegrated, a process hastened by Timur's devastation of its cities and by the rise of Lithuania and Muscovy. But the irresponsible feuds conducted by the clan chieftains and the military aristocracy in the name of impotent puppet-khans contributed, far more than external pressures, to the fragmentation of the khanate and Russian domination. Around the middle of the fifteenth century the original *ulus* of Batu had completely disappeared. In its place were independent khanates at Kazan and Astrakhan on the Volga and in the Crimea, in addition to the White Horde in Kazakhstan, the Noghay Horde north of the Caspian, and the khanate of Sibir centred on the Irtysh-Tobol basin with its capital near the future city of Tobolsk and ruled by the descendants of Batu's brother, Sibagan (later given the Arabic form of Shayban which will be used hereafter). The bitter internecine conflicts among these successor-states explains the ease with which the growing power of Muscovy overthrew its former Tatar overlords during the second half of the fifteenth and first half of the sixteenth century. Russian diplomacy proved extraordinarily skilful at pursuing a policy of *divide et impera* among the Tatar princes, at a time when the Tatars themselves were experiencing a relative decline in their military power. This was due partly to European developments in the art of fortification and the handling of artillery, of which they made insufficient use, and partly to a trend away from nomadism which reduced the mobility and regular training in steppe warfare of some of the more important Tatar communities. Under such circumstances, the Russian conquest of the Volga khanates met with little effective resistance. In 1552 Ivan the Terrible captured Kazan, and in the same decade Astrakhan was incorporated into the Russian state. The khanate of the Crimea survived for a further two centuries, but as an Ottoman protectorate. The greatest of Crimean rulers, Mengli Giray I (1466–1515), whose court at Baghchesaray constituted a culminating point in traditional Tatar culture, prudently made submission to Sultan Mehmet II, and in return for a nominal dependence obtained the service of disciplined Ottoman auxiliaries and artillery which were utilized with effect during the expulsion of the Genoese from Kaffa in 1475. Although as late as 1571 the troops of Devlet Giray I (1551–77) pillaged Moscow and compelled Ivan the Terrible to levy the ancient Tatar tribute, the khanate of the Crimea became progressively less able to face the growing might of Russia, and Catherine the Great took the final step of occupying and extinguishing it.

The extinction of the khanate of Sibir was an inevitable result of the Russian *drang nach osten* which followed the liquidation of the Volga khanates. This expansion eastwards, beginning with the crossing of the Urals in the late sixteenth century, was a complex movement in which Muscovy's need to secure stable frontiers, the formulation of a novel imperial ideology among her rulers and Russian superiority in firearms and artillery over the Tatars and other inhabitants of Siberia found a situation ripe for exploitation in the feuds of the Tatars themselves, the ambitions of the Stroganov family (semi-independent merchant-princes of Perm), the pioneering character of the earliest Cossack free-booters, and in the lure of the sable which drew men to Siberia as gold was later to draw them to California or diamonds to the Rand.[10] The Russian conquest of Siberia began when Ivan the Terrible ordered the Stroganovs to raise an army to overthrow Kuchum, the Shaybanid ruler of western Siberia, and it was this force, led by the Cossack Yermak, which captured the town of Sibir in 1583. Yermak himself was drowned in 1585, escaping from a night-attack on his camp by the indomitable Kuchum, but by then he had already won his legendary reputation as the conqueror of Siberia. In fact, the real founder of Russian rule in Siberia was Boris Godunov who, first as regent

125

and then as Tsar (1598–1605), consolidated Russian authority between the Urals and the Irtysh, founding the cities of Tyumen in 1586 and Tobolsk in 1587. Of Tatar ancestry himself and more than willing to conciliate the dispossessed Tatar princes, Boris Godunov sought to obtain Kuchum's voluntary submission, although the latter maintained an obstinate if ineffectual resistance until his murder by Noghay Tatars around 1601. In 1614, however, Kuchum's grandson, Arslan, was nominated khan of Kazimov (Gorodets-on-the-Oka) by Tsar Michael Romanov, and there his descendants reigned until the abolition of the puppet-khanate in 1681. The remnants of the old Siberian khanate which survived the Russian advance eastwards were finally eliminated by the onslaught of the Oirots in the middle years of the seventeenth century.

9

The Chaghatai Khanate

In the division of Chingiz Khan's empire Mawarannahr, Kashgaria, Semirechie and much of Jungaria formed the *ulus* of Chaghatai, his second son. Here his descendants ruled for nearly a century until early in the fourteenth century the *ulus* disintegrated; in Mawarannahr Chaghatai khans reigned as puppets of local Turkish amirs until the line was extinguished by Timur in the second half of the fourteenth century; in what remained of the original *ulus*, known as Mughulistan, Chaghatai khans maintained a nominal sovereignty down to the seventeenth century, succumbing thereafter to attacks by Oirots, Kazakhs and Kirghiz.

The history of the Chaghatai khans is extremely obscure and much of the chronology must be considered provisional: the source-material is inadequate and the numismatic evidence fragmentary. But it is clear that in this *ulus* the Chingizkhanids were able to retain their nomadic traditions far longer than in China, Iran or even the Dasht-i Qipchaq. So long as they controlled the steppes north of the Tien Shan which provided them with excellent grazing-grounds and a regular supply of horses and warriors they took little interest in the oases of Mawarannahr and Kashgaria except as sources of revenue. Wassaf records how Buraq Khan (1264–70) even plundered his own cities of Samarqand and Bukhara before crossing the Amu-Darya to raid Il-Khanid Khurasan.[1] Much of the region had suffered greatly during the foundation of the Mongol empire. Ibn Battuta, visiting Mawarannahr a hundred years later, was appalled by the decay or urban life. Tirmiz, for example, had been rebuilt upon a new site following its sack by Chingiz Khan, but Samarqand still contained extensive ruins, while in Khurasan Marv was still uninhabited and Balkh absolutely desolate.[2] The horrors experienced by the Muslim townspeople of Mawarannahr in the thirteenth and fourteenth centuries may perhaps account for their fanatical devotion to Sunni Islam. The dervish orders enjoyed great popularity and there was widespread veneration of descendants of the Prophet and his family (*sayyids* and *khojas*). Among the nomads, however, Islam spread very slowly and one of the most significant themes in the history of the Chaghatai khanate is the conflict between heathen Mongol traditions and the Muslim way of life, between the *Yasa* and the *Shari'at*, between the nomads and the settled population.

Chaghatai's original *ulus* consisted of the former Uighur and Qara-Khitan territories in Jungaria, Semirechie and the Tarim basin (the last being one of the few extensive areas in Central Asia to have escaped Mongol devastation) to which was added a substantial part of the possessions of the late Khwarazmshah made up of Mawarannahr and Khurasan (later transferred to the Iranian Il-Khans) but not Khwarazm proper which had been included in the *ulus* of Jöchi. It is impossible to define with any degree of accuracy the exact frontiers but they stretched from the Altai and the upper Irtysh to the Aral Sea and the Amu-Darya and for a time even extended south of the Hindu Kush to Ghazni and the Indus country. Chaghatai's subjects included followers of the Shamanist, Muslim, Nestorian, Christian and Buddhist faiths – and followed a wide variety of occupations. They included nomads, agriculturalists in the oases and the inhabitants of important commercial and manufacturing centres such as Samarqand, Bukhara, Kashgar, Yarkand and Aqsu. He himself took no direct interest in urban life. His principal encampments, whether in summer or winter, were close to the Ili and although the old Uighur city of Bishbaliq was the first seat of his administration it was soon replaced by Almaliq between the Tien Shan and Lake Balkhash.

With regard to Chaghatai himself the sources are contradictory. Juzjani declared that of all the Chingizkhanids he was

128

the most hostile to Islam and that it was because Chingiz Khan knew him to be cruel, malevolent and bloodthirsty that he did not nominate him as his successor.[3] Elsewhere he is described as a wise and energetic ruler, dignified, hospitable and open-handed, an able warrior, an enthusiastic hunter and a deep drinker. Chingiz Khan had made him responsible for enforcing the *Yasa*, and it was perhaps for this reason that he was re-membered as an enemy of Islam. By the standards of the age his government appears to have been exemplary, being founded upon co-operation with his younger brother, the *khaqan* Ögetei, who seems to have consulted him on major issues.[4] His rule had the reputation of being so firm and severe that the roads were free from bandits and escorts were unnecessary. In view of his reputation as an enemy of the Muslims it is interesting to note that during his reign Mawarannahr was in the charge of a Muslim governor, Mahmud Yalavach, a wealthy merchant from Khwarazm who was succeeded by his son, Mas'ud Bek, who later received charge of the entire *ulus* while another Mus-lim merchant, Habash 'Amid, also enjoyed Chaghatai's com-plete confidence, all of which suggests that the khan was shrewd enough to appreciate the usefulness of the Muslim merchant class.

Chaghatai died around 1241. A grandson, Qara Hülegü, suc-ceeded him, but failed to secure the approval of Güyük the *khaqan* who replaced him by Yesü-Möngke, Chaghatai's fifth son. In 1251 when Möngke became *khaqan* he re-instated Qara-Hülegü, who died before regaining the throne and for the remainder of the decade the *ulus* was governed by Qara-Hülegü's widow, Orqïna, who acted as regent for her infant son, Mubarak Shah, while administrative continuity was maintained by Habash 'Amid and his son Nasir al-din. This arrangement ended with the invasion of the *ulus* by another grandson of Chaghatai, Alghu, a partisan of Arïgh Böke against Qubilai, who by 1260 established himself as ruler, strengthening his position by marrying Orqïna. Alghu then abandoned his alliance with Arïgh Böke who in revenge ravaged Jungaria so thoroughly that during 1263–4 the population was decimated by famine. Now favoured by Qubilai, Alghu spent his last years fighting

129

Qubilai's rival, Qaydu, in eastern Jungaria, dying around 1264. He was succeeded by Mubarak Shah, the first Chaghatai ruler to become a Muslim, but his candidature was unacceptable to Qubilai, who replaced him with his cousin, Buraq, another great-grandson of Chaghatai.

The Chaghatai *ulus* was already less extensive than formerly; the founding of the Il-Khanate in Iran had converted the Amu-Darya into the south-western frontier of the khanate while the success of Qaydu against Qubilai in Jungaria meant loss of territory in the east. Buraq soon quarrelled with Qubilai and then found himself at war with Qubilai and Qaydu simultaneously. A defeat by Qaydu forced him to come to terms, and in the spring of 1269 he and Qaydu renewed the old alliance between the lines of Chaghatai and Ögetei against Tolui's descendants in China and Iran at a *quriltai* held beside the Talas. Whether Buraq became Qaydu's vassal or whether some sort of condominium was established is far from clear, but an attempt was made to define their mutual boundaries and to end the devastation of recent years: flocks and herds were to be kept away from agricultural areas, and the cities were to be free from interference and were not to be subjected to harsh taxation. As Buraq had complained that he lacked sufficient pastures it was agreed that he should invade Iran, and Qaydu was probably not unwilling to see his new ally preoccupied in the south-west.[5] Ravaging his own cities en route for the Amu-Darya (a barbarity which provoked a protest from the venerable governor of Mawarannahr, Mas'ud Bek) Buraq crossed the river in 1269 and penetrated Khurasan as far as Nishapur. His opponent, the Il-Khan Abaqa, proved himself to be the more skilful commander, however, and Buraq soon found his allies deserting him so that he was compelled to retreat in confusion back to Mawarannahr. There in Bukhara, he became a Muslim and began to intrigue against Qaydu's vassals. He died around 1270 and may have been poisoned at Qaydu's instigation.[6]

Two brief, unimportant reigns intervened before Buraq's son, Tuva, obtained his father's throne with the support of Qaydu, perhaps in 1274. Tuva was a vigorous ruler well-suited to be Qaydu's ally and together they fought Qubilai's generals and the White Horde to the north. In 1273–4 Abaqa avenged Buraq's incursion into Iran by a raid into Mawarannahr which ended in the sack of Bukhara. Tuva, however, returned to the attack, drove the Il-Khan's troops from Afghanistan and even sent raiders from Ghazni into the Punjab. Qaydu himself did not indulge in harrying his neighbours unnecessarily. Anxious to restore his territories to their former prosperity, he probably realized that he was strong enough to withstand Qubilai's attacks but not strong enough to take the initiative. His alliance with Buraq and then with Tuva indicates his unwillingness to fight on two fronts. The extent of his territory cannot now be determined with much accuracy. The centre of his power lay in Jungaria and Semirechie. Both his summer and winter camps were situated south of Lake Balkhash between the Ili and the Chu, and the Talas probably marked his frontier with the Chaghatai khanate, although he presumably exercised some sort of suzerainty over Mawarannahr and Kashgaria. North-east his authority stretched through the Altai to the upper reaches of the Irtysh and the Yenisei: to the east as far as Chagan-Nor and to the south as far as Lop-Nor.

Qaydu died sometime between 1301 and 1303 (the year when his son, Chapar, was enthroned) and for a while Chapar and Tuva maintained the traditional alliance between the two families. In due course, however, they drifted into war. Chapar was defeated and in consequence was forced to abandon his father's claim to some sort of suzerainty over the Chaghatai khanate. Tuva died around 1306–7 and his son and successor, Künjek, a year later in 1308. The throne was then seized by another of Chaghatai's descendants, Taliqu, whose open profession of Islam lost him the tribal support necessary for consolidating his position.

An extensive conspiracy against the usurper was led by Kebek, another son of Tuva, who eventually forced his way into Taliqu's tent and cut him down sometime around 1308–9. These conflicts among the descendants of Chaghatai tempted Chapar to recommence hostilities but his forces were completely annihilated by the superior power of Kebek, his people were absorbed into the Chaghatai tribes or the tribes of the White

Horde and the line of Ögetei passed out of history. In 1309 Kebek's elder brother, Esen-buqa, was enthroned as ruler of the reunited Chaghatai *ulus*. Esen-buqa was an indifferent warrior and when in 1315 he rashly crossed the Amu-Darya to raid Khurasan he was compelled to retire in confusion to protect his eastern marches from a Yüan invasion which penetrated as far as the Issyk Kul. In 1316, moreover, the Il-Khan Uljaytu invaded Mawarannahr, sacking Bukhara, Samarqand and Tirmiz. Esen-buqa died around 1318 and was succeeded by Kebek who reigned until 1326 and who, perhaps fearing a permanent occupation of Mawarannahr by the Il-Khans, made Nakhshab (Qarshi), south-west of Bukhara, his capital. Thus the political centre of the khanate was removed from Semirechie and Jungaria and now lay in Mawarannahr where heathen nomadic traditions were replaced by Irano-Islamic ones. Despite confused chronology, it appears that Kebek was succeeded by three more sons of Tuva – Eljigitei, Dura-Timur and Tarmashirin – who apparently contemplated an alliance with Sultan Muhammad b. Tughluq of Delhi against the Il-Khans.[7] Tarmashirin was a devout Muslim yet despite the spread of Islam among the tribes his religion was still unacceptable to many of the heathen tribal chieftains who in 1334 rebelled and deposed him. This event marked the beginning of a period of more than thirty years' anarchy in Mawarannahr, where local amirs fought each other in the name of rival puppet-khans of Chingizkhanid stock. This obscure period ended with the emergence of the Barlas Turk, Timur-i Lang (Timur the lame), as ruler of Mawarannahr in the second half of the century.

North and south of the Tien Shan events took a quite different turn. During the fourteenth century Semirechie and Jungaria reverted to a purely pastoral economy as a result of continuous warfare. Moreover, the shift of power to Mawarannahr when Kebek transferred the capital there, the gradual spread of Islam among the nomads in Mawarannahr and the lure of Irano-Islamic civilization for rulers like Tarmashirin all tended to strengthen the differences between the lands on one side of the Syr-Darya and those on the other. Not long after Tarmashirin's deposition, therefore, the amirs of Jungaria and

Semirechie consented to the resurrection of the former Chaghatai khanate where the traditions of the Chingizkhanids could be maintained unadulterated by Islamic influences. Among the Muslims of Iran and Mawarannahr this khanate was known as Mughulistan and its inhabitants were called Jats (robbers). Kashgaria was also included within it, and although at first Almaliq was the seat of government the cities of the south – Kashgar, Yarkand, Aqsu – proved increasingly attractive for the khans and their followers.

At first Mughulistan, like Mawarannahr, was divided by the quarrels of rival groups of amirs, but in 1348 a grandson of Tuva, Tughluq-Timur became ruler and reigned with distinction until his death in 1362 or 1363, his troops even entering Samarqand and Bukhara. Yet in one respect Tughluq-Timur failed to live up to his supporters' expectations: the attraction of Islamic culure proved irresistible and around 1353 he became a Muslim, his patronage of the religious classes contributing greatly to the spread of Islam in the khanate. Tughluq-Timur was also fond of urban life, making first Aqsu and then Kashgar his residence. His death was followed by a further upheaval in which the Dughlat family, from now until the middle of the sixteenth century the dominant factor in the history of Kashgar, murdered every descendant of Tughluq-Timur upon whom they could lay their hands. It was during this period that Timur five times invaded Mughulistan, and in 1389 his troops devastated the region so completely that it barely recovered from the catastrophe. Timur was unable to re-establish the original Chaghatai *ulus* by reuniting Mawarannahr and Mughulistan, and in 1389 he was content to recognize as ruler of Mughulistan a reputed son of Tughluq-Timur, Khizr-Khoja, who had been living in hiding since his father's death, first in the mountains between Kashgar and Badakhshan and later near the desolate Lop-Nor. An orthodox Muslim ruler, Khizr-Khoja's relations with Timur were not unfriendly and in 1397 Timur married his daughter. His death in 1399 resulted in further disorders which gave Timur's successors in Mawarannahr pretexts for interfering in the western part of the khanate, but eventually the throne was seized by Vays Khan (1418–28) a grandson or great-grandson of

Khizr-Khoja,[8] who passed most of his reign unsuccessfully fighting the Oirots in Jungaria. His death was followed by fresh disturbances among his amirs who formed rival factions in support of his sons, Esen-buqa and Yunus. In the trial of strength which followed Esen-buqa's faction proved the stronger and Yunus was taken by his supporters to Ulugh Beg, grandson of Timur and ruler of Samarqand, who sent him to Iran where he was educated by the historian Sharaf al-din 'Ali Yazdi, author of the *Zafar-nameh*, a celebrated account of Timur's campaigns. Esen-buqa's long reign (1434–62) was interrupted by frequent Oirot raids, by war with the Timurids in Mawarannahr and by internal revolts. At his death, the western parts of Mughulistan were easily occupied by the supporters of Yunus, the protégé of the Timurids, but it was not until 1472 that he conquered Aqsu and Turfan. Yunus was a strict Muslim and lavish in his support of the religious classes, especially members of the dervish orders (*silsileh*). He was also a polished product of fifteenth-century Iranian civilization, as befitted the maternal grandfather of Babur, the conqueror of the Delhi Sultanate and the first of the Great Mughuls. Calm, courteous and highly intelligent, Yunus was a scholar, a traveller, an amateur musician, a painter and a calligrapher as well as a brave soldier and far-famed archer. Yet not withstanding his impressive range of talents he made little headway in weaning his heathen followers from their nomadic ways and was no more successful than his father or elder brother in fighting the Oirots. Among his quarrelsome Timurid neighbours in Mawarannahr, however, his prestige was so great that he frequently acted as an arbiter in their endless disputes.

At his death in 1487 the khanate was divided. His eldest son, Mahmud, who had inherited his father's cultured tastes but little of his vigour, ruled in Tashkent while a younger son, Ahmad, a model Chaghatai ruler in the traditional mould, ruled in Aqsu. Ahmad was a tireless warrior, twice bringing the Oirots to battle and twice defeating them as well as three times overcoming Kazakh rebel armies. Against the Dughlat amir, Abu Bakr, however, he made no headway and failed entirely in his attempts to take Kashgar and Yarkand. When his elder brother Mahmud was threatened by the Uzbek conqueror, Muhammad Shaybani, Ahmad hurried to Tashkent to assist him. There Babur met him for the first time and left a vivid account of his arrival.

All his men had adorned themselves in Mughul fashion. There they were in Mughul caps; long coats of Chinese satin, broidered with stitchery, Mughul quivers and saddles in green shagreen-leather, and Mughul horses adorned in a unique fashion. . . . He [Ahmad] was a man of singular manners, a mighty master of the sword, and brave. . . He never parted from his keen-edged sword; it was either at his waist or to his hand. He was a little rustic and rough-of-speech, through having grown up in an out-of-the-way place.[9]

In 1503 both brothers were defeated and captured by Muhammad Shaybani, but although they were soon released they never regained their former eminence.

Ahmad's sons, however, were to prove themselves a formidable band of warriors who had inherited to the full their father's fighting instincts. The chief among them, Sa'id Khan, had been captured as a boy by the Uzbeks and had ridden into battle beside Muhammad Shaybani. At a later date he joined Babur in the conquest of Kabul and in 1514 led his brothers and followers, a total force of some 4,700 men against Kashgar, captured the city with ease and brought to an end the long rule of the Dughlat family. Abu Bakr fled into Ladakh and was there murdered.

Following Sa'id Khan's conquest of Kashgar his brothers launched attacks upon the cities to the east – Uch-Turfan, Aqsu, Bai, Kuchur, Qarashahr and Turfan – with the aim of reviving the former Mughulistan khanate as it had been during the lifetime of their grandfather, Yunus. Sa'id Khan fought the Uzbeks, the Kazakhs and the Kirghiz, and even embarked upon the conquest of Ladakh and Kashmir, regions where the Chaghatai khans had never before penetrated although Abu Bakr of Kashgar had recently set a precedent.[10] The Chaghatai army left the Kashgar region for the crossing into Kashmir sometime during 1531–2 under the command of Babur's cousin, Mirza Muhammad Haydar Dughlat, the celebrated author of the *Tarikh-i Rashidi*, the major surviving source for the history

135

of the Chaghatai khanate. Sa'id Khan himself followed soon afterwards, wintered in Baltistan and died in 1533 crossing the Suget pass on his way back to Kashgar. Mirza Muhammad Haydar Dughlat persevered for another season, campaigning under conditions of the greatest hardship, and is even reputed to have penetrated into Tibet until he was only eight days short of Lhasa and the Nepalese border when the harshness of the climate and the terrain forced him to withdraw. Then in 1536, fearing the enmity of Sa'id Khan's son and successor, 'Abdur Rashid, he fled to Badakhshan and thence to the court of the Indian Timurids, ruling Kashmir from 1541 until his death in 1551.

From the pages of the *Tarikh-i Rashidi* Sa'id Khan emerges as a brave soldier and an able, just and comparatively mild ruler although as he grew older his increasing devotion to Islam (the Tibetan expedition was justified as a *jihad* against idolaters) alienated many of his heathen followers. Like other Chaghatai rulers and the Uzbek conquerors of Mawarannahr, he patronized the followers of the celebrated saint, Shaykh Ahmad Yasavi.[11] His son, 'Abdur Rashid, maintained intact his father's conquests, but after his death (c. 1555–6) the Chaghatai khanate disintegrated as a result of the rivalry among various members of the ruling family, and external pressure from Uzbeks, Kazakhs and Kirghiz. The period from the middle of the sixteenth century to the middle of the seventeenth century is particularly obscure, but it was during this time that the Portuguese Jesuit, Benedict Goes, passed through Yarkand in 1603–5, the first known European to penetrate Kashgaria since Marco Polo.[12]

During the course of the sixteenth century the khanate of Mughulistan as it had existed during the middle years of the fifteenth century virtually disappeared for the Oirots had seized Jungaria, the Kazakhs had recently established themselves in Semirechie and the Kirghiz of the Tien Shan recognized no overlord. Only in Kashgaria did Chaghatai rule survive, growing increasingly feeble, until it was replaced – at least in the major centres of population – by quasi-theocratic regimes headed by an ambitious dynasty of Khojas from Mawarannahr.

The first of the line, an itinerant missionary and miracle-worker from Bukhara known as Hazrat-i Makhtum-i 'Azam, received from the reigning Chaghatai khan a handsomely endowed estate and died in Kashgar in 1540, an object of widespread popular veneration. In course of time his sons and grandsons, who soon split into two rival factions, came to exercise political as well as spiritual authority over the urban population of Kashgaria although outside the cities their influence was relatively weaker, especially in those areas dominated by the two rival confederacies of Kirghiz tribes known as the Aqtaghliq and Qarataghliq, with whom the rival Khoja factions eventually allied themselves.

In the latter part of the seventeenth century the last Chaghatai ruler to possess any real authority over the cities of the Tarim basin, Isma'il Khan, quarrelled with the leader of the Aqtaghliq Khojas, Khoja Hidayatullah, and sent him into exile. Unfortunately for Isma'il Khan, Khoja Hidayatullah, popularly known as Hazrat-i Afaq, was no mean adversary, being a man of commanding personality who was venerated by his followers as a saint possessing miraculous powers and as a prophet second only to Muhammad. Down to the early part of the twentieth century his tomb outside Kashgar contined to be a popular place of pilgrimage. Banished from Kashgar, he sought aid from the great Oirot chieftain, Galdan, who in 1678 invaded the Tarim basin, expelled Isma'il Khan and his family from Kashgar and installed in his place Khoja Hidayatullah as his personal representative. As a consequence of this revolution in the affairs of Kashgar the Khoja now exercised solid political power, in addition to widespread spiritual authority over the Muslim population of what is today Sinkiang. But it seems that he was still dissatisfied with his subordinate status, since he was soon intriguing with Isma'il Khan's brother, Muhammad Amin of Uch-Turfan, to secure the expulsion of the Oirots. In the ensuing struggle, the Oirots were defeated, and Muhammad Amin was shortly afterwards killed by one of his own supporters. Thus Khoja Hidayatullah was left as undisputed master of Kashgaria until his death, around c. 1693-4. After a further period of anarchy the Qarataghliq Khojas established themselves in

Yarkand while the Aqtaghliq Khojas retained Kashgar, resulting in an equilibrium between the two factions until in 1713 the Oirots, freed from the internal dissensions which had followed Galdan's death in 1697, reimposed their rule over Kashgaria and removed the leaders of both Khoja factions to their headquarters in the Ili valley. There Khoja Daniyal, leader of the Qarataghliq, won the confidence of Tsevan-Rabtan (1697–1727), Galdan's successor, who in 1720 sent him back to Kashgaria as sole ruler, a choice confirmed by the next Oirot ruler, Galdan-Tseren (1727–45). Nevertheless, after Khoja Daniyal's death the Oirots considered it prudent to divide the cities of Kashgaria between his five sons. In the chaos which followed Galdan-Tseren's death in 1745, these latter threw off their allegiance to the Oirots. Their obedience was savagely enforced by Amur-Sana, Galdan-Tseren's grandson, who thereafter gave his support to the Aqtaghliq faction. Once more rulers of Kashgaria, the Aqtaghliq Khojas now found themselves not only Amur-Sana's vassals but also vassals of his overlord, the Manchu emperor of China. But obligations to an infidel emperor many months' journey away from Kashgar meant little, and the Khojas were not slow to follow Amur-Sana into rebellion against Ch'ien-lung whose titular suzerainty over the Tarim basin cannot have been onerous. After the final defeat of Amur-Sana, Kashgaria was occupied by the Manchus during 1758–9, although not without fierce resistance from the Khojas and their followers.

Khoja rule in Kashgaria had, however, been far from stable and this may well have accounted for the apparent apathy with which the Muslim population of the region at first accepted Manchu rule. Their new infidel masters, although merciless in suppressing rebellion, were otherwise wholly indifferent to their 'barbarian' subjects who were left to continue their traditional way of life without interference from the aloof Manchu-Chinese colonial bureaucracy. Nevertheless, for a further hundred years or more the Khojas in exile beyond the Pamirs in Kokand had little difficulty in persuading their former subjects to rebel against Manchu rule – especially on a religious pretext.

138

In view of the paucity of source-material relating to the period between the decline of the Chaghatai khanate and the Manchu conquest of the Tarim basin it is still not possible to assess with any degree of precision the significance of the Khoja period for the history of Kashgaria. To their credit, the Khojas undoubtedly contributed to the spread of Islam throughout the region (including among their Kirghiz neighbours) and in the cities and larger towns they founded numerous *madrasehs* (Muslim theological colleges) and *maktabs*. If their rule was characterized, to a very great extent, by intellectual obscurantism and a total inability to provide conditions of political stability the fact remains that, at least down to the middle of the eighteenth century, the cities of Kashgaria retained a tenuous link with the Islamic world as a whole. Although the speech of the region was a form of Turkish (the origin of the Kashgari and Yarkandi dialects of modern times) derived ultimately from the Khaqani of the Qarakhanid period Arabic was naturally the language of religion while a knowledge of Persian must have been widely diffused among the upper classes as it was among the Uzbeks of neighbouring Mawarannahr so that, for example, the hagiologies of Hazrat-i Makhtum-i 'Azam and his descendants were written in the latter language. Even after the Manchu conquest of 1758–9 the Turks of Kashgaria continued to look westwards for the fulfilment of their political aspirations and one of Yakub Beg's first moves on seizing control of the area in 1867 was to establish diplomatic contact with the Ottoman Empire with the intention, in addition to more pressing motives, of re-asserting the place of Kashgaria in the *Dar al-Islam*.

10

The Kazakhs and the Kirghiz

At the foundation of the Mongol empire Shayban, the son of Jöchi and brother of Batu, received as his appanage an immense territory stretching from the Urals to the upper Irtysh. In the fourteenth century, this *ulus* adjoined the pastures of the White Horde which lay between the Sary Su and the Ala Tau range. From the reign of Tuqtamish, the khans of the White Horde became rulers of the Golden Horde, and their *ulus* emigrated in 1380 to the steppes of southern Russia. When Timur crossed the Ala Tau steppes in 1391, they were occupied by some Shaybanid tribes of diverse origin, Turkish and Mongol, all Turkish-speaking and already at that time given the collective name of 'Uzbeks'. At the beginning of the fifteenth century these nomadic tribes occupied the steppe-lands of what is today Kazakhstan while to their east lay the Oirot empire in western Mongolia and the Chaghatai khanate of Mughulistan in southern Semirechie. To the south lay the possessions of the Timurids and to the south-west the Nogay Horde which ranged between the Ural river and the Volga. For more than two centuries the history of the Kazakh Hordes was dominated by struggles against all these neighbours.

In 1428 a descendant of Shayban, Abu'l-Khayr Khan, having become paramount chieftain of the Shaybanid *ulus* (also known as 'The Uzbek Khanate'), succeeded in uniting all the nomadic tribes between the Ural river, the Syr-Darya, Mughulistan and the Tobol. An energetic ruler, Abu'l-Khayr tried to extend his possessions by attacking his southern Timurid neighbours. In

140

1430, profiting from the internal struggles which were destroying the descendants of the great Timur, he took possession of part of Khwarazm and sacked the ancient city of Urganj. In 1447 he seized the Syr-Darya region from the Timurids. This region was rightly held to be the key to the conquest of Mawarannahr and its thriving cities provided important marts for the exchange of goods between the nomads from the north and the sedentary population from across the river to the south. One of these cities, Sighnaq, he made his capital. At its height the empire of Abu'l-Khayr extended from the Syr-Darya to the Siberian forests where another Shaybanid prince, Ibak, had founded the allied khanate of Sibir.

In order to consolidate his authority Abu'l-Khayr aimed at establishing something like a centralized system of government and this in turn meant crushing the quasi-independent position of the Chingizkhanid chieftains who were his vassals. Such an aim – possible in a society which was sedentary or on the way to becoming sedentary – was doomed to failure when attempted in a society wholly nomadic. Two Jöchid princes, Karay and Janibek, broke loose, followed by a considerable number of clans, and sought refuge with Esen-buqa the Chaghatai khan of Mughulistan. These dissident clans received the name of 'Kazakhs'. Weakened by such major defections, in 1456–7 Abu'l-Khayr had to face an attack from the most formidable enemy which ever confronted the Muslims of Central Asia, the Mongol empire of the Oirots. This empire, founded at the beginning of the century in western Mongolia, had enjoyed a period of unrivalled power during the reigns of Esentaiji (1439–56) and his son Amasonji (1456–68). In 1449, the Oirot army had even defeated and taken captive the Ming emperor Ying-tsung, and besieged Peking.

These remarkable triumphs, which recalled the opening of Chingiz Khan's epic career, forewarned the nomads of the Kazakh steppes of sombre times ahead. In 1450 the Buddhist Oirots launched their first raids in the direction of the Muslim steppes, raids which were thereafter repeated periodically, and which were conducted with the utmost ferocity – being at times invested with the character of a veritable crusade. In 1456–7 the

141

Oirots penetrated deep into the steppes and inflicted upon Abu'l-Khayr a crushing defeat which was to prove an irreparable disaster for the Uzbek empire. The Syr-Darya region was ravaged from end to end, and Abu'l-Khayr's realm was never to be reconstructed.

The khans Karay and Janibek with their Kazakh clans were not slow to take advantage of this situation. Following the departure of the Oirot hordes, they returned in force onto the steppes and in 1468 defeated and killed Abu'l-Khayr in a great battle, fought to the north of the Syr-Darya. The son of Abu'l-Khayr, Shaykh Haydar, was killed in the same year by Yunus Khan of Mughulistan, and of the race of Shayban there remained only a young grandson of Abu'l-Khayr, Muhammad Shaybani. Muhammad Shaybani for many years led the life of a freebooter before assembling a band of followers at whose head he invaded Mawarannahr in 1500, occupying Bukhara and Samarqand. He founded on the ruins of the Timurid empire the last great empire of Turkestan – the Uzbek khanate over which his family were to rule for nearly a century and which was to be for the Kazakhs a most redoubtable adversary.

The migration of the Shaybanid clans into Turkestan left a vacuum on the steppes north of the Syr-Darya, a vacuum which was rapidly filled by the 'Kazakh' clans which had originally followed Karay and Janibek into Mughulistan and which now returned to their homeland. During the reign of Burunduk Khan (1488–1509), the son of Karay, and especially during that of Kasym (1509–18), the son of Janibek, the Kazakh tribes spread rapidly throughout the territory of the former khanate of Abu'l-Khayr. From this time onwards the terms 'Kazakh' and 'Uzbek' assume a new significance, the former designating the tribes remaining north of the Syr-Darya and the latter those which had followed Muhammad Shaybani and established themselves south of the river. Both were, however, derived from the same ancestral clans.

Under Kasym Khan the Kazakh empire remained unified and powerful, more than 200,000 horsemen being available to take the field when required, and its power was such that the Oirots, who during the sixteenth century experienced a prolonged eclipse, ceased to be a danger. The same was even more true of the Noghay Horde, weakened by internal dissensions, and of the Chaghatai khanate in Mughulistan, henceforward too enfeebled to challenge the warrior-tribes of the Kazakh steppes. The Kazakhs therefore enjoyed a century of prosperity and relative tranquillity, and during this period they took the opportunity of extending their territories southwards. There followed a protracted series of conflicts with the Shaybanids of Turkestan for possession of the cities of the Syr-Darya, conflicts from which the Kazakhs generally seem to have emerged victorious yet no nearer their objective of conquering Turkestan.

In fact, the feudal state founded by these nomads remained fairly fragile. At its head was a khan (in later years there were several), descended from Chingiz Khan. The office of khan was a hereditary one, confirmed by election but frequently contested, while actual day-to-day authority was concentrated in the hands of the theoretical vassals of the khans, the sultans, who were chieftains of important tribes. In practice, the clans – subdivisions of the tribes and headed by *biys* and *batyrs* – remained virtually autonomous. There was no regular army, only the *levée en masse*. Upon this nomadic society Islam had made only a superficial impression.

After the death of Kasym Khan, the fragility of the unified Kazakh state became obvious. The centralized empire broke up into three separate khanates or 'Hordes' ruled by a khan descended from Chingiz Khan: the Great Horde (*Ulu Zhuz*) in the Semirechie; the Middle Horde (*Orta Zhuz*) in the central steppe region; and the Little Horde (*Kishi Zhuz*), the most western of the three, east of the Ural river. For nearly twenty years the steppes witnessed a period of upheaval and futile warfare conducted by the sons of Kasym – Mamash (1518–23), Tagir (1523–33) and Buydash (1533–8) – against the Shaybanids of Turkestan and the khans of Mughulistan. In 1538 the last son of Kasym, Haqq Nazar (1538–80), re-established the unity of the three Hordes and even extended his authority over part of the Nogay country. He led several successful expeditions against the Shaybanids of Bukhara and in 1579 took possession of Tashkent. The Kazakh thrust southwards continued during the reign of Tevkkel Khan (1586–98) who occupied Tashkent yet again and then took Yasi and Samarqand, but was checked outside Bukhara in 1598. The attempt to occupy the rich lands of Mawarannahr was continued by Tevkkel's successors, Ishim (1598–1628), Jangir and finally Tauke (1680–1718) who fought with spasmodic success the new masters of Bukhara, the Astrakhanids (Janids), who had succeeded the Shaybanids in 1599. A warrior, administrator and legislator whose code (*Jety Zhargy*) gave the force of written law to nomadic custom (*adat*), Tauke was the last ruler of a unified Kazakh state.

But by this time the Kazakhs were threatened by a catastrophe which had been steadily gaining momentum since the opening years of the seventeenth century. The Oirots, repulsed by the eastern Mongol tribes who had reunited and grown powerful under Altan Khan (1543–83), were beginning to head westwards. One of their tribes, the Torghuts – to the number of 40,000 tents – penetrated Kazakh territory at the beginning of the seventeenth century and led by the khan, Khu Urluk, crossed from north-east to south-west, passing north of the Aral Sea and the Caspian. This migration of a whole people left behind it a blood-stained trail across the steppes. On their way the Torghuts fought the Kazakhs of the Little Horde near the Emba and the Nogays near Astrakhan before finally establishing themselves between the Ural river and the Volga where they founded a powerful nomadic state known as the Kalmyk Horde. In 1603 these Kalmyks ravaged the khanate of Khiva, and in 1639 subdued the Turkomans of Mangyshlak. Their khan Ayuka (1670–1724) became the nominal vassal of Russia and the Russians unleashed these Buddhist warriors against the khanate of the Crimea, the Bashkirs and the Nogays – all Muslims.

The establishment of the Kalmyk Horde on the southwestern confines of the steppe region presented a grave threat in the rear of the Kazakh Hordes since, at about the same time, another Oirot state was forming on the extreme north-east of the steppes in the Tarbagatai region. Its founder, the *khungtayji* Batur of the Choros tribe, aimed at re-enacting after an interval of four centuries the career of Chingiz Khan and it was during his reign that the Oirots began to direct their devastating raids

144

into the Kazakh steppes. At first these were only marauding expeditions with the object of stealing livestock, but they served as advance warnings of the great catastrophes which would decimate the Kazakh people for almost a century. In 1643 the *khungtayji* Batur led a great expedition into the Semirechie, which he occupied, and imposed his suzerainty over most of the clans of the Great Horde. After Batur's death in 1653, his son, the *khungtayji* Galdan, succeeded in imposing his authority over all the Oirot tribes and established a vast empire on the strength of what was for that epoch an impressive military machine, a well-disciplined force of 100,000 warriors. Galdan aimed to make himself master of all Central Asia and he nearly succeeded. He displaced the last Chaghatai rulers of eastern Turkestan, converted Kashgaria into a protectorate between 1678 and 1680, annexed Turfan and Hami in 1681, and finally swallowed up all that remained of the khanate of Mughulistan while between 1681 and 1695 Oirot armies made numerous raids into the Syr-Darya region where the city of Sairam north of Tashkent was taken and sacked. But Galdan's ambitions lay primarily in the east, as he demonstrated conclusively in 1688 when his Oirots overcame the Khalkha Mongols and established themselves in eastern Mongolia. In 1690 he attacked the Manchu empire in China in an effort to emulate the achievement of Chingiz Khan but the artillery of the emperor K'ang-hsi, cast by the Jesuits, settled the outcome once and for all and the defeated nomads fled back into Mongolia.

Repulsed by the Manchus, the Oirots turned their attention once again to their western neighbours and, during the reign of Tsevan-Rabtan (1697–1727), the nephew and successor of Galdan, there opened a truly sombre chapter in the history of the Kazakh steppes. Almost without interruption Oirot armies raided the whole region with impunity. Notwithstanding the efforts of Tauke Khan whose authority extended over all three Hordes, the Oirot raids began in 1698 in the direction of Lake Balkhash and were repeated in 1710. In 1716 an Oirot army left the Ili valley, marched towards the north of Semirechie and then descended towards the south-west. In the spring of 1718 it met the Kazakh tribes assembled beside the Aya Guz river north-east of Lake Balkhash and defeated them in a three-day battle, which left the way into the Syr-Darya plain undefended. Thrusting southwards the Oirots crossed the territory of the Middle Horde and won another bloody victory over the Kazakhs on the Arys river north of Tashkent. In 1723-5 yet another expedition reached southern Kazakhstan and the cities of the Syr-Darya – Tashkent, Yasi, Sairam – fell into Oirot hands and were sacked. At the same time the Kalmyks of the Volga began raiding into the Kazakh steppes to link up with their kinsmen from Jungaria. This was the age of the *aktaban shubrundy* (the Great Disaster) which imprinted itself in an uneffaceable manner upon the epic literature of the Kazakhs. Some of the tribes of the Great and Middle Hordes submitted to the Buddhists. Others attempted to escape into the amirates of Turkestan but were repulsed so that they turned back towards the north-west in the direction of the regions already under Russian control along the rivers Emba, Ural, Ilek and Or.

In the face of the mortal danger which threatened them the Kazakh tribes, so long divided, resolved to unite and form a common front. In 1728, near Chimkant, a general assembly of the tribes chose the khan of the Middle Horde, Abu'l-Khayr, as their supreme chieftain. In the same year the united Kazakh forces barred the path of the Oirot hordes heading towards the Aral Sea, and inflicted upon them their first defeat, close to the Chubar-Tengiz lake. In the following year the Kazakhs destroyed an important Oirot detachment in another great battle south of Lake Balkhash. But these two victories did not stop the Oirot expeditions, which continued for a further twenty years. In 1740-2 the Oirots succeeded once again in traversing the steppes from east to west and in reaching the Russian frontier near Orsk. Yet again the valley of the Syr-Darya experienced systematic devastation. It was not until the annihilation of the Oirot empire by the Manchus in 1757 that the Kazakhs were finally freed from the constant threat of their terrible neighbours.

This protracted and bloody struggle against an enemy of vastly superior strength had been the main obstacle preventing the emergence of a Kazakh state or nation. Even more serious, it had left the battered and exhausted khanates incapable of offering effective resistance to a new danger which, starting from the beginning of the eighteenth century, threatened them from the north and west – Russia.

The Russian advance was quite different from the raids of the Oirots. It was slow but inexorable, and was marked by the construction of forts: Omsk in 1716, Semipalatinsk in 1718, Ust-Kamenogorsk in 1719, the forts along the Irtysh between 1732 and 1757, Orsk in 1735, and the forts along the Ishim between 1752 and 1755. Moreover, far from seeking to oppose the Russians, the Kazakh khans time and again sought Russian help against the Oirots but always in vain. In 1731 the Little Horde, in 1740 the Middle Horde, and in 1742 part of the Great Horde had in fact accepted Russian protection but so far as the Oirot threat was concerned this protection remained purely nominal.

In the second half of the eighteenth century a final attempt was made by the khans of the Middle Horde, who had suffered least from the struggle with the Oirots, to reunite the Kazakh steppes and restore to the Kazakh Hordes something of their former greatness. Thus Abu'l-Khayr extended his authority over the Little Horde and part of the Great Horde, attacked Bashkiria (already in Russian hands) in 1737 and – taking advantage of Nadir Shah's defeat of the Khivans – temporarily occupied Khiva in 1740 and proclaimed himself its ruler. After Abu'l-Khayr's death in 1749 his son Nur 'Ali attacked the Russian frontier-posts but when in turn his successor, Ablay Khan, sought to add the Great Horde to his possessions, he clashed with the Manchus. As the successors of the Oirots in Jungaria, they regarded the Kazakh khans as their vassals, and in 1771 he was compelled to swear allegiance to the Manchu emperor.

By the close of the eighteenth century the Kazakh region, completely encircled on three sides by two Great Powers, Russia and China, and threatened on its southern frontiers by the amirates of Turkestan, had been converted into two protectorates – Russian in the west and Manchu in the east. This phase marked the final end of Kazakh independence. If the Manchu protectorate was purely fictitious and hardly

147

discernible, the Russian protectorate was steadily transformed into actual possession. The end of the eighteenth century and the opening of the nineteenth century were characterized in all three Hordes by social unrest, taking the form of tribal revolts against the authority of the khans and sultans, as well as against their Russian protectors. Such was the great rebellion of Batyr Srym in 1792–7. The authority of the khans proved incapable of surviving this period of upheaval, and when the Russians decided to intervene directly they met with virtually no resistance. Russian abolition of the authority of the khans began with the Middle Horde whose last ruler, Shir-Ghazi, was summoned to Orenburg in 1822; in 1824 the khanate of the Little Horde was suppressed; and in 1848 came the turn of the Great Horde. Thereafter a new phase of history began for the Kazakh tribes, once so formidable to their neighbours, which was to be a prolonged struggle for survival.

The Kirghiz Tribes

The history of the Kirghiz tribes, formerly known as *Kara-Kirghiz* to distinguish them from the Kazakhs who were then known as *Kirghiz*, is quite distinct from that of their Kazakh neighbours.

Inhabiting the mountainous region of the Tien Shan, the Kirghiz were the descendants of various Turkish tribes such as the Türgesh and Qarluq (Mongolized during the Chingizkhanid period) which had absorbed the Kirghiz of the upper Yenisei, who ever since the High Middle Ages had been infiltrating into the Tien Shan in whole clans, and which during the thirteenth century were incorporated into the Chaghatai *ulus*. The imposition of a nominal Mongol overlordship scarcely modified the very archaic social structure of tribes which had never known political power to be concentrated solely in the hands of chieftains and in which the clans were traditionally governed by *biys* or *manaps* ('elders'), while Islam, which penetrated Kirghiz society very slowly during the eighteenth century, made only a superficial impact.

During the fourteenth century the Tien Shan region was part of the Chaghatai khanate of Mughulistan which suffered appallingly from Timur's repeated invasions but which also rapidly recovered after his death during the reigns of the Chaghatai rulers, Vays Khan (d. 1428), Esen-buqa (1434–62) and Yunus (1462–87). The Kazakh khanate even at the height of its power never succeeded in extending its authority over the Kirghiz tribes – with the exception of a short period under Haqq Nazar. Between 1683 and 1685 the Tien Shan region was ravaged and then occupied by Galdan's Oirots, who finally extinguished the Chaghatai khanate. Certain Kirghiz tribes then emigrated into the country around Yarkand, Khotan and Kashgar in eastern Turkestan. In place of them the Oirots transferred the greater part of the Yenisei Kirghiz into the Tien Shan in 1702. After the destruction of the Oirot empire by the Manchus in 1758, the Kirghiz tribes, nominally Chinese vassals, regained their complete freedom. From the beginning of the nineteenth century the southern part of Kirghizia proper – the Farghana valley – was conquered by the khanate of Kokand, and a confused period followed during which the Kirghiz tribes attempted to throw off the Turkestani yoke.

Russian intervention began in 1855, and in 1862 Russia took possession of the fortress of Pishpek and occupied all the northern part of Kirghizia. The southern part was not annexed until 1867, following the liquidation of the Kokand khanate, and the conquest of the region was completed in 1876 by the occupation of the Alay valley. A fraction of the Kirghiz then emigrated into the Pamirs and Afghanistan.

11

The Timurid Empire and the Uzbek Conquest of Mawarannahr

The history of Mughulistan and the Kazakh steppes from the disintegration of Chingiz Khan's empire down to the advance of Russia and China into those regions has been related in the two previous chapters. It is now necessary to turn back to the second half of the fourteenth century to trace the course of events in Mawarannahr and, in particular, the career of Timur whose name has already appeared in different contexts, raiding across the frontiers of Mughulistan and challenging the supremacy of Tuqtamish of the Golden Horde. One of the boldest and most destructive conquerors in human history, Timur was born in 1336 near Shahrisabz, his father Taraghai being a Turkish amir of the Barlas clan, a devout Muslim and a friend to scholars and dervishes alike. As in the case of Chingiz Khan, Timur's early years were spent leading a band of adventurers and freebooters (at times perhaps little better than bandits), and establishing a reputation for daring, resourceful and intelligent leadership. During the 1360s he established a large military following and a position of exceptional strength among the amirs and chieftains of the Turko-Mongol Chaghatai clans which had dominated Mawarannahr since the Mongol conquests of a century and a half before and which, with the decline of the Chaghatai ruling house, aspired to rule through puppet-khans, who were distinguished only by their descent from Chingiz Khan. By 1369–70 he was *de facto* ruler of Mawarannahr although not officially recognised – coins con-

150

tinued to be minted and the *khutba* read in the name of the reigning Chaghatai khan, first Suyurghatmish (1370–88) and then his son, Sultan Mahmud (1388–1403 ?).[1] Having ruthlessly imposed his authority over the Chaghatai nobility and swept aside all potential rivals, Timur made Mawarannahr the centre of his far-flung empire and the base for campaigns against his neighbours. Samarqand, the city which he seems to have preferred to all others, became his capital, and the gardens and buildings with which he beautified it have been described by Clavijo, ambassador of Henry III of Castille, who saw them in 1403. Among those which have survived subsequent upheavals the Gur Amir mausoleum and the Bibi Khanum mosque provide ample evidence of the size and splendour of the earliest Timurid buildings.

The second half of the fourteenth century was a period peculiarly suitable for the emergence of a new Central Asian empire. The Chaghatai *ulus* had completely disintegrated, Mawarannahr had been in a state of anarchy since the death of Tarmashirin in 1334 and the khanate of Mughulistan, which had been a powerful state under Tughluq-Timur (1348–62/3), was also now the prey of feuding amirs. In the Dasht-i Qipchaq the Golden Horde was experiencing a period of similar dissensions between the death of Janibek in 1357 and the emergence of Tuqtamish around 1381. In Iran the death of the Il-Khan Abu Sa'id in 1335 had been followed by the rapid decay of his dynasty. Khurasan had passed into the hands of the Kart rulers of Herat while in the west the vigorous Mongol Jalayarids, destined to be Timur's most implacable opponents, ruled from Tabriz and Baghdad. In India the Tughluqid Sultans of Delhi who succeeded Firuz Shah (1351–88) were nonentities. Thus in the last decades of the fourteenth century Timur found himself surrounded by disintegrating states, and enfeebled dynasties, not unlike those which had confronted Chingiz Khan nearly two centuries before.

It is not possible to give a detailed account of Timur's military exploits here, but the following table of his campaigns indicates the immense energy and organizing ability with which he conducted his conquests:

c. 1370–80   A period of consolidation in Mawarannahr. Campaigns in Mughulistan and Khwarazm.

1380–2   Invasion of Khurasan. Capture of Herat.

1383   Campaigns in Khurasan and Sistan.

1384–5   Campaigns in western Khurasan, Mazandaran and western Iran. Ray and Sultaniyeh captured.

1386–8   Campaigns in Luristan, Azarbayjan, Georgia, eastern Anatolia and Fars. Isfahan sacked and Shiraz entered (1387).

1388–91   Campaigns against the Golden Horde. Urganj sacked (1388).

1392–4   Campaigns in Fars, Mesopotamia, Anatolia and Georgia. Baghdad entered (1393).

1395   2nd campaign against the Golden Horde.

1398–9   Invasion of north India. Sack of Delhi (1398).

1399–1401   Campaigns against Georgia, the Jalayarids and the Mamluks of Egypt. Sivas and Aleppo taken (1400). Damascus and Baghdad sacked (1401).

1402   Defeat and capture of the Ottoman Sultan, Bayazid I, at Ankara. Bursa and Izmir sacked.

1404–05   Projected invasion of China. Timur's death (1405).

This bald chronological skeleton conveys little idea of the extraordinary military genius displayed by Timur in these campaigns or of the unparalleled ferocity with which they were conducted.[2] Timur's ambition was apparently to reconstruct the thirteenth century empire of Chingiz Khan, the memory of which still remained vivid among the tribes of inner Asia, and in his methods of waging war, in his tactics on the field of battle and in the composition of the troops which he commanded he resembled a thirteenth century Mongol conqueror more than a contemporary Muslim ruler. He was evidently anxious to stress his connexion with the Chingizkhanids. After marriage with a daughter of the Chaghatai khan, Qazan, he assumed the title of 'son-in-law' which appears on his coins and which connected him to the Chaghatai sovereigns descended from Chingiz Khan. Another marriage with a daughter of Khizr-Khoja, ruler of Mughulistan, further strengthened his ties with the descendants of Chingiz Khan. Yet in Timur's career there existed a certain paradox. While he achieved his conquests as

152

the leader and manipulator of nomadic or semi-nomadic tribal forces such as have always been the driving-force of Central Asian empires, he himself (and to an increasing extent as he grew older) also came to exemplify the impact of Irano-Islamic civilization upon the Turko-Mongol peoples so that if he seemed a barbarous 'Tatar' to his victims in Herat, Shiraz or Baghdad, he was nevertheless also a strict Sunni Muslim, a generous supporter of *shaykhs* and dervishes, and a patron of Iranian art and letters who could fully appreciate the pleasure of Iranian city life. His court at Samarqand (as described by Clavijo) was very different from the encampments of the warlords of Jungaria and Semirechie, and was a measure of the rapidity with which Iran was able to tame this most savage of her conquerors.

Compared with Chingiz Khan, Timur emerges as a more cultivated and yet far less positive figure. If he was Chingiz Khan's equal as a warrior and a leader of warriors, as an empire-builder his career lacked the clarity and logic of the great Mongol conqueror's. In Timur's campaigns there seems to have been no obvious strategic pattern just as his empire contained within it no vision of a world order such as was envisaged in the promulgation of the *Yasa*, and no sense of permanence. Even economic motives seem to have been of little importance while Timur's conquests did nothing to spread knowledge or awareness of a wider world such as had resulted from Chingiz Khan's conquests. The fragility of the Timurid empire became apparent almost immediately after Timur's death at Otrar in 1405. He had decreed no order of succession designed to preserve the integrity of his conquests, as Chingiz Khan had done, and hence the empire rapidly dissolved into separate kingdoms, the ever-growing number of princelings who were his descendants recklessly fighting one another for some morsel of his heritage.

Of Timur's four sons, Jahangir, 'Umar Shaykh and Miranshah predeceased their father so that the throne passed – although not without opposition from Timur's grandsons – to the fourth son, Shah Rukh whose long reign (1405–47) marked a period of consolidation and relative tranquillity after his father's almost ceaseless campaigning. A devout Muslim and a passionate admirer of Iranian culture, Shah Rukh transformed Timur's Central Asian empire into an orthodox Islamic sultanate with its centre in Khurasan. Herat replaced Samarqand as the capital of the empire, and Mawarannahr became the charge of his son, Ulugh Beg. Shah Rukh's major preoccupation was western Iran where the security of the empire was most obviously threatened. There, and especially in Azarbayjan, the end of Jalayarid rule had left a dangerous vacuum, which during the fifteenth century was successively filled by two powerful Turkoman confederacies; the Qara-qoyunlu, former vassals of the Jalayarids, from north-east of Lake Van, and then the Aq-qoyunlu from the Diyarbakr region. Against the Qara-qoyunlu Shah Rukh achieved little of note and by the time of his death western Iran could no longer be counted as part of the Timurid empire.[3] Throughout the rest of his possessions, however, Shah Rukh's prestige was immense. With the assistance of his favourite wife, Gauhar Shad, he devoted much wealth and energy to the patronage of artists and writers, the support of the religious classes, the provision of religious endowments, and the building of shrines, mosques and *madrasehs* (Muslim theological colleges). The refined architectural taste of this period is exemplified by the surviving early Timurid buildings in Herat, Tayabad, Turbat-i Shaykh Jam, Kharjird and Mashhad. Among Shah Rukh's children, Baysunqar in Astarabad was one of the greatest bibliophiles in history and a discriminating patron of calligraphers and painters while the viceroyalty of Ulugh Beg in Mawarannahr is inseparably linked with the compilation of his astronomical tables and the construction of his observatory in Samarqand.

Shah Rukh's death was the signal for the beginning of a series of violent struggles for the vacant throne. Between 1447 and 1449 Ulugh Beg was nominal ruler of the empire but threatened by rivals or potential rivals, including his own son, 'Abd al-Latif, who certainly had a hand in his death and that of another son, 'Abd al-'Aziz. Shortly afterwards, 'Abd al-Latif was murdered by his cousin, 'Abdullah, another grandson of Shah Rukh, and he was then overthrown by Abu Sa'id, a grandson of

Miranshah. The reign of Abu Sa'id (1451–69) in Mawarannahr and Khurasan, despite the wars and rebellions which dominated the period, constituted the second phase of relative stability in the history of Timurid rule in Central Asia. One of the ablest of his family, Abu Sa'id emulated Timur and Shah Rukh in the generosity with which he patronized the dervish orders, especially the Naqshbandi. Towards the end of his reign, apprehensive of the rise to prominence of the Aq-qoyunlu in the west, he determined to reassert Timurid authority in Azar-bayjan. There he was captured by Uzun Hasan (1466–78) and handed over to a son of Gauhar Shad who had him killed in revenge for the execution of his mother in 1457.

During the last decades of the fifteenth century the only Timurid ruler of more than average ability (Babur excepted) was the celebrated Sultan Husayn Bayqara (Plate 29), a great-grandson of 'Umar Shaykh who, having made himself master of Khwarazm and Gurgan, finally conquered Khurasan and reigned in Herat from 1470 to 1506. Babur, the future con-queror of Delhi, who wrote a detailed account of the man and his court, described him as 'slant-eyed and lion-bodied, being slender from the waist downwards'.[4] At first, Husayn Bayqara appears to have favoured Shi'ism but he later became an orthodox Sunni, although he never fasted and, according to Babur, drank daily after the mid-day prayers for forty years. No mean soldier, he was reputedly the greatest swordsman of his dynasty and delighted in sports of all kind – ram-fighting, cock-fighting, pigeon-flying, etc. With so worldly a ruler setting the tone of social life it is not altogether surprising that the citizens of Herat during the late fifteenth century were considered pleasure-loving and debauched by their contemporaries.

In the history of Iran and Central Asia, however, Sultan Husayn Bayqara's importance rests upon the cultural sig-nificance of his court where musicians, poets, painters and scholars congregated and received lavish hospitality. The last great classical poet of Iran, Jami, lived under the protection of Sultan Husayn Bayqara. So did many lesser poets, the historians Mirkhwand and Khwandamir, Dawlatshah who composed Iran's best-known 'Lives of the Poets', and Mir 'Ali Shir Navai

155

who, more than any other single person, was responsible for the transformation of Chaghatai Turkish into a medium for literary expression. Complementary to the literary achievements of the later Timurid period were its attainments in the visual arts and the few buildings in Herat and Balkh which survive from the second half of the fifteenth century reveal a sophisticated taste for decorative effect which found its counterpart in the exquisite execution of detail which characterizes the miniatures of Bihzad and the whole Herat School, as well as in the ancillary skills of calligraphy and book-binding. Speaking of the reign of Husayn Bayqara, Babur wrote with feeling that 'the whole habitable world has not seen such a town as Herat had become under Sultan Husayn Mirza'.[5] Looking back to those times with nostalgia he wrote: 'His was a wonderful Age; in it Khurasan, and Herat above all, was full of learned and matchless men. Whatever the work a man took up, he aimed and aspired at bringing that work to perfection'.[6]

While Herat prospered under the rule of Sultan Husayn Bayqara, Mawarannahr was the scene of continual strife among Timur's remaining descendants – including Babur himself, descended from Timur through his paternal grandfather, Abu Sa'id, and from Chingiz Khan through his maternal grandfather, Yunus Khan. While Babur and his cousins were fighting for the thrones of Farghana and Samarqand, a formidable new power had established itself between the Syr-Darya and the Amu-Darya, that of the Uzbeks under Muhammad Shaybani, grandson of the unfortunate Abu'l-Khayr and through him, no less than Babur, a descendant of Chingiz Khan.

Muhammad Shaybani was born around 1451 and having been left without protection by the death of his father and grandfather in 1468-9, he was compelled to pursue the career of a freebooter, eventually entering the service of Mahmud b. Yunus, the ruling khan of Mughulistan. Having rapidly established his reputation as the leader of the formidable Uzbek clans dispersed at Abu'l-Khayr's death, he seized one by one the petty principalities which were all that remained of Timur's original conquests. The last generation of Timurid princes were too deeply involved in quarrels among themselves to be able to offer a concerted front against the usurper. The one ruler who still possessed the resources to crush Muhammad Shaybani, Sultan Husayn Bayqara, declined to aid his threatened kinsmen. By 1500, therefore, Muhammad Shaybani was undisputed master of Mawarannahr, having taken in that year Bukhara, Qarshi and Samarqand. A temporary set-back followed when Babur seized Qarshi and Samarqand but he failed to dislodge the Uzbeks from Bukhara, and from there Muhammad Shaybani launched a counter-attack, routing Babur at the hard-fought battle of Sar-i Pul. With Mawarannahr once again in Uzbek hands Muhammad Shaybani extended his conquests even further by the capture of Balkh and Qunduz while the defeat of his old patron, Mahmud, brought him Tashkent and the Farghana valley. During 1505–6 he occupied Khwarazm, a possession of Sultan Husayn Bayqara.

The attack on Khwarazm showed that he was ready to challenge the last remaining Timurid ruler of any importance but in May 1506 Sultan Husayn Bayqara died and a feeble condominium was hastily set up in Herat by his two feckless sons. Babur, who was in the course of carving out a new principality for himself in Afghanistan (Badakhshan, 1503; Kabul, 1504; Kandahar, 1507) hastened to Herat to assist his relatives against the impending Uzbek attack. He found there such evidence of incapacity that he judged sustained resistance to be impossible and he withdrew in disgust, quoting Sa'adi's dictum that ten dervishes may sleep under one blanket but two kings cannot share one country. Muhammad Shaybani advanced virtually unopposed to Herat where he seized the accumulated treasure of the former dynasty. Once in possession of the city, however, he acted with unusual leniency, perhaps hoping to outshine the late sultan as a magnanimous conqueror as well as a Maecenas. If Babur's account can be trusted, he even tried to instruct Bihzad in painting.

Kabul was now the last refuge of the Timurids, and when Muhammad Shaybani advanced as far south as Kandahar where the reigning Arghunid dynasty fled at his approach it must have seemed as if he intended to occupy Kabul and even march into India. But the extraordinary rapidity of his conquests demanded

157

a breathing-space in order to consolidate what had been won. Across the Syr-Darya the growing power of the Kazakhs under Burunduk Khan (1488–1509) and Kasym Khan (1509–18) was a constant threat to Mawarannahr, while in Iran the rise of Shah Isma'il (1502–24), founder of the Safavid dynasty, complicated the situation still further. Muhammad Shaybani's conquest of Herat had exposed Khurasan to Uzbek raiders who were soon plundering Mashhad, Turbat-i Shaykh Jam, Nishapur, Sabzavar, and even Damghan and Kirman. In fact, central and eastern Iran had been a vacuum since the break-up of the Timurid empire and it now seemed probable that the Uzbeks, like earlier invaders from the north-east, would rapidly fill it.

Clearly Shah Isma'il could neither acquiesce in the loss of Khurasan and its rich cities without a struggle nor – without serious loss of prestige – allow an enemy to penetrate his territory as far west as Damghan or as far south as Kirman. In the ensuing struggle between these two great fighters sectarian differences added an element of savage fanaticism to a rivalry already bitter enough, Shah Isma'il personifying the Shi'ite zeal of the Shaykhs of Ardabil while Muhammad Shaybani and his Uzbeks were rigid Sunnis. In 1510 Shah Isma'il entered Khurasan and occupied Mashhad unopposed. Muhammad Shaybani's movements in the preceding months are obscure, but it seems likely that he conducted a swift and successful campaign against the Kazakhs which was followed by another, commanded by his son, which ended in disaster.[7] It is probable, therefore, that he faced Shah Isma'il with exhausted and demoralized troops. The armies met in the December of that same year near Marv, and after a fierce contest Muhammad Shaybani was overcome and killed. Shah Isma'il ordered his skull to be set in gold and made into a drinking cup and the skin of his head, stuffed with straw, to be sent to the Ottoman Sultan, Bayazid II, the nominal ally of the Uzbeks against the Safavids (or, in another account, to the Mamluk Sultan of Egypt). In Marv, pyramids of skulls commemorated the Shah's victory.

Such was the end of Muhammad Shaybani, a brilliant leader

158

in the great tradition of Central Asian conquerors. He was also a man of considerable culture and versatility. In his native Chaghatai Turkish he wrote excellent poetry as well as instructions in the Muslim faith for the benefit of his son and his troops. He was also acquainted with Arabic and Persian, even writing indifferent verses in the latter. On his expeditions he was usually accompanied by a travelling library and although the Timurids may have considered him a barbarian he undoubtedly enjoyed the company of poets, scholars and theologians. In the case of the latter his court was a natural refuge for Sunni divines from Iran seeking sanctuary from Shi'ite persecution.

Following his advance into Khurasan and his victory at Marv Shah Isma'il, by the occupation of Herat and Balkh, once again made the Amu-Darya the frontier of Iran while Babur, now his ally, hurried northwards from Kabul, crossed the Amu-Darya and marched triumphantly on Qarshi, Bukhara and Samarqand which the demoralized Uzbeks quickly evacuated. In 1511 he received an enthusiastic welcome from the citizens of Samarqand, flattered to have again a descendant of the great Timur as their ruler. The honeymoon, however, did not last long. As the protegé of the Safavids, whose Shi'ite troops had accompanied him into Mawarannahr, Babur's popularity soon dwindled while the Uzbeks, now led by two vigorous commanders, Janibek and 'Ubaydullah (a cousin and nephew of Muhammad Shaybani), took advantage of this situation to return to the attack. 'Ubaydullah advanced against Bukhara with some 3,000 men and Babur immediately marched out of Samarqand with a larger force to meet him. The Uzbeks withdrew with Babur in pursuit, but at Kul-i Malik 'Ubaydullah turned at bay and won a resounding victory against heavy odds (1512). Having ruled in Samarqand for only eight months Babur now abandoned the city and fled to Hissar whence he appealed to Shah Isma'il for help. Joined by an Iranian force of 60,000 men, commanded by the Shah's *vakil*, Amir Yar Ahmad Khuzani, Babur had no difficulty in recapturing Qarshi where an indiscriminate massacre was ordered (which included one of 'Ubaydullah's cousins). The allied commanders then decided to besiege the fort of Ghajdivan, which contained a small Uzbek garrison, before advancing on Samarqand. 'Ubaydullah and Janibek assembled sufficient forces to come to its relief and in a pitched battle nearby, the Uzbeks were overwhelmingly victorious. Amir Yar Ahmad Khuzani was captured and executed on 'Ubaydullah's orders and Babur retreated to Kabul, never again to return to Mawarannahr. In these campaigns of the Timurids and Safavids against the Uzbeks, Shi'ite-Sunni hostility played an important part, so that even Mirza Muhammad Haydar Dughlat, a Sunni but also a cousin of Babur and no friend of the Uzbeks, could write of Ghajdivan: 'the claws of Islam twisted the hands of heresy and unbelief, and victory declared for the true faith. The victorious breeze of Islam overturned the banners of the schismatics'.[8]

In 1526 at the first battle of Panipat Babur became ruler of northern India and thereby laid the foundations of the Mughul Empire over which his descendants would reign until 1739, surviving as sovereigns of Delhi until 1857. For at least two centuries after Babur's invasion of India the Delhi court maintained regular contact with the courts of Central Asia through the stream of soldiers, officials, scholars, artists, adventurers and refugees from north of the Hindu Kush who sought wealth and fame in India. Moreover for more than a century after Babur's death in 1530 his successors continued to toy with the possibility of regaining their lost lands beyond the mountains, and not only from a desire to return to their ancestral patrimony. The defence of the north-west frontier against two such restless neighbours as the Uzbeks and the Safavids, and the fear that one day the Uzbeks might venture upon an invasion of India, necessitated Mughul control over the central Afghan *massif* while access to the trade-routes north of the Hindu Kush tapped the supply of fighting-men and horses which was a *sine qua non* for the survival of a foreign Muslim dynasty in India ruling a majority of alien Hindu subjects.

Such a dream never came near realization. After Panipat Babur was fully occupied in consolidating his conquests in northern India and was also probably too shrewd to risk another encounter with 'Ubaydullah. His son, Humayun, barely managed to retain his father's kingdom intact.[9] Akbar (1556–1605) was wholly preoccupied with his wars and administration in India, and during his reign Mawarannahr was ruled by one of the greatest of the Shaybanids, 'Abdullah II (1583–98) who expelled Akbar's Timurid relatives from Badakhshan and Tukharistan. Indeed, Akbar is reputed to have remained in northern India between 1585 and 1598 in expectation of an Uzbek attack upon Kabul and the Punjab.[10] His son, Jahangir, was probably too indolent to have contemplated campaigning beyond his north-west frontier, but military glory had a strong appeal for Shah Jahan (1627–59) and it was during his reign that the Indian Timurids made their last attempt to regain their former possessions in Central Asia. The occupation of Balkh in 1646–7 was however a disastrous failure and it is possible that when Shah Jahan's successor, Aurangzeb (1659–1707), himself a participant in that melancholy adventure, turned his whole attention to expansion southwards against the Deccan Sultanates, it was with the knowledge that further campaigns in Central Asia could only result in yet more ruinous losses in men and money.[11] Shah Jahan's attempts to take Balkh from the Uzbeks and Kandahar from the Safavids were, by seventeenth-century standards, fantastically costly undertakings and made a far from insignificant contribution to the mounting financial crisis of the empire in the second half of the century. Yet if the Great Mughuls were to prove no more successful than the British in their Afghan campaigns, pride in their Central Asian ancestry and in their descent from the mighty Timur survived down to the end. It is surely no accident that the celebrated *Mulfuzat-i Timuri*, a forgery if ever there was one, was written in Mughul India and at the court of Shah Jahan.

In the history of Central Asia the role of the Timurids was, in political terms, of little significance. The founder of the dynasty, although a supremely successful warlord, destroyed far more than he created and his career lacks the compelling fascination of Chingiz Khan's. His descendants, so long as they remained in Mawarannahr and Khurasan, proved themselves as often as not undistinguished and even inept rulers incapable of curbing their family feuds in the face of external danger and it was only much later in India that the administrative genius of the family manifested itself. In the cultural sphere, however, the contribution of the Central Asian Timurids is unique. They presided over the last great age of Persian literature and encouraged the development of Chaghatai Turkish as a literary language, their generosity provided the funds for the construction of the sumptuously decorated mosques and *madrasehs* of Herat, Mashhad, Bukhara and Samarqand, and their intelligent patronage of painters and calligraphers resulted in the execution of the finest Persian miniatures and manuscripts. No other dynasty in Central Asia has left behind it such a legacy.

12

The Shaybanids

A Central Asian empire had twice slipped from the grasp of the Uzbeks: first with the death of Abu'l-Khayr in 1468–9 and then again with Muhammad Shaybani's death at the battle of Marv. But the victory of Ghajdivan restored almost everything that had been lost in 1510. Thereafter Mawarannahr was parcelled out into appanages for the most important Shaybanid chieftains, and local regimes were established at Balkh, Bukhara, Samarqand, Tashkent and elsewhere. The eldest living Shaybanid khan, Küchkünchi, an uncle of Muhammad Shaybani, was acknowledged as paramount ruler and his name alone appeared on the coinage and was read in the *khutba*. Küchkünchi reigned from 1510 to 1530, followed by his son, Abu Sa'id, from 1530 to 1533, who was in turn succeeded by 'Ubaydullah who died in 1539. 'Ubaydullah had been the most influential figure among the Uzbek chieftains since the death of Muhammad Shaybani, and it was under his leadership that Uzbek rule in Mawarannahr was finally consolidated.

A major figure in Uzbek history, 'Ubaydullah was born in 1476 and at an early age acquired practical experience as a soldier and administrator since he was entrusted with the governorship of Bukhara during the lifetime of Muhammad Shaybani and was still only thirty-four at the time of the latter's death. In later life he earned the reputation of being, in addition to a model Sunni ruler, a man of some learning, a patron of scholars and poets, and himself – as Hasan-i Rumlu, a bitter Shi'ite opponent of the Uzbeks, grudgingly admitted – 'in

163

poetry unequalled'.[1] As a leader of unusual tenacity who enjoyed the distinction of having finally expelled the Timurids from their Central Asian homeland, 'Ubaydullah time and again invaded Iran in an attempt to incorporate Khurasan into the Shaybanid empire. His failure to overcome Shah Tahmasb (1524–76), however, was to prove decisive for the future of Central Asia.[2] By barring Uzbek expansion south of the Amu-Darya (or, when that was impossible, by containing it north of the Elburz and the Paropamisus) the Safavids effectively isolated Mawarannahr from the rest of the Islamic world, an isolation which was to blight her intellectual and cultural life down to the close of the nineteenth century.

It is often asserted that Chingiz Khan and Timur between them destroyed the prosperity of Khurasan. It seems more probable that the devastation which accompanied the Safavid-Uzbek wars of the sixteenth and seventeenth centuries had a far graver effect. The following summary of 'Ubaydullah's campaigns south of the Amu-Darya aptly exemplifies the misery which must have been experienced by both urban and agricultural communities in Khurasan as a result of Uzbek depredations which continued spasmodically down to the eighteenth century.

In 1515 'Ubaydullah and Janibek raided Khurasan. In 1521 and 1524 'Ubaydullah attempted to capture Herat. In 1526 he occupied Tus and Marv while a son of Janibek captured Balkh. In 1527 he raided further afield, penetrating as far west as Astarabad and Bistam before turning eastwards to winter near Herat which was again attacked in the following year (1528). Still unsuccessful, the result of lack of skill in siege-warfare and the absence of cannon, and learning that Shah Tahmasb was planning an advance into Khurasan, 'Ubaydullah retired to Samarqand to obtain reinforcements. Then he returned to Khurasan with greatly strengthened forces. A decisive victory for the Uzbeks seemed a foregone conclusion since the Shah was both young and inexperienced but when the two armies met near Turbat-i Shaykh Jam (1529) the Uzbeks suffered a crushing reverse. The bitter lesson of Caldiran – where, in 1514, the Safavid forces fell back in the face of Ottoman superiority in

164

artillery – had been well learnt and fifteen years later the possession of some cannon and rudimentary small-arms was a factor contributing to the Safavid victory at Turbat-i Shaykh Jam. Certainly the Uzbek failure to appreciate the importance of artillery resulted in their gradual relegation to a place among the minor military powers of Asia.[3]

Although the battle of Turbat-i Shaykh Jam enormously enhanced the prestige of the young Shah it appears to have in no way lessened 'Ubaydullah's appetite for Khurasan since no sooner had the Safavid army withdrawn again westwards than he returned to the attack, re-crossed the Amu-Darya, and with extreme rapidity captured first Mashhad and then Herat, which was ferociously plundered, still in 1529. Early in the following year, while wintering in Khurasan, he learnt that Shah Tahmasb was returning eastwards with a strong army and having been refused reinforcements by his suzerain, Abu Sa'id, who presumably dreaded any further increase in the power of his ambitious relative, he was forced to abandon his conquests and withdraw beyond the Amu-Darya. He returned to the neighbourhood of Herat (but was foiled in an attempt to take the city) in 1532–3 and from there swept westwards in a lightning raid through Mashhad, Sabzavar, Bistam and Astarabad before once again beating a hurried retreat at the news of the Shah's approach. Finally, in 1535 he captured Herat for the second time, sacked it and then, as usual, abandoned it in the face of an advancing Safavid relief-force. Not long afterwards he met with an ignominious defeat at the hands of one of his own kinsmen, the ruler of Khwarazm, and died in 1539 at the age of sixty-three.

'Ubaydullah had been the one chieftain capable of maintaining even a semblance of unity among the warring Uzbek clans and for at least two decades after his death each Shaybanid khan, at constant warfare with his neighbour, endeavoured to convert his possessions into an independent principality. This anarchic phase gradually disappeared with the emergence to a position of unchallenged supremacy of a grandson of Janibek, 'Abdullah Khan, who during the reigns of his uncle and father, Pir Muhammad I (1556–61) and Iskandar (1561–83), exterminated all potential rivals and seized their fiefs so that when he finally succeeded his father he controlled an area little less extensive than had Muhammad Shaybani at the height of his power. In the history of Mawarannahr the reign of 'Abdullah Khan II (1583–98) was long remembered as a period when public order was ruthlessly enforced after decades of anarchy and when, in consequence, commerce and agriculture began to revive and the burdens on the people became lighter. As a corollary to all this, in the country between the Amu-Darya and the Syr-Darya, and especially in Bukhara, the fame of 'Abdullah Khan assumed a legendary proportion comparable with that of his near-contemporary, Shah 'Abbas I, in Iran so that even down to very recent times it was usual to attribute the construction of any otherwise anonymous caravansarai, bridge, *madraseh*, garden or other amenity in or around Bukhara to the munificence of this larger-than-life figure.

Like his predecessors, Muhammad Shaybani and 'Ubaydullah, 'Abdullah Khan was bent on extending his frontiers in every possible direction, crossing the Syr-Darya to penetrate the inhospitable Kazakh steppes, asserting an authority (however transitory) from Astarabad in the west to Kashgar in the east, and taking Badakhshan and Tukharistan from Timurid relatives of Akbar. But his greatest triumphs were won against the Safavids. In 1585 he sacked Herat and Marv, and in 1588 – a year after the accession of Shah 'Abbas (1587–1629) – intervened so effectively in Khurasan that he enabled his allies, the Ottomans, to close their long war of 1578–90 against Iran with a highly favourable peace. In due course Shah 'Abbas became 'Abdullah's most formidable antagonist but before that time arrived the list of cities in Khurasan plundered by 'Abdullah's troops – Herat Fushanj, Turbat-i Shaykh Jam, Marv, Sarakhs, Mashhad, Nishapur, Sabzavar, Isfarayin, Tun, Tabas and Khwaf – is eloquent testimony of the way in which the Uzbek occupation of Mawarannahr brought destruction to northeastern Iran.

'Abdullah was a strictly orthodox ruler, even to the extent of expelling the students of philosophy from Samarqand and Bukhara, and sending an embassy to Akbar to enquire into rumours of the emperor's heterodoxy.[4] Too responsive to the spiritual atmosphere of late sixteenth century Bukhara to be a patron of scholarship he proved an indulgent paymaster of architects and painters. Yet 'Abdullah lived to see the beginning of the decline of the empire which he had won amid plague (which swept Mawarannahr in 1590–1), Oirot raids and the rebellion of his son, 'Abd al-Mumin. An alliance between Khwarazm and Iran resulted in the capture of Mashhad, Marv and Herat by Shah 'Abbas in 1595–6, and the appearance of Iranian troops on the north bank of the Amu-Darya symbolized the end of Shaybanid rule in Mawarannahr (although not in Khwarazm where a collateral line ruled). 'Abdullah died in 1598 and neither 'Abd al-Mumin nor his cousin Pir Muhammad II survived for more than a few months. The throne then passed to 'Abdullah's sister's husband, Jani Khan, a descendant of the former khans of Astrakhan, who declined it in favour of his son, Baqi Muhammad (1599–1605), with whom the Janid or Astrakhanid dynasty began.

It was the achievement of the Shaybanids to make Mawarannahr the permanent home of the Uzbeks, but the simultaneous rise of the Safavid dynasty in Iran and the firm hold which the Indian Timurids retained on the region south of the Hindu Kush prevented even the greatest Shaybanid rulers from re-enacting Timur's conquests. Instead, a balance of power was established between these three dynasties in which the superior mobility of the Uzbeks was off-set by their failure to develop an artillery arm comparable to that of their rivals. All the ablest Shaybanid rulers aspired to the permanent occupation of Khurasan but the only result of this ambition, which they lacked the resources to implement, was protracted and exhausting warfare with the Safavids, represented by both sides as a sectarian conflict, which weakened the Uzbeks on the line of the Syr-Darya (where they had assumed the role of the Timurids as champions of Islam and wardens of the marches) where they faced their dangerously mobile Kazakh kinsmen. Neither the Safavids whose line expired in 1720 with the Ghilzai Afghan occupation of Isfahan, nor successive Uzbek dynasties could muster sufficient strength to retain the whole of Khurasan and by the second half of the eighteenth century Herat and Balkh had already been incorporated into the Afghan empire of Ahmad Shah Durrani, remaining ever since in Afghan hands. A revival of Uzbek ambitions south of the Amu-Darya in the last quarter of the eighteenth century resulted in the capture and retention of Marv by Shah Murad, founder of the Mangit dynasty. Thus the Qajars who, shortly afterwards, were to found a new dynasty in Iran had to content themselves with only the southern and western parts of what had once been one of the largest and richest provinces of the mediaeval Caliphate and its eastern successor-states. This partition was confirmed by the frontier demarcations of the late nineteenth century and today Khurasan is still divided between Iran, Afghanistan and the Soviet Union.

It was in the course of the sixteenth century and under Shaybanid rule that Mawarannahr became finally isolated from the rest of the Islamic world as a direct result of the relentless Sunni-Shiʻite conflict between Shaybanids and Safavids which made it difficult for contacts to be maintained with the Sunni states beyond Iran. To the south-east, it is true, lay Mughul India but the Timurid rulers of Delhi were – with good reason – wary of contacts with the Uzbek courts while the stream of soldiers, scholars and adventurers from Mawarannahr and Khurasan who made their way into India during the sixteenth and seventeenth centuries was a one-way traffic, a sort of medieval 'brain-drain' from Central Asia and Iran which benefited India alone. To the north-west, the Muslim successor-khanates of the Golden Horde were, with the solitary exception of the Crimea, passing into Christian Russian hands throughout the sixteenth century while relations with the Ottoman empire depended upon the arduous and dangerous crossing of the Caspian Sea and the Caucasus. During the lifetime of ʻAbdullah Khan this isolation of the Uzbeks had already become a matter of concern in Istanbul as well as in Bukhara.

But politics alone do not explain the growing cultural isolation of Mawarannahr which, in earlier centuries, had so often produced the intellectual and spiritual 'pace-setters' of mediaeval Islam. One highly significant but also relatively intangible factor to take into account is the luxuriant growth during the sixteenth and seventeeth centuries of dervish orders (*silsileh*) which, although they had flourished well enough during the Chaghatai and Timurid periods, found the Uzbek regimes peculiarly well-disposed towards them and which were, for the most part, antipathetic to the spread of higher Muslim culture. The members of these orders inspired intense veneration among almost all classes of the population, whether nomads or oasis-dwellers, although perhaps not among the *ulama* of the larger towns, and several of the most influential orders such as the *Naqshbandiyeh* maintained close relations with the reigning chieftains in a manner not wholly dissimilar from the way the Jesuits of seventeenth and early eighteenth century Europe established intimate contacts with the ruling Catholic dynasties. These chieftains, for their part, were better able to retain their hold over their sometimes heterogeneous subjects by identifying themselves with the spirit of popular religion – however debased it might be – and notable examples of such a course among the Uzbeks were 'Abdullah Khan in the sixteenth century and Shah Murad two centuries later.

The dervishes represented Islam at the level of the lowest common denominator. At a much more sophisticated level, among the educated classes of urban Mawarannahr there was an excessive preoccupation with the study of theology at the expense of other disciplines (excessive when compared to the intellectual milieu of Samanid or Seljuqid times) which imposed an absolute sterility upon the intellectual life of important centres of population such as Bukhara the *Qutb al-Islam* (the Pillar of Islam) where in any case the *ulama*, their social and economic position secured by extensive holdings in *vaqf* (*mortmain*), exercised immense influence over public affairs and undoubtedly inhibited cultural life in general.

It is likely that the intensity of religious feeling of the Muslims of Central Asia at this period may have had its roots in their exposed position on one of the most vulnerable frontiers of the Muslim world, the frontier which received the full weight of the Mongol invasions of the thirteenth century; which experienced two centuries of turmoil and upheaval during the lifetime of the unstable Chaghatai khanate; and which then, not long after the tumultuous career of Timur had come to an end, endured the onslaught both of the Uzbek and Kazakh Hordes from the north and of the infidel Oirots from the east. Against this background of endemic invasions and political instability, however, the great task of converting the nomads to Islam proceeded slowly but nonetheless inexorably – the achievement not so much of the Muslim Establishment as of individual dervishes and *pirs*, and in this respect the spread of Islam on the steppes followed a course parallel to its spread in northern India where the main impetus for conversion also came from the dervish orders, and especially the *Chishtiyeh*. For the nomads living on the fringes of the *Dar al-Islam* it was the emotional appeal of Islam (and, of course, the opportunity to be assimilated into a superior culture) rather than its theology which mattered, while the reverence with which nomadic communities would receive itinerant dervishes and accept their assertions of miraculous power implies that, at least to some extent, they identified these newcomers with their own ancestral shamans.

Thus it was the dervish rather than the town- or village-based *mulla* who moulded the shape of Islam as a popular faith in Central Asia and at least some of the reasons for this can readily be deduced. In contrast to the typical *mulla, madraseh*-trained, an Arabic scholar perhaps, strictly orthodox in his beliefs, rigid in his obedience to the requirements of the *Shari'at* and meticulous in his ablutions, the wandering dervish, begging his way from one encampment to the next, easily established a faithful following among relatively unsophisticated, only half-converted nomads who minded not at all his illiteracy, his lack of orthodoxy or his disregard for personal cleanliness so long as his reputation for sanctity and for the possession of super-natural power agreed with their own pre-conceived notions of what a spiritual counsellor – that is to say, a shaman – should be. With good reason, therefore, were the dervish 'monasteries' (*khanqah*) frequently sited on the edge of the steppes, within easy access of the nomads' regular encampments and it is no accident that the shrine of Shaykh Ahmad Yasavi at Yasi, located in close proximity to the southernmost extension of the Kazakh steppe, should have been a major place of pilgrimage for both Uzbeks and Kazakhs alike. Deriving their support, therefore, from the most turbulent and indeed barbarous elements in the population both of Mawarannahr and of the country beyond the Syr-Darya the dervish orders met with few obstacles to their pretentions from the better-educated and wealthier inhabitants of the towns who had good cause to fear their greed and enmity when even powerful khans judged it expedient to placate them.

Under such circumstances it is hardly surprising if Muslim Central Asia under Uzbek rule contributed so little to Islamic civilization in general although an exception must be made where the emergence of Chaghatai literature is concerned. During the Timurid period Chaghatai Turkish had developed rapidly as a language of polite learning and, blossoming under the patronage of Sultan Husayn Bayqara of Herat and Mir 'Ali Shir Nava'i, greatest of Chaghatai poets, in the last decades of the fifteenth century, had become by Shaybanid times a mature vehicle for literary expression and complementary to Persian which, however, it failed to replace as the language of the cultural elite. Chaghatai poetry was warmly patronized, and indeed written, by a number of Shaybanid rulers, including Muhammad Shaybani and 'Ubaydullah, while further afield Babur chose it in preference to Persian as the language in which he composed his memoirs and Bayram Khan, the great Turkoman *amir* who won back for the Mughuls (Timurids) their Indian empire at the second battle of Panipat (1556) and acted as regent during Akbar's minority, wrote poetry as fluently in Chaghatai as in Persian. Later and coinciding with the passing of the Shaybanid dynasty there was a marked decline in the quality of Chaghatai poetry after the end of the sixteenth century but under the Janids and Mangits there developed a tradition of historical prose writing which foreshadowed the emergence of a modern Uzbek literature.

In the visual arts the well-established traditions of Timurid times were maintained, although with declining vigour, throughout the greater part of the sixteenth century. With regard to miniature painting, the famous Herat School did not disappear as a result of Muhammad Shaybani's conquest of the city in 1507 but it was thereafter dispersed and while Bihzad and some

171

of his pupils emigrated to Shah Isma'il's court at Tabriz others entered the service of the Shaybanids and were transferred to the new provincial capitals of Mawarannahr, but mainly to Bukhara. Neglected by art-historians who have tended to concentrate their attention on Timurid, Safavid and Indian Mughul miniature painting, the Bukhara School, although an unmistakable off-shoot of the parent school in Herat, possessed its own distinctive style characterized by elaborate composition and a fondness for sumptuous colour. Its splendour, however, proved short-lived and it is unlikely that more than one generation of painters of real merit succeeded the original refugees from Herat.[5] In architecture the traditions of the previous century survived far longer – in fact, well into the nineteenth century – but on a fast-declining scale so far as quality was concerned. The Shaybanids, however, constructed a number of fine mosques and *madrasehs* in both Bukhara and Samarqand, *kashikari* (the decoration of surfaces with coloured tiles) continuing, as it had been under the Timurids, the principal form of architectural decoration.[6] In one minor field of the arts, however, the Shaybanids improved upon their predecessors: in comparison with the coarse, carelessly-minted coinage of the Timurids the Shaybanid issues were of distinctly superior design. In fact, the Shaybanids of the sixteenth century were certainly no barbarians – notwithstanding the understandable abuse which Babur in his memoirs heaps upon Muhammad Shaybani – and the genuine love of learning and patronage of the arts displayed by their leading princes, coupled with their unswerving support of the Sunni *ulama*, probably made the transition from Timurid to Shaybanid rule relatively palatable for the urban *literati* of the larger towns and cities of Mawarannahr.[7]

From the sixteenth century onwards Turks probably formed a majority in the racial composition of the population of Mawarannahr and it seems likely that there was also an increase in the proportion of nomads to sedentary cultivators or townsfolk. Iranian culture and the Persian language continued, however, to exercise a pervasive influence on the ruling elite and from quite early in the seventeenth century Uzbek clans which had entered Mawarannahr more than a century before as nomadic cattle-breeders were beginning to settle in the oases as cultivators and even city-dwellers, apparently assimilating themselves without undue difficulty with the existing sedentary population, whether Turkish or Iranian (Tajik). In cities like Bukhara there continued down to the nineteenth century a prevalent of Iranian racial types – descendants of the ancient inhabitants of the oases reinforced by generations of captives from Iran, prisoners-of-war or the victims of slave-raids. While the Uzbeks largely succeeded in coming to terms with agricultural and even commercial life, the Turkomans, the Kara-Kalpaks and the Kazakhs retained down to the period of the Russian conquest their traditional nomadic life as stock-breeders, continuing their ancient quarrels with the inhabitants of the oases who were now as often of Uzbek origin as of Tajik.

Uzbek rule in Mawarannahr coincided with the steady decline of the trans-continental caravan-trade which had always been the main source of the prosperity of the oasis-cities of Central Asia and their principal *raison d'être* for while Muhammad Shaybani had been conquering the remnants of the Timurid empire, a Portuguese seaman on the other side of the world had unwittingly set the seal on the economic eclipse of Central Asia, an eclipse which was to last until the twentieth century. Prior to Vasco da Gama's circumnavigation of Africa in 1498, and the discovery of the sea-route between Europe and the Far East, Central Asia had been the meeting place of the commerce and civilizations of China, India, the Middle East and Europe. As a consequence of these discoveries, the old Central Asia trade-routes declined in importance; this in turn implied the economic decline of Central Asia itself. When Russia revived the overland trade with China two centuries later the caravans travelled far to the north of the old routes, through Siberia and Mongolia. The gradual decay of the caravan-traffic meant an enormous loss of wealth to those Central Asian rulers whose main source of revenue had been the tolls levied on goods passing through their territories. This, in turn, must have meant a real decline in their power since they were no longer able to maintain a following such as their predecessors had done or purchase firearms, now becoming for the first time a factor of some importance. As a result of these changes rulers ceased to have much incentive to keep the old routes open and safe for a declining volume of merchandise. It is possible that this trend was already becoming apparent before the end of the sixteenth century – Bukhara under 'Abdullah Khan, for example, was almost certainly less prosperous than it had been a century before[8] – but until further work is undertaken on the economic history of mediaeval Central Asia the problem of the economic decline of the area in the post-Timurid period must remain a matter for speculation.

13

The Decline of the Uzbek Khanates

The Janids ruled Mawarannahr from Bukhara for the whole of the seventeenth century and the greater part of the eighteenth century, while a branch of the Shaybanids continued to reign in Khwarazm (Khiva). Under the later Janid rulers Mawarannahr experienced marked economic and cultural stagnation. Significant of the cultural decline is the statement made in the *Shajareh-ye Turk*, an account of the descendants of Chingiz Khan, by the historian, Abu'l Ghazi Bahadur Khan (ruler of Khiva, c. 1644–63), who writes:

As a result of the carelessness of our ancestors, due to the ignorance of the people of Khwarazm, there does not exist down to the present time a single history of our family from the time when our ancestors separated from the ancestors of 'Abdullah Khan. I originally intended to entrust someone with the responsibility of writing this history, but I found no one capable of carrying out this task. That is why I am compelled to write this work myself.[1]

Around 1700 the establishment of an independent khanate at Kokand removed the Farghana valley from the control of the Bukhara government while both Bukhara and Khva were further weakened by the invasion in 1740 of the Iranian conqueror, Nadir Shah, who once again made the Amu-Darya the frontier of Iran. Towards the close of the eighteenth century, however, extensive tracts in the Amu-Darya/Syr-Darya region began to show signs of recovery, due in part at least to the emergence of relatively vigorous new dynasties: the Mangits in Bukhara, the Qungrats in Khiva and the Mins in Kokand. All three regimes endeavoured, with varying degrees of success, to impose a greater degree of administrative centralization than had hitherto existed in the area; as a result, in addition to an obvious growth of political cohesion in each khanate, it became possible to undertake the construction of useful public works and, in particular, irrigation-projects.[2]

Twelve Janid rulers reigned in Mawarannahr between 1599 and 1785, a period during which Bukhara remained the seat of government while Balkh, as an outlying principality, was usually the residence of the heir-apparent, at least until the time of Nadir Shah's invasion. From Balkh, which continued to maintain tenuous commercial relations with Mughul India, a trickle of outside influences penetrated to Bukhara where one or two rulers still managed to retain the semblance of a cultured court amid a society otherwise subjected to unbridled fanaticism. For the most part, however, Mawarannahr in the seventeenth and eighteenth centuries was almost wholly isolated from the rest of the Muslim world.

The Janids inherited from their Shaybanid predecessors a territory which closely corresponded with the heartlands of the old Timurid empire of the fifteenth century – Mawarannahr itself, Balkh, Badakhshan, the Farghana valley but not Khwarazm – and for the first century of their rule they maintained this heritage virtually intact. Under the greatest ruler of the dynasty, Imam Quli Khan (1608–40), Bukhara enjoyed a final Indian summer of relative peace and prosperity, exemplified by the construction of the Shirdar *madraseh* in Samarqand (1619–36). Imam Quli Khan was the first of several Janid rulers to resign the throne for a devotional life in the Holy Cities of Arabia, but so great was the unpopularity of his pleasure-loving brother and successor, Nadir Muhammad (1640–7), that he was compelled to hand over the government of Bukhara to his son, 'Abd al-'Aziz (1647–80), retaining only Balkh as his personal appanage. These family quarrels invited the attention of Shah Jahan (1627–59), the Mughul ruler of India and a great-great grandson of Babur, who now attempted to reconquer at least a part of his Timurid patrimony north of the Hindu Kush. In 1645 a Mughul army invaded Badakhshan and in 1646, under the command of Shah Jahan's youngest son, Murad Bakhsh, occupied Badakhshan and entered Balkh almost unopposed, Nadir Muhammad fleeing first to Mashhad and then to the Safavid court at Isfahan. It was not long, however, before Murad Bakhsh and his Indian troops, finding their position untenable, withdrew to Kabul while Shah Jahan, as soon as the news reached him, dismissed Murad Bakhsh from his command and in 1647 sent in his place Aurangzeb, his third son and the future emperor (1659–1707). Aurangzeb was compelled to fight every mile of the way from Kabul to Balkh, and it was only his iron will-power and the respect of the Uzbeks for his musketry which enabled his forces to reach the shelter of the walls of Balkh. Opposing him were the two able sons of Nadir Muhammad, 'Abd al-'Aziz and Subhan Quli, and with these Aurangzeb was soon forced to negotiate. On the 1 October 1647 the citadel of Balkh was formally handed over to two grandsons of Nadir Muhammad, and Aurangzeb began his retreat. Winter came early that year on the Hindu Kush and the exhausted Mughul army, unaccustomed to the harsh climate, laden with baggage yet short of supplies, harassed by Uzbeks in open country and by Hazaras in the passes, struggled back to Kabul a mere remnant of the expeditionary force which had set out from there only a few months before. The losses in men and beasts had been appalling and immense sums had been squandered – all to no purpose. No new territory had been acquired; no conceivable political advantage had been gained; Mughul prestige on their unstable north-west frontier had been sadly shaken; and the same family ruled in Balkh after Shah Jahan's intervention as had ruled there before it. This was the last attempt of the Mughuls to regain their former possessions in Central Asia, and thereafter they were content to restrict contact with their northern neighbours to formal diplomatic exchanges.

Aurangzeb's campaign of 1647 exemplified in striking fashion the relationship, which existed even at this late date, between the Uzbeks and their Mughul and Safavid neighbours, between combatants who had to a certain extent retained the military traditions of their nomadic forebears and those who fought with forces cumbersome in comparison and far less mobile. Less hardy than the Uzbeks and numerically weaker, Aurangzeb's forces (and he was already by that date an experienced commander) held their own only when their artillery and musketry could be used effectively. Yet had their superiority in firearms been supported by the kind of mobility which Nadir Shah's armies possessed nearly a century later, the outcome of the encounter might have been very different. As it was, the Uzbeks proved invincible in open country and in harrying an enemy on the move, repeatedly demonstrating against the unwieldy Mughul army (as they had done previously with the Safavids) that the baffling and unnerving mobility of nomads or semi-nomads could only be defeated by the greater mobility of peoples like the Kazakhs or the Oirots, or by the effective use of firearms such as the Russians and the Manchus deployed in the pacification of the tribes.

The long reign of 'Abd al-'Aziz, followed by that of Subhan Quli (1680–1702), marked the climax of Janid rule in Mawarannahr. Subhan Quli was a scholarly figure who wrote a treatise on medicine, and was probably the last ruler of his house to play the host to embassies from Delhi and Istanbul. During the second half of the seventeenth century, Janid patronage of the arts exemplified by the 'Abd al-'Aziz *madraseh* in Bukhara (1652) and the Tala Kari *madraseh* in Samarqand (1646–60) compares not unfavourably with that of the later Safavids in Isfahan. Yet the surface splendour was deceptive. The dynasty, constantly divided against itself by family rivalries, was unable to control the more turbulent clans while the spasmodic contests with the Safavids, although generally fought on Iranian soil, tended to enhance the power of the semi-independent chieftains and freebooters of the marches at the expense of the Bukhara government. Then the conflict with Shah Jahan, though brief, had been fierce and it was followed by a protracted struggle with the ruler of Khiva, the much-travelled historian, Abu'l Ghazi Bahadur Khan. There was always potential danger from the Kazakhs across the Syr-Darya and after the turn of the century the khanate of Kokand was an additional threat. Finally, the great Iranian conqueror, Nadir Shah (1736–47) destroyed the surviving prestige of the Janid state in much the same way that he destroyed what remained of the prestige of the Mughul empire in India, so that although the reigning Janid sovereign (like Muhammad Shah in Delhi) survived his visitation he exercised only a nominal authority, control of the administration having passed into the hands of the family of Muhammad Rahim Bey, a chieftain of the Mangit tribe which traced an illustrious lineage back to Mongol times, and which in Mawarannahr now occupied lands near Qarshi and on the lower Amu-Darya.

It was during the reign of Abu'l-Fayz (1705–47), a colourless son of Subhan Quli, that Muhammad Rahim Bey, attained the highest office in the Bukhara state, that of *Hakim Ataliq*. One of the leading chieftains of the Mangits, in 1737 he led the Janid forces against Riza Quli Mirza, the son of Nadir Shah, who had taken advantage of his father's absence on his Afghan and Indian campaigns to win some glory for himself by crossing the Amu-Darya and marching on Qarshi. Here he was confronted by Muhammad Rahim Bey, and here too he received an angry command from his father to withdraw south of the river. Riza Quli Khan was recalled because he had exceeded his father's orders but in 1740, following his return from India, Nadir Shah resolved to crush the Uzbek khanates of Bukhara and Khiva, the source of so many invasions of Iran. Setting out from Balkh he descended the south bank of the Amu-Darya to Charjui and then crossed into Bukharan territory. Abu'l-Fayz, leaning on the advice of Muhammad Rahim Bey, was willing to submit to the Shah but he was over-ruled by the pro-war group at court. An army was therefore rapidly assembled and led against the invaders but the Uzbeks, unnerved by the Iranian artillery, suffered a humiliating defeat and Abu'l-Fayz hastened to make peace. The terms were surprisingly mild: a matrimonial alliance was arranged between the two rulers; all territory south of the Amu-Darya formerly belonging to Bukhara was to be incorporated into Nadir Shah's empire; 30,000 Uzbeks were to serve in Nadir Shah's army. Before marching off to attack Ilbars Khan of Khiva, Nadir Shah formally entered Bukhara as a conqueror and had his name read in the *khutba* and stamped on the coinage. The city itself, however, was spared the horrors of the recent sack of Delhi.

179

Nadir Shah's rapacity was apparently not aroused by the sight of the decayed capital of the Uzbeks. The wheel had indeed come full circle. Two centuries before, exiles amid the dust and heat of the Indian plains, Babur and his followers had longed to return to those splendid cities of the north – Balkh and Herat, Bukhara and Samarqand. Now another great soldier, gorged with the loot from the Mughul capital of Babur's descendants, scorned to plunder the petty provincial town which had once been *Bukhara-ye Sharif*, Bukhara the Noble.[3]

After Nadir Shah's departure the Janids survived for another forty-five years although the Mangits were the real rulers of the country. Muhammad Rahim Bey eventually murdered Abu'l-Fayz, probably in 1747, and between 1753 and 1758 assumed full sovereignty. Following his death, however, the Janid line endured for nearly thirty years more in the person of Abu'l Ghazi Khan (1758–85), a *roi fainéant* in the hands of a relative of Muhammad Rahim Bey, Daniyal Bey. The latter died in 1785 and one of his sons emerged from the ensuing anarchy as undisputed master of Bukhara, pensioned off Abu'l Ghazi Khan and the remaining Janid princes, and became the first full sovereign of the Mangit dynasty, Amir Ma'sum Shah Murad.

During the reign of Shah Murad (1785–1800) Bukhara enjoyed a short period of prosperity and military power such as she had scarcely known since the sixteenth century. Nevertheless, the character of the new ruler (popularly known as Begi Jan) fully exemplified the stultifying traditions of dervishism which had for so long blighted the intellectual life of Mawarannahr.[4] Shah Murad's early life had been spent training as a theologian in the college attached to Bukhara's ancient Kalan Masjid where he had acquired a great reputation for sanctity. Even after mounting the *masnad* of Bukhara he continued to be an object of intense popular veneration, and this may partly be attributed to the fact that, as ruler, he retained the dress and manners of the dervish fraternities, even leading his troops into battle astride a meanly equipped pony such as no *amir* or *khan* would normally consent to ride. As a military leader, however, he possessed unusual talents and once he had consolidated his hold over his own subjects he vigorously pushed forward the frontiers of the

Bukhara state at the expense of Khiva and Kokand. He never managed to wrest Balkh from the Durrani rulers of Afghanistan, but against Iran he was more successful, year after year crossing the Amu-Darya to harry the inhabitants of Khurasan, the last of a long line of rulers of Mawarannahr to invade Iran. His principal objective was Marv, once a famous centre of Iranian civilization but now a decaying frontier-town garrisoned by a Qajar chieftain, Bahram 'Ali Khan, who was distantly related both to the Janids and to Aqa Muhammad Khan, founder of the Qajar dynasty in Iran. He put up a determined resistance but was finally killed and his head nailed to the gallows of Bukhara. However, under his son, Muhammad Husayn Khan, supported by Timur Shah Durrani of Afghanistan (1773–93), Marv held out until 1788 when the city was finally taken. Muhammad Husayn Khan was at first imprisoned in Bukhara but he eventually escaped to Tehran where he became a great favourite with his kinsman, Fath 'Ali Shah (1797–1834). After Shah Murad's troops had sacked Marv they proceeded to destroy the elaborate irriga-tion-system on the Murghab river which had for so long given life to the oasis so that both the city itself and the surround-ing countryside soon reverted to that desolate condition so eloquently described by nineteenth-century European travellers. The occupation of the oasis was followed by the systematic deportation of its Iranian inhabitants, who so glutted the slave-markets of Bukhara that prices fell to a level unknown in living memory and by the close of the eighteenth century the Iranian population of northern Khurasan had been replaced by Turkomans, even in the oases.[5] Aqa Muhammad Khan threat-ened vengeance for Shah Murad's treatment of the Marv Qajars, but he was prevented from attacking Bukhara by the Russian invasion of Azarbayjan in 1796, and his successors lacked the resources to restore Marv to the Iranian crown. As a direct result of Shah Murad's career, therefore, the present frontier of north-eastern Iran is not the Amu-Darya but the northern escarpment of the Elburz, the Kopet Dagh.

The inhabitants of Bukhara revered Shah Murad as much for his strict enforcement of the *Shari'at* as for his military triumphs. His son and successor, Amir Haydar (1800–26), likewise combined the roles of prince and dervish with some success, but following his death the Bukhara state was involved in a fratricidal struggle among his sons from which the third son, Nasrullah, eventually emerged victorious. The name of Nasrullah was notorious among mid-Victorian Englishmen for the brutal imprisonment and execution in Bukhara in 1842 of (among other Europeans) two East India Company officers, Colonel Charles Stoddart and Captain Arthur Conolly.[6] But although Nasrullah undoubtedly deserved his reputation for treachery and cruelty which made him the terror of his subjects and his neighbours, his long reign (1827–60) cannot by the standards of former rulers of Bukhara be judged wholly unsuccessful. If he had not had the misfortune to live in an age when Muslim rulers everywhere were sinking into fatuity and helplessness in the face of European aggression, he would probably have left behind him the reputation of having been one of the most able and certainly one of the most successful post-Shaybanid rulers of Bukhara. For the first thirteen years of his reign he appears to have governed prudently under the guidance of an experienced Mangit chieftain, Husayn Beg, crushing the independence of the tribal chieftains and supporting the clerical classes, a policy which inevitably won him popularity among the townsfolk, while beyond his frontiers his aim was to expand his possessions at the expense of Khiva and Kokand. His ultimate ambition seems to have been the conquest of all Mawarannahr, and perhaps the reconstruction of Timur's never-forgotten empire, an ambition encouraged by an Azarbayjani adventurer, 'Abd al-Samad, who managed to supplant Husayn Beg as Nasrullah's chief adviser and procure his execution in 1840. 'Abd al-Samad possessed some knowledge of how to train regular troops and how to cast cannon, talents which were put to good effect in the war against Kokand between 1839 and 1842. He also had first-hand experience of Russian penetration in north-western Iran and British expansion in India and Afghanistan, and since he seems to have exercised a wholly evil influence over Nasrullah, playing upon his deeply suspicious nature, he had little difficulty in stimulating his dread of Europeans approaching his frontiers. Nasrullah had, indeed, some excuse for believing that the arrival of Europeans, whether merchants, missionaries or envoys, in the parts of Asia of which he had any knowledge generally heralded the establishment of some form of European protectorate. Nevertheless, he himself was never directly threatened by the Russians who were pre-occupied with Khiva and Kokand throughout his reign. In 1868, however, his successor, Muzaffar al-din, was compelled to establish treaty relations with Russia, and although the amirate of Bukhara survived until 1920 as a protected state analogous to Hyderabad or Kashmir in British India the econ-omic life of the country became increasingly bound to that of the Russian Empire.

In comparison with Bukhara the khanate of Khiva, isolated in the remote oases of Khwarazm and protected by the Kara Kum, Ust Urt and Kizil Kum deserts, played a far less significant role in Central Asian history during the three and a half centuries of Uzbek rule. For the greater part of that time her military power was weaker than Bukhara's, her foreign relations less significant and her cultural life even more retarded, the histor-ical writings of Abu'l Ghazi Bahadur Khan constituting an almost unique phenomenon.

In Khiva, the traditional tension between nomads and cultiv-ators and between Uzbeks and Tajiks, was further complicated by the presence of the Turkomans. The Turkoman language belongs to the group of Oghuz or western Turkish languages which include Ottoman and Azeri, the Turkish spoken in Azarbayjan, and the fact that it is not closely related to the eastern Turkish languages has tended to isolate the Turkomans from the other Turkish peoples of Central Asia. In earlier times Turkoman dynasties and Turkoman tribal confederacies had played an important, sometimes even a preponderant part in the history of Iran and its neighbours but by the time the Uzbeks had consolidated their occupation of Mawarannahr all Turkomans east of the Caspian Sea had ceased to have more than local significance, except in so far as they constituted an element of instability in the frontier-relations of Iran, Khiva and Bukhara. From the sixteenth century onwards these states endeavoured to dominate the Turkomans, with varying degrees of success, while the latter passed from one allegiance to another in accordance with the relative military strength of their neighbours. In the time of rulers such as Shah 'Abbas I and Nadir Shah they were compelled to acknowledge Iranian suzerainty. Similarly when Bukhara expanded her frontiers, as in the reigns of 'Abdullah II and Shah Murad they gave allegiance to her. In the latter part of the seventeenth century when both the Safavid and Janid dynasties were becoming enfeebled they were subdued by two vigorous rulers of Khiva, Abu'l Ghazi Bahadur Khan and his son Anusha (1663–87). For most of the time, however, the most warlike Turkoman tribes enjoyed *de facto* independence, enabling them to attack lines of communication and caravan-routes in their vicinity with relative impunity. Incorrigible slave-raiders, they were still a scourge in the north-eastern provinces of Qajar Iran during the second half of the nineteenth century. Down to the period of the Russian annexation, most Turkoman tribes remained either nomadic or semi-nomadic, but some Turkoman agriculturists were to be found in the valley of the Gurgan river. Islamic civilization exercised only a limited influence on their way of life, although when fully exposed to alien cultural influences they were far from impervious to their attractions. The skill and sense of colour displayed by Turkoman rug-weavers requires no emphasis while a few highly Iranicized members of the ruling elite even earned for themselves a place in Persian literary history: Iskandar Munshi, author of the *Tarikh-i 'Alam ara-ye 'Abbasi*, a history of the reign of Shah 'Abbas I written in 1616, was a Turkoman and so was the architect of the early Mughul empire, Bayram Khan, who in addition to his qualities as a statesman and general during Akbar's minority, was an accomplished writer in both Persian and Chaghatai. These were Turkomans who established their reputations in foreign courts and wrote in foreign languages, but by the close of the eighteenth century a Turkoman literary language was beginning to emerge which, consolidated by poets such as Makhtum Quli and Mulla Azadi, gave the Turkomans, perhaps for the first time, a sense of cultural unity and positive achievement.

Both the amirate of Bukhara and the khanate of Khiva had a continuous independent history from the beginning of the sixteenth century until their extinction in 1920. In contrast, the khanate of Kokand had a history which dated back only to the first decade of the eighteenth century when a reputed descendant of Chingiz Khan, Shah Rukh Beg, established a regime at Kokand which survived under a succession of some twenty rulers until 1876 when it was annexed to the Russian Empire. At its height early in the nineteenth century the khanate comprised the Farghana valley, Kokand itself, Khojand to the west, and Tashkent and Chimkant on the north bank of the Syr-Darya, with a total population reaching perhaps three-quarters of a million. Territorial growth was determined by the geography of the Farghana valley which directed expansion westwards down the Syr-Darya, resulting in conflict with Bukhara over the Khojand, Ura-Tyube and Qarategin districts and with the Kazakhs in the country beyond Tashkent. As was the case in Bukhara and Khiva, the khans of Kokand found their authority checked both by the ambitions of local Uzbek chieftains and by the immense influence wielded by the dervish orders. During the first decade of the nineteenth century, however, a ruler of quite exceptional determination and ruthlessness, 'Alim Khan, embarked upon a vigorous policy of centralization which included the establishment of a mercenary force of Qarategin mountaineers in place of the traditional tribal levies. Having strengthened his position inside the khanate, 'Alim Khan proceeded to push forward his frontiers, occupying Ura-Tyube, Khojand and Tashkent. His successor, Muhammad 'Umar Shaykh, a devout Muslim and a generous patron of the arts, continued this policy and having penetrated north into Kazakh territory, built Aq Mechet as a fortress against the tribes on the north bank of the lower Syr-Darya. Under Muhammad 'Umar Shaykh (d. 1822) and during the early years of the reign of his son, Muhammad 'Ali, Kokand reached the zenith of its short-lived splendour. But Muhammad 'Ali proved no match for the energetic Nasrullah of Bukhara, whose destructive raids into Kokandi territory, culminating in the capture of Kokand itself and the death of Muhammad 'Ali in 1842, left both states hopelessly weakened for the approaching struggle with Russia. Kokandi resistance to Russian aggression, however, was more determined than that of Bukhara or Khiva, despite the fact that like them the khanate suffered from internal conflicts between Uzbeks and Tajiks and between the nomads (including the Kirghiz) and the settled population.

The period of a century and a half in which the Farghana valley and its western approaches enjoyed a political history independent of the surrounding country was, however, far from inglorious: irrigation projects were initiated, a considerable amount of public building was undertaken in traditional styles derived from Iran, and craftsmanship of some quality survived wherever it found adequate support. Few non-Muslims found their way to the Kokand khanate but those that did seem to have been impressed by evidence of modest prosperity and commercial activity, impressions which were certainly not shared by contemporary visitors to Bukhara or Khiva.

14

The Turks under Tsarist and Soviet Rule

1. *The Heirs of the Golden Horde under Russian rule*
The three successor-states of the Golden Horde in Russia, the khanates of Kazan, Astrakhan and the Crimea, were conquered and incorporated into the Russian state in 1552, 1554 and 1783 respectively.

From the time of its annexation there is nothing to relate about the former khanate of Astrakhan except for the fact that descendants of its khans sought refuge in Turkestan and there even founded a dynasty, the Astrakhanids (Janids), which reigned in Bukhara during the seventeenth century. The region of the lower Volga, moreover, supported only a sparse Muslim population which was rapidly reduced to the level of a negligible minority and which had no history. Yet the town of Astrakhan retained a certain Muslim character and after 1905 even revived as an Islamic cultural centre of some importance. On the other hand, the Tatars of Kazan and of the Crimea experienced after the Russian conquest an evolution which affected the history of the whole Muslim world.

(a) *The Tatars of Kazan under Russian rule*
On the 2 October 1552 the forces of Ivan the Terrible stormed Kazan, capital of the khanate and heir of the former realm of Great Bulgaria and of the Golden Horde. No longer vassals of the Mongols they obtained a dazzling revenge over the descendants of their former masters and the Muslims of eastern Russia were to live for more than four centuries under this 'infidel' domination.

The conquest, accompanied by large massacres, was followed by a systematic occupation of the territory which was annexed to Russia under the name of 'The Kingdom of Kazan'. There the Russians enforced for two centuries a brutal policy which aimed at russifying completely the former khanate and integrating the Muslim community into their own society.

The first stage in carrying out the 'detatarization' of the Middle Volga was the expulsion of the Tatars from all the important cities, in particular from Kazan which remains today a city with a Russian majority. The most fertile land situated beside the rivers was redistributed to the Russian nobility and monasteries. Fortresses were built at strategic points and a flood of Russian peasants swept over the region where the indigenous population of Muslims and animists were very rapidly reduced to the status of a minority. This expropriation was accompanied by a policy of enforced conversion to Christianity. The Muslim clergy were deprived of their rights, *vaqfs* (property in *mortmain*) were despoiled, mosques and Koranic schools destroyed or closed down. The conversion of the indigenous population to Christianity was inaugurated in 1555 by the first bishop of Kazan, Mgr. Gurii, and brought into the fold of Russian Orthodoxy an important fraction of the Muslim Tatar and animistic Finnish population. Finally the Russians embarked upon the destruction of the class which seemed to them to be the most dangerous, the Tatar feudal nobility who were to lose their privileges unless they became converts to Christianity.

Tatar resistance was violent and prolonged. It showed itself as early as December 1552 in bloody revolts which lasted until 1610, led by the feudal nobility who hoped to re-establish the former khanate with the help of the Crimean khanate, then at the height of its power. During fifty years ten risings can be enumerated of which the most tragic were those of Husein Seit in 1552, of Mamysh Berdy in 1556–7, and the great revolt of 1572–4 which synchronized with the raid of Devlet Giray, khan of the Crimea, against Moscow, as well as these of 1608 and 1610. All were crushed with extreme ferocity and in them the Tatar nobility was almost completely exterminated.

The first years of the seventeenth century marked the

beginning of an era of peasant risings which lasted almost without interruption from 1608 to 1615 and which resulted in fresh massacres. The Tatars also took an active part in the civil war led by the Cossack Ataman, Stepan Razin, against the Muscovite state in 1670-1.

The situation of the Volga Muslims did not improve with the accession of the Romanov dynasty. A new campaign of forcible conversion, more determined than any which had preceded it, was launched in 1731 by Luka Konashevich, bishop of Kazan, and the misery of the Tatar peasants drove them to fresh revolts. The most spectacular was that of Batyrsha in 1755, conducted as a 'Holy War' against the 'Infidels', and, above all, that of Pugachev in 1773-4, whose troops included a considerable proportion of the *allogènes*, Tatars, Bashkirs, Volga Finns and Kazakhs.

Complementary to these desperate upheavals the Tatar people also experienced a profound modification of their social structure. Driven from the towns, nobles and artisans spread into the countryside where they eventually formed a new class of merchants who slowly spread eastwards, establishing everywhere prosperous commercial communities. Reduced to impotence in their own country, the Tatar people steadily became a Diaspora race, dominated by its new commercial bourgeoisie.

The accession of Catherine II produced a radical change in Russian policy towards the Tatars. Anxious to avoid any recurrence of troubles such as the revolt of Pugachev, and fully appreciating the advantages to be gained by having Tatar trading communities in the marches of the empire, the Tsarina undertook various measures to improve the status of the Tatars. She ended the religious persecution and established a Spiritual Assembly at Orenburg for the use of the Muslims of Russia and Siberia. The surviving nobility were given equal rights with the Russian nobility, and Tatar merchants were granted favours which allowed them to be intermediaries between the growing Russian industry and the markets of Turkestan which were still closed to non-Muslims. In this way the Tatar bourgeoisie experienced an unprecedented economic prosperity which lasted for more than a century. Having become 'partners' of

Russian imperial policy but remaining deeply attached to Islam and conscious of their duty towards their nation, these merchants proved themselves enlightened patrons, without whom the reform movement and the 'Tatar Renaissance' of the nineteenth century could neither have emerged nor developed.

The period of co-operation between Russian and Tatar capitalism came to an end in 1860 with the permanent conquest of Central Asia by Russian armies. This opened the region to Russian industry which thereafter by-passed Tatar intermediaries. In the reign of Alexander II the Russian authorities reverted to a policy of repression against the Muslims. The old policy of conversion to Christianity, abandoned by Catherine II, was revived but with more subtle and effective methods. It has been reckoned that nearly 200,000 Tatars were converted during the course of the nineteenth century. Further very severe legislative measures were taken with a view to neutralizing the economic and cultural hold of the Tatars over their co-religionists in the Urals, the Kazakh steppes and Turkestan.

This double offensive which threatened the Tatars both with regard to their national integrity and their material interests, provoked a vigorous reaction and the reform movement was its direct result. In order to survive, the Muslims had to reawaken their retarded culture in an attempt to reconcile Islam and progress. This work of cultural revival was carried out by a brilliant group of religious thinkers, Abu Nasr Kursavi (1783–1814), Shihabeddin Marjani (1818–89), Rizaeddin Fahreddin (1859–1936) and Musa Jarullah Bigi (1875–19?), the boldest figures and the most profound theologians of their time. It was also necessary to reconstruct the backward educational system, and the first to attack this problem was the language-reformer, Abdul Kayyum Nasyri, followed by a number of writers who made illustrious what is usually described as the 'Tatar Renaissance' of the close of the nineteenth century. At the same time some disciples of Ismail bey Gasprinski (see below under Crimea) were introducing into the Tatar region their modern educational methods. At the beginning of the twentieth century Kazan and the other Tatar towns, Orenburg, Troitsk and Astrakhan, with their *madrasehs*, their printing-works and their

Press in the Tatar language were returning to life as brilliant cultural centres whose influence spread far beyond the country of the Tatars and even beyond the limits of the Russian Empire.

But the Tatars possessed an additional advantage which could preserve them from Russian domination: their linguistic kinship and religious communion with the other Turkish peoples of Russia which enabled them to extend their influence and propagate in all directions Pan-Turkish and Pan-Islamic ideas. In this way the Tatars placed themselves in direct rivalry to the Russians at the forefront of the nationalist movement which embraced all the Muslim peoples of Russia.

The first Russian revolution provided the leaders of the Tatar nationalist movement with the opportunity of voicing openly their demands at three Muslim Congresses held in 1905 and 1906 at Nizhni-Novgorod and St Petersburg. Their demands were still modest, seeking only equality of political rights together with religious and cultural freedom, and not yet seeking independence.

In February 1917 began a new page in the history of the Tatar people. Political autonomy, formerly a distant dream, appeared with the fall of the monarchy to be near at hand. Two groups disputed for leadership of the Tatar nationalist movement: the 'unitarians' who sought for all Russian Muslims extra-territorial autonomy within a unified Russian state (this programme corresponded with the interests of the moderate bourgeoisie), and the more progressive 'federalists' who demanded the territorial independence of a Volga-Ural state within a federal Russian state. At the Pan-Russian Muslim Congress held in Moscow on 1 May 1917, the federalist trend took the lead but the October Revolution and the outbreak of the civil war in 1918 utterly crushed their hopes.

Meanwhile, the struggle of the Tatars for their national autonomy did not come to an end with the establishment of the Soviet regime. A considerable number of Muslim intellectuals, former militants of the reform movement, entered the Communist Party in 1918, all remaining convinced nationalists. The creation of a Tatar Socialist Republic on the 27 May 1920 was unable to satisfy them since the Tatars represented scarcely

51 per cent of the population, and half their community found themselves outside the frontiers of their own state. The struggle against Russian centralization was then pursued from within the Communist Party. It was led by a group of Tatar Communists, headed by Mir Said Sultan Galiev, who clamoured for the creation of a great Turkish state – Turan – embracing the Muslim territories of the Volga-Ural region, Kazakhstan, Kirghizia and Turkestan, the population of which would add up to more than twenty million inhabitants. Other demands were for the creation of an autonomous Muslim Communist Party and the recognition of the uniqueness of Muslim culture within the Socialist world. The action of these 'Nationalist Communists' took the form of a 'deviation' which, under the name of 'Sultangalievism', was condemned for the first time in 1923 and finally in 1928. Sultan Galiev and his colleagues were liquidated and harsh repression descended upon the Tatar intelligentsia.

Since the war there have been no major crises for the Volga Tatars, despite anti-religious propaganda pursued without intermission for more than forty years and the general 'deislamization' of the younger generation. In general the position of these people, formerly leaders of Russian Islam, is rather precarious, dispersed as they are over an immense area of the Soviet Union and therefore most vulnerable to Russian assimilating influences. Today the Tatar people find themselves approaching a new turning-point in their history.

(b) The Crimea under Russian Rule

The khanate of the Crimea was, after Kazan, Astrakhan and Sibir, the fourth Muslim state to fall under Russian domination. Ravaged in 1736 and in 1737–8 by Russian armies, the Crimea was occupied for the first time in 1771. The treaty of Küchük-Kainardji (1774) put an end to the Ottoman protectorate over the Crimea and made the khanate theoretically independent. Nevertheless, the treaty recognized that the Sultan, in his capacity as Caliph, was the spiritual leader of the Tatars, thereby regulating the spiritual bond between the Tatars and the Sublime Porte. Some years later, profiting from the dissensions between the khan, Shahin Giray, and the partisans of Turkey,

Russian troops finally took possession of the peninsula. The manifesto of Catherine II, dated 9 April 1783, proclaimed quite simply the annexation of the khanate to the Russian Empire. Officially, Turkey did not recognize the annexation until the treaty of Jassy, 6 January 1792.

The Russian occupation opened a new and sombre chapter in the history of the Tatar people, once so formidable to their northern neighbours. The manifesto of 9 April nevertheless granted the Muslim population, who then numbered nearly 400,000, security of person and property, and freedom of religion, together with equal rights with the Russians, but from the conquest onwards contact with the new masters of the country caused the fortunes of the Tatar community to deteriorate. The feudal system in the former khanate disintegrated, the principal revenues of the ruling class having been provided by military expeditions and not by exploitation of the soil. Deprived of their revenue and closely assimilated to the Russian aristocracy the Tatar nobility faced a ruin slow but certain. Only some ten great families continued to enjoy the actual privileges of their class and while they became increasingly russified, the remainder sank down to being known as 'nobles en sabots' (*chabataly mirza*).

The Muslim clergy were, from the beginning, protected. A *muftiat* was set up at Simferopol in 1794, the *mufti* being chosen by the Muslim community although from a list approved by the Russian government. The *vaqfs* (property held in *mortmain*) which assured the clergy's material well-being were maintained, but the Russians little by little absorbed large numbers of them. In 1917 they comprised only 100,000 hectares of land against more than 460,000 hectares in 1783.

The peasants and artisans who formed more than 96 per cent of the Tatar population were the chief victims of the conquest. From 1784 Prince Potemkin, governor-general of Tauris, introduced the policy of confiscating the most fertile land for the benefit of members of the Russian nobility and this policy was pursued for nearly a century. Finally, aiming to 'detatarize' the country, the Russians sought to attract foreign colonists (Germans, Greeks, Bulgars, Balts) and then Russians (retired soldiers and Zaporozhian Cossacks). In 1800 these already numbered 30,000. It was during this time that the despoiled Tatar peasants were driven back into the arid tracts of the central Crimea.

Condemned to increased misery, subdued by a regime which, without being actually tyrannical, showed itself oppressive, incapable of accepting their decline since the glorious past still lived in their memories, the Tatars turned all the more naturally towards the Ottoman Empire. But no help was forthcoming, so emigration to Turkey seemed to them to be the only solution. Hence between 1783 and 1893 the history of the Crimean Tatars is merely a long and tragic succession of migrations, undertaken in the worst conditions, in the course of which thousands of emigrants perished from disease or hunger.

The exodus which began in 1784 was one of individuals. In 1788 nearly 8,000 people, particularly members of the nobility, left the country. During the Russo-Turkish war of 1787 the Tatars in the coastal districts were driven into the interior and from the time of the treaty of Jassy (1792), emigration assumed the character of a mass movement, more than 100,000 Tatars from the southern Crimea leaving the country. During the Russo-Turkish war of 1808–11 the situation grew much worse: a revolt occured at Baghchesaray and a number of nomadic Noghays from the Perekop region took the road into Turkey. At the beginning of the nineteenth century there remained no more than about 80,000 Muslims out of a total population of 200,000, the gaps having been filled by foreign settlers.

In the course of the first half of the nineteenth century, no outstanding event altered the position of the Muslim community and it remained calm during the war of 1829. The influx of new immigrants continued but due to their naturally rapid birth-rate, the Tatar population had reached the considerable figure of 300,000 by about 1850, of whom nearly 50,000 were Noghays.

A new tragedy descended upon them with the Crimean War. Although the Tatars remained outside the conflict during the allied occupation they were unable to hide their sympathy for Turkey. In consequence, fear of reprisals resulted in another

194

large-scale exodus, at first tolerated and then actually encouraged
by the Russians. It has been estimated that 135,000 Tatars,
two-thirds of the community, and 46,000 Noghays left for
Turkey between 1859 and 1863, leaving behind them nearly 800
deserted villages. This time the Russian authorities became concerned at the extent of the emigration and tried to stop it, but
in vain, for in 1875 a new wave of departures began which
lasted until 1880 and which involved more than 60,000 emigrants.
Finally, between 1891 and 1893 a last wave carried some
20,000 Tatars into Turkey.

By the end of the nineteenth century the Tatars represented
only a minority in the Crimea. According to the census of 1897
there were 187,000 (out of a population of 523,000), an impoverished community with a very feeble cultural level – one of
the lowest of all the Muslim groups of European Russia. The
glorious memories of the khanate seemed to be completely
forgotten.

Nevertheless, this backward people was destined to experience once again a period of intellectual re-awakening and to
illuminate its history with a last, brilliant ray of light. This
glory was due to an exceptional personality.

The person responsible for the great revival of Tatar culture
was Ismail Bey Gasprinski (Gaspraly), a member of the lesser
nobility. After completing both a traditional and a Russian
education and a long residence in France and Turkey, he returned
to his motherland in 1877 and threw himself with enthusiasm
into the work of rejuvenating his own people and the Turkish
peoples generally. A prolific and profound writer and thinker,
a convinced supporter of progress, Gasprinski sought to
reconcile Islam with the modern world. He proved himself a
teacher of genius; his 'New Method' of education was at first
applied in his model *madraseh* in Baghchesaray and then
gradually introduced into the majority of Muslim schools in
Russia. It then spread into Turkey and other Muslim countries,
including distant India. Last and most important of all, he was
the promoter of the Pan-Turkish Movement which aimed at
uniting Turkish peoples 'from the Balkans to China' through
a common ideology and language which he expounded and

195

propagated in his paper, '*Terdjuman*', which during thirty-five years between 1882 and 1914 was the best and most widely read Muslim paper of its time. Beyond any doubt Gasprinski was one of the figures who most deeply affected Islam at the beginning of the twentieth century. In Russia itself he aroused the political consciousness of his compatriots by making them conscious of their unity. In the Crimea his work attracted the best representatives of the Muslim intelligentsia of Russia and Turkey. Baghchesaray became one of the cultural centres of the Muslim world where a brilliant constellation of young writers and political thinkers assembled together.

The disciples of Gasprinski were, after the 1905 Revolution, much more radical than their master. Influenced by the Young Turks and by Russian Socialism, they were not content with merely cultural reform, but put forward political and economic demands. This group of 'Young Tatars' founded the '*Milli Firka*' ('The National Party') at the beginning of February 1917 and attempted to seize power. In March 1917 they convened at Simferopol an Assembly (*Kurultay*) which established the constitution for a Tatar government and the formation of Muslim military units. Unfortunately, the Tatars in the peninsula constituted only a small minority confronted by a more vigorous and dynamic Russian majority. During the four years between 1917 and 1920 the Crimea was rent by rival parties struggling for power – Reds, Germans, the Allies, the White Armies of Denikin and Wrangel – before being finally occupied by the Red Army in November 1920.

On 18 October 1921 a decree of the Supreme Soviet created the Soviet Republic of the Crimea, the government of which represented a coalition of Russian Communists and Tatars, former militants of the *Milli Firka*. The Muslim community enjoyed a certain amount of autonomy: during the first years of the Soviet regime the Tatar language was recognized, jointly with Russian, as the official language of the Republic; Tatar schools were opened and various Tatars were appointed to official posts. But real power remained in Russian hands. In 1921 the Communist Party of the Crimea included only 192 Tatars in a total membership of 5,875.

The alliance between Russian Communists and Tatar Nationalists ended tragically in 1928 when the government in Moscow began the liquidation of Tatar 'bourgeois nationalists'. The President of the Council of People's Commissars of the Republic, Veli Ibragimov, and a large number of his followers were then condemned and executed.

Under Soviet rule the Crimea continued to receive a regular influx of Russian immigrants. In the census of 1926 the total population of the Republic had risen to 875,100 inhabitants, of which only 23 per cent were Tatars.

During the Second World War the peninsula was occupied by the German army. When it was recaptured by Soviet forces in 1944 all the Tatar community, accused of 'collaboration' during the occupation and of 'treason', were deported to Siberia and Central Asia, and the peninsula was incorporated into the Ukrainian Republic. With this deportation the history of the Tatar people of the Crimea ended catastrophically. The survivors of the deportation were never rehabilitated nor permitted to return to their old country. At present they are dispersed throughout the Central Asian Republics where there is every reason to believe that they are being absorbed into the Turkish nations of Turkestan. A newspaper in the Tatar of the Crimea still appears in Tashkent, the last pitiable remnant of a long and glorious history.

2. *The Kazakh Steppes under Russian Rule*

The acquisition of the immense territory of the Kazakh steppes and the Kirghiz mountains was not achieved, as in the case of the other Muslim regions, by military conquest. At the beginning of the eighteenth century a very loose protectorate was established over the Kazakh khans who sought Russian aid against the Oirot invasions. During the first half of the nineteenth century there followed the construction of fortified lines and fortresses at first on the fringe and then in the heart of the steppes. Finally, the Russians took over the direct administration of the area.

The dates of the conquest may be reckoned from when the power of the khans was suppressed in the three Hordes; 1822 for the Middle Horde, 1824 for the Little Horde, 1845 for the Horde of Bukey and 1848 for the Great Horde. Finally, in 1864, the Russians occupied the Syr-Darya region which was in the possession of the Turkestan amirates but which was peopled by Kazakhs.

The establishment of Russian rule was carried out slowly and prudently. The government in St Petersburg did not give the status of subjects to the Kazakhs who remained *allogènes* (*inorodtsy*, aliens). They were excused military service, retained some of their own customary laws and, although their nobility was deprived of its feudal rights, kept their self-government at local level with 'councils of elders'. In their dealings with the Kazakhs the Russian administration utilized the services of the Tatars of Kazan until 1860, who benefited by increasing their political and economic influence and by strengthening the Muslim faith among the still semi-animistic nomads.

Meanwhile relations between the Russians and the Kazakhs rapidly deteriorated. From the end of the eighteenth century the settlement of Cossacks on the western, northern and eastern edges of the steppe, and then in the nineteenth century the appearance of the first rural colonies of Russians and Ukrainians, led to a continuous reduction in the unoccupied land essential for the movement of the nomads' flocks. Very soon, even before the establishment of direct administration, anti-Russian revolts broke out, mostly led by the greater or lesser nobles, now dispossessed, and sustained by the khanates of Khiva and Kokand. In little less than a century between 1783 and 1870, eight really important revolts can be enumerated.

The first to raise the standard of revolt was a lesser nobleman (*batyr*) of the Little Horde, Srym Datov, who in 1783 led a guerrilla war against the fortified line of the Ural. Srym Datov was only finally defeated by the Russians in 1797; he fled to Khiva and was assassinated there in 1802.

In the Middle Horde the resistance to the establishment of Russian administration began in 1825 after the suppression of the khanate. It was led by the descendants of dispossessed rulers, Sarzhan Kasymov and Ubaydullah Valikhanov, grandsons of Ablay Khan. Defeated by the Ural Cossacks who pursued them into the steppes, the two khans fled to Kokand. Sarzhan tried to return to the steppes between 1831 and 1834 with troops recruited in Kokand, but he was defeated yet again. The struggle was resumed in 1837 with another grandson of Ablay Khan, Kenesary, a fine organizer and a brave warrior, who during ten years of spasmodic conflicts and short truces, succeeded in restoring his authority over the Middle Horde and even over some of the tribes of the Great Horde. In order to put an end to the murderous raids which he launched against the regions directly under their control (Petropavlovsk and Akmolinsk), the Russians built the fortresses of Turgai and Irgiz deep in the heart of the steppes. In 1846 they succeeded in driving Kenesary back towards the south, and in 1847 obliged him to take refuge in the Tien Shan mountains where he was defeated and killed by the Kirghiz. Thus ended the only serious attempt of the former rulers to reunite the nomad tribes and lead them against their conquerors.

In the same period a movement directed simultaneously against the Russians and the power of Jangir Khan arose among the Kazakhs of the Horde of Bukey, who pastured their flocks between the Volga and the Ural rivers. The insurgents led by a *bey*, Isatay Taymanov, and a folk-singer, Mahambet Utemisov, besieged Jangir's capital, Khanskaya Stavka, in 1837 but were defeated by a Russian detachment and forced to flee towards the territory of the Little Horde. Isatay was killed in 1838, Mahambet in 1846.

In 1855 another *batyr*, Eset Kotibarov, led into revolt the Shekly clan who pastured their flocks west of the Aral Sea. This revolt was crushed three years later. Also in 1855 the *batyr* Janhodja Nurmuhammedov led the resistance of the southern Kazakhs against the first Russian colonies to be founded along the Syr-Darya.

The final anti-colonizing disturbances took place in 1867–8 in the Uralsk and Turgai regions, where the struggle of the tribes was conducted under the banner of Islam and assumed the character of a 'Holy War' against the 'Infidels', and was only crushed following the intervention of an imposing Russian force. Another revolt occurred in the same period in the

Mangyshlak region on the eastern shores of the Caspian, where the rebels attacked Russian villages before being dispersed by military units transported by sea from Baku.

After 1875 the old feudal nobility, bled white, was no longer able to resist the Russian presence with force. The Kazakh country appeared to be 'pacified'. But under the influence of Pan-Turkish and Pan-Islamic ideas spread by the Tatars, it became evident that the Kazakhs had acquired the feeling of belonging not only to a clan or to a tribe, but also to a 'nation'. The Russians, disturbed by this new feeling of nationalism but hoping to turn it to their own use, initiated in the 1870s a new policy aimed at neutralizing Tatar influence. Measures were taken to eliminate Tatar instruction in Kazakh educational establishments and Russo-Kazakh schools were founded. This aided the emergence of a new 'Westernized' intelligentsia, which saw co-operation with the Russians as the only available way of leading the Kazakhs in the direction of progress. The most typical representatives of this new intelligentsia were three great writers, Chokan Valikhanov (1835–65), an officer in the Russian army and an orientalist; Ibray Altynsaryn (1841–89), ethnographer and educationalist; and Abay Kununbaev (1845–1904), a talented philosopher who was won over to liberal ideas. Other intellectuals, descended from the nobility and educated in Russian schools – Ali Bukeykhanov, Ahmed Baytursun, Mir-Yakub Dulat, etc. – from the beginning of the twentieth century followed in the footsteps of these three Kazakh 'kulturträger'. With them the nationalist movement acquired a fully 'Kazakh' tone and was not merely Pan-Turkish – at times even opposing the aspirations of other Muslims in Russia, the Tatars in particular.

But the dream of fruitful co-operation with the Russians was utopian. In the years 1891–2 a vast wave of colonists burst upon the country, attracted by the virgin steppe-lands. More than a million peasants came from Russia and settled in the Turgai, Akmolinsk, and Semipalatinsk regions and in Kirghizia, causing a reduction in livestock and a catastrophic fall in living standards, already very low among the nomads. The daily conflicts between Russian settlers and Kazakhs thereafter constituted the background to life on the steppes. A crisis became inevitable and exploded with unusual savagery in 1916.

If economic difficulties were the remote cause of the great revolt of the Kazakh tribes, the immediate cause lay in the promulgation of a decree of 25 June 1916 mobilizing the *allogènes*, conscripting them not for military service but for labour-gangs. The disturbances began in the Uzbek country, at Khojand and Jizak, and spread rapidly throughout Kazakhstan and Kirghizia, assuming the character of a national uprising. Some thousands of settlers and tens of thousands of Kazakhs and Kirghiz were massacred, not including the very large number who died of hunger and disease. More than 300,000 nomads, fleeing from this repression, found refuge in China. Everywhere the revolt was savagely crushed, except in the black lands of Turgai where the insurgents, led by Amangeldy Imanov and Alibiy Jangildin held out until the Revolution of February 1917.

Following the fall of the Tsarist monarchy the Kazakh chiefs formed a national party, the *Alash-Orda*, with a liberal programme. After the October Revolution the *Alash-Orda* at first allied itself with the anti-Bolshevik forces of the Orenburg, Ural and Semirechie Cossacks, and set up a national government. The authority of this government was, however, purely nominal and without the possession of sufficient armed forces it was unable to prevent the civil war spreading to the steppes. In March 1919, because of the systematic hostility of the Whites" to their aspirations, the leaders of the *Alash-Orda* decided to join the 'Reds', and signed an agreement with the Soviet government by means of which they hoped to safeguard the interests of the Kazakh nation. After the civil war the Soviet government granted the Kazakhs and the Kirghiz regional autonomy. The former territory of the Kirghiz of the Tien Shan was formed into an Autonomous Region and then into the Kirghiz Soviet Republic (5 December 1936). The Kirghiz, numbering some 837,000 in 1959, only constitute 40.5% of the total population.

For their part, the Kazakhs had their own republic, at first autonomous, then Soviet (5 December 1936). The former leaders of the *Alash-Orda* at first played a more important role n the government than the Communist Party. They were able to maintain power until around 1928, dominating the cultural life of the country and striving to preserve the cultural integrity and the unique character of Kazakh society. From 1924, however, they opposed the Russian Communists in a number of disputes, above all those relating to the problems of the settlement of the nomads and the destruction of the property-owning classes whom they sought to protect. In April 1928 they were denounced as 'bourgeois nationalists' and almost all liquidated.

The terrible famine which decimated the steppes in 1921, and even more the brutal policy of settling the nomads which was applied after 1928, were heavy blows for the Kazakh nation. Between 1926 and 1939, it lost nearly a million people. At present the Kazakh population numbers only a little more than 3,500,000 as against more than 4,600,000 in 1926. Since the end of the Second World War the influx of Russian and Ukrainian peasants and workers has continued at an accelerated rate. Today the Kazakhs represent no more than 29.6% of the population of their own republic.

3. *Turkestan under Russian rule*

Turkestan was belatedly conquered by Russian armies in the sixties and seventies of the nineteenth century, though the first contacts between Russia and the Central Asian khanates go back to the beginning of the eighteenth century. In fact it was in 1714 that by order of Peter the Great a Russian expedition penetrated the Trans-Caspian steppes for the first time. Three years later another expedition led by Prince Bekovich-Cherkasskii even tried to reach Khiva from Astrakhan, but his column was ambushed in the desert and destroyed, and he himself was killed. In 1715 another column commanded by Bukholz set out from Tobolsk in Siberia, and tried to reach Turkestan from the north. It came into contact with the Oirots, then at the height of their power, and was compelled to turn back. Again in 1840 General Perovskii, governor of Orenburg, led a strong Russian detachment against Khiva but the expedition was a total failure.

The real conquest of Turkestan only began after 1847, that is to say after the suppression of the revolt of the Kazakh khan, Kenesary, who between 1837 and 1847 blocked the way to the Syr-Darya to Russian forces. In 1847 the Russians built near the mouth of the Syr-Darya the fort of Raim, their first military base on the frontiers of Khiva. In 1855 they won from the khanate of Kokand the fortress of Aq Mechet on the middle course of the Syr-Darya, and forthwith undertook the construction of a fortified line along the length of the river. At the same time another offensive, starting from Semipalatinsk threatened Turkestan from the north-east. This resulted in the building of Vernyi (now Alma-Ata) in 1854.

No power seemed able to oppose the Russian advance into Turkestan. The three principalities into which the country was divided, Khiva, Bukhara and Kokand, were weakened by internal struggles and revolts by the nomads. Moreover the backward economy and the absence of modern troops hampered any serious resistance to the organized might of Russia. But the Russian conquest was delayed by the Crimean War, and by the resistance of the Kazakh tribes and the war in the Caucasus. It was only after the final defeat of the *imam* Shamil which freed the forces engaged in Daghestan, that annexation could be undertaken in a systematic manner. In 1864 a column under General Cherniaev, setting out from Vernyi, captured the town of Turkestan (Yasi), then Chimkant, and in May 1865 Tashkent, which belonged to the khan of Kokand. Two years later the Russians attacked Bukhara. In May 1868 they took Samarqand and in June of the same year defeated Bukharan troops at the battle of Zerabulak. On the 18 June 1868 the amir of Bukhara signed a treaty which placed his state under a Russian protectorate. In 1873 it was the turn of Khiva. The capital of the khanate was taken and on the 12 August a treaty put an end to its independence.

Finally Kokand was invaded in 1875. The capital surrendered on the 29 August and on the 19 February 1876 the khanate, the most dangerous opponent of Russia in Central Asia, was extinguished and its territory annexed to the governor-generalship of Turkestan. The conquest was completed between 1873 and 1874 by the occupation of the Turkoman country

203

which ended with the capture of the Geok-Tepe oasis by General Skobelev (in 1879) and the conquest of the Marv region in 1884.

With the exception of the territory of the two protected States, Turkestan was converted into a governor-generalship placed under military administration responsible to the Ministry of War. Towards the Muslim population the Russians maintained a 'colonial' attitude. Contrary to the means employed in other Muslim countries conquered from Turks, they did not attempt to russify the indigenous population, nor even initiate them into European civilization. The Turkestanis were not considered citizens of the empire nor eligible for military service. They preserved their own legal system in accordance with Muslim law and retained their own local administration. The Russian authorities attempted to preserve the most traditional forms of a society which was dominated by extreme Islamic conservatism and was impervious to the influence of the outside world. They especially opposed contact between the Turkestanis and their more advanced co-religionists of the Volga, and rejected the claims of the Tatars to extend to Turkestan the jurisdiction of the Muslim Spiritual Assembly of Orenburg. For all these reasons the awakening of national consciousness among the Turkestanis was far slower than among the other Turks in Russia.

Turkestan was a land of oases and so, in contrast with the Kazakh steppes and the Kirghiz mountains, it was not suitable for colonization. Such as there was, was on a very modest scale, the land available for cultivation being very scarce. But even this small influx of settlers was sufficient to provoke conflicts between Russians and natives in the countryside. Meanwhile Russian workers were arriving to help in the building of railways and the establishment of a textile industry. Consequently the cities of Turkestan rapidly acquired the character of colonial cities comprising a modern 'European' quarter side by side with the old 'Native' town.

Resistance to Russian colonization began in the eighties of the nineteenth century and the movements assumed a religious character, a 'Holy War' against 'Infidels' sometimes aiming at the restoration of the former khanate of Kokand. Its leaders originated almost always from a religious milieu, often from the Sufi orders, whose followers were drawn from peasants and city artisans. Anarchistic and spontaneous, without external support, they were all easily crushed.

The first rebellion was that of the dervish Khan Töre in the Farghana valley in 1885, followed in 1891 by disturbances in Namangan and in 1892 by riots in Tashkent and in the neighbourhood of Kokand. In 1898 the growing disaffection led to a more important movement organized by the Sufi brotherhood of Naqshbandis, the revolt of Ishan Madali, who having gathered together more than 2,000 fighting men, proclaimed a Holy War. The rebels attacked the Russian garrison in Andizhan (Andijan), but after some initial successes were defeated and suffered severe punishment.

At the beginning of the twentieth century the vigilance of the Russian authorities discouraged all further inclination to rebel. Henceforward resistance to Russian pressure manifested itself only in the guise of the reform movement.

Despite censorship, reforming and Pan-Turkish ideas began to penetrate into Turkestan at the end of the nineteenth century – in the first place deriving impetus from the personal initiative of Ismail Bey Gasprinski and his Crimean disciples. From 1905 onwards the movement was activated by the Volga Tatars and, finally, after 1908 it came under the influence of the Young Turks. The victory of Japan over Russia opened a new phase in the relations between Russians and Turkestanis. The former no longer seemed invincible and the latter embarked little by little upon a course of political demands. Some secret or semi-secret societies were formed which published and diffused nationalist works. Other political groups, the Young Bukharans and the Young Kievans, threw themselves openly into revolutionary activity.

The revolution of February 1917 gave the Turkestanis the opportunity to express their demands openly. In March 1917 they convened at Tashkent a Muslim congress and appointed a National Committee, the first stage of a national government. When the October Revolution broke out the National Committee tried to seize power and formed in Kokand a Muslim government for Turkestan. This attempt was short-lived, the Kokand government having at its disposal neither a cadre of administrators nor, above all, troops capable of preserving its existence. In January 1918 the Russian Soviet of Tashkent despatched its troops, composed of Russian workers, against Kokand and the city was taken on the 19 February and sacked.

The first two years of the Soviet regime in Turkestan were characterized by the complete domination of the Russian Communists of Tashkent over the native Muslims. The principal concern of the Soviet authorities, isolated from the rest of Russia by the 'White Armies', was not merely to fight their counter-revolutionary enemies, which they did with savage energy, but to keep their distance from the Muslim revolutionaries. According to the formula of one of the leaders of the Tashkent Soviet, 'since the Revolution has been made by Russians, it is they and they alone who should benefit from it'. At the end of 1919 the Red Army, advancing from the Volga, reached Central Asia and its commanders immediately proceeded with the extinction of the khanates of Khiva (December 1919) and Bukhara (February 1920). The two principalities were transformed into the People's Republics of Khorezm and Bukhara.

Despite its victory, the position of the Soviet power in Turkestan remained difficult since it had to face a double threat, external and internal. On the one hand, it had to fight the Basmachis, Muslim guerrillas numbering more than 20,000 combatants who were entrenched in the mountainous region of eastern Bukhara (now Tajikistan). This was part of a more general resistance by the rural population, directed as much against the Russians as against Communism. By 1925, before the intervention of well-armed Russian forces, the movement had begun to decline. One group of insurgents took refuge in Afghanistan but isolated groups held out in the mountains until 1936.

The other danger originated with the former reformers who after 1920 joined the Communist Party *en masse*. Becoming Communists but remaining Nationalists and Pan-Turks, for some years they dominated the political life of Turkestan, opposing the Russians and aiming to create 'Muslim' national Communism and a vast Turkish state which would embrace Turkestan, Kazakhstan, Kirghizia, Bashkira and Tatarstan, thus approaching the project for a Turanian state elaborated at this same period by Sultan Galiev in Kazan.

The Russians first reacted cautiously in ousting, after 1921, the native Communists from positions of responsibility. In 1924, despite opposition from the latter, Turkestan was truncated into national republics – Uzbekistan, Tajikistan and Turkmenistan – which put an end to the dream of a unified Turkish state. Finally, in 1930 there began the massive purges which continued almost without interruption until 1938 and in the course of which there perished the greater part of the native intelligentsia which had rallied to the Communist regime after 1919.

Nevertheless, despite the destruction of the separatist and autonomous aspirations of the Turkestanis, Central Asia today is the last Turkish bastion of the Soviet Union. On account of the geographical configuration of the country (deserts and oases) Russian colonization is still feeble. It was, in fact, estimated that in 1959 there were less than 15% non-Muslims in Uzbekistan and Tajikistan, and less than 20% in Turkmenistan. It seems that of all the regions which were once part of the vast Mongol empire Turkestan is the one where the future can still belong to Turkish races.

15

The Russian Conquest and Administration of Turkestan (to 1917)

The rise of Russian power, coincident with growing weakness and disunity in the states of western Central Asia (Turkestan), might have foretold the fate of the latter as early as the seventeenth century. However, after an initial surge forward at the expense of the khanates of Kazan, Astrakhan and Sibir, preoccupation elsewhere forced Russia to employ a defensive strategy on her south-eastern frontiers. A long line of Cossack colonies from the Caspian Sea to the Altai mountains, based on Orenburg, Petropavlovsk, Omsk, Semipalatinsk and Ust-Kamenogorsk, was established to prevent Kazakh inroads in the Volga region and western Siberia.

This defensive policy was never satisfactory. The Kazakhs, though nominally subject to Russia from the 1730s, frequently broke through the lines to attack settlements. The khanate of Khiva encouraged Kazakh revolts, gave refuge to rebel leaders, and offered a ready market for Russian captives. Russian trade with the Central Asian states remained undeveloped because of Kazakh attacks on caravans.

In the 1820s Russia finally sought a more stable frontier. Kazakh independence was undermined by the abolition of the khanates of the Middle and Lesser Hordes (1822 and 1824) and the establishment of smaller units ruled by sultans under Russian supervision. Outposts were established in the steppe: Kokchetav and Karkaralinsk (1824), south of Orenburg; and Kokpekty (1820), Baian-Aul (1826) and, following explorations by Alexander von Humboldt, Sergiopol (1831), south of

Semipalatinsk. The missions of N. N. Muraviev to Khiva (1820) and of A. Negri to Bukhara (1820), and the expeditions of Colonel F. F. Berg and E. Eichwald (1825–6) secured valuable information about the regions beyond. During the 1830s Fort Novo-Aleksandrovskoe was established (1834) on the Mangy-shlak peninsula, while mounting demands for the protection of trade and the need to counter British influence in Afghanistan led to a major expedition against Khiva led by General V. A. Perovskii. The winter march, undertaken in 1839, ended in the loss of nearly a thousand men and most of the expedition's transport. Perovskii's disaster underlined the need for more advanced bases in the steppe. During the 1840s several small forts were established south of Orenburg: Turgai and Irgiz (1845), Atbasar and Ulutavsk (1846). Raim (Aralskoe, 1847), placed at the mouth of the Syr-Darya, gave clear notice of Russian intentions in that area. In the east, the founding of Kopal (1847) at the foot of the Ala-Tau mountains secured the region north of the Ili river.

Russia was now encroaching on lands claimed by the khanate of Kokand which were virtually undefended. In 1853 Perovskii regained his laurels by leading Russian forces from Aralskoe up the Syr-Darya to establish Fort No. 1 (Kazalinsk) and then went on to take the Kokandi fort of Aq Mechet (renamed Perovsk). In the east, Russian forces occupied the region south of the Ili river, founding the town of Vernyi, modern Alma-Ata (1854).

Plans of the Russian government for connecting these two southerly extensions of its power were halted by the Crimean War (1854–6). A period of consolidation ensued. The western part of the Kazakh steppe was organized in 1859 into the *oblast* (province) of the Orenburg Kirghiz, administered from Orenburg. The eastern part of the steppe became the *oblast* of the Siberian Kirghiz, administered from Omsk, and the *oblast* of Semipalatinsk, organized in 1854 and administered from the town of Semipalatinsk.

The need for an alternative supply of cotton, which suddenly became acute during the American Civil War (1861–5), led to the renewel of operations. In May 1864 Colonel M. G.

209

Cherniaev set out from Vernyi with a force of 2,600 men, and Colonel N. A. Verevkin from Perovsk with 1,600 men. On 4 June Cherniaev's force stormed the city of Aulie-Ata (now Dzhambul), winning it at a cost of only 3 men wounded, whereas the native garrison of about 1,500 men, poorly armed, badly led and undisciplined, suffered 307 killed and 390 wounded. Verevkin took the city of Turkestan (Yasi) with similar ease. The two forces then joined under Cherniaev's command and after a four-day siege stormed the citadel of Chimkant on 22 September. Most of the native garrison of 10,000 men fled; the Russians lost only 2 men. With this action the Russians occupied the entire Chu valley and enclosed the Kazakh steppe with a line of Russian forts.

The news of these operations caused concern in the capitals of the European Powers, especially in Great Britain, who feared for her Indian possessions. Prince A. M. Gorchakov, the Russian Foreign Minister, allayed fears in a skilfully worded circular letter to the Powers on 21 November 1864. Gorchakov stated that Russia's chief motive was simply to secure an effective boundary, one that could be defended against border raids. The Russian Empire had therefore to advance until it reached the boundaries of settled states. There Russia would halt, building a line of forts to hold this boundary, teaching the marauding tribesmen that trade was better than pillage, and bestowing upon them the benefits of 'western civilization'.

Early in 1865 the newly won territories were organized as the *oblast* of Turkestan, under a military governor in charge of both military and civil affairs and responsible to the governor-general of Orenburg. Cherniaev, appointed military governor, was ordered not to advance, but upon his own initiative undertook to seize the Kokandi city of Tashkent. In late April 1865 he seized Fort Niaz-bek on the river Chirchik, the main source of irrigation-water for Tashkent, and a few days later took that city itself with only minor losses.

In order to placate Britain the Russian government recalled Cherniaev, but gave him high honours, and his successor, General D. I. Romanovskii, continued his programme. Invading Bukharan territory in the following spring, Romanovskii and a

210

small force of 3,600 routed a force of nearly 40,000 Bukharans and Kazakhs from entrenched positions at Irdzhar, on the road to Samarqand. He then moved up the Syr-Darya into Kokandi territory, seeking to drive a wedge between Kokand and Bukhara. He took the Kokandi fort of Nau without resistance and the city of Khojand on 24 May after artillery bombardment. The Russians lost five men and the defenders 2,500. This brought the khan of Kokand, Khudayar Khan, to terms. He acknowledged himself a vassal of the Tsar, agreed to the Russian conquests, consented to let Russians trade throughout his realm, and undertook the payment of an indemnity which would reimburse the Russians for the expense incurred in defeating him.

There were indications that the amir of Bukhara was also disposed to make peace, but the Russian government was determined to put him in a position which would leave no room for doubt as to his future conduct. The Amu-Darya, not the Chu or the Syr-Darya, was now seen as the logical southern boundary of Russian authority. In August 1866 General N. A. Kryzhanovskii, the governor-general of Orenburg, assumed command and prepared a new campaign. He led his troops first against the fortress of Ura-Tyube which he captured on 2 October. The Russians lost seventeen men, the natives at least 2,000. A few days later, on the 18 October, Kryzhanovskii took Jizak. There the Russians lost six men and the natives 6,000.

An Imperial decree of 11 July 1867 declared the formation of the governor-generalship of Turkestan, centred at Tashkent, comprising all lands taken in the region since 1847, divided between the *oblasts* of Syr-Darya and Semirechie. General K. P. von Kaufman, previously governor-general of the North-West Region, a part of Russia's share of Poland, was appointed to the new post with broad powers to carry on military operations and diplomatic negotiations. Arriving in Tashkent early in November 1867, Kaufman set about his complex tasks, organizing the region on a pattern which was to endure for the next half-century. 'Old Turkestanis' in later years over-idealized his thirteen-year tenure of office as a golden age, but even

211

Britain's Lord Curzon paid him grudging tribute as having 'undoubted, though limited, greatness'.

Under Kaufman's rule the region was organized on the model of the civil administration of European Russia, and except for the highest posts, was governed almost exclusively by civilian bureaucrats. After a census the two *oblasts* were divided into *uezds* (counties) and these into *volosts*. Each *volost* was made up of several nomad *auls* (patriarchal family groups, each consisting of up to 200 *kibitkas* or households) or of several *kishlaks* (villages) of the sedentary population. Each village and *aul* chose its elder and a group of electors who helped elect a *volost* headman responsible to the Russian *uezd* commandant. In the judiciary, the authority of the *Adat* (customary law) and of the *Shari'at* (Muslim canonic law) was preserved. Only lawsuits involving Russians and the more serious criminal cases were tried in Russian courts. Aside from the abolition of corporal punishment, the chief Russian innovation was the election of judges, formerly appointed by the head of state. The native system of taxation was reformed and brought into line with Russian practice and a limited land reform was put into effect. Efforts were made to study the burdensome system of *vaqfs* (property donated in trust to mosques and charitable institutions) and the complex system of water law with a view to reform, though this was never accomplished.

Kaufman purposely left native customs unchanged. Though deploring the inferior status of native women and certain other attributes of the Muslim way of life, he preferred to follow a policy of calculated neglect rather than arouse native wrath by a direct attack on such problems. This was not indifference but expediency, under a theory that gradual change through the effect of a good example could accomplish more than coercion. To this end he opposed the efforts of the Muslim religious administration at Ufa to extend its control over the Muslim institutions of Turkestan. Out of fear that it might arouse and harden Muslim opposition he even forbade the Russian Orthodox Church to send missionaries to the region or to establish an Orthodox bishopric in Tashkent.

Hearing in the spring of 1868 that the amir of Bukhara was

1 A 'city' of yurts (canvas, dustproof tents) in Mongolia—a typical nomad encampment.

2 Caravansarai and bazaar, Aqcha, northern Afghanistan. Both institutions were indispensable for the Central Asian caravan trade.

3. Landscape near Shibarghan, northern Afghanistan. In Central Asia the distinction between desert and steppe is often indefinite and even seasonal.

4 (*opposite*) Landscape in the Orkhon country, Mongolian People's Republic.

5 'Pointed-cap' Sacae in an Achaemenid tribute-procession, eastern staircase of the Apadana, Persepolis, c. 485 BC.

6 (*opposite*) Pile-carpet in the Achaemenid tradition from Pazyryk in the Altai. Fourth century BC. Hermitage Museum, Leningrad.

7 Double decadrachm of Amyntas, c. 120 BC.
Graeco-Bactrian treasure of Qunduz.
Kabul Museum; actual size.

8. The Lion-Capital from Mathura, India. This monument appears to
be a memorial to the Indo-Scythian king Maues (97–c. 77 BC.)

9. Indo-Scythian tetradrachm of Azes (c. 58 BC) showing armoured Saca
horseman. Obverse and reverse. British Museum; twice actual size.

10 Statue of Kanishka I (AD 128–51) in red sandstone. Mathura Museum.

11 Gold casket from Bimaran, an early example of Gandhara metalwork, c. AD 70. British Museum.

12 Silver dish of the Kidarite period, c. AD 400. British Museum.

13 (*opposite*) An Uighur prince, part of a fresco from Bäzäklik, Sinkiang, c. eighth to ninth century AD. Indische Kunstabteilung, Staatliche Museen, Berlin.

14 Part of the *mihrab* of the shrine of Yahya b. Zayd at Sar-i Pul, Afghanistan. The Sayyid's name appears in Kufic script above the point of the *mihrab* arch.

16 Seljuqid caravansarai of the early twelfth century, Ribat-i Sharif, north-east Iran, on the caravan-route between Nishapur and Marv.

17 Hülegü, first Il-Khan of Iran (d. 1265). From a miniature in the British Museum.

15 (*opposite*) The minaret of Ghiyath al-din Muhammad b. Sam (AD 1162–1202), Firuzkuh, Afghanistan.

18 (*above and left*) A bowl excavated at New Saray (Saray-Berke), capital of the Golden Horde. Black, blue and white on grey. First half of the fourteenth century AD. Hermitage Museum, Leningrad.

20 (*opposite*) Gold brocade made for the Mamluk Sultan of Egypt, al-Malik al-Nasir. Despite its Chinese design this fabric was probably manufactured in one of the cities of the Golden Horde. Early fourteenth century AD. Marienkirche, Danzig.

19 Part of a letter in pre-classical Mongolian from Arghun, Il-Khan of Iran (1284–91), to Philip the Fair, King of France, dated 1289. Archives Nationales de France.

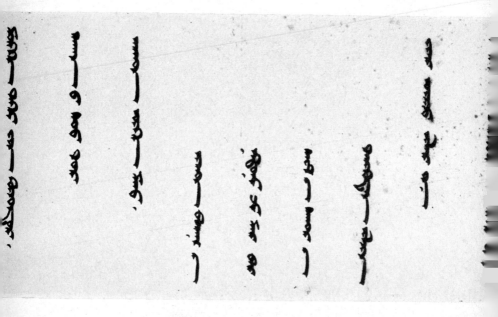

21 The shrine of Shaykh Ahmad Yasavi (d. 1166) in Turkestan, formerly Yasi. The cult of Shaykh Ahmad Yasavi played a great part in the diffusion of Islam in the Chaghatai Khanate and the present shrine, built by Timur in 1397, rapidly became an important pilgrimage centre for both Uzbeks and Kazakhs.

22 An ornamental page from a Quran written and illuminated for the Il-Khan Uljaytu (1304–16) in Mosul, c. 1310. British Museum.

23 Wooden Quran stand, made in 1360 by Hasan b. Sulayman of Isfahan. Despite the craftsman's birth-place, this master-piece of Iranian wood-carving of the Mongol period shows distinct Far Eastern influence and may have been carved in Mawarannahr. Metropolitan Museum of Art, New York.

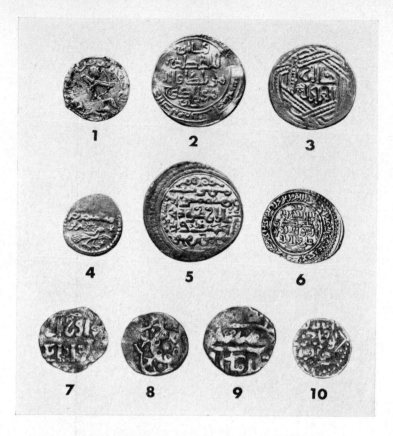

24 Examples of Chingizkhanid coinage (Editor's collection.
Nos. 1–6, silver; nos. 7–10, copper).

(1) Töregene Khatun, widow of Ögetei, Tiflis (n.d.)
(2) Hülegü (Il-Khanid), as viceroy of the *khaqan* Möngke, Baghdad (n.d.)
(3) Abaqa (Il-Khanid), as viceroy of the *khaqan* Qubilai, no mint (n.d.)
(4) Arghun (Il-Khanid), as viceroy of the *khaqan* Qubilai, Tabriz (n.d.)
(5) Ghazan (Il-Khanid), Baghdad (AH 702)
(6) Uljaytu (Il-Khanid), Kayseri (n.d.)
(7) Uzbek (Golden Horde), Saray-Berke (n.d.)
(8) Jani Bek (Golden Horde), Saray-Berke (n.d.)
(9) Khizr Khan (Golden Horde), Saray-Berke (n.d.)
(10) Tuqtamish (Golden Horde), Saray-Berke (AH 789).

25 Detail of the entrance to the tomb of the Chaghatai khan, Buyan Quli (AD 1348–58), Bukhara.

26 The mausoleum of the Il-Khan Uljaytu (1304–16), Sultaniyeh, north-west Iran.

27 Detail from the *madraseh* of Ulugh Beg, Samarqand, 1417–20.

28 Detail from the Gazar Gah, Herat, 1428–9.

29 (*opposite*) A Timurid prince, Sultan Husayn Bayqara of Herat (AD 1470–1506). From a miniature of the Herat School.

30 Title-page of the *risaleh-ye ma'arif-i shaybani*, a treatise on Islam written in Chaghatai Turkish by Muhammad Shaybani for his son in AD 1507–8. The calligraphy is attributed to a pupil of Sultan 'Ali Mashhadi. The manuscript is dated Mashhad, AD 1510–11. British Museum.

31 Muhammad Shaybani
(d. 1510). Miniature
of the Herat School.
Metropolitan Museum
of Art, New York.

32 'Abdullah Khan of
Bukhara (1583–98).
Miniature of the Bukhara
School.

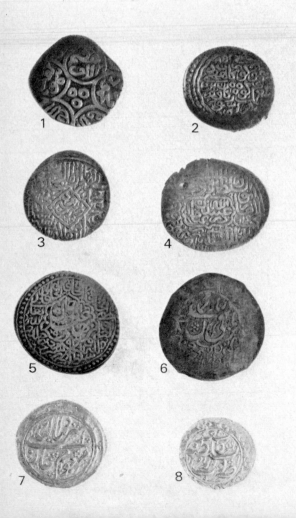

34 Examples of Muslim coinage in Central Asia (British Museum. Nos. 1–6, silver; nos. 7–8, gold).

(1) Timur, in the name of the Chaghatai khan, Mahmud (1388–1402?), no mint (n.d.).
(2) Ulugh Beg (Timurid), Herat (AH 852).
(3) Muhammad Shaybani (Shaybanid), Herat (AH 914).
(4) 'Ubaydullah Khan (Shaybanid), Samarqand (AH 940).
(5) 'Abdullah Khan (Shaybanid), Bukhara (AH 993).
(6) Baki Muhammad (Janid), Samarqand (n.d.).
(7) Shah Murad (Mangit), Bukhara (AH 1206).
(8) Yakub Beg, Kashgar (AH 1291).

35 A Kazakh bride, c. 1877.

36 Idealized portrait of Tsong Khapa, Tibetan religious reformer and
founder of the so-called 'Yellow Hat' Gelugpa sect. Origin unknown.
American Museum of Natural History, New York.

37 Painted gold bronze
statue of a Tibetan
sorcerer, a disciple of
Padmasambhava.
Western Tibet. Probably
sixteenth century.
Rijksmuseum voor
Volkerkunde, Leyden.

38 A street scene in Urga (now Ulan-
Bator) during the time of Przhevalsky's
visit, c. 1870.

39 A Mongol woman of the Chahar
tribe, wearing traditional ornamental
head-dress.

40 The main square of Kuldja, showing a Dungan mosque built in the Chinese style. From a drawing made at the time of the Russian occupation, c. 1880.

41 The principal Taranchi mosque in Kuldja, c. 1880. The Chinese style of the building is a measure of the extent of Chinese cultural influence among the Muslims of Jungaria. 'Taranchi' was the name by which the Uzbeks of Sinkiang were known in the nineteenth century.

42 Yakub Beg, Ataliq Ghazi, receiving the British tea-planter and explorer, Robert Shaw, at a nocturnal durbar in Kashgar, 1869.

43 A multiple prayer-rug from Khotan, second half of the nineteenth century. This design, unusual among Khotanese rugs, developed in Anatolia during the eighteenth and nineteenth centuries and may have found its way into Kashgaria as a result of Yakub Beg's diplomatic exchanges with the Ottoman Empire.

44 Members of the Turkoman Militia established in Marv in 1885 by the Russian administration.

gathering his forces at Samarqand with apparent hostile intent, Kaufman invaded Bukharan territory. On 2 May he took Samarqand and then the towns of Urgut and Katta-Qurghan. A month later, on 2 June, his army came to grips with the main Bukharan force on the Zerabulak heights near Katta-Qurghan. Though possessing over 6,000 infantry, 15,000 cavalry and fourteen light cannon in excellent positions, the Bukharans were put to flight with heavy losses. This forced the amir to capitulate. In a treaty of 18 June 1868 Bukhara ceded Samarqand, Katta-Qurghan, Khojand, Ura-Tyube and Jizak, and agreed to pay a 500,000 rouble indemnity. As in the case of Kokand, Russian subjects were accorded free access to Bukhara and trade within its boundaries, while only an insignificant tax was to be levied on Russian goods. The ceded territories were incorporated into the Turkestan governor-generalship as the Zarafshan District, later the *oblast* of Samarqand. The amir asked for permission to abdicate but Kaufman deemed it useful to have in Bukhara a ruler who had learned to recognize Russian supremacy. The Russians therefore not only confirmed the amir as ruler of Bukhara but even assisted him in the suppression of uprisings against his authority.

Russia next acquired Chinese territory in the upper Ili valley. In 1862 a rebellion had broken out in Jungaria and spread to the Ili region where in 1864 the local Dungans (Chinese Muslims) and Taranchis (Uzbeks of Chinese Turkestan) united to throw off Chinese rule. The Russian consulate in Kuldja and a Russian factory in Chuguchak were destroyed, commerce ceased and refugees poured over the frontier into Semirechie.

Meanwhile, Yakub Beg, a Kokandi general who had led the defence of Aq Mechet against Perovskii in 1853, had raised a rebellion in Kashgar, ousted the Chinese and carved out a khanate for himself. This new native state threatened to upset the balance of power in Central Asia. Yakub Beg was friendly towards England, causing the Russians some consternation. If he should spread his rule to Jungaria he might menace the adjoining *oblast* of Semirechie. This could lead to a major extension of British influence which would outflank Russian positions and ultimately might even threaten communications between European Russia and Siberia. In June 1871, to forestall this and to put an end to the prevailing anarchy, Kaufman ordered the occupation of the upper Ili valley. The occupation of the Ili province (as it was known to the Chinese) or the Kuldja district (as it became known to the Russians) was treated by Russia as a purely temporary affair as far as international opinion was concerned. The Chinese were assured that the occupation would last only until they could regain control over the rebel provinces in Kashgar and the rest of Jungaria. The Russians appear to have assumed that this would never occur but in 1877 Yakub Beg was defeated in battle with the Chinese, his realm crumbled and the Chinese regained mastery. After some months of diplomatic parleying, Russia finally relinquished control in 1883, though on condition of an indemnity and cession of part of the territory. In the words of the British ambassador in St Petersburg: 'China has compelled Russia to do what she has never done before, disgorge territory that she had once absorbed.'

However, Russian attention had meanwhile been drawn towards larger objectives, the first of which was the khanate of Khiva. Three expeditions by the Ural Cossacks in the seventeenth century, Prince Bekovich-Cherkasskii's expedition in 1717 and Perovskii's expedition in 1839 had all met disaster against this ancient foe. When, early in 1873, Kaufman proposed settlement of the problem once and for all by military action permission was readily granted. The British government was assured that only punitive measures were contemplated.

In size and technology Khiva was hopelessly outmatched. Her chief asset, as always, lay in her geographical situation. An advance from several directions was therefore planned to ensure success as well as more laurels for commanders. The main column was to set out from Tashkent, another column from Orenburg, another from Krasnovodsk and a fourth from Fort Aleksandrovskii on the Mangyshlak peninsula. The entire expedition, amounting to 13,000 men and sixty-two guns, was under the command of Kaufman who accompanied the Tashkent column. As it turned out, a smaller force would have sufficed. Hampered by its size, the Tashkent column narrowly escaped disaster in the desert before it reached the Amu-Darya (12 May). The Krasnovodsk column suffered so greatly from heat and lack of water that it had to turn back to its base. Sixty men died of sunstroke and the detachment's supplies, including artillery, had to be abandoned. Both the Orenburg and Mangy-shlak columns, on the other hand, arrived without difficulty and soon had the city softened up by artillery fire and ready for storming by the time Kaufman's column arrived (29 May). The city was taken with only minor losses by the attackers. The khan of Khiva fled but was called back by Kaufman to rule under Russian guidance. The population was well treated; the Russian troops were kept under strict discipline. At Kaufman's order the khan proclaimed the abolition of slavery in his realm. In a treaty signed on 12 August Khiva ceded its possessions on the right bank of the Amu-Darya, agreed to pay an indemnity, renounced the right to conduct independent relations with foreign Powers, and granted the Russians right of residence and tax-free trade. The British government protested but finally agreed to the conquest on condition of Russian recognition of Afghanistan as a British protectorate.

Of the three major Central Asian states thus reduced to Russian vassalage, only in Kokand was Russian power uncertain. Khudayar Khan the ruler was unpopular because of his cruelty and exactions, and because of his ties with the Russians. In July 1875 an uprising broke out against him and he had to flee to the protection of the Russian army. The rebels set up his eldest son, Nasir al-din, as the new khan. In August the rebellion spread to former Kokandi possessions held by Russia. Proclaiming a holy war, the rebels entered Khojand and besieged the Russian garrison in the citadel. Kaufman hastened to the relief of Khojand and then invaded Kokandi territory. On 22 August he attacked the main rebel force, estimated at 30,000 to 50,000 men, occupying the fortress of Makhram, and routed them. The natives left ninety dead in the fortress and Cossacks led by Colonel M. D. Skobelev pursued the fugitives along the banks of the Syr-Darya for several miles and killed over 1,000 more. The Russians lost six men. Kaufman then retook Kokand and other towns with little difficulty and on 23 September

215

concluded a peace treaty at Margelan (Marghinan) with Nasir al-din Khan. The latter promised to pay Russia an indemnity of 3,000,000 roubles, to cede all the lands of Kokand on the right bank of the Syr-Darya, and to give up the right to conduct diplomatic relations or to carry on military activities without permission of the governor-general. The entire eastern part of the khanate, however, was still unsubdued. Andijan went over to the rebels. When Major-General V. N. Trotskii tried to storm Andijan his force was beaten off with a loss of at least fifty men. Skobelev, by that time a Major-General, was then placed in command and after a series of hard-fought engagements forced the rebel leaders to capitulate in January 1876. The Russian government, unwilling to attempt any new restoration of native rule, on 19 February annexed Kokand as an *oblast* bearing the ancient name of Farghana.

Russia had already gained a foothold in the Transcaspian region, south of the Amu-Darya. At the end of 1869 a force from the Caucasus region led by Colonel N. G. Stoletov established a fort at Krasnovodsk. The adjacent area was annexed to Russia as part of the *oblast* of Daghestan under the governor-generalship of the Caucasus. More territory was annexed in 1873 when Krasnovodsk became one of the bases for the operation against Khiva. The desolate region had little to recommend it save a certain strategic value from possession of coastal strongpoints, useful in relations with Iran and Great Britain. Turkoman raids soon necessitated Russian counter-measures and the establishment of advance posts inland. In 1879 General I. D. Lazarev, commander of the First Army of the Caucasus, led a strong detachment against the unruly Akhal group of the Tekke Turkomans. Lazarev died on the march but his second-in-command, Lomakin, pressed on to the oasis. There on 9 September 1879 he found nearly all of the population of the oasis, some 20,000, taking refuge behind the earth walls of a fortress on the hill of Dengil-Tepe (sometimes known as Geok-Tepe). The fort could have been reduced by artillery and rocket fire but Lomakin, eager for glory, ordered an early halt to the bombardment so that the infantry could take the fort by storm. This gave the Turkomans their chance, so that when the Russians charged they met with such resistance that they were forced back with the heaviest losses yet experienced in Central Asia. Of 3,024 Russian troops engaged, nearly 200 were killed and more than 250 wounded.

Fearful that the defeat would shatter Russian prestige, the government quickly appointed General Skobelev, just back from a glorious role in the Russo-Turkish War, to head another expedition. By early November 1880 Skobelev had assembled a force of 11,000 men at Krasnovodsk and other coastal points. The army had already begun construction of a railroad from Krasnovodsk but as this was not finished in time to be of any use, some 20,000 camels were used for transport. Late in November 1880 Skobelev's force, by then about 7,100 after the detachment of others to man the supply lines, reached the Akhal-Tekke oasis and laid siege to the fortress. The defenders resisted as stubbornly as before but Skobelev continued the bombardment relentlessly and had sappers mine the fortress walls. Finally, on 12 January 1881, the Russians set off their mines and stormed the fortress. The demoralized defenders streamed out of the gates on the other side in headlong flight. The victors followed in hot pursuit, cutting down all, regardless of age or sex, and killing several thousand. Inside the fortress were found the corpses of 6,500 persons. The Russians killed all males who had not succeeded in escaping but spared about 5,000 women and children and freed 600 Iranian slaves.

The slaughter at Dengil-Tepe broke the Turkoman resistance. Convinced of Russian might, the Tekke became devoted subjects of the Tsar. A few days later, Colonel A. N. Kuropatkin occupied Ashkhabad, Kaakha and other points. On 6 May 1881 Transcaspia was declared an *oblast* of the empire, subordinate to the viceroyalty of the Caucasus. Skobelev was made governor of the new province but was soon removed, apparently to assuage British opinion, and replaced by General A. V. Komarov.

On 18 February 1884 Komarov occupied Marv, centre of the important Tejen oasis and in May the fortress of Sarakhs. Early in 1885 his soldiers gained possession of the Zulfikar pass on the road to Herat and in March they engaged the Afghans in battle and took Kushka. The apparent threat to India brought Great Britain and Russia perilously close to war. The diplomats of the two empires, however, secured a joint commission to settle the question. The Russo-Afghan Boundary Convention of 1887 confirmed the Russian conquests.

Another crisis, caused in 1891 by Russian attempts to occupy the Pamir plateau, was amicably settled in the Anglo-Russian Convention of March 1895, by which a commission was appointed to survey the region and mark the boundary line. Russian claims to part of the Pamir region were upheld and another part was given over to the sovereignty of the amir of Bukhara.

The settlement of the Pamir question left all boundaries clearly delineated and thus completed the remarkable movement by which, during less than half a century, Russia had gained a region comparable in size to western Europe. The cost in men was relatively low – only about 800 died in battle; most of the operations were little more than tactical exercises. The potential gain, economically and strategically, was enormous.

In the wake of their conquest the Russians brought European administration, economic practices and culture to the heart of Asia. Their settlements, which for reasons of health and defence were built beside rather than within native cities, became models of careful planning. At Kaufman's orders the Russian section of Tashkent was laid out with tree-lined avenues and imposing public buildings. He established an observatory, a museum, a public library and a newspaper, and encouraged exploration and the study of the region's natural history and resources. Other towns followed the same pattern.

Colonization, essential for consolidating the Russian hold on the region, occupied official attention from the first. There were no free lands in Turkestan, so Kaufman and his successors allowed the Russians who came there to settle only in the cities. In the steppe, where grain-farming and animal husbandry offered great possibilities, colonization was of prime importance. The government first relied on Cossacks, by 1867 settling nearly 12,000 in the foothills of Semirechie *oblast*. However, this means proved too slow. The movement of peasants to the region was at first restricted to prevent 'harmful mobility' of the population after the emancipation of the serfs in 1861, then tolerated. Finally, when agrarian distress in southern Russia and the resultant pressure became acute, official policy changed to open encouragement. The Trans-Siberian railroad, built in the 1890s, was designed in part to help peasants to get to the new lands. The Resettlement Administration (*Pereselencheskoe upravlenie*), established in 1896, found and prepared suitable land and helped peasants to get established. With this encouragement thousands of would-be colonists poured over the Urals annually, their number reaching a peak of 665,000 in 1908. The majority settled in the Kazakh steppe.

This aspect of the Russian conquest proved more detrimental to the native population than any other, as the land-hungry peasants were allowed to settle on the best lands, dispossessing and impoverishing the Kazakh and Kirghiz nomads. By the time World War I halted the movement, the influx had already altered the ethnic composition and way of life of large areas. In the steppe *oblasts* and in Semirechie the ethnic balance was tipping in favour of the newcomers. In 1911 40 per cent (1,544,000) of the total population of the four steppe *oblasts* of Uralsk, Turgai, Akmolinsk and Semipalatinsk (approximately 3,834,000) were settlers from European Russia. In Semirechie 204,000 or 20 per cent were Russian.

The irrigated lands of the governor-generalship of Turkestan presented a different picture, however. There, out of a total population of 5,090,000 in 1911, only 202,000 or a trifling 4 per cent were Russians. Even of this number 177,374 represented urban population, leaving only about 25,000 as rural population in the entire region. This population imbalance was regarded with apprehension by the Imperial administration, which saw the Russian element lost in 'an endless sea of natives'.

But even though comparatively few Russian colonists appeared in Turkestan Russian rule transformed the economy. Cotton had been grown in the region since ancient times but the quality was low and methods of processing and transportation were primitive. In 1883, after earlier experiments initiated by Kaufman, the government introduced the American

219

Upland variety (*Gossypium hirsutum L.*), and American machinery for processing it. Production increased rapidly until by 1914 Russia was able to supply half the cotton needs of her industry. The Trans-Caspian railroad, Central Asia's first rail connection with the outside world, reached Samarqand in 1888, making large shipments possible. Low freight rates, combined with protective tariffs, made the Turkestan product competitive with foreign cotton. The Orenburg-Tashkent railroad, built in 1899–1905, enabled the import of cheap wheat from the Ukraine and Western Siberia, which encouraged the natives to devote more land to cotton. The Turkestan-Siberian railroad, started just before 1914, and not completed until 1930, would have carried the economic transformation of the region still farther. The undesirable feature of this one-crop economy, however, was the growing indebtedness and tenantry of the native peasants.

Other agricultural innovations were successful, but of more limited scope. Experiments were made in drying fruit and in shipment of fresh fruit by rail to European Russia. The ancient silk industry was improved by modern methods of inspection and control, and by experimental stations. Grape-growing and wine-making proved successful in the Samarqand area. Sugar beet was grown near Tashkent. In the steppe, mowing machines and other modern farm machinery were introduced and experiments were made with refrigerator-cars for the transport of meat.

Russian rule also enabled the construction of the first major irrigation works to be undertaken in Central Asia for several centuries. After unsuccessful attempts by Kaufman and his successor Cherniaev to irrigate the so-called Hungry Steppe south-west of Tashkent, the Grand Duke Nikolai Konstantinovich, who lived in exile in Taskhent, succeeded with a less ambitious project. This was absorbed in 1900 by the ambitious Romanov Canal project, aimed at the irrigation of 50,000 hectares. In the *oblast* of Transcaspia a series of dams on the Murghab river provided irrigation for 27,250 hectares near Marv. Other projects of greater magnitude never attained reality. One of the most persistent envisaged diverting the Amu-Darya back to its ancient bed so that it would flow again into the Caspian Sea, a prototype of the abortive Main Turkmenistan Canal Project of the early 1950s. There were several projects for a canal to irrigate extensive areas of the eastern part of the Kara Kum desert with water from the Amu-Darya, a forerunner of the present-day Kara Kum canal. But most ambitious of all was a proposal for regional development put forth in 1912 by A. V. Krivoshein, head of the Resettlement Administration and right-hand man of Prime Minister P. A. Stolypin. Combining economic and political aims, Krivoshein urged vast irrigation works to reclaim an area nearly the size of the Netherlands which would make Russia self-sufficient in cotton and help achieve Russian ethnic dominance in Central Asia by enabling the settlement of 1,500,000 peasants in the region.

The mineral resources of Central Asia drew Russian interest from the time of Peter the Great, who sent large expeditions up the Irtysh and to Khiva to seek rumoured gold deposits. Mining of the Ridder lead and silver deposits in the Altai region near Ust-Kamenogorsk began in 1784. Working of lead and silver mines in what was later the Akmolinsk *oblast* began in the 1830s. Coal-mining began at Karaganda in the 1850s; copper-mining at Spasskii and at Iuspenskii, further south, a few years later. The Dzhezkazgan copper deposits, among the richest in the world, were first noted in 1771 and work was begun in the 1850s. In Turkestan, coal, lead, gold, sulphur, oil and salt deposits were known long before the coming of the Russians. For all of these deposits, however, the story was nearly the same: because of insufficient capital, lack of a trained labour force, and inadequate or non-existent transportation facilities, none were exploited on a major scale, and most remained untouched.

Russians, like the representatives of other colonial powers of the same period, justified their presence in Central Asia on humanitarian grounds and thought of their expansion as a civilizing mission. Behind this, however, lay the practical but less openly admitted considerations of economic and strategic advantage. But whatever the reason for their dominion, the Russians, like other colonial powers, sought somehow to reconcile the natives to foreign domination. Russia had already faced this problem many times and thanks to numerical predominance, relative cultural superiority, and general absence of legal or even psychological discrimination, had gone far towards the cultural and ethnic amalgamation of many of the peoples she had overrun. Nineteenth century nationalism and colonial rivalry, however, brought to an end the relatively easy-going ways of earlier times. From the mid-nineteenth century the Russians began a campaign to draw their subjects closer, to instill in them sympathy and loyalty, to teach them the Russian language and culture, and if possible to convert them to Orthodox Christianity.

The Kazakhs, because of their primitive way of life and situation, and their imperfect practice of Islam, appeared particularly suited for Russian cultural penetration. Starting in the 1860s, the orientalist and nationalist, N. A. Ilminskii, aided later by his pupil, the Kazakh educator Ibrahim (Ibray) Altynsary, laid plans for schools in the Kazakh *auls*. The instruction was to be in Kazakh, with courses in Russian. From the *aul* schools the pupils could advance to the *volost* schools or to the 'Russian-Kirghiz' schools, each comprising two years of study. From there they could go to a Russian city school, to the Orenburg Kirghiz Teachers' School, or other institutions of higher learning.

The development of Kazakh schools was slow and uneven, depending on the interest of the local administrators and the funds that were available. The greatest effort was made in Turgai *oblast* where Altynsarin served as the *oblast* inspector of schools from 1879 until his death in 1889 under like-minded Russian officials; in some other *oblasts* scarcely anything was done. Ultimately, about 2,000 Kazakhs benefited from these facilities annually, though most never got beyond the primary level.

The sedentary natives of Turkestan presented a more difficult problem. These peoples already had a system of education. At the end of the nineteenth century there were about 5,000 Muslim primary schools and 400 *madrasehs* in Turkestan, comprising about 75,000 pupils. Kaufman regarded these schools as against Russian interests but instead of attempting to abolish them he followed the same policy of calculated neglect which he employed towards other Muslim institutions in the region. He felt that withdrawal of state support and the end of the former dominant position of the higher Muslim schools in filling public office would weaken them to a point where they would fall into disuse or undergo drastic change. To fill the vacuum which would be left by the hoped-for decline of the native schools, Kaufman encouraged the development of a system of bilingual elementary schools for Russian and native children. The first of these opened in 1884 and by 1915 there were more than 90 such schools in the entire Turkestan region. Of these, some 65 were in Syr-Darya *oblast*, with 3,410 pupils. Even the latter figure represented, however, only about 2 per cent of the native children as compared to approximately 95 per cent of the more than 10,000 Russian children of school age in the *oblast* who were receiving an elementary education at the same time. Fewer still of the native children went on to higher levels of schooling. Of 415 students who completed their studies at the Tashkent Teachers' Seminary in the twenty-five years from 1879 to 1904 there were only 65 natives. Of these, only 11 were Uzbeks, Turkomans and Tatars. and 54 were Kazakhs and Kirghiz. Modest though these results were statistically, the few who did take advantage of the facilities provided by the Russians for natives to receive western schooling formed the beginning of a native intelligentsia.

The formation of this intelligentsia could be regarded as the long-sought 'drawing closer' at which the Russians aimed. It could also herald more effective native opposition to Russian rule. For, contrary to Russian declarations then and now, the natives did not accept foreign rule freely. Active resistance was hopeless, as shown by the history of the Russian conquest and the snuffing-out of minor flare-ups such as the three-day Andizhan (Andijan) revolt of 1898. Russia had from the first exempted the natives from military service, considering it unsafe to raise militant feelings and teach them European military organization and the use of modern arms. Russia wanted no mutinous Sepoys.

There remained for the natives the usual paradoxical alternative of the conquered, of modernizing so that they could cope with the intruder but thereby transforming themselves, abandoning the very way of life they were defending. As for the Russians, they were transmitting the means which might eventually spell the end of their own dominion in the region.

Towards the end of the century Central Asians receptive to new influences displayed the growing restlessness found among other Muslim peoples then living under infidel rule, becoming increasingly aware that while the rest of the world had moved on they had been left behind. Thus some of the Muslims of Central Asia became adherents of Jadidism, the new method of schooling originated by the remarkable Crimean Tatar, Ismail bey Gasprinski. His programme was welcomed in Central Asia by the handful of native thinkers who had begun to entertain reformist views. The first Jadid school in Turkestan opened in Tashkent in 1901 and in spite of government surveillance and the opposition of conservative Muslims, others followed. The Russo-Japanese War and the 1905 Revolution gave the native reform movement greater impetus. Actual political representation, in which Central Asian deputies sat among other Muslim deputies in the First and Second Dumas, proved shortlived but reform flourished in the cultural sphere of Muslim life. By 1914 there were over a hundred Jadid schools in the region. Native newspapers appeared. In Orenburg several Kazakh intellectuals involved in the production of the newspaper *Kazakh*, which appeared in 1912, criticized the government for its russification policies and the displacement of Kazakhs by Russian colonists. The paper attacked conservative circles for Pan-Islamism, urged military service for the Kirghiz and Kazakhs, demanded more schools, and the transition of the nomads to a settled life. Devoting attention first to economic problems, the newspaper turned gradually to political ones – though following the line taken by Russian liberals.

Where this trend towards native self-assertion would have led, or whether the Russian hold on the region would have tightened with additional economic development, cultural penetration and colonization, can only be conjectured. Economic development, the spread of new ideas and the revolutionary unrest of

1905 had all portended change but with the outbreak of World War I the end of the old order was really at hand. For Russian Central Asia, as for the rest of the world, many of the ideals and values of preceding decades were to be set aside or irrevocably modified; many trends were to be stifled or distorted. The effects of the war were soon felt. Taxes rose, inflation set in. Native yurts, carts and livestock were requisitioned; the rifles of Russian settlers were called in to supply troops at the front. The flow of settlers ceased but in their place came large numbers of evacuees from the theatre of war. Many of them died in epidemics. Following the Russian victories in Galicia in September 1914, about 225,000 Austro-Hungarian prisoners-of-war were sent to camps in the steppe and Turkestan. Some 40,000 of the prisoners died of disease and privation before the efforts of foreign Red Cross workers got most of them moved to camps in Siberia.

By 1916 deterioration of the military situation and the growing manpower-shortage caused government scrutiny of the long-standing exemption of the natives from military service. In June an Imperial decree ordered a special draft of the native male population of Central Asia, Siberia and parts of the Caucasus for construction of defence works and communication lines in the rear of the fighting forces. Conceived in desperation and executed in haste without proper explanation, the mobilization decree touched off a wave of riot and rebellion. In Semi-rechie, Kazakh and Kirghiz tribesmen killed more than 3,000 Russian peasants. In near panic at the prospect of a general uprising, the Russians struck back and many natives – estimates run as high as 200,000 – died in reprisals. Many others – again the estimates are around 200,000 – fled over the border into Chinese Central Asia.

To deal with the situation, General A. N. Kuropatkin, veteran campaigner and administrator in the region, was sent to Turkestan as governor-general. His stern measures, aimed at protecting colonists and natives alike, established an uneasy peace. Then, in February 1917, the Tsar abdicated. Soviets sprang up almost at once in all the towns in the region and began to harass the representatives of the government. A

225

vociferous left demanded a more complete revolution, one which would bring about a government not by the 'bourgeoisie' but by the 'toilers'. Kuropatkin, as the lawful head of the government, tried to retain control but after four weeks he was arrested by the Soviets and sent back to Petrograd. Thereafter, as in the rest of Russia, the agencies of the Provisional Government steadily lost power. The Bolsheviks finally gained control of the Soviet and on 31 October their forces seized Tashkent. By the end of the year the new regime was in control of the entire region.

16

The Russian Revolution
and Soviet Policy
in Central Asia

In Central Asia the Revolution of 1917 had a specific character closely bound up with social conditions in the area. This was to affect relations between the native population and the new authorities emerging from the revolution for a long time to come. The peasants and nomads of Central Asia had been widely dispossessed of their lands by Russian colonists and despite some restrictions on colonization, especially after 1905, the situation in that part of the world on the eve of the revolution was on the verge of catastrophe. In spite of often bloody repression, the Russian authorities had never entirely succeeded in suppressing the revolt which since 1916 had shaken the whole region from the Kazakh steppes to Transcaspia. Russian colonists, armed by the government, were everywhere fighting for survival and adding to the tragic nature of the revolt. In the towns, the specific cause of dissension between Russians and natives was differentiation in employment. The nascent industries of Turkestan certainly employed a comparatively high proportion of local labour (around 70 per cent), but this consisted almost entirely of unskilled, manual workers who were particularly ill-paid by reason of the seasonal nature of their employment. The skilled workers, as well as all permanent employees and managerial staff, were Russian. In its anxiety to prevent the infiltration of revolutionary ideas among the local populations, the imperial government had systematically favoured the Russians and discouraged the creation of any proletarian trained personnel or indeed of any regular indigenous proletariat. Consequently, on the eve of the Revolution, there was a complete dichotomy between the Russian proletariat and the semi-proletarian natives for whom their Russian comrades constituted a privileged class. The towns of Central Asia was full of artisans whom Russian competition had deprived of a livelihood, of peasants dispossessed by colonists looking for work and, at the same time, of illegal Russian immigrants waiting for land and ill-disposed towards the wretched workless natives. From 1908 onwards the local intelligentsia had begun to rally, in Turkestan around the pan-Islamic revolutionary Abd ur-rauf Fitrat, who was to lead the reformist movement in Turkestan, and in the Kazakh country around men like Baitursunov and Tanyshbaev. The first of these groups soon adopted an attitude of violent hostility to Russia while the second maintained until 1924 a more equivocal attitude.

The revolution of February 1917 found Central Asia in a state of complete political disintegration. The great revolt of the nomadic tribes in 1916 which convulsed the region of the steppes and the government of Turkestan in general had been suppressed with the utmost harshness: large numbers of the local inhabitants were killed and whole villages deported, and even where order had been restored there remained deep wounds and grievances. The representatives of the various Central Asian peoples made known their tragic predicament at the 'Congress of Nationalities' held in Lausanne in June 1916 and one, a delegate from Bukhara, actually stated for the first time the demand for complete independence for the entire region and the eventual aim of a sovereign state of Turkestan.

The men who came to power in February 1917 received an enthusiastic welcome from a region which had suffered so much under the imperial regime and had risen wholeheartedly against it, but even so they proved incapable of finding a solution to its problems and rapidly lost all hope of doing so. Before coming to power the February leaders had been, for the most part, supporters of the idea of national self-determination, but once the fate of Russia was in their hands they rejected its application. Unanimously determined on continuing the war, they postponed the solution of national problems to a later date. The *Declaration of Rights* of 19 March 1917, which asserted the equality of all individuals, had no bearing on national individuality.

The Provisional Government was at grips with countless difficulties, and when the Bolsheviks charged it with pursuing a policy of recognizing national aspirations, it quickly decided to identify the demands of the oppressed nationalities with counter-revolution. When, in September 1917, it realized its mistake and finally admitted the legitimacy of nationalist aspirations, it was too late. The Bolsheviks' hour had come. In Central Asia the Provisional Government's general policy of suspicion with regard to the nationalities was intensified by the fact that Central Asia was a region colonized by Russians. This in itself was enough to give the Revolution there a special character. Essentially it was a revolution which united the Russians in their primary aim of checking the nationalist demands of the indigenous population. When the Revolution broke out, political administrators of the imperial regime, colonists and even Russian workers all spontaneously supported it, but their alliance was more a defensive move directed against the local population than a specifically pro-revolutionary one. The Governor-General of Turkestan, General Kuropatkin, declared for the Revolution and offered to organize the defence of the Soviet settlers in the event of a native rising. In Turkestan, more than anywhere, the Provisional Government's order to the military and civil officials to remain at their posts was thoroughly appreciated. The first Soviets alloted only the minimum number of seats to natives of the region but included the very Russian generals who had put down the revolt of 1916. It was not until April 1917 that the tsarist officials were finally placed under arrest and new political figures emerged. These were Schepkin, Preobrazhenski, Elpatiev, Shkapski, and Litapolski and, together with four Muslims, General Davletchin, Sadri Maksudov, Tanyshbaev and Bukeikhanov, they formed the *Turkestan Committee of the Provisional Government*, under the presidency first of Schepkin and later of the orientalist Nalivkin. It was to be expected that the government committee set up in Tashkent under the control of the constitutional democrats, should have

229

included Tatar or Kazakh Muslims, most of whom were not Turkestanis, rather than the traditionalist religious leaders who had such a hold over the local masses, or the principal leaders of the reformist movement. Among the latter were such men as Behbudi, Chokaev, and Munevver Qari, who had a large following among the intelligentsia, the educated urban populations and native craftsmen. In the event the indigenous population resorted to the organization of purely Muslim bodies. The conservatives, under the leadership of Mulla Said Ali Lapin, organized themselves into an assembly of *ulema* (*Ulema Jamiy*), while the reformists formed a Muslim council (*Shura-i Islamiyeh*). These two organizations met together from the 16 to 23 April 1917 in the first regional Muslim Congress at Tashkent to formulate the native attitude to the future of Turkestan. However vague their position with regard to Russia, the Muslim delegates' demands in other respects were quite clear: they wanted an end to colonization, the restoration of all sequestered lands to their original owners, and they wanted the future of Turkestan to be decided, not by the Russians alone, but by the inhabitants themselves. The Congress set up a Central Muslim Council of Turkestan (*Turkistan musulman merkezi-shurasi*) or National Centre (*Milli-Merkez*), headed by Mustafa Chokaev, whom the delegates regarded as their representative in future discussions with Russia. At the same time, the first socialist Muslim organizations appeared, the most effective of which was the *Ittihad* of Samarkand.

On the political level, therefore, a split occurred between Russians and Muslims in the first months of the Provisional Government which was further aggravated by the economic situation in Central Asia. Since its conquest, the agriculture of the region had been directed towards the intensive cultivation of cotton and a consistent reduction of the acreage under corn. Turkestan was thus nearly dependent on the import of food-stuffs from Russia. In the summer of 1917 these imports came to an end and famine was widespread. Subsequent clashes between natives and Russian peasants, which were aggravated by the fact that the natives suffered more in practical terms than the Russians, reached their peak in July 1917. The Russian

230

colonists, alarmed by rumours that the Dungans who had emigrated to China were returning to Turkestan, succeeded in arming themselves against the natives and massacred large numbers of Kirghiz.

When October came, the unarmed natives made no move and once again revolution was brought about by the Russians alone. Just as in February, the Revolution meant different things to the Russians and to the indigenous population, and the gulf between them deepened accordingly. To the Russians it meant chiefly bread and liberty. To the natives, who had already suffered from one revolution which had been only too clearly Russian and oppressive in character, the October Revolution undoubtedly meant bread, but above all it meant the national liberty which had been a part of the Bolshevik programme since April 1917.

However, in its initial manifestations the new government displayed the same thoroughly Russian attitude as the Provisional Government. The first organ of the Bolshevik government established in Tashkent after the October Revolution did not include a single representative of the indigenous population.

In the Steppe Region, where the change-over was not so sweeping, the political problems which arose between February and October 1917 were less serious. The Tsarist officials and *oblast* governors gradually disappeared, but the administrative structure survived under the control of executive committees of the Provisional Government. The leaders of the nationalist movement, *Alash-Orda*, still believed that the future of the peoples they stood for lay in a federal-based Russian state: their demands were basically concerned with the problem of land, the use of their own language and a share in the administration of the region. But they were sufficiently clear-sighted to realize that in a predominantly nomadic region, the people were too far from any real national consciousness for autonomy to be immediately practicable. First and foremost was the problem of settlement, and here too they knew it was necessary to proceed slowly and cautiously.

In spite of the nationalist principles maintained by the Bolsheviks at the VIIth Congress, the Bolshevik revolution in

Central Asia, in the words of G. Safarov, 'took a colonialist direction'. Just as the revolution had been Russian, so too was the government. The disappointed native population had to choose between anti-Bolshevik national governments and vain attempts at co-operation with an authority which persisted in ignoring them. The Bolsheviks also had to contend against the Russian opponents of the Revolution who endeavoured to make use of the rebellious nationalist movements to support their own counter-revolutionary activities. The history of Central Asia from 1917 to 1924 involved a long, hard struggle between the Bolsheviks and these two equally hostile forces.

The process of embodying in the Soviet state a Turkestan divided into national units began in the summer of 1920 by which time two such units – the People's Republics of Bukhara and Khorezm (Khiva) – already existed as sovereign states. Aware that the Revolution in the West had suffered a check, the Soviet authorities were compelled to modify their policy and to resign themselves to a long and lone struggle in a world dominated by the capitalist countries. After negotiating with the *Alash-Orda*, reconquering the Turkmen region and checking the nationalist elements in the Republic of Turkestan, the Soviet authorities were free to begin thinking about the reorganization of Central Asia. The ultimate aim of this reorganization was to destroy the unity of the region and thus eradicate the nationalist tendencies which had built up during the Revolution. Reorganization was in the first place territorial; later it was to become national and sociological.

To begin with the government approached the problem by means of economic measures. Thanks to the NEP, the government was able, in 1921–2, to achieve some improvement in the material conditions of the local population of Turkestan. It also embarked on a number of placatory measures aimed at depriving the opposition, and the Basmachis in particular, of the support of the masses. In 1922–3, the *vaqf* lands confiscated in 1919 were restored to their original owners. At the same time the measures taken against Islam two years earlier were repealed. Muslim educational establishments were reopened and courts of *shari'at* law resumed their sessions. The Republic of Turk-

estan, appeased by these measures, could now become the basis
of Soviet policy for the region. In March 1923 came the first
conference of the Central Asian Republics (Turkestan, Bukhara
and Khiva) which stated the principle of a common economic
policy for the participating states, and to this end set up an
Economic Council for Central Asia. This was to become a
powerful instrument towards the integration of the independent
republics. This integration began with the reunification of
Central Asia, since irrigation, commerce, agriculture and planning were to become common to the whole of Central Asia
under the control of the newly established council. Currency,
transport and telecommunications in the two People's Republics
were directly connected to the Soviet system. The seeds of these
changes were already present in the Soviet treaties with Bukhara
and Khiva in 1921 but despite these alterations Bukhara and
Khiva both remained legally independent states. This independence, however, tended to become more and more nominal.
Moreover, the process of economic integration was accompanied
by a process of political integration after 1923, when all possibility of resistance by the nationalist elements was progressively
eliminated. In 1921 the Republic of Khorezm had undergone a
drastic purge. The inter-tribal squabbles which were endemic in
Khiva had facilitated the intervention of the Soviet authorities,
ostensibly in defence of the aspirations of the Turkmen minority
in the Khorezmian state towards self-determination. On this
pretext, the Soviet representatives urged the removal – and
subsequent liquidation – of the nationalist leaders. The power
of the Khorezmian government between 1922 and 1924 was
more theoretical than real and any action was prevented by the
succession of purges during the last two years of the Republic's
existence. A nationalist government managed to survive in
Bukhara until 1923, but it was paralysed from the outset by
the contradictory conditions of its birth in 1920. Supported by
the mass of the people who wanted agrarian reform and a total
reconstruction of the state, the government, composed largely of
reformists, was unable to carry out its plans for lack of administrative personnel. Dependent on the administrators of the old
Uzbek State, fearful of running counter to social and religious

233

tradition, it could not set in motion the reforms which were the dream of the government, no less than of the poorest of the people whom it disappointed beyond redress. After 1922, the Communist Party of Bukhara became affiliated to the Russian Communist Party (Bolshevik), and in the middle of the same year it underwent its first purges, like the other Communist organizations in Central Asia. When Stalin denounced the Bukhara government as reactionary in June 1923, the masses it had disappointed did nothing to save it. The nationalist members were arrested and the Communist Party, drastically purged and dependent on the Russian party, took power and set about the socialization of the ancient emirate. By September 1924 when the delegates to the Vth Pan-Bukharan Assembly (*Kurultay*) voted unanimously in favour of the dissolution of the People's Republic to make way for a Soviet Republic, Bukhara had already, despite its maintenance of legal independence, long passed under the control of the Russian Communist Party and hence of the Russian Communist element in Turkestan. Economically there was no further reason for the continued existence of the national states after 1923, and once the nationalist leaders were no longer in a position to exercise their responsibilities, there was not even the political machinery to sustain it.

Nevertheless, the economic unification of 1923 had its dangerous side from the point of view of the Soviet authorities. It encouraged the dreams of Central Asian unity, or of widespread internal regroupings in Central Asia cherished by the local nationalist leaders. From 1920 to 1924 native aspirations were very far removed from the Russian plans. The Kazakh nationalists maintained the idea of a great Kazakhstan, which was matched by the Kirghiz and Uzbek dreams of a great Kirghizia and Uzbekistan. The nationalists of Khiva had visions of combining with the Uzbeks of Turkestan to found a Khorezmian state, while the Bukharans were divided between the supporters of an independent Muslim state, bounded by the frontiers of the ancient emirate, and those favouring a Turkestan which would include the Uzbeks, the Bashkirs and the Kirghiz.

The measures adopted in Central Asia made it clear at a very early stage that the Soviet authorities were anxious to prevent any extensive regroupings in the region. To forestall any aspirations to unity they implemented the policy of dividing the nationalities. The creation of an autonomous Turkmen region in 1921 and of a Kirghiz region in 1922 paved the way for this policy. When the Khivans and Bukharans put an end to their respective national states in 1924, their representatives, the new elite which had emerged from repeated purges, finally conformed to Soviet policy by voicing the hope that the various races which had made up the old Central Asian Khanates would form their own national states. In October 1924 the Central Executive Committee of the USSR voted the creation of two socialist republics: Uzbekistan (made up of the central portion of the old emirate of Bukhara, the southern part of the Khanate of Khiva, and the former regions of Samarqand, Farghana, Amu-Darya and Syr-Darya which had previously come under the general government of Turkestan) and Turkmenistan (covering the Turkmen regions of western Bukhara, Khorezm and what had been the Transcaspian region). The same vote further provided for the creation of two autonomous republics: Tadjikistan (from the mountainous region of what had formerly been Bukhara with a Persian-speaking and basically Shi'ite population), and Kazakhstan which replaced the republic created on 26 August 1920 from people previously called Kirghiz, and controlled for a while by Baitursunov. Finally two autonomous regions were also established: the Kirghiz and the Karakalpak. The latter was originally part of the Kazakh autonomous republic but then in 1932 became the autonomous republic of Karakalpak and was affiliated to the RSFSR before becoming in 1936 a part of the Uzbek Republic. In the following years, the reorganization of Central Asia along national lines was completed by the successive promotion of the republics and autonomous regions to the rank of federal socialist republics. On 5 December 1929, Tadjikistan became the seventeenth republic of the Union. On 5 December 1936, the Republics of Kirghizia and Kazakhstan were admitted to the same status within the Soviet system. This finalized the existence of the socialist nations and, simultaneously, the disappearance of a

235

name, Turkestan, which had covered a vast common heritage belonging to the races divided by the revolution. Thus ended the dream of unity cherished equally by the modern intelligentsia and the traditionalist elements of Central Asia.

Even so, these territorial redistributions were still insufficient to destroy the bonds which united the peoples of Turkestan. These bonds were political, cultural, religious and social. From a political point of view, there were two organizations which had played a part in encouraging the disappearance of the national states by making it possible for them to reform under Soviet control. These were the Economic Council for Central Asia and the Communist Party's Central Asian Bureau. These organizations, although their usefulness to the Soviet authorities prior to 1924 had been considerable, were later to be viewed by the indigenous populations simply as a means of halting the nationalities policy. Men like the Uzbek, Faizullah Khojaev, who realized as early as 1923 that there was no possibility of saving the national states from the process of integration towards which these organizations tended, were already thinking (as F. Khodjaev stated at his trial) of the subsequent need to use them to safeguard the unity of Turkestan, or at least as a means of working out a common policy for the indigenous peoples against the Russians. For ten years the Soviet authorities were obliged to tolerate the existence of nationalist elements in Central Asia. Too violent action against barely pacified peoples was ruled out by the precarious state of the Union which, in Central Asia, was aggravated by constant trouble with the indigenous population. (The resistance of the Basmachis, despite the defeats they suffered in 1922, persisted underground until 1930 when it broke out more violently in the form of resistance to collectivization.) In 1934, the time of the great purges in the USSR, both these organizations were suppressed.

Another political bond of union was the continued existence in the various Central Asian republics of national 'establishments', which had in common their attitude towards Russia and their views on the future evolution of the peoples of Central Asia and which had had moreover the same political past. From 1924 onwards, the Soviet authorities set out to eliminate the intelligentsia throughout the area, but did not do so openly and on a large scale until the years 1934–8. As early as 1924 the former leaders of *Alash-Orda* were beginning to come into conflict with the Soviet authorities in the steppes. The heads of *Alash-Orda* were determined to preserve the integrity of Kazakh life; for this reason they opposed any rough-and-ready attempts to force the nomads to settle down, and fought against the introduction of what they regarded as an artificial class struggle into a society where such differences as yet hardly existed. In November 1927 the Soviet authorities embarked on the elimination of these leaders on the pretext that they supported the Trotsky-Zinoviev opposition. The purge began within the party, with the replacement of native officials, the secretariat being held successively by Goloshchokin, a Russian, and Mirzoian, an Armenian. The latter set about replacing the indigenous government agents by Europeans, thus completing the denationalization process which had been begun in the local party in 1927–8. From this time onwards the nationalist intelligentsia disappeared from Kazakh political life. The fate of the Kirghiz nationalists was little better, although Stalin introduced a Kirghiz, Turar Ryskulov, into the Commissariat of Nationalities in 1922. Between 1928 and 1930 the nationalists were wiped out nearly everywhere. In Uzbekistan, the Uzbek intelligentsia remained in power a little longer than in the steppes, but from 1930 onwards there was open conflict between the local administration and the Russian authorities, and as in the steppes it hinged on Soviet social and economic policies. In 1938, Faizullah Khodjaev, a former president of the Central Executive Committee of the USSR, and Ahmed Ikramov, First Secretary of the local CP, were accused of sympathizing with the right-wing, Trotskyite bloc. Their execution on 13 March 1938 marks the end of the co-operation between the Russians and the indigenous population which had been inaugurated in the 1920s. Any such co-operation had been rendered impossible by the almost total disappearance of all nationalist elements in the republic in circumstances often less spectacular than the trial of Khodjaev, but nonetheless effective. The purge of the Tadjiks was carried out in two stages. In 1933 the President of

237

the Republic, Nasratullah Maqsum, and his prime minister, Abdurrahim Khodjibaev, were charged with sabotaging the agrarian policy by their nationalist, chauvinist and anti-Russian deviationism. A great many local administrators disappeared with them, and in 1937 the remaining survivors, in particular the new President of the Republic, Shotemar, and his prime minister, Rahimbaev, were eliminated. These, like their Uzbek colleagues, were charged with Trotskyism and Bukharinism. In Turkmenistan, the purges were directed first against the intellectuals who from 1930 to 1934 had taken the lead in a nationalist resistance movement with a cultural basis. Once the leading Turkmen writers had been convicted of hostility to Russia, it was the turn of the politicians to be accused of sabotaging Soviet policy, especially with regard to collectivization. In 1939, the President of the Turkmen Supreme Soviet, Aitakov, was executed, and with him the last of the nationalists perished.

Despite the largely imaginary nature of the accusations brought against the leaders of the indigenous populations – Trotskyism-Zinovievism first, and then Trotskyism-Bukharinism – it is clear that the struggle from which the Soviet authorities emerged victorious in 1938, was no fiction. For as long as they could, the intellectuals of the region fought to defend their integrity and to resist any measures aimed at integrating them still further into the Soviet system. On a cultural level, one of the principal bonds of unity between the various peoples of Central Asia was that of language. In 1917 all the Turkish-speaking peoples had their own dialects, but aspirations towards linguistic unity occupied a prominent place in the objectives of Muslim intellectuals of the early twentieth century. In Turkestan, the idea of the unification of all Turkish-speaking peoples around Chaghatai was firmly established even before the revolution, and it should not be forgotten that one of the first acts of the nationalist heads of the Peoples' Republic of Bukhara in 1920 had been the abandonment of Persian, the language of the court and the Bukharan nobility, in favour of Uzbek. Here, too, Turkic influence was gaining ground. This policy to bring together the Turkic-language-speaking races with a lingua franca as the first step towards the dream of Turkestan unity, was shattered in 1924 by the creation of the national states, and the firm establishment of national languages based on the various local dialects. The Soviet policy of linguistic differentiation met with fierce opposition from the local intelligentsia, especially in the Turkmen region. From 1930 to 1935, the Turkmen intelligentsia united to demand that Turkmen should be dropped in favour of Anatolian Turkish or some more literary language such as Chaghatai. This was the fundamental reason for the purge of Turkmen writers. However, although divided by dialects, the people of Central Asia still had, in 1924, a common writing which united them, and preserved their link with Islam, thus cutting them off from the western races. The Soviet authorities were well aware of the importance of this, and of the psychological effects of a different way of writing, and they decided in 1926 to abolish the Arabic alphabet on grounds of convenience. In March 1926, the Congress of Turcology, meeting at Baku, decided to replace the Arabic alphabet by the Latin. This was a half-measure which had the dual advantage in 1926 of appearing neither harsh nor tending towards russification, and of having a reputable precedent in the Turkey of Kemal Ataturk. This was, however, a dangerous precedent since, although the adoption of the Latin alphabet set the seal on the different national languages of Central Asia, and the break between these languages and the sacred language of Islam, it also provided a link between the cultural development of Central Asia and that of Turkey which had already, since the beginning of the century, provided an inspiration for the local intelligentsia. This was, in fact, only a first step towards the fundamental reform which was to enclose the Muslim peoples of the USSR within a predominantly Russian state: the adoption of the Cyrillic alphabet. On 13 March 1938, the teaching of Russian was made compulsory throughout the Union. Inevitably, this meant the disappearance of the Latin alphabet in favour of the Cyrillic. The change-over took place comparatively quickly (by 1942 it was already complete) and met little opposition in as much as it came about at a particularly dark period in Soviet history. With the nationalist intelligentsias out of the way and the purges threatening every citizen of the Union, resistance was impossible.

Of all the unifying factors among the indigenous populations, the most powerful, and the one which most clearly marked them off from the rest of the Soviet Union, was Islam. The restriction of the power of Islam in the life of Central Asia was a formidable task, since the Muslim faith and institutions were indissolubly bound up with every aspect of daily life.

The government had to find a means of removing two factors from which Islam derived vast temporal power. These were the *vaqf* possessions and the *shari'at* law. The problem of the *vaqfs* was bound up with the whole question of property, with which they vanished in 1930. The suppression of the canon law was accomplished in stages. After some hesitation and back-peddling during the civil war years, the Soviet authorities decided in 1924, during the political and territorial reorganiza-tion of Central Asia, to restrict the authority of religious courts by bringing their functions into line with those of Soviet courts of law. Between 1925 and 1927, the number of Soviet courts was greatly increased and religious ones curtailed. Finally, on 21 September 1927, a decree was passed which effectively put an end to their existence by relieving them of the power to implement their sentences. Much against the will of the indigenous populations, Soviet law was established every-where. But however offended in its religious beliefs, and divided nationally and linguistically, Central Asian society had still to lose its last trace of individuality, its last traditions and finally conform to the Soviet mould. The settlement of the nomads and the increased cultivation of cotton were to play a decisive part in bringing this about. As far back as 1925 the policy of agrarian reform based on the confiscation of the great estates and the redistribution of land had been put into operation in all recently settled areas. At the same time the authorities were proceeding with the intensive cultivation of cotton which was to lead to serious clashes with the local politicians. In the course of the civil war, the politicians experienced some of the dis-advantages of single-crop cultivation which left Central Asia dependent on Russia, and they were fiercely opposed to the

240

THE RUSSIAN REVOLUTION

Soviet plan to extend cotton cultivation. The conflict was all the more tragic because both sides were fully aware that what was at stake was in fact a degree of economic and hence of political independence for Central Asia. Successive purges broke the back of local resistance. In the steppes, where nomadic life still persisted, the work of settlement was begun in 1928. The extreme brutality with which the policy was enforced resulted in considerable loss of human life, the destruction of the greater part of the flocks and herds and a bitter conflict between the nationalists and the representatives of the Soviet authorities, from which the latter emerged victorious in 1930. Resistance to the economic integration of Central Asia into the Soviet Union was most lasting in Tadjikistan, where it persisted until 1935 in the form of armed opposition to collectivization.

Once the intelligentsia of Central Asia had been wiped out in its entirety in the tragic years before the Second World War, what remained of the cultural, political and economic individuality of the region? Despite the massive influx of Russian and Ukrainian colonists into the Kazakh region, which changed the whole face of the land, the total assimilation of the area which had formerly been Turkestan was clearly very far from complete. Central Asia may have been economically-speaking closely linked to the Soviet Union, but its social and economic life was likely to remain very different from that of the USSR so long as Muslim women continued to remain at home rather than going out to work. Despite the unceasing efforts of the Soviet authorities to change matters, this appears still to be very generally the case. Furthermore, a strongly nationalist intelligentsia does exist which testifies, sometimes vociferously, to its attachment to its own values. It was in Central Asia that at the end of the Stalin era, the greatest conflict between Soviet government and national intellectuals acting in defence of their cultural heritage took place. In the 1950s the whole of Kirghizia refused to accept the condemnation of its national epic, *Manas*, by the Soviet authorities, and in the end *Manas* was rehabilitated. There was an unquestionable link between the intelligentsia liquidated in 1937–8 and the new elite, Soviet in appearance but profoundly nationalist in feeling. It is no accident that the Tadjik, Saddrudin

Aini, is regarded as the greatest contemporary poet of Central Asia. It is true that he denounced the pre-revolutionary social and political system, but at the same time the greater part of his work had been devoted to a recreation of the figure of Ahmad Donish, the father of reformism and modern nationalist ideas in Turkestan. It looks now as though it is in 'the most backward of all Muslim regions of the Empire', where national consciousness was slowest and least adept at finding its expression, that Turkic national pride has found its firmest and surest refuge.

17

Lamaistic Civilization in Tibet and Mongolia

In the preceding chapters the history of the western part of Central Asia, predominantly Turkish in its racial composition and Muslim and Iranian in its culture, has been traced from the disintegration of Chingiz Khan's empire down to the Russian annexation and the establishment of the five soviet republics which are an integral part of the USSR. The remaining four chapters describe the history of eastern Central Asia during the same period. Here, where Turks, Tibetans and Mongols mingle on the arid frontiers of China, Tibetan Buddhism has been a more significant factor than Islam (despite the Uighurs and the Dungans) while the presence of China has generally been the decisive factor in moulding the destinies of all these peoples.

In 1368 the Yüan dynasty was overthrown by the native Ming dynasty and the last Mongol emperor of China became a fugitive in the Gobi. By no means all the Mongols in China followed him. Many were incorporated into the resuscitated Chinese armies of the new regime where they provided a welcome addition of strength. Some also remained in administrative and diplomatic employment. It was thus under the Ming dynasty that the final sinification of the Mongols took place.[1]

During the Ming period (1368–1644) successive tribal confederacies in Mongolia struggled to reconstruct the Mongol polity and empire of the thirteenth century, but although several rulers came near to success the ultimate goal always eluded them. A major element in their failure was the Ming government

243

itself which steadily pursued a policy of setting tribe against tribe and chieftain against chieftain. The establishment of the Manchu dynasty in China (1644–1911) radically altered Mongol-Chinese relations. The likelihood of a second Mongol conquest of China (which under the Mings had been a possibility) disappeared entirely with Manchu expansion into the Chinese frontier-zone. This extension of Manchu power coincided with the gradual Russian advance across Siberia to Transbaikalia and the Mongols, overawed by Manchu and Russian artillery, were forced back into a steadily contracting (although still vast) area. Yet neither Manchu nor Russian encroachment on the Mongol homeland, nor the failure of Mongol leadership to combine in the face of these dangers, was the most significant development in Mongol history in the post-Yüan period. This was provided by the spread of Lamaistic Buddhism from Tibet throughout Mongolia which grafted Tibetan civilization upon alien Mongol traditions, thereby tending to transform, albeit very gradually, an aggressive and predatory society (with the warrior as its social ideal) into one where the contemplative life and acquiescence in a pre-ordained destiny shaped important areas of human relations.

During the period of Ming and Manchu rule in China the Mongols occupied four clearly defined areas: the area north of the Gobi in what is now the Mongolian People's Republic; Inner Mongolia south of the Gobi; the Koko-Nor region of Tibet, far to the south and the region west of the Gobi, which stretches into Jungaria. Under Chingiz Khan's successors the Mongol tribes had been divided into two wings, a left wing comprising the eastern Mongols (among whom the Khalkhas were the most important), ruled directly by the *khaqan*, and a right wing comprising the western Mongols such as the Ordos and Tümet tribes as well as the Oirots, all of whom were ruled on behalf of the *khaqan* by a *jinong* or viceroy, an office which soon became hereditary. With the fall of the Yüan dynasty the tribes which formed these two wings engaged in disastrous rivalry for the Yuan heritage in Mongolia, the capacity for discipline, cohesion and military organization which had characterized the tribes in the time of Chingiz Khan, his sons and grandsons, having almost entirely disappeared. These conflicts may have reflected a certain racial and cultural division, the eastern Mongols being more sinified while the western Mongols probably contained a considerable Turkish element.

During the second half of the fourteenth century the most important tribal confederacy among the Mongols was centred on western Mongolia and Jungaria, and was dominated by the Oirots. The evolution of the Oirots exemplifies the fluid course of tribal history in Central Asia. Early in the thirteenth century they had practised a semi-pastoral, semi-hunting economy in the region of the upper Yenisei and its tributaries; by the early fourteenth century they had become horse-breeders in the Altai; before the close of the fourteenth century they were making a bid for the Chingizkhanid inheritance and were to do so again in the seventeenth century. In 1399 they murdered Elbek, *khaqan* of the eastern Mongols and descendant of the Yüans, and for the next half century were masters of Jungaria, overawing the divided eastern Mongols and harrying their Turkish Uzbek and Kazakh neighbours to the west in the Semirechie as well as the Chaghatai rulers of Mughulistan. During the reign of their khan Esen (1439–56) the Oirots even raided China with immunity and in 1449 captured the Ming emperor Ying-tsung (1435–49), a feat which justified Esen's assumption of the title of *khaqan*. His death soon afterwards, however, led to a rapid decline of Oirot power. There followed a revival of the eastern Mongols under Dayan Khan (1470–1543), a descendant of Chingiz Khan, whose long reign gave to Mongolia a temporary unity unknown since the first Yuan emperors. So great was Dayan Khan's prestige among the tribes that he unwisely planned the succession regardless of the fissiparous trends of the past two centuries, and he nominated a grandson as *khaqan* and personal sovereign of the eastern Mongols and one of his sons as *jinong* of the western tribes. This settlement foreseeably floundered on the rock of traditional hostility between the two Mongol wings, but his empire was revived on a more modest scale by another grandson Anda, usually known as Altan Khan (1543–83), who based his power upon the loyalty of the western Mongol Ordos and Tümet tribes in what is now the Suiyüan province of Inner Mongolia. Altan Khan campaigned in Jungaria, in Koko-Nor and northern Tibet but his greatest efforts were directed against China, now incapable of serious resistance to an invader, and he was able to penetrate to the walls of Peking. Diplomacy restored what pusillanimity had lost, and the Ming emperor granted the khan the honorific title of 'Loyal and Obedient Prince' and a golden seal! Altan Khan's success against the Chinese was due to traditional nomadic mobility and tactical superiority, but despite the fact that his power rested on his tribal cavalry, he himself lived a semi-sedentary life at Kuku-khota (Kweisui) west of Kalgan. In addition to pastoral nomads, his subjects included many agriculturists, while the revenue he received from commercial activities of various kinds was probably little less important than the profits derived from marauding expeditions. Like his Chingizkhanid ancestors, he endeavoured to expand commerce in the territories under his control, and it is significant that his negotiations with the Chinese included arrangements for the establishment of fairs where surplus pastoral produce could be exchanged for Chinese commodities.

Altan Khan's power was based on tribes living close to the Chinese frontier and therefore more exposed than the Khalkhas or the Oirots to the blandishments of Chinese civilization. This may account for the encouragement which he gave to the re-introduction of the Tibetan form of Buddhism among his people, although an element of personal piety need not necessarily be excluded. As a result the close of the sixteenth century marked a sudden blossoming of Mongol culture under Tibetan influences. Nearly four hundred years after the thirteenth-century *Secret History of the Mongols*, literature sprang to life again with translations into Mongol of the Tibetan Buddhist *Kanjur* and *Tanjur* under the patronage of the Chahar Mongol prince, Ligdan (1603–34),[2] and with the composition of historical chronicles such as the *Altan Tobchi*, and the *Erdeni-yin Tobchi* of Sagang Sachen.[3]

Tibetan Buddhism had first reached the Mongols in the thirteenth century, though without taking root under a dynasty so eclectic in religious matters as the Chingizkhanids.[4] Chingiz

Khan never invaded Tibet although he fought the Tibetan Tanguts, but there is a tradition that he corresponded with the celebrated Sakya Pandita (1182–1251), abbot of the Sakya monastery which had been founded in the second half of the eleventh century and had soon established itself as a centre of religious learning. It was among the lamas of Sakya that the concept of a theocratic state such as was later to emerge with the Dalai Lamas, was first propounded and the Sakya Pandita himself combined with spiritual functions the day-to-day administration of extensive estates. Some time during the 1240s the Sakya Pandita was nominated viceroy of Tibet by the Mongol prince Godan, a son of the *khaqan* Ögetei and governor of Kansu. In 1253 his nephew Phagpa (1235–80) was granted similar authority by Qubilai, together with the title of *tisri*. Phagpa exercised great influence over Qubilai, and it was during this period that the Mongols first became familiar with Tibetan Buddhism. Phagpa provided the Mongols with an alternative script to the Uighur one adopted by Chingiz Khan and also undertook the internal re-organization of Tibet, neither Qubilai nor the later Yüan emperors apparently taking any interest in the country which they left in the charge of *tisris* who were invariably lamas.

The collapse of the Yüan dynasty was followed by the temporary disappearance of Buddhism among the Mongols. It also led to the restoration of the Tibetan monarchy (c.1350–c.1642). Tibetan relations with the Ming court were formal, not unfriendly but irregular and lacking the intimacy which had existed between the *tisris* and the Yüan dynasty. A tenuous connexion was maintained, however, by means of the Buddhist ecclesiastical hierarchy in both countries so that from time to time the Ming emperors received lama missions (viewed by the Chinese as acts of homage) and were able to intrigue in Tibetan affairs through lamas who had received Chinese honours and titles. Regular commercial relations were also maintained, Tibet's supply of tea coming from China. Meanwhile, the spiritual life of Tibet was being transformed through the work of Tsong Khapa (1357–1419), a reformer from Amdo (the Kum Bum monastery commemorates his birth-place). His aim was to

247

purify and rejuvenate Tibetan Buddhism and he founded the Gelugpa or 'Yellow Hat' sect which was eventually to establish the theocratic regime of the Dalai Lamas and to proselytize Mongolia.[5] Tsong Khapa's work was continued by his nephew Gedün Truppa (1391–1475) who founded the monastery of Tashilhunpo near Shigatse and who was identified posthumously as the First Dalai Lama. The Second Dalai Lama, incidentally, Gedün Gyatso (1476–1542), was also recognized only posthumously.

It was perhaps a combination of missionary zeal and political acumen which took the Third Dalai Lama, Sonam Gyatso (1543–88), to Mongolia where in 1578 he converted Altan Khan who first gave him the title of Dalai Lama which all his subsequent incarnations have held. Thereafter the Gelugpa sect spread rapidly in Mongolia, assisted by the foundation of numerous lamaseries (Erdeni Dzu, near Qaraqorum, was founded in 1586). Equally rapidly appeared that peculiar feature of Tibetan Buddhism in Mongolia – the proliferation of incarnations known as *khutukhtus* (the Mongol word means 'Blessed and Holy') and generally styled 'Living Buddhas' by later European writers. Like the lamaseries, the Mongolian *khutukhtus* were already established by the close of the sixteenth century.

Following Sonan Gyatso's death in 1588 at Kuku-khota, his incarnation was discovered in the person of a great-grandson of Altan Khan, the Fourth and only Mongol Dalai Lama, known by his Tibetan name of Yontem Gyatso (1589–1616).[6] When the latter went to Tibet in 1600 he sent another *khutukhtu* to Mongolia in compensation. It was by such means that powerful part-religious, part-political links were forged between the Gelugpa ecclesiastics in Tibet and the Mongol princes resulting both in the rapid spread of Buddhism among the Mongol tribes throughout Mongolia and the adjacent regions and in the complete triumph of the Gelugpa sect over all its rivals within Tibet itself. These links were to prove of crucial importance. In the early decades of the seventeenth century the Gelugpas themselves had been in real danger of extermination at the hands of the older, unreformed sects and it was only the far-sighted action of the reigning Dalai Lama in seeking military aid from the Mongols which ensured their survival and, ultimately, their supremacy.

It was the Fifth and greatest Dalai Lama, Ngawang Lobzang Gyatso (1617–82), who broke the vicious circle of sectarian rivalry by summoning to his aid Gusri Khan, ruler of the Qosot Mongols who had been infiltrating into Tsaidam and the Koko-Nor region since the beginning of the sixteenth century. Gusri Khan, a notable warrior and supporter of the Gelugpas, invaded Tibet in 1642, overthrew the monarchy and the Karmapa sect (chief rival of the Gelugpas), and proclaimed himself king in Lhasa, a title retained by his descendants until 1720. Gusri Khan died around 1655–6. By then, however, the Fifth Dalai Lama had been installed as undisputed spiritual ruler of Tibet and was, in addition, steadily absorbing all temporal authority into his own hands. Tireless in his efforts to swell the power and prestige of his office it was he who first began building the Potala on the site of Song-tsen Gampo's palace in Lhasa.

Ngawang Lobzang Gyatso established with the line of Gusri Khan (subsequently to be replaced by the Manchu rulers of China) that subtle and intangible relationship of priest and patron which originated in the understanding between Phagpa and Qubilai four centuries earlier and he also initiated a concordat between Tibet and the new Manchu regime in China by his visit to Peking in 1652. The Manchus were concerned with the control of the Mongol tribes on China's northern frontiers and were therefore anxious to have an understanding with their spiritual head.

But there was one action taken by the Fifth Dalai Lama, a profound scholar as well as an outstanding administrator, which – although doubtless unforeseen – was to prove a perpetual thorn in the flesh of his successors. This was his recognition of his teacher and abbot of Tashilhunpo, Lobzang Chökyi Gyaltsen (1569–1662), as an incarnation of the Bodhisattva Amitabha to whom he gave the title of Panchen Lama – the First or Fourth, according to disputed reckonings. In later times this incarnation often became a rallying-point for opponents (both Tibetan and Chinese) of the Dalai Lamas but theologically there could be no question of rivalry. Whichever incarnation was older was assumed to be tutor and mentor of the younger.

The Fifth Dalai Lama died in 1682 but vigorous government was maintained for some years by his reputed son, Sangye Gyatso, who was regent from 1679 until his death in 1705 and who concealed the death of the Fifth Dalai Lama by announcing that he had withdrawn from the affairs of the world in order to follow a life of meditation. Eventually, however, the fraud was uncovered and the Sixth Dalai Lama, Tsang-yang Gyatso, was enthroned in 1697 (he had been identified as early as 1683). The new Dalai Lama rapidly acquired a reputation for debauchery which may have meant that he (and perhaps the regent) subscribed to Padmaistic Tantric practices abhorrent to the Gelugpas, but his activities precipitated the conflict over Tibet between the Manchus and the western Mongol Oirots, now deeply engaged in a protracted struggle for control of the Chinese borderlands. Tsang-yang Gyatso's ineptitude tempted Lhabzang, great-grandson of Gusri Khan and nominal king of Tibet, to overthrow the regent and, in 1706, to depose the Dalai Lama himself – although not without provoking bitter resentment, even among those who had deplored the latter's vices. Between 1706 and 1717 Lhabzang was master of Tibet but his position was such that he felt the need to come to terms with the Manchu emperor K'ang-hsi (1661–1722) partly out of fear of the Oirot menace to the north. Whatever his motives were in drawing closer to Peking, it triggered off the very event which it was intended to prevent for in 1717 the Oirot ruler, Tsevan-Rabtan, successfully invaded Tibet and in the course of the struggle Lhabzang was killed.

At first the Oirots were not unwelcome to Lhabzang's numerous enemies – many of whom considered his treatment of the Dalai Lama sacrilegious – but the savagery of the Oirots who sacked Lhasa and desecrated the Potala soon produced a violent reaction. When K'ang-hsi intervened to prevent the addition of Tibet to the extensive Oirot empire he was assuming the role of a liberator. In 1718 his armies were beaten back by the Oirots.

but in 1720 they captured Lhasa with only slight resistance – the presence with the Manchu army of the Seventh Dalai Lama, Kezang Gyatso (1708–58), greatly enhancing the emperor's popularity. In this way Tibet became a Manchu protectorate, and in the pacification which followed a further period of upheaval between 1723 and 1728, a pattern for Manchu-Tibetan relations was established which survived (with some modification) down to the twentieth century. This relationship was based upon the presence in Lhasa of two Manchu *ambans* (comparable in their functions to the Residents attached to the courts of Indian rulers in British India), supported by a small Manchu garrison. Their task was to observe, to advise, and to uphold the prestige and rights of their imperial master in every possible way. Throughout the eighteenth century Manchu control over Tibetan affairs tended to increase, especially after the Gurkha invasion of western Tibet in 1791–2 when the position of the *ambans* was immeasurably strengthened. They were placed on terms of equality with the Dalai and Panchen Lamas (now forbidden to memorialize the emperor direct) and they were made responsible for defence and foreign relations. Foreign trade and the entry of strangers into the country were now strictly controlled, and so was the nomination of the higher ecclesiastical dignitaries who previously had often been selected from the families of the nobility.

Enforcement of these regulations would have ultimately converted Tibet into a Manchu province (albeit a remote one) but the military decline of the empire during the nineteenth century, the disintegration of the imperial system, the great rebellions in the western and north-western provinces and, above all, the role of the European Powers in Chinese affairs resulted in Tibet being left to look after itself. Thus Tibetan indigenous institutions remained intact despite the increased power of the *ambans* and even outlived the Manchu dynasty itself. Yet Manchu neglect of Tibet during the nineteenth century did not lead to any immediate revival of the Dalai Lama's authority. None of the Dalai Lamas from the Ninth to the Twelfth inclusive reached maturity (perhaps due to foul play) and real power was therefore exercised by a succession of regents. In these circumstances, the

Panchen Lamas at Tashilhunpo (whom the Manchus assumed to possess temporal jurisdiction over the neighbouring districts) preserved a tradition of independence and hostility towards the Lhasa government which was to develop most dramatically during the upheavals of the twentieth century.

The establishment of a Manchu protectorate over Tibet early in the eighteenth century had its counterpart further north in the gradual expansion of Manchu suzerainty over Mongolia. For the Mongols themselves, the most important event of the seventeenth century was the rise of the Oirot empire in western Mongolia and Jungaria with its centre in the upper Ili valley. The Oirots had not been alone in making a bid for Mongol hegemony but they came nearest to success. Early in the century the Chahar ruler, Ligdan (1603–34), in an endeavour to reassert the idea of a great khan ruling over all the Mongol tribes, had established himself as a potential empire-builder close to the Chinese frontier until he was dislodged by the Manchus in 1634. Next, the Tushetu Khan Gombodorji, grandson of Abadai Khan who had introduced Buddhism to the Khalkhas, formed a Khalkha confederacy north of the Gobi in Outer Mongolia. With him emerged a new variation on the theme of priest and patron, his own son becoming the first Jebtsundamba Khutukhtu of Urga.[7] Defeated by the Oirots in 1688, the Khalkhas were compelled to seek the protection of the Manchus, and in 1691 the Jebtsundamba Khutukhtu and his brother, the new Tushetu Khan, submitted to K'ang-hsi at Dolun-Nor. Thereafter the division of the Chinese frontier-region into 'Inner' and 'Outer' zones was exemplified on its Mongolian section by the distinction between those Mongol tribes living close to the zone of cultivation, and firmly controlled by the Manchus, and those like the Khalkhas, whose relationship with their suzerain was more remote and had less effect upon every-day life. That the eastern Mongols, and in particular the Khalkhas, preferred Manchu suzerainty rather than subordination to the Oirots decisively affected the future history of the Mongol people as a whole, since thereafter it became impossible for a Mongol confederacy outside the Chinese frontier to unite against the Manchus within. Thus, despite the ferocity of the Manchu-

Oirot conflict, there was never any likelihood of the Oirots replacing the Manchus as rulers of China. In 1691, however, when the Khalkhas submitted at Dolun-Nor, the Oirot threat to China still seemed a serious one.

The Oirot confederacy of the seventeenth and eighteenth centuries was formed from the same western Mongol tribes which had formed the nucleus of the Oirot confederacy of the fourteenth and fifteenth centuries, and Muslim writers do not seem to distinguish between them.[8] The foundations of this new nomadic power were laid by the great warrior Khotokhotsin, the *khungtayji* Batur (1634–53), but it was his son Galdan (c.1644–97) who made the Oirots masters of the greater part of Central Asia. Galdan spent his early life in Lhasa training to become a lama but by 1673 he was back in the Ili valley and in possession of his father's inheritance, which he soon extended to Lake Balkhash in the west, to the Siberian forests in the north and at the expense of the Khalkhas in the east. The conquest of Koko-Nor in 1677 brought Tibet within his reach while in 1678 his suzerainty was recognized in the Tarim basin. Aggression against the Khalkhas, however, resulted in conflicts with the Manchus and in 1696 he was defeated by K'ang-hsi in a battle south of Urga where Manchu artillery decided the issue.

Galdan was not defeated by the Chinese but by the Manchus, though ever since their capture of Peking in 1644 the latter (a Tungusic people like the Jurchids) had come to represent Chinese civilization *vis-à-vis* the frontier peoples. In the initiative which they took in Tibet, eastern Turkestan and Mongolia they were to outdo the most aggressive of native dynasties. Their predecessors, the Mings, had never possessed sufficient strength to make much headway on the frontier and had directed their diplomatic efforts to the perpetuation of tribal divisions through diplomacy, while pursuing a traditional policy of demanding submission from the more vulnerable or accommodating tribes. The tribute-bearing missions from the latter brought China no material benefit and involved her in great expense, but she was content with the prestige which they were supposed to confer. The nomads, however, having little to fear from the Ming regime, profited from the lavish gifts (in reality bribes) which they received from the Chinese in recompense for their 'tribute', and which far exceeded in value anything which they themselves had to offer. These missions stimulated commerce between the two economies, pastoral and agricultural, which were really complementary, thereby discreetly bringing the nomads into further contact with Chinese culture.[9] The Mings also tried to promote Buddhism among the nomads, a less hazardous means of pacifying warlike peoples than the despatch of costly military expeditions. In the sixteenth century one shrewd Chinese frontier-official, observing Altan Khan's preoccupation with Buddhism, reported to Peking that 'we must promote the diffusion of Buddhism and help it in every way'.[10] The Manchus followed the Mings in encouraging tribute missions and the spread of Buddhism, although such methods had little success with the Oirots. Neither Galdan's defeat in 1696 nor his death in 1697 toppled the Oirot empire, but during the reign of his nephew and successor, Tsevan-Rabtan (1697–1727), Oirot pressure swung away from the east towards Tibet, the Tarim basin and the Kazakh steppes. The Oirots remained, however, a constant threat to China's frontiers, so that the Manchus ultimately had no option but to accept the implications of a direct confrontation. The final destruction of the Oirot empire came in 1758 when the last Oirot ruler, Amur-Sana, was defeated by the Manchu emperor, Ch'ien-lung (1735–96), after a hard-fought campaign over a vast area which had involved the Manchus in maintaining an enormously extended line of communications. Amur-Sana died a refugee in Russian Tobolsk and the Manchus took a savage vengeance on his people. Over a million Oirots (the figure is, of course, almost certainly an exaggeration) of both sexes and all ages were reputed to have been massacred, only a small number escaping to their kinsmen, the Volga Kalmyks.[11] In the upper Ili valley, the heart of the former Oirot empire, the Manchus founded Kuldja as a military colony to which they deported a large number of Chinese convicts and some genuine Chinese settlers, as well as Muslim Dungans from Kansu and Shansi. After 1771 the nomadic element in Jungaria increased slightly as a result of the return of some Kalmyks from Russia,[12] but it did not affect the newly established distribution of power in Jungaria which was the result of the recent decimation of the nomad population during the course of the Oirot-Manchu struggle and the merciless pacification which followed it.

It was the Oirot threat to China which led the Manchus to embark upon these costly and difficult campaigns, but the outcome produced incalculable effects upon the subsequent history of eastern Central Asia, including a legacy of frontier-problems which still remain in dispute today. First, so long as their military power remained undiminished, the Manchus brought peace to the frontier-regions of China. They established a protectorate over Tibet and absorbed both Jungaria and the Tarim basin as far as the Pamirs into their empire, governing these distant dependencies through colonial-type administrations. They established close control over the eastern or 'Inner' Mongols and a vague suzerainty over the western and northern Mongols, which resulted in a tendency among the latter, restless under Manchu tutelage, to turn to the advancing power of Russia for protection. Above all, their policy sharply accentuated the historic division between 'Inner' and 'Outer' Mongolia. With all the frontier-peoples, but especially with the Mongols, the Manchus assumed an ambivalent attitude. Mongols and Manchus had much in common: both belonged to the 'barbarian' world outside the pale of Chinese civilization; both (alone among invaders) had conquered the whole of China; both were frontier peoples with considerable knowledge of each other since some eastern Mongol tribes had served as auxiliaries of the Manchus. Yet it was the Mongols' past which also made them objects of suspicion to the Manchus. If the Mongols had conquered China once they might do so again in the future. Manchus and Mongols had once been allies but they might well become rivals in the future. Indicative of Manchu awareness of this danger was the existence, even before the conquest of China was completed, of a Mongolian Office (*Mêng-ku Ya-mên*) which in 1638 became the Board of Frontier Dependencies (*Li Fan Yuan*).[13] Pursuing a similar frontier-policy to the Mings – but from a position of strength – the Manchus manipulated Mongol tribal politics by taking advantage of traditional

255

feuds and rivalries, and by boosting the prestige of theocratic institutions at the expense of secular Mongol leadership. The first Jebtsundamba Khutukhtu of Urga, who had been instrumental in bringing the Khalkhas into the Manchu tributary system, had been a high-ranking Mongol prince, and so was his successor. But the possession of such spiritual authority by a member of one of the great princely families of Mongolia immeasurably increased that family's ambitions and capacity for uniting the clans and tribes under its leadership, and hence the Manchus quickly recognized the danger of aristocratic Mongol incarnations. After the death of the second Jebtsundamba Khutukhtu in 1757, the discovery of incarnations among Mongol princes was forbidden. All subsequent Jebtsundamba Khutukhtus were located in Tibet.

The Manchu emperors proved easy masters and their suzerainty in Mongolia, as in Tibet, was largely nominal. It is impossible to generalize about Manchu interference in Mongolian affairs, but the mailed fist was usually carefully concealed in the silk glove. The Mongols were regarded by the Manchus as useful auxiliaries and, in theory, were carefully segregated from the Chinese. Chinese entry into Mongol territory was limited to officials and traders possessing authorized permits. As vassals of the Manchu emperors, the Mongol princes had no organic relationship with the Chinese state, and their vassalage was little felt since they retained the two principal attributes of sovereignty – the administration of justice and the collection of revenue. Their tribute-bearing missions to the imperial court were occasions of happy expectation rather than humiliation, since the outcome was invariably the despatch of valuable Chinese luxuries and novelties from Peking into Mongolia. Moreover, there was an additional reason why the Manchu connexion was not so distasteful to the Mongol princes as might have been expected. The economic systems of Mongolia and northern China – extensive pastoralism and intensive cultivation – have always been complementary to each other and after the Mongol economy had provided Mongol society with its basic requirements – food, clothing, shelter, fuel and transport – there was usually a surplus of wool, hides, leather and meat to exchange for such Chinese commodities as tea, cloth and ironware. For the Mongol princes therefore, participation in commercial relations with China became an extremely attractive proposition once it had become clear that the Manchu regime itself was far too powerful to tolerate the frontier-raiding of former times. A taste for the amenities of civilization developed quickly among members of the Mongol aristocracy as a result of friendly relations with the Manchu court, closer contacts with the Chinese way of life and under the influence of Tibetan culture, and this taste could only be satisfied by an increase in their purchasing power. The Mongol princes, therefore, began evading the restrictions placed by the Manchus on the movement of their Chinese subjects in Mongolia in order to encourage Chinese traders to bring their wares to the Mongol encampments and to attract Chinese artisans and craftsmen to Mongolia to build palaces, temples and monasteries.

There was, however, a limit to northern China's ability to absorb Mongolia's surplus produce so long as inadequate communications prevented the establishment of commerce with more distant provinces of the empire, so the Mongol princes, in search of fresh sources of revenue to pay for their requirements, introduced Chinese cultivators into those parts of 'Inner' Mongolia which were suitable for agriculture (often the very parts which had hitherto been used for winter pastures).[14] As a result, by the nineteenth century a new relationship had grown up between Mongols and Chinese (the Manchus, forbidden to engage in trade, had no part in this relationship). The Chinese settlers, gaining a tight grip upon the economy of 'Inner' Mongolia, established a peculiarly oppressive hold over their Mongol neighbours. The Mongol herdsmen were chronically indebted to Chinese money-lenders while their princes, also in debt, were forced to raise more and more revenue, which in turn meant further colonization.[15] The result was intense hardship for the herdsmen who, driven from good pastures to poorer ones and forced to change from extensive to restricted grazing, were compelled to reduce the numbers of their beasts, generally by selling them at a loss to Chinese traders. The export of Mongol produce to China, as well as the import of Chinese commodities in return, became the monopoly of Chinese merchant-houses which also monopolized the transport-system and provided credit facilities at exorbitant rates of interest.

These developments were accompanied by other unpalatable changes in Mongol-Chinese relations. After the beginning of the nineteenth century the extent of Chinese colonization in Mongol areas was so great as to necessitate the appointment of Chinese officials to administer the colonists, thus breaking down the traditional Mongol administrative and legal framework. At the same time, the Imperial government began to replace both the Manchu bannermen and the once-famous Mongol cavalry by despised Chinese troops who nevertheless enjoyed an over-whelming advantage in possessing European-manufactured firearms. In 'Outer' Mongolia the position was different, but even there– around Urga, Kobdo and Uliassutai (the seats of the Manchu *ambans*) – Chinese colonists appeared. Although these latter were minute islands of Chinese commerce in an ocean of nomadic pastoralism, and enjoyed none of the advantages of the colonists in 'Inner' Mongolia who were able to radiate out-wards from a well-established belt of cultivation, they never-theless controlled much of the 'Outer' Mongolian economy by the end of the Manchu period.[16]

This situation explains both Mongol hatred for the Chinese and the readiness with which, at the beginning of the twentieth century, the Mongols of 'Outer' Mongolia turned to Russia for protection. Mongol history in the twentieth century must be interpreted in relation to this strong anti-Chinese feeling. Under Manchu rule the Mongols – notwithstanding the special rela-tionship they enjoyed with the Manchu dynasty – became the victims of a peculiarly oppressive colonial system based upon ruthless economic exploitation that had no mitigating concept of imperial obligation.

The growth of this sombre relationship between Mongol and Chinese should not be allowed to obscure the positive achieve-ment of the Manchu period – the triumph of Tibetan civilization in Mongolia. During the Manchu protectorate, Mongolia and Tibet witnessed the zenith of Lamaistic civilization, characterized in Tibet by the theocracy of the Dalai Lamas and in Mongolia by the cult of *khutukhtus*. In both countries the lamasery with its great estates, the yellow-robed celibate lama with his prayer-wheel and the prevalence of a ritual in which Buddhism and Shamanism were inextricably mixed, gave a distinct religious tone to a society where every family aspired to have at least one son a lama. Lamaistic society in Tibet has been discussed too often to require further interpretation here. It was first described in detail for European readers by the Jesuit Ippolito Desideri and other Roman Catholic missionaries early in the eighteenth century, accounts which were supplemented in the nineteenth and twentieth centuries by those of Anglo-Indian officials concerned with Indian frontier-problems, and of an increasing number of European explorers and specialists in Tibetan culture.[17] Some praised Lamaistic society for its emphasis on the spiritual life embodied in its theocratic state-system. Others identified it with ignorance, laziness and apathy, and with a feudal system in which the monasteries combined with the secular aristocracy to exploit the cultivators and herdsmen. Most observers stressed that Lamaism was a degenerate form of Buddhism far removed from the spirit of the early Buddhist faith, and noted the problems arising from extensive celibacy such as monasticism in Tibet and Mongolia demanded. Critics of Lamaistic society did not always recognize that in artificially depressing the birth-rate Lamaism contributed towards giving both Tibetans and Mongols – notwithstanding the rigours of the harsh climatic conditions in which both peoples live – a higher standard of living than that of their more prolific neighbours.

It is more rewarding to turn to the positive achievements of Lamaism. One indication of the enduring quality of Tibetan civilization has been its capacity to inspire and sustain a distinct tradition in the visual arts, especially in painting.[18] Another has been the vigour with which it spread to distant Mongolia, taming a people formerly objects of justifiable terror to their neighbours. From the middle of the sixteenth century to the beginning of the twentieth century Mongol society underwent a profound change as a result of the influence of Tibetan culture.

259

The adoption of Tibetan religion and ritual, the spread of Tibetan customs and manners, the acquisition of a knowledge of the Tibetan language and of Tibetan literature among the literate classes and the appearance in Mongolia of Tibetan arts and iconography produced a cumulative effect which, taken *in toto*, involved a total transformation of traditional Mongol society. The principal agency in bringing about this gradual revolution was the lamasery. No doubt the occupants of the latter were often idle and ignorant (the same may be said of the monasteries of mediaeval Europe) but, taking a long view, the role of the Mongolian lamasery as a civilizing agent was of the greatest significance, contributing towards a softening of manners and a diffusion of literacy, providing educational facilities of a modest kind, encouraging learning and the arts, and creating a limited demand for craftsmanship and skilled labour. Lamaseries also participated in a varied range of economic activities. They owned countless flocks and herds. They encouraged cultivation. They engaged extensively in commerce, turned money-lenders, and even played a part in the organization of the caravan-trade.

It has been said that the spread of Lamaistic civilization into Mongolia (supposedly with the blessing of the Ming and Manchu dynasties) resulted in the degeneration of the Mongols but their conversion to Buddhism certainly did little to reduce their belligerence – as the history of the Oirots clearly shows. By the end of the sixteenth century traditional Mongol society was already disintegrating under the strain of constant tribal warfare. The traditional culture was bankrupt and the social system, dominated by hereditary princes descended from Chingiz Khan, was fast becoming ossified, a tendency which the Manchus encouraged. In such circumstances Lamaistic civilization acted as a rejuvenator, injecting much-needed stability into society. It enabled the rule of a rigid hereditary aristocracy to be supplemented by a parallel ecclesiastical hierarchy, wherein the pursuit of a career open to talent as well as to birth permitted a certain amount of flexibility and social mobility comparable to that of mediaeval Christendom. Even more important, throughout the Manchu period Lamaistic civilization bound the

Mongols together, giving them a common cultural identity by means of which they were able to resist the pressure of sinification. Despite a natural tendency to gravitate towards Chinese culture the Mongols of the Manchu period were able to reorientate themselves towards Tibetan culture, thereby preserving their national identity.

The changes brought about by the introduction of Buddhism into Mongolia did not entirely efface older traditions and ways of life. The Mongols remained almost wholly nomadic in spite of the building of lamaseries and a few towns. Urga (modern Ulan-Bator) was founded in 1649 but in 1820 it was still largely a city of tents with a population not exceeding 7,000 of whom one-fifth were lamas.[19] Even smaller were Uliassutai and Kobdo, garrison-towns with resident *ambans* originally founded by the Manchus to control the western Khalkhas and Oirots. Notwithstanding Buddhist injunctions against violence and the taking of life, the Mongols continued to indulge in desultory fighting (when their Manchu suzerains did not intervene to prevent it) as an alternative to the traditional pastimes of hunting, wrestling, horse-racing and archery. Some European travellers in Mongolia during the Manchu period, such as Przhevalsky, were far from impressed with what they saw there and their accounts are largely taken up with describing the prevailing poverty, ignorance and superstition.[20] Others, however, were more impressed by the sleek herds, by the signs of comfort and sometimes even luxury in the encampments, and especially by the proud bearing of the Mongols themselves. The Russian explorer G. N. Potanin, writing in 1881, was most favourably struck by the positive achievements of Lamaistic culture:

What we find them [the Mongols] possessed of shows that, even in so poor and desert a country as Mongolia, people can create for themselves the conditions of a peaceful and cultural existence. The traveller is astounded by the sight of these nomad monasteries, nomad altars with their numerous pantheons, nomad libraries, transportable temples of felt several fathoms high, primary schools housed in nomad tents, nomad physicians, nomad hospitals at the mineral-water springs—all these are things that you by no means expect to find in the nomad life. But as regards primary education the Mongols are incontestably the first nomad people in the world. They are no savages like the Turkomans or even our own Kirghiz [i.e. Kazakhs]. Whoever has seen both peoples, Mongols and Kirghiz, must involuntarily wish to compare them. The Mongol princes are from an Asiatic point of view highly educated. They are often able to speak several languages of the Empire to which they belong, can write in Mongol and Tibetan, and sometimes even learn Sanskrit; many of them have dwelt for a year or more in Peking, the capital of this country. They rival one another in the building of monasteries and temples, in enriching them with costly vessels and metal statues of the Gods, the mere transport of which costs much money; they seek to acquire books. Amongst our own Kirghiz the Sultans are little educated, they carry on their correspondence through hired secretaries—runaway Tatars or Turkestanis—for they consider hunting with *berkuts* (golden eagles) and falcons the only occupation worthy of their position. The Kirghiz Sultans have neither libraries nor schools.

Life among the Mongols proceeds quietly, their ways are gentle, brutal treatment of women and children is unheard of; crimes, especially murders, are of rare occurrence. . . . The foreigners can travel in safety throughout the country, Russian salesmen go alone from camp to camp with their goods, nor ever complain of injury.[21]

Potanin may have been guilty of some exaggeration – it is interesting to note that another great explorer, Douglas Carruthers, took the opposite point of view and considered the way of life of the Muslim Kazakhs (whom he termed Kirghiz, as was customary in his day) far superior to that of the Buddhist Mongols[22] but Potanin's tribute to the influence of Tibetan civilization cannot be wholly disregarded. The conversion of the Mongols to Lamaistic Buddhism, closely followed by the establishment of numerous monastic foundations throughout Mongolia, resulted in the diffusion over a vast area of a distinctive civilization which, at least to some extent, tamed a society hitherto dominated by the ideals of the warrior, gave it new values, enriched its outlook, stimulated delight in the visual arts, spread some degree of literacy and provided its new readers with a written Mongolian literature. In all these respects the role of the lamasery, whether in Tibet or Mongolia, was strikingly similar to that of the Christian monasteries of early mediaeval Europe.

18

Tibet and Great Power Rivalry

The last phase of Tibetan history began with the despatch by the British East India Company of missions across the Himalayas; Warren Hastings sent George Bogle to the third Panchen Lama, Lobsang Palden Yeshe (1730–80), at Tashilhunpo in 1774–5, and Bogle's mission was followed by that of Samuel Turner in 1783 and that of Thomas Manning in 1811. None of these missions had any permanent effect upon the subsequent course of Anglo-Tibetan relations, although they did provide limited information about the unknown country north of the Company's possessions in Bengal. In retrospect, however, they mark the first stage of the 'opening' of Tibet.[1]

It was during the second half of the nineteenth century that Tibet became an object of increasing interest to the Indian Government (despite the disapproval of the British Legation in Peking), partly as a result of mounting Russophobia following the Russian annexation of Kokand in 1867.

In 1861 the British established treaty-relations with Sikkim which was a vassal-state of the Lhasa government, so that the Tibetans were bound to try to terminate the 1861 agreement whenever they felt strong enough to coerce the Sikkim Durbar. In 1876 an article in the Sino-British Convention of Chefoo specified Chinese protection for a British exploratory mission into Tibet; in 1885 a mission was formed under Colman Macaulay, but in 1886 it was disbanded as a condition of Chinese recognition of the British annexation of Upper Burma, which followed the Third Burmese War. The cancellation of this

263

mission seems to have given the Tibetans the impression that the British were afraid of the Chinese, for in 1888 they entered Sikkim and constructed a fortress at Lingtu. The British promptly expelled the Tibetans from Lingtu in the same year, and in 1890 a Sino-British convention, signed by the Viceroy of India and the Manchu *Amban* of Lhasa, recognized the British protectorate over Sikkim and demarcated the frontier between Sikkim and Tibet. In 1893 representatives of the British and Chinese governments met at Darjeeling and agreed to the opening of a trade-mart at Yatung on the Tibetan side of the border, on or before 1 May 1894. The Tibetans protested that the Chinese had no right to make this arrangement without consulting them beforehand yet they refused to negotiate directly with the British, maintaining that the conduct of Tibetan foreign relations was the responsibility of the Chinese. At Yatung no mart was established and the Chinese were unable, even if they had been willing, to coerce the Tibetans.

Meanwhile, in 1895 the local government of Bengal urged upon the Indian Government the occupation of the Chumbi valley, a strip of Tibetan territory between Sikkim and Bhutan (which had become a British protectorate in 1865), in order to compel the Tibetans to fulfil the obligations which the Chinese had agreed to on their behalf. This was the policy finally adopted during the viceroyalty of Lord Curzon (1899–1905) who sanctioned the despatch of the Younghusband expedition. Several factors influenced Curzon in his decision to adopt an aggressive policy towards Tibet. First, there was his fear of Russian intrigue in Lhasa (stimulated by the reception of the Dalai Lama's Buriat tutor by Tzar Nicholas II in 1900[2]). Then the Tibetan action in Sikkim in 1885 had never been punished. Finally, since Chinese suzerainty over Tibet appeared to have no practical significance, the Tibetans had to be coerced into accepting the 1890–3 agreements. The objectives of the mission, therefore, were to establish British prestige in Lhasa upon a proper footing, to ensure a permanent diplomatic link between Calcutta and Lhasa (thereby avoiding the confusion and pre-varications of past decades) and, finally, to open the Tibetan tea-market to British planting interests.

TIBET AND GREAT POWER RIVALRY

The story of the Younghusband expedition, really a commercial mission with a sufficient military escort to impose terms on the Tibetans if they should prove recalcitrant, has been described by British writers, including Sir Francis Younghusband himself, in considerable detail. The approach of the mission did nothing to make the Tibetans more willing to negotiate and by April 1904 the mission had occupied Gyantse, one of the few comparatively large towns in Tibet, while the Tibetans continued to resist the British terms. After desultory fighting in which some 1,700 Tibetans were killed, Younghusband led his forces into Lhasa on 3 August 1904. As a military exploit the advance had been remarkably easy since the Tibetans lacked both the weapons and discipline necessary to withstand European-trained troops equipped with modern firearms. In Lhasa Younghusband negotiated a Convention with the regent and abbot of the Ganden monastery, the Tri Rimpoche, which was signed on 7 September 1904 in the presence of the Manchu *Amban*. The Thirteenth Dalai Lama, Nga-wang Lob-sang Tup-den Gya-tso (1875–1933), had already fled to Urga in Outer Mongolia. The Convention of Lhasa imposed upon Tibet an indemnity of seventy-five lakhs of rupees to be paid in seventy-five annual instalments (reduced almost immediately to twenty-five lakhs), British occupation of the Chumbi valley for three years, and the opening of trade-marts at Gyantse and Gartok. These terms appeared to envisage ultimately some form of British protectorate yet within a short space of time after Younghusband's departure from Lhasa British policy had reverted to the recognition of Manchu (i.e. Chinese) suzerainty. The cause of this *volte face* was the Anglo-Russian convention of 1907 which specifically concerned Iran, Afghanistan and Tibet, and in which Britain and Russia agreed to abstain from direct relations with Tibet and to recognize Chinese suzerainty. Anglo-Tibetan commercial agreements already in force were to continue; British and Russian Buddhist subjects were permitted to have dealings with Tibetan ecclesiastics on purely spiritual matters. Startling as this change of British policy was, it had much to recommend it at that time. Tibet was a power-vacuum which Britain could neither annex

265

nor convert into a protectorate, partly on account of the financial liabilities involved and the strength of anti-expansionist feeling in Britain but principally because of Russian hostility to further British penetration into Central Asia. Similarly, a Russian advance into Tibet would arouse comparable hostility in England. On the other hand, Britain had nothing to fear from a revival of Chinese suzerainty over Tibet since the moribund empire of the Manchus was itself in a state of disintegration.

Meanwhile the Chinese themselves had reacted with remark-able energy (considering the internal state of China herself) to the British advance on Lhasa – reasserting their former position as suzerains in a manner comparable to the administrative changes which followed the Nepalese invasion of 1791–2. Within three days of the signing of the Anglo-Tibetan con-vention in Lhasa, the Chinese government proclaimed that the Dalai Lama was nothing more than the spiritual head of the Yellow Church while the *Amban* in Lhasa possessed complete temporal authority. Recognizing in the Tibetan indemnity to Britain and the British occupation of the Chumbi valley the key to Britain's new relationship with the Tibetans, the Chinese government promulgated an Imperial Decree in November 1905 for the immediate repayment by China of the Tibetan indemnity, which was followed by the British evacuation of the Chumbi valley. China then took the initiative in earnest. In 1908 a Chinese army under the command of General Chao Erh-feng invaded Tibet and captured Batang, while a new *Amban*, Lien-yu, made his way to Lhasa. As frontier commissioner in eastern Tibet, Chao Erh-feng stripped the lamaseries of their temporal authority, and replaced Tibetan local authorities by Chinese district magistrates in an attempt to separate the eastern provinces from the Lhasa government. During 1908–9 he brought his campaign to a successful conclusion with the capture of Chamdo, Markham, Draya and Derge, and in February 1910 entered Lhasa. At the first news of the Chinese invasion the Dalai Lama had again fled to Urga. From there he made his way to Peking where he was received as a subordinate vassal by the emperor and the empress-dowager, Tzu Hsi. In December 1909 he returned to Lhasa but his relations with

Lien-yu were strained from the outset and on the day when Chao Ehr-feng's troops occupied his capital he fled into India.

The Manchu conquest of Tibet between 1908 and 1910 was the last military undertaking of a dying empire. It did not, in fact, initiate a Chinese occupation of the country but rather precipitated the end of the traditional relationship between the Dalai Lamas and China's Manchu rulers. Between the declaration of the Chinese Republic in 1912 and the Communist invasion of Tibet in 1950, Tibet was *de facto* independent, although the Chinese Republic always maintained that Tibet was an integral part of China. As early as 12 April 1912, President Yuan Shih-k'ai proclaimed that Tibet, Sinkiang and Mongolia were Chinese and were to be treated on the same basis as the Chinese provinces; Tibet was allotted seats in the National Assembly and the black bar in the five-coloured flag of the Republic represented Tibet.

It was the arrival of the news of the revolution in Peking late in 1911 which led directly to the expulsion of the Chinese from Tibet: the Chinese garrison in Lhasa began to mutiny; some Chinese troops deserted; others began to loot Tibetan property. This provoked the Tibetans and sporadic fighting began whereever there were Chinese garrisons. For a time General Chung Ying, Lien-yu's successor as *Amban*, maintained a precarious foothold in the capital. The British were requested to mediate but refused. At last a compromise settlement was reached through the good offices of the Nepalese government, and towards the end of 1912 the Chinese troops were shipped back to China via Calcutta. The Dalai Lama returned to Tibet in 1912 and re-entered Lhasa in January 1913. Sporadic fighting continued between Tibetan and Chinese troops in the east until 1919. On the whole, the Tibetans retained the initiative, and were able to make the Yangtze their north-eastern frontier and prevent any restoration of Chinese authority west of it, their success being partly due to their acquisition of a small quantity of modern arms supplied by Britain between 1914 and 1916, and partly to the continuing chaos within China itself.

In 1913–14 the British endeavoured to clarify the status of Tibet in a conference at Simla attended by Tibetan and Chinese as well as British plenipotentiaries. The conference achieved little, due to the refusal of the Chinese government to ratify the final agreement, but from these discussions emerged the concept of an 'Inner' and 'Outer' Tibet comparable to that of 'Inner' and 'Outer' Mongolia enunciated in the Sino-Russian declaration of 1913. 'Inner' Tibet – the region bordering Kansu, Szechuan and Yunnan – was incorporated into China. 'Outer' Tibet – the remainder of the country administered from Lhasa – enjoyed virtual independence under an informal British protectorate, since the Thirteenth Dalai Lama, a shrewd politician and bitterly hostile to the Chinese, was quite content to see Tibet draw closer to its powerful southern neighbour. Thus by the end of the First World War Britain had acquired with very little effort a footing in Tibet equal to anything envisaged by Curzon or Younghusband and thereafter Anglo-Tibetan relations developed smoothly and amicably thanks to the goodwill of the Dalai Lama and the discretion of the British officials posted in Lhasa, notably Sir Charles Bell and F. M. Bailey.

It was Bell who described the rule of the Thirteenth Dalai Lama as being 'far more orderly than the government of those parts of Tibetan territory which are occupied and administered by China; it is far more orderly than Chinese administration in China itself'.[3] One of the greatest figures in Tibetan history, he faced internal problems which, in part at least, arose from his friendship with the British. This friendship brought about the appearance of certain elements of western civilization in Tibet, which unnerved the more conservative elements in Tibetan society. In fact, changes were on a very small scale and could not be compared with contemporary reforms in Turkey, Iran or even Afghanistan, yet for most Tibetans they must have seemed very great. A telegraph line was constructed from Gyantse to Lhasa; a small hydro-electric plant was installed in the capital; in 1924 a small English school was opened in Gyantse for the children of wealthy Tibetans and four Tibetan schoolboys were sent to Rugby. A small number of Europeans were permitted to enter the country and attempts were made to establish a *gendarmerie* in Lhasa and a small modern army. The latter, officered by lay nobles, brought the traditional conflict between the nobility and the monks into the open once more, for now that the Dalai Lama possessed an army officered by the nobility, he could challenge the pretensions of the turbulent lamaseries of Drepung, Sera and Gaden. Nor did the Thirteenth Dalai Lama, wilful and overbearing as he was, improve matters by his harsh treatment of the Sixth Panchen Lama, the mild Chökyi Nyima, who became a fugitive in China and Mongolia.

Between 1925 and his death in 1933 the Dalai Lama's enthusiasm for the British connection steadily cooled, although he showed no increase of friendship for Republican China, represented by the neighbouring warlord-governors of Szechuan and Chinghai (Sining). On the whole he had been disappointed by the British. He had found their support to be half-hearted: he had expected them to compel China to ratify the Simla Convention and they had not done so; he had expected them to supply him with modern arms and these had not proved forthcoming. The fact was that in neither London nor Delhi did Tibet arouse much interest. At no stage in Anglo-Tibetan relations had there been any question of annexing Tibet to British India, and it happened that ever since the time when Tibet had thrown off Chinese rule in 1911 Britain had been fully preoccupied with more urgent matters – the maintenance of Anglo-Russian friendship, the First World War and the problems of post-war reconstruction – while the Government of India was almost wholly absorbed in attempts to contain the self-sustaining growth of the independence movement.

Faced with internal opposition to innovations and lack of interest by the British the Dalai Lama abandoned further schemes for modernization. The *gendarmerie* and army were allowed to deteriorate, the Gyantse school was closed and a motor mail-service to the British Trade Agencies was stopped. When the British offered to mediate on behalf of the fugitive Panchen Lama their offer was curtly refused.

The Thirteenth Dalai Lama had maintained Tibetan autonomy by combining friendship with British India (unpopular with extreme conservatives) with restrained hostility towards China (popular among most sections of the nation). Predictably, his death in 1933 triggered off a bitter struggle for the *de facto* control of the country since the next Dalai Lama had yet to be located and would, in any case, be a child while the Panchen Lama was still in exile. Eventually a fairly stable and conservative regime was established under the regency of the incarnate lama of Reting but, as was to be expected under the circumstances, neither the regent nor the *Kashag* (the executive council of state) felt inclined to initiate major innovations at a time of such uncertainty.

China, moreover, had never abandoned her claims to Tibet during the period of autonomy under the Thirteenth Dalai Lama. In 1933 the Chinese government, stronger than it had been in recent years and rightly assuming that the interim government in Lhasa would prove less intransigent than its predecessors, sent a mission of condolence to the regent on the death of the Dalai Lama. The negotiations conducted by this mission in Lhasa proved abortive, but at least diplomatic relations of a sort had been re-established and when it finally departed it left behind a small staff with a wireless-transmitter which, in addition to acting as a source of information for the Chinese, took to making regular payments to various Tibetan officials. Meanwhile the problem of the Panchen Lama came to the fore again when the Chinese threatened to send him back to Tibet with an armed Chinese escort. It looks, therefore, as if the Kuomintang were contemplating active intervention in Tibetan affairs when the Sino-Japanese war broke out in June 1937. The Panchen Lama died in the following December but the hardening Chinese attitude had not passed unnoticed in Lhasa where there had been a corresponding move in the direction of closer relations with British India. As early as 1936 Sir Basil Gould had headed a fresh British mission to Lhasa and on its withdrawal there remained a wireless-transmitter and a skeleton-staff headed by the notable Tibetan scholar, H. E. Richardson. With Indian independence in 1947 this mission became the responsibility of the Republic of India.

Even at the height of the war with Japan, Chinese interest in Tibet did not diminish, and a major step forward in the integration of Tibetan territory into China was made in 1939 when Kham became the Chinese province of Sikang. It is clear that throughout the Second World War the Kuomintang never relinquished its determination to absorb Tibet into the motherland and when, for example, the British suggested the creation of a supply route through Tibet as an alternative to the Burma Road, and urged the Chinese to assuage Tibetan suspicions by a declaration of autonomy, Chiang Kai-shek's government refused. In 1949 the Tibetans requested the withdrawal of all Chinese officials from Lhasa on the grounds that they had been guilty of intriguing with various factions in the capital; they had also been interfering quite openly in the selection of Tibet's two principal incarnations. In 1938 the Fourteenth Dalai Lama, Tenzin Gyatso, had been discovered in Amdo (which was now in the Chinese province of Chinghai) where the Muslim governor and local warlord, Ma Pu-feng, placed innumerable obstacles in the way of his transfer to Lhasa – as also did the great Kum Bum monastery. After protracted negotiations he was eventually taken to Lhasa and enthroned in February 1940. The choice of the new Panchen Lama proved more complicated, there being ten potential candidates in 1942. In 1944, however, it was announced that one of these had been acknowledged and enthroned in China, and in 1949, just prior to its collapse, the Kuomintang gave this candidate official recognition.

The Chinese Communist People's Republic was inaugurated in October 1949, and in October 1950 a rejuvenated China, determined to reassert her authority in the borderlands which had acknowledged the sway of Ch'ien-lung, invaded Tibet. On 7 November 1950 Tibet appealed to the United Nations against Chinese aggression, neither party being member-states and only Britain and India possessing first-hand experience of the problem of Chinese *de jure* suzerainty and Tibet's forty years of *de facto* independence. Of the handling of the Tibetan case in the United Nations, H. E. Richardson has written pungently in *Tibet and its history*.[4]

Having established themselves in Tibet without much serious military opposition the Chinese began to negotiate with the Tibetans from a position of strength. The outcome was the Sino-Tibetan agreement of May 1951 in which Tibet was incorporated into the Chinese motherland but was granted national regional autonomy. The agreement was to be implemented by a military and administrative committee in Lhasa. The Tibetan army was to be integrated with that of China. In return, China pledged herself not to alter the traditional Tibetan system of government nor to interfere with the status of the Dalai Lama. Reforms were not to be forced upon the Tibetans without their consent, and religious customs were to be left intact. In this way Tibet was brought into the framework of the Chinese state.

Thereafter, the Chinese moved cautiously. A military occupation was swiftly but unostentatiously imposed, and immense efforts were made to develop adequate communication with China (without which the Chinese position remained insecure), roads and air-strips bringing Tibet for the first time into contact with mechanized transport on a considerable scale. With regard to the civil administration, the Chinese were at first content to utilize the ruling classes, the lamas and the lay nobility, in their traditional roles as administrators, while taking every opportunity to reduce their influence. The Dalai Lama, still only sixteen but already invested with full authority because of the critical situation, remained the titular head of the country but his powers were steadily circumscribed while the status of the Panchen Lama was deliberately raised to a point where the two incarnations seemed to be exercising a sort of condominium. While the great lamaseries were treated with open hostility by the Chinese a number of lamas and lay nobles were taken to China on official visits, and some of these decided that co-operation with the new China was unavoidable. Some young monks and nobles received scholarships in schools and colleges in China but whether this experience made them pro-Chinese or anti-Chinese is unknown. With the Tibetan peasantry the Chinese appear to have had little success.

At first the Chinese were not remarkably overbearing or high-handed, but it must be remembered that in official Chinese eyes the Tibetans were reclaimed citizens, not conquered aliens. Inevitably, however, the more normal relationship between conquerors and conquered came to the fore. The Tibetans themselves had a long-standing suspicion of Chinese motives, and this was reinforced by the innovations which accompanied the Communist occupation. Some of these were in themselves valuable (such as agricultural improvements and better medical and educational facilities) but to the lamas, in particular, the changes were hateful, and clashes between Tibetans and Chinese became frequent, especially following the announcement that 40,000 Chinese farming families would be settled in Tibet. The completion of the military road to Lhasa from China in 1954, which enabled the Chinese to strengthen their military hold, further aggravated relations. It was in April 1954 that the Chinese and Indian governments signed the agreement defining the conditions of trade and pilgrimage between Tibet and India, in which no mention was made of former agreements between Tibet and India, and in which Tibet was referred to as 'the Tibet region of China'. Thus the Indian government apparently assumed unqualified Chinese sovereignty over Tibet. This agreement was preceded by the *Panch Shila* or Five Principles of peaceful co-existence and friendly co-operation.

Between 1954 and 1956 the situation remained deceptively calm, and in the autumn of 1954 both the Dalai Lama and the Panchen Lama visited Peking. Yet dissatisfaction was mounting, especially among the eastern tribes. Attempts to disarm the latter, new forms of taxation, attacks upon religion and the traditional class structure, the introduction of new educational institutions (education having been the age-old preserve of the lamaseries), and the brutal punishment of recalcitrants bred bitter resentment and by the summer of 1956 there was an active guerrilla movement among the tribes in Amdo and Kham. There followed merciless reprisals on villages in this area and the destruction of the monasteries of Changtreng, Litang and Batang. Repression merely stiffened Tibetan resistance and soon the two provinces of Chinghai and Sikang were ablaze. The conduct of the Chinese forces operating in these areas is recorded in *Tibet and the Chinese Peoples Republic*, a report published by the International Commission of Jurists in Geneva in 1960.

Between the end of 1956 and the beginning of 1958 there was a lull in the fighting; in November 1956 the Dalai Lama and the

Panchen Lama visited India and held conversations with Pandit Nehru and also with Chou En-lai who happened to be visiting India at the same time; in February 1957 Mao Tse-tung denounced 'Great-Han chauvinism', banned the implementation of further reforms for Tibet for another five years, and made some conciliatory gestures towards Tibetan nationalist feeling. Early in 1958, however, the Tibetans determined to resist any further encroachments upon their traditional way of life – their determination being strengthened by the presence in central Tibet of many Khamba tribesmen and dispossessed lamas from the east. By the autumn of 1958 the guerrillas had increased in numbers, experience and morale, and controlled most districts south of the Tsang-po.

From the time when China first invaded Tibet in 1950, there had always been the possibility that the Chinese might seize the Dalai Lama as a hostage for Tibetan good behaviour. As opposition to the Chinese occupation mounted this possibility became increasingly strong, and in March 1959 the Dalai Lama, now twenty-four, fled from his capital to the safety of India. His escape was followed by a reign of terror for the inhabitants of Lhasa who had so resolutely guarded him prior to his absence. The absence of the Dalai Lama brought the traditional administrative institutions to a standstill and the Chinese took the opportunity of replacing them by a military dictatorship which functioned through those lamas and nobles (including the Panchen Lama) who were still willing to co-operate. Order was enforced by Chinese troops and the grim paraphernalia of tyranny established: secret police and paid informers; propaganda and forced labour; compulsory identity-cards and police check-points; food rationing according to work-output, the separation of children from parents and the billeting of Chinese troops on the villages. An all-out effort was made to eradicate the hold of religion on Tibetan life and the lamas were persecuted, evicted from their monasteries, and sent to swell the labour-force. After the lamas it was the turn of the nobles and those who had not escaped to India with the Dalai Lama were liquidated; so were many yeomen and tenant-farmers. These measures – the overthrow of government by the Dalai Lama, the assault upon Tibetan religious institutions and the destruction of the traditional social order – marked the end of the unique culture of Tibet as it had evolved for the past thousand years.[5]

Tibet was too remote for these events to arouse much international concern and at that date Afro-Asian states took little interest in cases of colonial exploitation in which the guilty party was not European. India, however, could hardly remain ignorant of what was happening across her northern border, especially after the flight of the Dalai Lama from Lhasa and his arrival on Indian soil, which had been followed by a mass exodus of Tibetan refugees, and there can be no doubt that the rape of Tibet carried very sinister overtones indeed for the future security of India's Himalayan frontier. In July 1959 the International Commission of Jurists published in Geneva an interim report on Chinese aggression in Tibet, *The Question of Tibet and the Rule of Law*, and late in August the Dalai Lama appealed to the United Nations. By October Tibet was on the Assembly's agenda and the pattern of 1950 re-emerged with Britain and India as 'expert' witnesses. The Tibetan people gained nothing from the four-day debate except a brief period of publicity, although in many countries there was a prompt and generous response to the plight of the Tibetan refugees in camps scattered throughout the foothills of northern India. Whatever can be salvaged from the wreck of Tibetan civilization and the traditional Tibetan way of life will be preserved by these exiles, with the Dalai Lama at their head, for there can be no doubt that with the almost total pacification of Tibet by the Chinese Communists in 1959 the history of the Tibetans as an independent people was brought to a violent and irrecoverable conclusion. The future of the country, such as it is, will henceforth be decided not in Lhasa but in Peking.

19

The Mongols in the
Twentieth Century

In 1900 the position of Outer Mongolia was in several ways comparable to that of Tibet, both being Manchu protectorates inhabited by non-Chinese peoples possessing strong cultural traditions of their own, and being sufficiently remote from China not to suffer much from their loose attachment to the crumbling Manchu regime. Tibet was protected by uninviting terrain from the Chinese colonists who were beginning to penetrate Inner Mongolia, and Outer Mongolia was protected from such intruders by the Gobi desert. Tibet and Outer Mongolia also had powerful neighbours, British India and Russia, who had scant respect for Chinese susceptibilities where their own commercial or strategic interests were concerned so that while some Tibetans looked to the government of India as an alternative 'patron' to the Manchu emperor many Khalkhas (the most important tribe in Outer Mongolia) looked to Tsarist Russia. Both these Great Powers welcomed the existence of Tibet and Outer Mongolia respectively as buffers between them and China. Neither considered the annexation of Tibet or Outer Mongolia as worth hastening the ultimate disintegration of the Manchu empire, and neither considered the cost of large-scale military intervention justifiable in terms of the estimated commercial return. In this situation the Tibetans and the Mongols of Outer Mongolia enjoyed considerable room for manoeuvre in their relations with China, yet during the first half of the twentieth century the history of these two peoples who had shared a common cultural heritage since the

276

sixteenth century sharply diverged. Tibet, *de facto* independent between 1911 and 1950, now exists only as a province of China, and with its traditional culture on the brink of extinction while Outer Mongolia (now the Mongolian People's Republic) is a member-state of the United Nations whose people have continued to manifest within the limits imposed by an orthodox Communist regime both a sense of pride in their historic past and a rigorous nationalist outlook. The existence of a Mongolian People's Republic today is due partly to the resolution of the Khalkhas themselves, partly to Russian, Chinese and Japanese rivalry in north-east Asia, and partly to the existence of Chinese colonization in Inner Mongolia, a factor which, perhaps more than any other, determined the nature of Outer Mongolia's relations first with Tsarist Russia and then with the Soviet Union. While Outer Mongolia in the twentieth century has functioned as a welcome buffer between Russia and China along one section of their immense frontier, Inner Mongolia has been subjected to intensive Chinese settlement which has meant for its indigenous Mongol inhabitants the ruthless expropriation of their grazing-lands. During the last decades of their rule, the Manchus, increasingly identified with their Chinese subjects, reversed their predecessors' policy of excluding Chinese influence from Mongolia and deliberately fostered Chinese colonization as a barrier to Russian penetration, a policy likewise pursued in Manchuria. With the fall of the Manchus this colonizing movement gained further momentum as a result of railway construction. The Peking-Süiyüan Railway, for example, which had reached Kalgan in Chahar by 1909, had reached Paotow in Süiyüan, via Kweisui and Sarachi (two of the principal centres for Chinese colonization in Inner Mongolia), by 1923. Railways assisted the transportation of colonists, enabled farm-produce from the new lands to be distributed to centres of population deep inside China proper, and led inexorably to the physical subjection of Mongols to Chinese. Colonization of under-populated Mongol lands (which reached its peak in Inner Mongolia between 1928 and 1931 and in Manchuria between 1928 and 1931) was due not to any genuine pioneering movement by the Chinese peasantry but to the efforts of frontier officials and landowners. Under the patronage of local warlords and often with the connivance of the more sinified Mongol princes, destitute peasants were recruited from famine areas inside China and were settled on expropriated Mongol grazing-lands, where they could be exploited and rack-rented on a vast scale. Possessing few modern fire-arms, the Mongols were compelled to acquiesce and withdrew to poorer pastures. The result, so profitable to local officials and land-speculators, was the establishment of inefficient agriculture on land best-suited to a pastoral economy leading in turn to desiccation and soil-erosion, excessive crop-renting, absentee landlordism and for the settlers a standard of living probably below that in China itself. The Mongols, however, were the chief sufferers. As a result relations between Mongols and Chinese rapidly deteriorated, and lawlessness and banditry became endemic wherever the traditional frontier-relationship between sinified Mongols and Mongolized Chinese was replaced by the racial antagonism inherent in the new system of ex-propriation.

The example of Inner Mongolia compelled the Khalkhas of Outer Mongolia to recognize that Russia was less of a threat to their national survival than China. No doubt they were sus-picious of Russian activities in the area but Chinese colonization of Inner Mongolian pastures was an uncomfortable reality and this accounts for what has been described as 'the tendency for power in Mongolia to gravitate into the hands of those Mongols who can get on best with the Russia of the time, whatever the time may be'.[1] Regardless of the price the Mongols have had to pay for Russian protection in the twentieth century it has at least preserved them from the fate of the Mongols of Inner Mongolia for whom the Chinese colonists who ploughed up their pastures and the Chinese money-lenders who reduced whole families and even clans to debt-slavery proved to be scourges far worse than the former Manchu *Ambans* with their isolated garrisons, turning traditional Mongol contempt for the Chinese into justifiable fear and loathing.

Towards Russia there was no comparable animosity. For some three centuries the Mongols had experienced irregular contacts with the Russians beginning with the journey across Mongolia of the remarkable Moldavian scholar and adventurer, Nikolai Gavrilovich Spathary, who was sent as Russian envoy to the court of K'ang-hsi in 1675. Spathary drew the attention of the Russian government to the fact that the route into China south of Lake Baikal via Kiakhta and Urga was preferable to the dangerous journey across the steppes or to the long Amur route. By the close of the seventeenth century the Buriat Mongols had been incorporated into Russia's expanding Siberian empire, a process completed by the demarcation of the Sino-Russian frontier in the treaties of Nerchinsk (1689) and Kiakhta (1727). The latter permitted Russians to trade in Mongolia, but for nearly a century and a half thereafter their influence was insignificant. A change came, however, after the Sino-Russian convention of 1860 which placed Russian commercial activity in Outer Mongolia on a proper footing and led to the opening in 1861 of a Russian consulate in Urga and especially after the 1881 treaty of St Petersburg which regulated the transit trade across Mongolia and gave the Russians the right to open consulates in Kobdo (Jirgalantu) and Uliassutai (Jibhalanta) whenever they wanted. By 1911 when the Chinese Revolution severed the Khalkhas' allegiance to their Manchu suzerains, the extent of Russian economic penetration into Outer Mongolia and Urianghai seemed to foreshadow the establishment of some sort of Russian protectorate, perhaps even annexation, but for the Khalkhas, fearful of Chinese colonization which already showed signs of spreading into Outer Mongolia, increasing Russian interest in their country was probably not unwelcome. Moreover Russian influence was beginning to make itself felt among some of the younger generation while personal contact with individual Russians was to give at least a few Khalkhas their first experience of foreigners other than the hated Chinese.

Predictably in the case of a society where there was no definable commercial middle class and virtually no urban life, Mongol nationalism in the early twentieth century (whether in Outer Mongolia, Inner Mongolia or Manchuria) was the preserve of a small minority drawn mainly from the ranks of the hereditary princes and the aristocracy whose political activities, while principally motivated by fear of China, were for the most part determined by family and local interests which tended to give incipient Mongol nationalism a narrow, parochial character. This parochialism was reinforced by a tendency for Mongol nationalism to acquire distinctive regional character-istics so that, for example, the nationalist aspirations of the Buriats differed in their priorities as well as in emphasis from those of the Khalkhas or of the Mongols of Barga or Inner Mongolia. Naturally enough, the most vigorous expression of nationalist feeling came from those Mongols living on the fringes of the Mongol world, such as the Buriats or the Mongols of Inner Mongolia, who were most exposed to external pressures of one kind or another.

The two most important factors in the growth of a nationalist movement among the Mongols were (1) a sense of racial cohesion and unity, notwithstanding their sparse distribution over an immense area, and (2) the Mongol language. In com-parison, the contribution of religion as a unifying factor was slight, partly because the Tibetan origin of Buddhism in Mongolia worked against a total identification of Mongol church with Mongol nation, partly on account of the undynamic quality of Mongol religion in the early twentieth century, and partly because the Mongols in general lacked the Tibetans' deep-rooted respect for the ecclesiastical hierarchy. Far more influential was the memory of the heroic past of the Mongol people. Under the Manchus the *khungtayjis* (descendants of Chingiz Khan) had preserved the traditions of the Mongol empire of the thirteenth century and of the age-old struggle with China. In the twentieth century (despite official disapproval in the Mongolian People's Republic[2]) the glorification of Mongol history and traditional culture has continued unabated – the growth of the scientific study of Mongol literature, archaeology and folklore in the last hundred years, first by Russian scholars and then by their Mongol pupils as well as by a few European and Japanese scholars, having given fresh impetus and direction to this sense of pride in the Mongol past.

During the early twentieth century these factors stimulated

the Mongols' sense of nationality in proportion to the extent to which they were threatened by Chinese colonization and by Great Power rivalry in north-east Asia. Nevertheless, there were also powerful factors working against Mongol nationalism and, more especially, against Mongol unity. First and most important of all, there was the Gobi desert which separated Inner Mongolia from Outer Mongolia. Secondly, there were the traditional tribal and clan rivalries which were most strongly perpetuated wherever, as in Inner Mongolia, princely leadership and feudal institutions were most vigorous. Thirdly, there was the presence in Inner Mongolia of the Chinese colonists, disrupting the traditional administrative framework and traditional social relationships, and bringing in their wake Chinese military domination. Fourthly, there was the steady growth of Russian influence in Outer Mongolia from 1911 onwards which, especially after the Russian Revolution of 1917, caused Outer Mongolia to develop along very different lines from Inner Mongolia. There the Chinese authorities operated through Mongol feudal institutions and strengthened the power of the Mongol princes in order to prevent the emergence of a Pan-Mongol nationalist movement directed at the independent unification of all Mongol-inhabited territories. All these circumstances deflected Mongol nationalism into separate channels corresponding to the existing geographical and political divisions of the Mongol people. The Buriats, for example, long accustomed to Russian rule, were the first Mongols to produce a westernized intelligentsia, so that Buriats educated in Russian schools in Irkutsk and Chita, and even in Kazan and St Petersburg, acted as natural intermediaries between Russian civilization and the Mongols of Outer Mongolia. Yet, paradoxically, the extent of their russification tended to isolate them from their fellow Mongols, a trend which was strengthened after the replacement of Tsarist by Soviet rule. Those Buriats who deeply disliked the latter regime fled to Inner Mongolia or Manchuria where the Japanese enlisted their services during the 1930s.

From 1911 onwards nationalism in Inner and Outer Mongolia pursued divergent courses, the contrast between the two movements growing greater after the Russian Revolution and

281

especially after the Japanese invasion of Manchuria in 1931. This led to the creation of the state of Manchukuo in 1932 with a descendant of the Manchu dynasty, P'u Yi, as Chief Executive and to the annexation of Jehol to Manchukuo in 1933. The Mongols in Manchuria were both nomads and agriculturists and the fall of the Manchu empire had left them at the mercy of local Chinese warlords against whose modern weapons they had no defence, and of Chinese colonists fanning out from the railways. Hence they welcomed the arrival of the Japanese while the elevation of P'u Yi to the rank of Emperor of Manchukuo in 1934 awakened dormant Mongol loyalty (especially among the princes) for the old dynasty which had ruled them with so light a hand. A Manchu emperor of Manchukuo was also a focal point of attraction for the princes of Inner Mongolia, restless under the rule of a Chinese Republic incapable of protecting them from exploitation by its local officials. The Japanese attached great strategic importance to Inner Mongolia as a wedge between China and the USSR, while Inner Mongolian nationalism was clearly a useful weapon against the Chinese. Their Mongol policy in Manchuria was therefore initiated partly with the intention of wooing the Mongols of Inner Mongolia. The first stage in this policy was the creation on the western frontier of Manchuria of an autonomous Mongol province of Hsingan, with an area of 148,000 square miles and a population of 90,000, where further Chinese colonization was forbidden and where the Mongol princes were left to rule their own territories, assisted by Japanese advisers.

In dealing with the Mongols the Japanese clearly enjoyed considerable advantages over the Chinese. The Japanese had no tradition of conflict with the Mongols. Like the Chinese in Inner Mongolia, they used the Mongol princes and the most influential lamas as their agents but they did so more effectively. They furthered Mongol education and the study of Mongol culture, sent a number of young Mongols for training in Japan, and possessed the inestimable advantage of having a body of genuine specialists in Mongol affairs who were able to win the confidence of the princes. If any Great Power could have given meaning to Pan-Mongol dreams, and done so with advantage to itself, that Power was Japan. Yet Japan's Mongol policy ultimately proved a failure. Strangely reckless in their interference with Mongol traditions, the Japanese displayed chronic suspicion of their Mongol subjects and allies, ferociously punishing those suspected of disloyalty. The Mongols themselves had less contact with Japan's Mongol specialists than with the Japanese counterparts of the speculators, petty extortioners and bullies who were to be found among the Chinese officials in Inner Mongolia. Moreover, one of the principal attractions of Mongol territory for the Japanese was its potentiality as a wool-producing area which could replace Japanese dependence on the Australian market. To establish large-scale wool production, however, it was necessary to interfere in the traditional nomadic life of the Mongol herdsman by converting him into a ranch-hand under Japanese management. All these factors contributed in varying degrees to a rapid Mongol disenchantment with their overbearing overlords.[3]

The failure of Japan's Mongol policy in Manchuria was matched by a similar failure in Inner Mongolia where virulent hatred of the Chinese had produced the most violent manifestations of Mongol nationalism, a situation seemingly ripe for Japanese exploitation. When Outer Mongolia declared its independence in 1911 Inner Mongolia had been unable to follow a similar course. As soon as Outer Mongolian independence became a reality the Chinese Republic (dedicated to the assimilation and sinification of its minorities and represented on its Inner Mongolian frontier by semi-independent Chinese warlords) took steps to prevent the Mongols of Inner Mongolia from pursuing a similar course. The Chinese ruthlessly suppressed any nationalist moves, aided by their control of the railways and their possession of modern firearms. In 1928, as part of a policy of *divide et impera*, the Nanking Government divided the historic area of Inner Mongolia into four separate provinces – Ninghsia, Süiyüan, Chahar and Jehol – where they sought to win the support of the more important Mongol princes and lamas so that Chinese policies could be carried out with the co-operation of and even through the agency of traditional Mongol rulers. These rulers were now granted rights and privileges such as they had never previously known; they were invested with judicial authority and were held responsible for enforcing the payment of the debts of their Mongol subjects to Chinese firms and money-lenders. Most important of all, they were even given the backing of Chinese troops. Some were persuaded to participate in the expropriation of their own tribal grazing-lands in favour of Chinese cultivators, the princes concerned (often scarcely distinguishable from Chinese landlords) sharing the profits with the local Chinese officials. Similarly, Mongol ecclesiastics were compromised by accepting Chinese titles and favours. In this way Chinese policy succeeded in destroying tribal unity and any potential cohesion inherent in Inner Mongolian nationalism, assisted – paradoxically – by developments in Outer Mongolia. Between 1911 and 1921 the princes of Inner Mongolia were wary of drawing closer to Outer Mongolia for fear of being overshadowed by the powerful Khalkha princes. Those with interests in Chinese commercial ventures in Inner Mongolia disapproved of the Outer Mongolian government's abrogation of Chinese debts. After the establishment of Soviet influence in Outer Mongolia from 1921 onwards, co-operation with Outer Mongolia seemed even less desirable. The weak Chinese Republic was easier to deal with than revolutionary Russia and while Soviet ideology was coming increasingly to dominate the Urga government Inner Mongolia was moving in the opposite direction, making *rapprochement* even more difficult. At the time of the Japanese occupation of Manchuria, Mongol society in Inner Mongolia was far more feudalized than in any other Mongol-inhabited area of north-eastern Asia.

Since some of the princes in Inner Mongolia acted as agents of Chinese colonization and political dominance, Inner Mongolian nationalism developed radical elements bitterly hostile to the privileges and status of the traditional aristocracy. Yet, paradoxically, it was from the ranks of the *khungtayjis* that some of the most important leaders of the nationalist movement in Inner Mongolia were recruited, including Prince Demchukdongrob (usually known by his Chinese title of Teh Wang), who during the 1930s led a movement for Inner Mongolian autonomy which attracted supporters from Jehol in the east, through Chahar and Ordos to the Ala Shan in the west. A cautious moderate in politics, Teh Wang's aims, represented after 1934 by the Pailingmiao Inner Mongolian Autonomous Political Council (PIMAPC), seem to have been thoroughly realistic: to bargain with the Chinese Republic on behalf of the PIMAPC from a position of strength (the result of the Japanese presence in Manchuria) in order to obtain for Inner Mongolia a meaningful autonomous status subordinate to a central government in which the Mongols, as a minority, would have adequate representation. Yet even this moderate programme, which was envisaged at a time when circumstances seemed peculiarly favourable to Inner Mongolian aspirations, failed utterly.

The fact is that the Nanking government never took the Mongol problem in Inner Mongolia seriously, with the result that the PIMAPC was unable to establish those influential contacts in high government circles which alone could have counter-balanced its weakness in dealing with the Chinese provincial authorities in Inner Mongolia, who were determined to prevent the Mongols coping directly with their distant superiors. Moreover, the PIMAPC was an amorphous coalition of parties with conflicting interests. Amongst its members there were a few honest and able leaders, those composed of hereditary princes and lamas who were implacably opposed to Chinese colonization, some Manchurian Mongols who disliked living under the Japanese regime across the border, a few Mongol supporters of the Kuomintang, and representatives of the newly emerging radical intelligentsia. The latter tended to be influenced by the contemporary course of events in Outer Mongolia and were generally hostile to the hereditary ruling classes. The princes, unsympathetic to the intelligentsia and dreading the spread of Outer Mongolian revolutionary fervour to Inner Mongolia, looked to Japan for a solution similar to the Hsingan autonomous Mongol province in Manchuria, or else sought a compromise with China (the pro-Chinese princes had already founded in 1934 the Süiyüan Inner Mongolian Autonomous Political Council as a rival to the PIMAPC). In these circumstances the local Chinese authorities had no difficulty in

285

exploiting the inherent weaknesses of the PIMAPC, splitting its leadership and isolating Teh Wang. The Japanese completed the process when they occupied Inner Mongolia and established a Federative Autonomous Government of Inner Mongolia ('Mengchiang'), dividing the territory into administrative districts with Teh Wang in charge of one only, thus reducing his position from that of a national leader to that of a local administrator acting on behalf of Japanese interests. The fact that Japan failed to evolve a Mongol policy in Inner Mongolia comparable to her Mongol policy in Manchuria seems strange in retrospect but it should be remembered that by the late 1930s Japan was already preoccupied with the conquest of China itself. The opportunity for creating another Manchukuo in Inner Mongolia had already passed.

With the collapse of the PIMAPC and with the successful Japanese manipulation of some of the most vigorous nationalist leaders, Inner Mongolian nationalism lost its impetus. Eventually the region became involved in the larger conflicts of the Second World War, and with the establishment of a Communist government in China a new Inner Mongolian regime emerged with a similar Marxist ideology. Subsequently the new rulers of China established an Inner Mongolian Autonomous Region in 1947 and although it is unlikely that the Mongols under Chinese Communist rule can expect any substantial degree of independence it is possible that, as a result of the growing strain in Sino-Russian relations, the Chinese Communists may be prepared to pay more lip-service to Inner Mongolian autonomy and may give greater encouragement to Mongol culture than did the Kuomintang.

Separated from China by Inner Mongolia and the Gobi desert, the Khalkhas of Outer Mongolia were better placed for national survival than the Mongols on the Chinese frontier and during the period of anarchy inside China between 1911 and 1926–7, they were able to establish and maintain a *de facto* independence, assisted by the possession of a limited quantity of modern weapons acquired from Russia, an advantage denied to the Mongols of Inner Mongolia.

With the fall of the Manchu empire in 1911 the Khalkha

princes declared Outer Mongolia independent, established a national government with the Eighth Jebtsundamba Khutukhtu (1870–1924) as head of state, and despatched a delegation to St Petersburg requesting Russian protection. A barrier was raised to future co-operation with the new China by the Outer Mongolian government's total repudiation of Mongol debts to Chinese firms and individuals. Coming at a time when the Great Powers were still preoccupied with the probable disintegration of China, the Mongol request for protection seriously embarrassed the Russians, since the recognition of an independent Outer Mongolia might initiate a European scramble for the rest of China. Even if that did not happen there was still the danger that if Russia accepted some sort of protectorate over Outer Mongolia she might find herself at some later date compelled to defend the Khalkhas against their erstwhile overlords. Sazonov the Russian Foreign Minister warned the Duma on the 13 April 1912:

The Khalkhas are not prepared by their history for independent government. Being nomads, for centuries accustomed to obey the Peking Government, the Mongols of Khalkha possess neither a military nor a financial organization, nor leaders, without whom an independent state is impossible.[4]

Russia therefore moved cautiously, but in a Russo-Mongol agreement of 3 November 1912 Outer Mongolian autonomy was given *de facto* recognition, and this was reiterated in both a Sino-Russian declaration of November 1913 and in the tripartite treaty of Kiakhta between Russia, China and Outer Mongolia of June 1915, although China never renounced her historic claims to suzerainty. Meanwhile the first phase of Outer Mongolian independence (1911–17) was characterized by the steady consolidation of Russia's hold over the economic life of the new nation. In July 1914, for instance, Russia lent the Outer Mongolian government three million roubles on condition that a Russian financial adviser should reside in Urga, and the two governments signed an arms agreement in which the Mongols accepted Russian military instructors and agreed not to acquire arms from any country other than Russia. In September 1914 Russia acquired a monopoly on railway construction and in

1915 established the National Bank of Mongolia, later incorporated into the Siberian Commercial Bank. Russian economic influence was further strengthened during the First World War by the large-scale purchase of Mongolian cattle to feed her huge armies.

While growing contacts with Russia injected new life into the Outer Mongolian economy, a sense of nationalism was gradually emerging although, for the most part, restricted to Urga with its small foreign community of Russians and Chinese, where the Russian consulate had long been a hive of intrigue. Since 1911 the Jebtsundamba Khutukhtu's government had been based upon an alliance between the more energetic and intelligent Khalkha princes and those higher ecclesiastics who shared with them their hostility to Chinese ambitions in Outer Mongolia and also opposed with equal vigour any local challenge to their authority. Together with the Jebtsundamba Khutukhtu it was they, not the two-chamber parliament founded in 1914 nor the ministries with their small staffs of untrained officials, who constituted the driving-force of the administration, and their authority rested ultimately upon traditional leadership. Yet if Mongol society after 1911 continued to function traditionally with regard to social status and political power there were factors which were encouraging the spread of new attitudes. The implications of Outer Mongolia's new status as a virtually independent country did much to stimulate a sense of nationality. The early years of independence happened to be prosperous ones for the stock-breeders which, taken with the cancellation of the iniquitous Chinese debts, meant a rising standard of living among a people who were still mainly pastoralists. Figures were emerging on the political stage who to some extent constituted an intelligentsia such as Outer Mongolia had hitherto lacked. The majority of these were young princes or lamas but a few like Sukhe Bator (1893–1923) and Choibalsan (1895–1952) were of humble birth. Most had been influenced in some way by Russia. Some had attended Russian schools or institutes, some had been trained in the new army where they had Russian instructors, and others had been employed in Russian trading companies or by Russian officials.

288

Meanwhile, the formative years after 1911 when Outer Mongolia acquired practical experience of running her own affairs came to an end with the Russian Revolution of 1917. The Bolsheviks had denounced Russia's former treaties, including that of Kiakhta (1915) which had set the seal on an informal Tsarist protectorate over Outer Mongolia, and hence the Jebtsundamba Khutukhtu began fresh negotiations with the Soviet government. In Urga itself radical and revolutionary groups began to appear which were hostile both to the princes and the Buddhist hierarchy. Russia's weakness after 1917, however, gave China the opportunity to resume old claims to Outer Mongolia. On 22 November 1919 she unilaterally cancelled Outer Mongolian autonomy, a Chinese force under General Hsü Shu-ch'eng occupied Urga and Chinese military, political and economic domination was temporarily reasserted. Unsupported by Russia, Outer Mongolia was incapable of resistance and the Chinese at once pressed for the restoration of the former debts owed by Mongols to Chinese, together with compensation for the losses which followed the 1911 revolution and the accumulated interest of eight years of Mongol autonomy! China was bent on reducing Outer Mongolia to the same state of dependence as Inner Mongolia and she might well have succeeded but for the eruption into Outer Mongolia of the White Russian adventurer, Baron von Ungern-Sternberg. His capture of Urga in February 1921 in command of a mixed force of 5,000 Russians, Buriats, Mongols and Tibetans brought Chinese influence in Outer Mongolia to an abrupt end. Ungern-Sternberg seems to have aimed at harnessing his career to Pan-Mongol slogans but his insane violence soon made his presence as odious to the Mongols as the Chinese had been, so that the Soviet Red Army forces which fought their way into Urga in July 1921 had little difficulty in overcoming him. Between 1921 and 1924 an interim government containing some liberal as well as revolutionary elements was in power, with the Jebtsundamba Khutukhtu remaining as head of state. Thus some degree of continuity was maintained with the 1911–17 period, and softened the shock of the transition from a regime dominated by hereditary princes to one unmistakably revolutionary in character. With the death of the Eighth Jebtsundamba Khutukhtu in 1924, however, the discovery of a new incarnation was forbidden, the Mongolian People's Republic was established in November of the same year, and the tenacious rule of hereditary princes and lamas at last came to an end.[5] Conscription for a People's Revolutionary Army, the nationalization of land, mineral wealth and other natural resources and the creation of a state monopoly in foreign trade revealed the extent of Soviet Russian influence which was, however, less blatant than later Japanese control over the Mongols of Manchuria, and was quite different from Chinese exploitation of Inner Mongolia. Chinese economic activities in Outer Mongolia virtually came to an end.[6]

The actual status of Outer Mongolia remained ambiguous, as did Russia's attitude towards its protegé, exemplified by the statement of Chicherin the Soviet Commissar for Foreign Affairs in 1924:

We recognize the Mongolian People's Republic as part of the Chinese Republic, but we recognize also its autonomy in so far-reaching a sense that we regard it not only as independent of China in its internal affairs, but also as capable of running its foreign policy independently.[7]

In October 1945 a plebiscite established complete independence for the Mongolian People's Republic, which was recognized by China in January 1946. A Russo-Mongol treaty of amity and mutual assistance followed in February 1946, and Outer Mongolian independence was reaffirmed in the Sino-Russian treaty of February 1950. Thereafter China maintained diplomatic representation at Ulan-Bator (formerly Urga), and in October 1961 the Mongolian People's Republic became a member-state of the United Nations.

The modern history of Outer Mongolia is still an obscure subject. It appears that between 1925 and 1928 there was a tendency for the Mongolian People's Republic to move closer to China, but this was followed by a swing in the opposite direction between 1929 and 1932, coinciding with a period of feverish sovietization. It was during these years that government policy concentrated – with a very great degree of success – on rooting out traditional Lamaistic beliefs and attitudes but the attempted collectivization of flocks and herds proved a failure, the nomads preferring to slaughter their beasts rather than surrender them. The revolutionary fervour with which these innovations were pursued was considerably modified by the appearance of Japan in Manchuria and Inner Mongolia. Predictably, relations between the Mongolian People's Republic and Manchukuo (where many Outer Mongolian princes and lamas had lived as refugees since 1924) steadily deteriorated until fighting broke out between the two states, reaching a climax with the Mongol victory at Nomonhan during the summer of 1939. Throughout the Second World War Outer Mongolia lay dormant but in August 1945 well-equipped and well-disciplined Mongol troops formed the right wing of a combined Russian and Outer Mongolian force which defeated the Japanese in Inner Mongolia and Manchuria. China's subsequent recognition of the Mongolian People's Republic may have been partly due to the performance of these troops.

In the words of a distinguished western scholar of Mongol culture, 'Mongolia emerged after the war, and more particularly in the early 1950s when outside observers were re-admitted, as a semi-modernized state well on the way to possessing a fully socialized economy and society'.[8] Today the Mongolian People's Republic is a state run by Mongols for Mongols, but where Russia occupies a commanding position with regard to international trade, industrial development and defence. Without Soviet support Outer Mongolia would once again become a Chinese dependency although it is by no means certain that such is China's present objective. The government of the Mongolian People's Republic closely follows the Soviet Russian pattern.[9] All power is invested in the Mongolian People's Revolutionary Party where, although the higher echelons are largely Russian-trained, the rising generation of party officials now receives its training in the Sukhe Bator Higher Party School and the Choibalsan State University. The administration is highly centralized; there is no unofficial press; cultural and intellectual pursuits are subject to official scrutiny and

291

interpretation. Russian influence is very strong in the educational field. The Mongol language now has a Cyrillic alphabet, Russian is the only foreign language taught in schools, and while the State University teaches Russian, Chinese, Manchu, Tibetan and English, the majority of the small number of Mongol students educated abroad go to Moscow and very few to Peking. The Mongol intelligentsia, however, remains surprisingly preoccupied with the glories of the Mongol past which is also well represented in contemporary drama and the arts.

Outer Mongolia today has lost much of its former isolation, being linked with its neighbours by air-routes to Irkutsk and Peking, by the Trans-Mongolian railway which links the Trans-Siberian railway to the Chinese system, and by steamers on the Selenga and Orkhon. A more significant kind of isolation is, however, implied by the Republic's limited diplomatic contacts which are restricted for the most part to fellow Communist regimes and a few neutralist states such as India, Burma and Indonesia although there is now a *chargé d'affaires* in London.

As in the case of other Asian countries the future development of the Mongolian People's Republic is closely linked with the rapid expansion of existing educational facilities and the effective utilization of available natural resources. The majority of Mongols are still stock-breeders living nomadic or semi-nomadic lives, despite government planning and support for mechanized agriculture, industry and mining. The Mongolian People's Republic enjoys a great advantage as compared with most Asian countries, being under-populated, and so far only a small minority of Mongols have taken to urban life – 150,000 in Ulan-Bator; 20,000 in Choibalsan; 10,000 in Tsetserlik; 10,000 in Kobdo; and 10,000 in Sukhe Bator. At present many Mongols enjoy a material standard of living (and for those in the less remote areas, educational and medical facilities) which probably compares favourably with the rest of Asia. Further progress, however, and the future of the Republic itself are inextricably bound up with the future course of relations between China and the Soviet Union.

One region long attached to Outer Mongolia, Urianghai, separated from Siberia to the north by the Sayan ranges and from Outer Mongolia to the south by the Tannu-Ola, has evolved along rather different lines. The majority of its Tuvinian inhabitants were originally Turkish reindeer-herdsmen and hunters of the forests but dominated by cattle-breeding nomads of the steppes whose culture was predominantly Mongol. Between 1757 and 1911 Urianghai was a remote appanage of the Manchu empire governed from Uliassutai (now Jibhalanta), its chieftains being subordinate to the Outer Mongolian princes who were themselves Manchu vassals, and its tribute to Peking being levied in furs. It was furs too which first brought the Russians to Urianghai where their presence was regulated by the Sino-Russian treaty of 1860. Settlers followed the fur-traders and by the beginning of the First World War there were probably some 12,000 Russians in Urianghai compared to some 56,000 Tuvinians.

In 1911 Urianghai, following the example of Outer Mongolia, declared its independence but Russian troops promptly occupied the capital, Kyzyl (then Byloczarsk). In 1914 a Russian protectorate was established; in 1917–18 a Soviet regime was set up; and in 1921 the People's Republic of Tannu-Tuva and the Tannu-Tuvinian Revolutionary Party were founded. Thereafter Tannu-Tuva survived as a Soviet satellite for over twenty years, wholly isolated from Outer Mongolian influences and exposed to systematic russification. On 11 October 1944 it was officially incorporated into the Soviet Union as the Tuvinian Autonomous Oblast. The growth of Russian settlement would suggest that the region is now rapidly becoming more Russian than Tuvinian in racial composition while its known mineral wealth gives it a considerable importance for the Soviet economy as a whole. Of the present population of 172,000, some 80,000 are Russians, many of whom live in Kyzyl which has a population of upwards of 34,000.[10]

20

Sinkiang under the Manchus and the Chinese Republic

Chinese Turkestan, a region of over 600,000 square miles of territory which in the 1880s came to be known as Sinkiang, consists of two distinct parts separated from one another by the Tien Shan range. North of the Tien Shan lies Jungaria, bordering on Russian Semirechie and Mongolia, with Kuldja on the Ili and Urumchi as its main towns. South of the Tien Shan lies Kashgaria, the land of the six cities (*Alty Shahr*) of Kashgar, Yangi Hissar, Yarkand, Khotan, Uch-Turfan and Aqsu. To the west and north Kashgaria touches on Russia, to the south it borders on India and Pakistan (the successor-states to British India) and Tibet.

The histories of these two parts of Chinese Turkestan have tended at times to follow rather different courses. Jungaria can in many ways be considered as a westward extension of Mongolia. In the seventeenth century, on the eve of the Manchu conquests, it was inhabited by the Eleuths (Olots) or Western Mongols (sometimes also referred to as Kalmyks) who were culturally and politically closely related to the Mongols to their east. Kashgaria, on the other hand, was predominantly populated by Turkish peoples usually described as Uighurs, Islamic in religion and following the life of settled cultivators in the oases surrounding the main cities. Where Jungaria looked towards Mongolia in the east, Kashgaria tended to have close relations with the Islamic Central Asian khanates to the west, such as Khiva, Bukhara and, in the nineteenth century, Kokand. In both Han and T'ang Dynasty times the Chinese had extended their influence into Jungaria and Kashgaria, and both regions also formed part of the Mongol empire founded by Chingiz Khan in the thirteenth century. In Ming times these regions remained outside the Chinese empire; and they might well have done so in the Manchu era had not the evolution of Central Asian politics made it impossible for Peking to ignore Turkestan. The Manchu conquest of Turkestan was the result of the emergence of an Eleuth empire during the course of the seventeenth century.

The Eleuths were a group of Western Mongol tribes, which included the Khoshots (Qosots), Torghuts, Derbets and Oirots. Early in the seventeenth century there was a period of movement and unrest among these tribes. One of them, the Torghuts, migrated westwards to the banks of the Volga. Another, the Khoshots, established itself in the Koko-Nor region on the north-eastern border of Tibet, whence, under Gusri Khan, it acquired in alliance with the Fifth Dalai Lama control over much of Tibet and came under the influence of Tibetan Buddhism. Yet another group, the Oirots gained control over the Urumchi region under the leadership of Khotokhotsin (also known as the *khungtayji* Batur). The Oirots, like the Khoshots, were much influenced by Tibetan Buddhism and many of their young men went to study in Lhasa.

By the time of his death around 1653 Khotokhotsin had greatly expanded the power of the Oirots. He had entered into diplomatic relations with the Russians, from whom he acquired firearms, and he had established the basis upon which his son Galdan, when the latter took over the Oirot leadership in 1673, set out to create an Oirot empire in emulation of the achievements of Chingiz Khan. In 1677 Galdan brought many of the Khoshots under his control and with them much of the state which Gusri Khan had created. In 1678 Galdan invaded Kashgaria. In 1679, with the occupation of Hami and Turfan, he completed his domination of the region which was later to become Sinkiang.

Kashgaria on the eve of Galdan's conquest had been ruled by a number of Muslim dynasties, heirs of the former Chaghatai Khanate. Galdan made no attempt to reorganize the Kashgarian

295

administration, contenting himself with the establishment of an Oirot governor at Yarkand to collect tribute. The Oirot presence, however, seems to have acted as a catalyst in Kashgarian politics, bringing about the rise of the Khojas, a family which claimed descent from the Prophet Muhammad. Under Khoja Hidayatullah, the Khojas turned Kashgaria into something very like an Islamic theocracy under Oirot suzerainty.

The rise of Galdan did not escape the notice of the Manchus. In 1677 a group of Khoshot tribesmen, refusing to accept Oirot rule, moved towards the Chinese border in Kansu which they were barely prevented from crossing by the Chinese general Chang Yung. At this moment the San-fan rebellion against the Manchus was raging in China and, accordingly, Chang Yung was ordered not to take any but defensive action against the Eleuths who were disturbing the peace of the frontier. In 1679 it seemed as if Chinese intervention might be avoided entirely when Galdan sought Chinese recognition for his empire.

In the 1680s, however, the Eleuths once more appeared a serious danger in Chinese eyes. A civil war had broken out among the Khalkhas (the Eastern Mongols) and Galdan showed a close interest in these events to his east. In 1686, at an assembly attended by both the Chinese and Galdan, the Khalkhas agreed to a truce. In the following year, however, the truce was broken and this time Galdan actively sided with one of the Khalkha factions. In 1688 Galdan's faction defeated its opponents but political troubles in Jungaria prevented Galdan from exploiting his victory. In 1690 Galdan returned to Mongolia with a large force with which, it seems, he intended to march to Peking and overthrow the Manchus, but he was defeated by a Chinese army and obliged to withdraw once more. He thereupon hastened to patch up a truce with the Manchus though he declined the Emperor K'ang-hsi's request in the following year to come to Peking to seek formal Imperial pardon.

In 1696 the Manchus under K'ang-hsi finally felt themselves strong enough to seek a permanent solution to the Eleuth problem. K'ang-hsi, personally leading the central wing of an army of over 80,000, took the field against Galdan and defeated him decisively near Urga. Galdan managed to escape capture by the Chinese but his power was broken and he died in 1697 before he could restore his fortunes.

The Oirots had now been cured of their interest in Mongolia but the Chinese had not undertaken the physical occupation of Jungaria. Under Tsevan-Rabtan, Galdan's nephew who had sided with the Chinese in 1696, the Oirots once more became a major Central Asian power. They now turned towards Tibet where in 1705 the Khoshot chief Lhabzang Khan, following in the footsteps of Gusri Khan, had become the dominant figure. Control of Tibet, Tsevan-Rabtan appreciated, would mean control of the Tibetan Buddhist Church and hence the acquisition of great influence among the Buddhist princes of Mongolia. This the Manchus could not permit to happen. Accordingly, when in 1717 the Oirots launched a daring raid on Lhasa from Kashgaria (using a route across Western Tibet later followed by a Chinese Communist army in 1951), K'ang-hsi was bound to intervene. The Oirots took Lhasa and managed to hold it against a Chinese army sent from Sining in 1718. In 1720, however, a more powerful Chinese force expelled them from the Tibetan capital.

While planning his Tibetan venture, Tsevan-Rabtan was also busy increasing Oirot control over Kashgaria where the Khoja rulers had become virtually independent once again following Galdan's defeat. During this period the Oirots expanded westwards towards Lake Balkhash and Lake Zaysan in what was later to become the Russian province of Semirechie, coming into hostile contact with Russian outposts in the process.

The Chinese, although they had been able to expel the Oirots from Tibet, still did not have the power to penetrate the Oirot heartland, despite much skirmishing on the Sino-Oirot border in Kansu. In 1727 Tsevan-Rabtan died and in 1738–9 the Chinese patched up a truce with his son and successor, Galdan-Tseren. With the temporary suspension of the war with the Chinese, the Oirot empire enjoyed a period of peace and internal prosperity which finally came to an end a few years after Galdan-Tseren's death in 1745. In 1750 an Oirot faction rebelled against Galdan-Tseren's son and successor Tsevan-Dorji. The Chinese decided to exploit this opportunity to put an end, once and for all, to the Oirot menace on their borders. Using as their spear-head Amur-Sana of the Khoit tribe of Eleuths who was, through his mother, a grandson of Tsevan-Rabtan, they undertook in 1755 the conquest of Jungaria.

After initial successes the main Chinese forces were withdrawn, the process of consolidation being left to Amur-Sana who promptly declared himself the head of the Oirot state and threw off his allegiance to the Manchus. In 1756 the Chinese once more entered Jungaria, forcing Amur-Sana to flee from Ili. Again the Chinese withdrew and again the tribes arose in support of Amur-Sana. This time the Manchu emperor, Ch'ien-lung, sent one of his best generals, Chao-hui, who soon forced Amur-Sana to take refuge in Russian territory where he died of smallpox. During 1757–8 Chao-hui undertook the drastic pacification of Jungaria, executing potential rebels and making it clear that this time the Chinese would tolerate no further trouble. He also sent envoys to Kashgaria to bring the Khoja rulers under Chinese suzerainty.

One of Chao-hui's envoys was murdered by the ruler of Yarkand, an act which the Chinese did not intend to let go unpunished. In October 1758 Chao-hui with a force of 3,000 men struck across the desert from Aqsu to Yarkand by forced marches. He was too weak to take the Yarkand citadel but he was able to establish himself in a fortified camp nearby where, under attack from Yarkandi forces, he awaited reinforcements. In February 1759 he was relieved by a Chinese army which soon enabled him to take both Yarkand and Kashgar, the latter city falling in July. Chao-hui then pursued some of the remaining supporters of the Khojas into the Pamirs, in the process bringing many of the chiefs of Farghana under Chinese rule.

Once the conquest was completed, the Chinese set about creating an administration in Turkestan which aimed at maintaining Manchu influence while not bringing the new territories within the provincial structure of China. A Manchu governor-general was stationed at Kuldja on the Ili, where Ch'ien-lung founded a new city. *Ambans*, or lieutenant-governors, were located at Urumchi and Yarkand to look after the two main divisions of Turkestan. In Jungaria the Manchus endeavoured to establish agricultural colonies, especially in the fertile Ili valley, in order to weaken the predominance of the nomads, and agriculturists of Uighur stock from Kashgaria were encouraged to settle north of the Tien Shan. In Kashgaria the Manchus took care not to offend Islamic sentiments and the bulk of the local administration was left in the hands of local Muslim chiefs who collected taxes and administered justice on behalf of the Manchus. On the whole, in the early years of Chinese rule, government was carried out with efficiency and moderation, bringing with it peace and prosperity.

During the first half of the nineteenth century, however, Chinese rule in Turkestan began to decline because the Empire itself became embroiled in internal upheavals such as the Taiping and Nien rebellions. During this period the Muslim peoples of Turkestan were stirred by religious movements, perhaps inspired by the Wahabis, which created opposition to the Manchus. This development was encouraged by the Khoja family, now in exile in the rising khanate of Kokand in Farghana. Kokandi merchants in Kashgaria fomented rebellion against China, while at the same time they came to dominate the Kashgarian foreign trade to such an extent as to oblige the Manchus to give them special privileges, thus strengthening their position and undermining Manchu influence even more.

The Manchus were further weakened during this period by the advance of Russian power in Central Asia. In the decade 1850–60 the Russians acquired the treaty right to trade and reside in Ili and Kashgaria. At the same time Russian posts like Vernyi in Semirechie brought Russian military power south of Lake Balkhash towards Ili.

All these developments created a state of unrest throughout Chinese Turkestan, and in Kashgaria, this situation was exploited by the Khojas. There were Khoja risings in 1825, 1830, 1846 and 1857, each suppressed with increasing difficulty by the Manchus. At the same time there was growing discontent with Chinese rule among the Muslims of Jungaria and in the neighbouring Chinese province of Kansu, where a focal point of rebellion was provided by the Dungans, a group sometimes described as being of mixed Chinese and Turkish ancestry.

299

In 1862 a major uprising against the Manchus broke out among the Dungans of Kansu which spread rapidly into Jungaria. The communications between China and Kashgaria were cut, and this provided the opportunity for yet another Khoja rising. By the beginning of 1864 the Chinese had lost control of much of Kashgaria which was on the point of reverting to Khoja rule. This was an opportunity which the Kokandi adventurer Yakub Beg was able to seize.

Yakub Beg, who was born in Kokand territory in 1820, had fought against the Russians and had become deeply involved in Kokandi politics. In order to get him out of the way, the Kokandi ruler sent him early in 1865 to join the suite of Buzurg Khan, the head of the Khoja family, on the latter's return to Kashgaria from his Kokandi exile.

During the course of 1865 the military ability of Yakub Beg enabled Buzurg Khan's party to dispose of the remaining pockets of Manchu strength and consolidate Khoja rule throughout Kashgaria, Buzurg Khan, however, soon grew jealous of his successful subordinate and began plotting his downfall. In self-defence, Yakub Beg was forced to make Buzurg Khan a prisoner and, in 1867, to exile him. By 1873 Yakub Beg was undisputed ruler of all territory south of the Tien Shan range. North of the Tien Shan a group of Dungan tribesmen had acquired control of much of Jungaria with the exception of the Ili valley which the Russians had occupied in 1872, ostensibly to maintain peace on their frontier.

Yakub Beg, who assumed the title of *Ataliq Ghazi*, established at Kashgar, which he made his capital, a regime of pronounced Islamic character which in many respects reflected the traditions of Khoja times. His government was autocratic in the extreme. He felt strongly the need for some external support and recognition for his rule. Thus he opened diplomatic relations with the Ottoman Empire, sending envoys to Constantinople whence he was able to obtain arms and military instructors. He also, though perhaps with some reluctance, entered into relations with both the Russians and the British. In 1872 he negotiated with Baron Kaulbars a commercial treaty between Russia and Kashgaria, and early in 1874 he signed a similar treaty with

Douglas Forsyth, then in Kashgaria on his second mission to investigate on behalf of the Government of India the commercial possibilities of Central Asia. The first Forsyth mission to Kashgaria had taken place in 1870 but had produced no treaty.

Yakub Beg, it is clear, hoped that by dealing with both the British and the Russians he would prevent either Power from attempting to take over his kingdom. It seems likely that in the event of an attempted Chinese reconquest of Kashgaria he was hoping to count on Russian and British neutrality, if not on their active help to his cause. In the event, when the Chinese attack finally did come, foreign aid availed him nothing.

The Chinese recovery of Turkestan was entrusted to Tso Tsung-t'ang, who was appointed in 1866 as governor-general of Shensi and Kansu where the Muslim rebellions had started in 1862. By 1873 Tso had pacified both Shansi and Kansu, and was ready to tackle Turkestan. This step, however, was opposed by a number of leading Chinese politicians, notably Li Hung-chang, who felt that the task was then beyond Chinese powers and who believed that the emergence of a series of independent Muslim states would serve to protect the Central Asian frontiers. Anglo-Russian rivalry, it was thought, would serve to keep both Powers out of places like Kashgaria. It was with some difficulty that Tso secured permission from Peking to start the reconquest, and with permission came very little practical aid. Tso was forced to raise his own loans in the Shanghai money-market and to find his own sources of supply for his army. To feed his troops, he ordered them to plant crops and he also managed to purchase grain, at a very reasonable price, from the Russians.

By 1876 Tso had reoccupied most of Jungaria north of the Tien Shan except, of course, the Kuldja region on the Ili which was still in Russian hands. In the spring of 1877, on the Kashgarian border, Tso defeated the army of Yakub Beg who died in obscure circumstances in May of that year. In December Kashgar was taken and by the beginning of 1878 the destruction of Yakub Beg's kingdom was complete. There now arose the problem of getting Ili back from the Russians.

When they occupied Ili in 1871 the Russians had justified their action on the grounds that they needed to preserve the peace on their borders and they promised to withdraw from Ili as soon as the Chinese had regained control of Turkestan. In January 1879 Ch'ung Hou, a Manchu diplomat, was sent to St Petersburg to try to persuade the Russians to give up Ili. By the Treaty of Livadia the Russians agreed – but at a price. The Chinese would pay for the expenses incurred by Russia during the occupation; Russia would retain the upper Tekkes valley, a fertile tract in the Ili basin; and the Russians would also be granted commercial and diplomatic concessions in Chinese Central Asia. Ch'ung Hou's treaty was promptly denounced in Peking and its negotiator only escaped sentence of death as a result of the intervention of the Powers through their representatives in China. For a while it looked as if China would rather go to war with Russia than come to terms over Ili. A crisis, however, was finally avoided by Tseng Chi-tse, Chinese Minister in London, who early in 1881 signed a fresh agreement with the Russians, the Treaty of St Petersburg, by which the Chinese regained Ili but had to pay an inflated compensation to the Russians for their occupation-costs.

In 1880 Tso Tsung-t'ang was recalled to Peking but until his death in 1885 he remained an influential adviser on Turkestan affairs. He urged that the reconquered territory should no longer be governed by indirect Manchu rule but should be converted into a new Chinese province. This step was formally taken on 11 November 1884 when an Imperial Decree announced the creation of Sinkiang (*Hsin-chiang*), 'The New Dominion'. The capital was to be at Urumchi (Ti-hua). The new province was divided into four circuits, each under a lieutenant-governor (*taotai*). Beneath the circuits were over forty administrative districts under Chinese district officers. All these posts were now open to Chinese – hitherto Turkestan had been very much a Manchu preserve. The first governor-general of Sinkiang was Liu Chin-t'ang, one of Tso Tsung-t'ang's generals. At the lowest levels of administration matters were still left very much in the hands of tribal chiefs who collected taxes and administered justice much as they had in the days before Yakub Beg. Chinese rule was reinforced by a permanent garrison of about 8,000 troops.

The Sinkiang government, as it was established in the 1880s, continued without major changes until the Chinese Revolution reached the province in 1912. It was a moderately corrupt but, as many foreign observers thought, not too oppressive a regime, being tolerant of local custom and based on the support of the local feudal leaders. The Chinese officials kept themselves very much apart from the local population. The government was not one to bring about radical social or economic change. Nonetheless, by including Sinkiang within metropolitan China, the creation of the new province made Turkestan much more accessible to foreigners. A few European missionaries established themselves there. The Russians opened a Consulate at Kashgar; and from 1890 the British maintained a representative there, George Macartney, who was recognized by the Chinese as possessing Consular status in 1908. Macartney acquired enormous influence in Sinkiang which continued until his retirement in 1918. This was based not upon the physical strength of the Consular escort, which was virtually non-existent, but on his personality and his understanding of the Chinese, perhaps derived from his Chinese mother and from his father, Sir Halliday Macartney, who had been for many years the trusted adviser to the Chinese Legation in London. During the last decade, as a result of pressure exerted by Macartney, the Chinese were induced to abolish formally the institution of slavery in Sinkiang.

Macartney's personal influence was not backed by any overwhelming British economic influence in the province. Traders from British India, faced with the long route over the difficult passes of the Karakoram, were far less favoured than the Russian traders. The Russian advantage was further increased at the end of the century when the Russo-Asiatic Bank, established in Kashgar, helped finance the construction of a cart road from the Russian border to that city. Perhaps the most important British traders in Sinkiang after the defeat of Yakub Beg were the Hindu money-lenders from Shikarpur in India who lived in Yangi Hissar and whose high interest rates won them little love from the Kashgarian people. Apart from a brief experiment in the 1880s by the Central Asiatic Trading Company, British European capital did not make any serious venture into Sinkiang in Manchu times.

Although the Chinese had come to terms with Russia in 1881 over Ili and had secured a definition of the border between Russian territory and Jungaria in 1884, in the years between the creation of Sinkiang and the outbreak of the Chinese Revolution, the province remained continually under the threat of a Russian advance. In the early 1890s the Russians penetrated into the Pamirs and as a result of the Anglo-Russian Agreement of March 1895 were confirmed in possession of considerable territory there which the Chinese had previously thought of as being under their sovereignty. After 1895 the Sino-Russian border in the Pamirs was still undefined by any treaty, although in practice it came to be accepted as following the Sarikol range. It seemed likely that the Russians might make a further extension of their territory in this quarter; this was certainly one implication of the establishment of a Russian post at Tashkurghan on the Chinese side of the Sarikol range in 1899.

The Russians, however, despite their close interest in Sinkiang which lay so near to their borders and the foreign trade of which they dominated, refrained from further territorial advances. It is possible that they were restrained by the knowledge that any forward movement here would arouse considerable British opposition, a consideration which became all the more important following the signing of the Anglo-Russian Convention of August 1907. While the Convention made no specific reference to Sinkiang it implied a renunciation by both Britain and Russia of provocative policies in Central Asia in the neighbourhood of the Indian border. Thus, when the Chinese Revolution broke out in 1911, both Jungaria and Kashgaria were still Chinese although many foreign observers of Central Asian politics wondered how much longer this state of affairs could continue.

In the winter of 1911–12 the revolution which was taking place in metropolitan China also had its consequences in Sinkiang. The Manchu governor at Urumchi, Yuan Ta-hua, was unable to maintain his authority and was obliged to resign in favour of Yuan Tseng-hsin, an official of Yunnanese origin who was then in command of the Urumchi regional administration and who controlled Muslim troops personally loyal to himself. Yang, however, was not to find it easy to preserve Sinkiang's unity in the face of revolutionary stresses. Ili threatened to set up its own government. Troops from Outer Mongolia, which was then attempting to establish its complete independence from China, undertook the invasion of the Altai region on the eastern border of Sinkiang. Chinese troops in many parts of the province, and particularly in Kashgaria, had been much affected by secret societies in Manchu times and these looked as if they would break away from the control of Urumchi. In Hami (Komul) the Muslims had risen against the Manchus and seemed likely to continue in arms against the Republic.

All this not only threatened the unity of Sinkiang; it also made it likely that the Russians would intervene to annex the province or take it under their protection. In late Manchu times the Russians had acquired great influence through their Consuls at Kashgar and Kuldja. With the Chinese Revolution, the Russians, arguing the need to protect their subjects, had greatly increased the size of their Consular escorts. By the middle of 1912 there were nearly 1,000 Cossacks in Sinkiang. Had Yang Tsen-hsin seriously lost control of the situation it is more than likely that this augmentation of Russian military strength would have resulted in the establishment of at least a Tsarist protectorate comparable with the regime which emerged at this time in Outer Mongolia.

Yang Tsen-hsin, however, kept control. By June 1912 he had come to terms with the Ili revolutionaries. The Mongol threat to the Altai was answered by the end of 1913 when Yang, with Russian diplomatic help, secured a Mongol withdrawal and the stabilization of the Mongol-Sinkiang border. The problem of the secret societies, which had produced mutinies in several Chinese garrisons in Kashgaria and also attacks on Russian subjects, was met by Yang with a mixture of ruthlessness, tact and guile. By the end of 1912 he had established his authority over all Chinese troops in Kashgaria. In 1912 also, Yang

Tseng-hsin, applying diplomatic persuasion, brought the Muslim revolt in Hami to an end.

As governor of Sinkiang and recognized as such by Yuan Shih-k'ai, the President of the Chinese Republic, Yang Tseng-hsin was no revolutionary and he showed no great enthusiasm for the Republic. His policy was to regard Sinkiang as a more or less autonomous region. The administration which he established retained much from Manchu practice and relied to a great extent on local chiefs in the lower levels of government. To important civil and military posts he appointed as many Yunnanese as he could, either his relatives or young men of promise from the province of his birth. In 1916, however, Yang lost some of his enchantment with Yunnanese when some of the men whom he had appointed plotted his overthrow. This plot was provoked by his refusal to side with the Yunnanese warlord Ts'ai Ao in the latter's armed opposition to Yuan Shih-k'ai's attempt to found a new Chinese monarchy. On learning of the plot, Yang Tseng-hsin invited his Yunnanese officials to a banquet where he treacherously put two of them to death. Many of the remainder he banished. In this, as in other issues, Yang was very careful to frustrate any challenge to his authority. It was his policy, for example, to keep all Sinkiang communications, such as the press and the telegraph system, under his personal control and he prohibited newspapers in Uighur and the other local Sinkiang languages.

While conservative in his political outlook, Yang made a number of attempts at social and economic reform during his rule of Sinkiang which lasted until 1928. He abolished certain commercial monopolies, including that over sericulture. He prohibited the obligatory provision of transport by the local population for travelling government officials. He tried to place a limit on interest-rates charged by money-lenders. He sought methods to make the province economically self-sufficient and experimented unsuccessfully with paper currency. He thus brought about serious inflation.

In foreign policy Yang was mainly concerned not to provoke the Russians. He was thus faced with a serious problem when in 1916 the Kazakhs rose against Russian conscription and over

300,000 fled into Sinkiang. Through clever diplomacy Yang managed to secure the repatriation of most of them to Russia, where they were promised an amnesty. He allowed a few Kazakhs to remain in Sinkiang where they settled down beside their fellow-tribesmen under Chinese rule. This Kazakh crisis served to emphasize the great problem of the Sinkiang-Russian border which for long stretches, and particularly in Ili, marked no clear division between ethnic groups.

In 1920, after the outbreak of the Russian Revolution, Yang Tseng-hsin faced another crisis on this border when defeated White Russian troops under General Anyenkov and their followers, some 7,000 persons in all, withdrew into Sinkiang. Yang did not try to obstruct their entry into the province but promptly disarmed and interned them, thus satisfying the Bolsheviks who made no attempt at pursuit into Chinese territory. Eventually the Bolsheviks agreed to an amnesty for the bulk of the refugees and the greater part of them were repatriated to Russia.

One group of White Russians, however, was not so easy to dispose of. A number of troops under General Baschich established themselves in the Altai where they were joined in 1921 by General Novikov and some 3,000 men. On their refusal to leave his province, Yang Tseng-hsin decided to collaborate with the Bolsheviks in their expulsion. In September 1921 a joint Sino-Soviet operation forced Baschich to retire into Outer Mongolia where he ceased to concern the Sinkiang authorities. While thus opposing the prolonged presence in Sinkiang of White Russian troops, Yang was quite sympathetic to individual Russian refugees who wished to make their home in his dominions so long as they did not involve themselves in plots against the Bolsheviks.

The foreign trade of Sinkiang had long tended to be orientated towards Russian territory, a fact which provides another explanation for Yang's attitude towards the Bolsheviks, with whom he made a commercial agreement in 1920. In 1924–5 he permitted the opening of five Russian consular posts in Sinkiang, including those at Kuldja and Kashgar which had been abandoned since 1918. In 1927, when Chiang Kai-shek broke off diplomatic relations with the USSR, Yang Tseng-hsin did not follow suit and the Sinkiang consulates remained open.

In 1928 Yang Tseng-hsin formally acknowledged some relationship with the Kuomintang – a step which he had so far avoided taking – and he accepted the Kuomintang flag as being also the flag of Sinkiang. By this time Yang had been in power for seventeen years and was seriously thinking about retiring, having transferred much of his fortune to foreign banks. Before he could withdraw from active politics, however, he was assassinated by one of his own officials, Fan Yao-nan, Commissioner of Foreign Affairs. Fan hoped to take over the government but he was unable to win the support of the majority of Yang's former subordinates. Fan and his supporters were arrested and executed by Chin Shu-jen, Chief of the Political Department of Sinkiang, who then declared himself governor.

Chin Shu-jen, an official of the old school like Yang Tseng-hsin, showed no great aptitude for government. His regime was nepotic, corrupt and inefficient, and it did not last long. In 1933, following an Uighur rebellion which started in Hami and then spread into Kashgaria, combined with an attack by Muslim Dungans from Kansu under Ma Ch'ung-ying and with a mutiny of White Russian mercenaries who had been recruited into the Urumchi garrison, Chin Shu-jen was overthrown. His place was taken by Sheng Shih-ts'ai, a soldier who had been born in Manchuria and who, before he came to Sinkiang, had been a follower of the warlord Chang Hsueh-lang with whom he had fought against the Japanese. Sheng Shih-ts'ai was without doubt a most exceptionally able soldier, politician and administrator, and by 1937 he had managed both to frustrate Dungan attacks from Kansu and suppress Uighur risings, thereby bringing a measure of peace to the province.

As a young man Sheng had spent a short time in Japan, where he flirted with Communism and became alarmed at the threat to China posed by Japanese expansionist ambitions. From the outset he seems to have seen in his control of Sinkiang the opportunity to achieve two objectives: to keep the province free of Japanese agents (in which category he placed Ma

Ch'ung-ying and his followers) and to bring about some improvement in the lot of the non-Chinese population. In 1933 he declared that his policy of government would embody eight points: equality between nationalities; religious freedom; agrarian reform; financial reform; administrative reform; education; the development of self-government; and reform of the judiciary. In 1935–6 he re-defined these eight points with the proclamation of his 'Six Great Policies' which included the substance of the eight points of 1933 together with 'anti-imperialism' (which meant opposition to Japan and the British) and 'kinship to Soviet Russia' (which meant that he would look to Russia rather than to the Chinese Central Government). The 'Six Great Policies' contained a recognition of the need to base Chinese rule on the support of the non-Chinese peoples who were a majority in Sinkiang, and that such support required a significant measure of social and political reform.

In the first few years of his administration there can be no doubt that Sheng Shih-ts'ai did introduce real reforms. His government was far less corrupt than had been that of either the Manchus or Yang Tseng-hsin. There was a rapid expansion in the facilities for the education of the non-Chinese population. Local languages were encouraged and newspapers were permitted to be published in them. The currency was stabilized with the help of a Russian loan. Again with Russian help, communications were improved, factories built and a refinery set up to exploit the potential of the Karamai oilfield near Urumchi. In 1937 Sheng announced the commencement of a Three Year Plan for economic development on the Soviet model, which was followed by a second Three Year Plan in 1941.

Up to 1941 Sheng Shih-ts'ai relied upon Russian assistance to a degree which, in the years following the Second World War, would have earned Sinkiang something like the title of a Russian satellite. In 1941, however, following the German invasion of the USSR, Russian aid was abruptly curtailed. Sheng then found himself obliged to turn towards Chiang Kai-shek and the Kuomintang, of whom hitherto he had been virtually independent. This change seems to have produced a marked decline in the liberal nature of his rule. Uighur and other non-

Chinese groups were once more repressed. Communist advisers and officials, hitherto enjoying great influence, were now interned along with Chinese civil servants of liberal, but definitely non-Communist, views. In 1944 there were said to be over 80,000 political prisoners in Sinkiang.

In 1943 the Russians withdrew their remaining technicians from Sinkiang, shut off the Karamai oil wells, and closed down the refinery, removing most of the machinery. At the same time the Kuomintang Government at Chungking began to send its officials and troops into the province, undermining the personal power of Sheng Shih-ts'ai. In desperation Sheng attempted to obtain Russian support such as he had enjoyed up to 1941, at the same time imprisoning Kuomintang officials. He is even said to have asked Stalin to take Sinkiang into the Soviet Union. The Russians, however, refused to help and Sheng, who had lost his local support with the abandonment of his liberal policy in 1941, had no choice but to surrender Sinkiang to Chiang Kai-shek, accepting as a face-saving measure a ministry in the Chungking Government.

The assertion of the control of the Chinese Central Government over Sinkiang for the first time since Yang Tseng-hsin took power in 1912 was not entirely welcome to the non-Chinese population. In November 1944 a Kazakh rebellion broke out in Ili which soon gained support from the Uighurs. At Kuldja, an Eastern Turkestan Republic, independent of Urumchi and claiming to represent the right to self-determination of the non-Chinese inhabitants of Sinkiang, was declared. It appeared to be receiving Russian support and the Kuomintang found itself unable during the course of 1945 to suppress it. Negotiations were accordingly opened between Urumchi and Kuldja which, in the summer of 1946, produced a compromise by which the Kuldja Group leaders entered the Urumchi government on the understanding that there should now begin a period of liberal administrative reform in Sinkiang. On this basis General Chang Chih-chung became Chairman of the provincial government at Urumchi.

General Chang appears to have made a serious effort to live up to the terms of the agreement with Kuldja. A new basic law for the province was promulgated. Tax arrears were cancelled. Political prisoners were released. Attempts were made to put the provincial finances in order. General Chang, however, did not go far enough to satisfy Kuldja and he was rather too liberal for Chiang Kai-shek who sought to undermine his influence. In 1947, in the face of increasing distrust by the Kuldja faction under the leadership of Akhmedjan, Chang was replaced as chairman by Masud Sabri, the first non-Chinese (he was an Uighur) to head the Sinkiang Government since Yakub Beg. He was an extremely conservative member of an old landowning family and of less liberal views than General Chang, who still remained in the provincial government. Continued opposition by Akhmedjan and the threat of civil war obliged the Kuomintang in December 1948 to replace Sabri by Burkhan, a non-Chinese of rather more flexible views. But by this time the power of the Kuomintang was obviously waning rapidly in the face of the Communists, towards whom both the Kuldja Group and many members of the Urumchi government, including General Chang, began to lean. In September 1949 both Chang and representatives of the Kuldja Group attended the People's Consultative Council which the Communists summoned to Peking and in this way Sinkiang passed into Communist hands without major fighting. On 17 December 1949 a Provisional People's Government was established in the province.

The ease with which the Communists acquired Sinkiang was to a great extent the product of their declared policy towards minorities, echoing some of the ideas of Sheng Shih-ts'ai from the period of the 'Six Great Policies', and contrasting with the reluctance of Kuomintang officials to permit the non-Chinese any participation in the higher levels of government. While it cannot be said that since 1949 the Chinese Communists in Peking have sacrificed any of the substance of their control over Sinkiang they have, nevertheless, been very careful to create and maintain the shadow of regional autonomy. In 1954, for instance, they organized Ili, the centre of the Kuldja Group, into the Ili Kazakh Autonomous *Chou* (or district) and on 1 October 1955 the whole of Sinkiang became the Sinkiang-Uighur Autonomous Region, with a political structure similar to that

311

developed in the Inner Mongolian and Kwangsi Chuang Autonomous Regions.

Shortly after the Communist acquisition of Sinkiang the province was used as a base for the Chinese occupation of Tibet. An army was sent into Western Tibet from Khotan by way of Aksai Chin along a route which the Oirots had used for their attack on Lhasa in 1717. This route the Chinese later developed into a motor road, the opening of which in 1957 marked an important stage in the evolution of the Sino-Indian boundary dispute since the Indian Government regard the Aksai Chin through which it passes as Indian territory. This dispute reached serious proportions in 1962 when Chinese troops based on Sinkiang clashed with Indian forces at the same time as the Chinese staged a major military demonstration along another section of the disputed Sino-Indian border, the McMahon Line separating Tibet from Assam.

Since 1962 another sector of the borders of Sinkiang, namely that which separates Chinese from Russian territory in the Ili region, has also been disturbed. As in earlier times, the problem here has been the presence of the same ethnic groups on both sides of the border, a fact which lends itself to disturbances, particularly in times of strained Sino-Russian relations. The Ili is a particularly sensitive area because the Chinese feel that their territory here should really extend far further north than it does at present. Chinese Communist maps have appeared showing as Chinese a tract right up to the shores of Lake Balkhash and including the Russian city of Alma-Ata.

One sector of the external border of Sinkiang has given less trouble in recent years than might have been expected. On the Pakistan side of the border the Sinkiang authorities have long possessed claims of a rather theoretical nature over the mountain state of Hunza which became a Chinese tributary in the eighteenth century and which continued to pay some form of tribute to the Chinese in Kashgar until the 1940s. The Chinese Communists could have reasserted the Hunza claim easily enough but they have declined to do so. In the Sino-Pakistan boundary agreement of March 1963 they have, to all intents and purposes, abandoned their rights over Hunza to which their

Manchu and Republican predecessors had clung with some tenacity.

With the coming of the Communists Sinkiang entered upon a period of economic development which, in many ways, continued from where Sheng Shih-ts'ai's Three Year Plans had left off. New roads were built. The railway was pushed on from Lanchow in Kansu to Urumchi, and thence to the Russian border; and a further line was projected towards Kashgar. Irrigation schemes were put in hand. The Sinkiang oilfields, abandoned by the Russians in the 1940s, came once more into production. Collectivization of both cultivators and herdsmen proceeded rapidly. Schools and centres of higher learning, with much emphasis put on local non-Chinese languages and cultures, were built. The power of the old feudal chiefs, which had survived under the previous regimes since the outbreak of the Chinese Revolution in 1911, was broken once and for all. In contrast to Tibet, all this appears to have been carried out in the face of surprisingly slight local opposition.

Abbreviations used in the Notes and Bibliography

BABesch	Bulletin van de Vereeniging tot Bevordering der Kennis van de antieke Beschaving te 'S-Gravenhage.
BSOAS	Bulletin of the School of Oriental and African Studies.
CAJ	Central Asiatic Journal.
CAR	Central Asian Review.
CRAI	Académie des inscriptions et belles-lettres (comptes rendus).
EI	*Encyclopaedia of Islam*, new edn., Leiden, 1960–.
HJAS	Harvard Journal of Asiatic Studies.
JA	Journal Asiatique.
JNSI	Journal of the Numismatic Society of India.
JRAS	Journal of the Royal Asiatic Society.
MDAFA	Mémoires de la Délégation archéologique française en Afghanistan.
NC	Numismatic Chronicle.
PA	Pacific Affairs.
PBA	Proceedings of the British Academy.
RCAJ	Royal Central Asian Journal (and predecessors).
RMM	Revue du Monde Musulman.
SA	*Studia Altaica. Festschrift für Nikolaus Poppe*, Wiesbaden, 1957.
SJA	Southwestern Journal of Anthropology.
TG	W. W. Tarn, *The Greeks in Bactria and India*, 2nd edn., Cambridge, 1951.
TP	T'oung Pao.
ZDMG	Zeitschrift der Deutschen mörgenlandischen Gesellschaft.

Notes

Introduction

1 M. A. Stein, 'Innermost Asia: its geography as a factor in history', *The Geographical Journal*, 1925, 489, but cf. E. Huntington, *The Pulse of Asia*, London, 1907.

2 For the disputed course of the Amu-Darya see V. V. Bartold, *Nachrichten über den Aral-See und den unteren Lauf des Amu-darja von den ältesten Zeiten bis zum XVII. Jahrhundert*, Leipzig, 1910; B. Spuler, *EI*, sv. 'Āmū-Daryā'.

3 In Han times this route crossed the Lop-Nor to Kurla. Stein, *op. cit.*, 394–5.

4 I am indebted to the Librarian of the Zoological Society of London for these figures.

5 N. M. Przhevalsky, *Mongolia, the Tangut country and the solitudes of northern Tibet*, 2 vols., London, 1876, I, 64.

6 F. B. Pegolotti, *La Practica della Mercatura*, ed. A. Evans, Cambridge, Mass., 1936.

7 D. Carruthers, *Unknown Mongolia*, 2 vols., London, 2nd edn., 1914, II, 446.

8 E.g., R. B. Ekvall, *Cultural relations on the Kansu-Tibetan border*, Chicago, 1939, 81.

9 For the population of Sinkiang in 1953 and Soviet Central Asia in 1959 see W. A. Douglas-Jackson, *Russo-Chinese Borderlands*, Princeton, 1962, 12. For further details of the demography of Soviet Central Asia see L. Krader, *Peoples of Central Asia*, 171–218.

10 Most Dungans (today known as Hui) live in the Ninghsia Hui Autonomous Region, Kansu and Shensi while less than half a million live in Sinkiang and even fewer live in Soviet territory. While G. F. Hudson, 'The Nationalities of China', *St Antony's*

Papers, VII, London, 1960, 60, accepts the figure of four million. Soviet estimates have been much higher. Cf. 'The Dungans in China', *CAR*, 1961, 201.

11 The Mongols are divided approximately as follows: in Outer Mongolia just over one million; in Inner Mongolia and Barga less than two million; in the Buriat ASSR less than 300,000. To these may be added 100,000 Kalmyks who were re-established in the Kalmyk Autonomous Oblast in 1956 and a similar number of Oirots in Sinkiang.

12 This figure is deceptive as, in addition, between two and three million Tajiks live in Afghanistan.

13 The following articles may be recommended as introductory reading: J. L. Myres, 'Nomadism', *Journal of the Royal Anthropological Institute*, 1941; R. Patai, 'Nomadism: Middle Eastern and Central Asian', *SJA*, 1951; E. E. Bacon, 'Types of Pastoral Nomadism in Central and Southwest Asia', *SJA*, 1954; L.Krader, 'Principles and Structures in the Organization of the Asiatic Steppe-Pastoralists', *SJA*, 1955; idem, 'Ecology of Central Asian Pastoralism', *SJA*, 1955; idem, 'Ecology of Nomadic Pastoralism', *International Social Science Journal*, 1959.

14 Ekvall, *op. cit.*, 80–2.

15 B. Laufer, *Chinese Clay Figures*, Chicago, 1914, 249–50.

Chapter 1

1 Herodotus, IV, 11; cf. E. D. Phillips, 'New light on the ancient history of the Eurasian steppe', *American Journal of Archaeology*, LXI, 1957, 269–80.

2 E. D. Phillips, 'The Argippaei of Herodotus', *Artibus Asiae*, XXIII, 1960, 124–8; idem, 'The legend of Aristeas; fact and fancy in early Greek notions of East Russia, Siberia and Inner Asia', *Artibus Asiae*, XVIII, 1955, 161–77.

3 For support of this identification see W. Samolin, 'Historical ethnography of the Tarim basin before the Turks', *Palaeologia*, IV, Tokyo, 1956, 38.

4 Herodotus, I, 201.

5 Arrian, *Anabasis*, III, 27; Strabo, XV, 724.

6 Pliny, *Natural History*, VI, 92.

7 E. Benveniste, 'La ville de Cyreschata', *JA*, 1943–5, 163–6.

8 By this name Herodotus seems to refer to the Jaxartes.
9 According to Arrian, *Anabasis*, VI, 29.
10 R. G. Kent, *Old Persian*, 1953, 134.
11 Not necessarily identical with the well-known city of Capisa.
12 The Seleucid Era is called the Era of Alexander by the Arab astronomer, al-Biruni, *Chronology of ancient nations*, trans. Sachau, 121.
13 W. B. Henning, *Zoroaster, Politician or Witch-Doctor*, Oxford, 1951.
14 Kent, *op. cit.*, 144.
15 The tribute was paid in silver bullion, a talent of the Babylonian standard amounting to 30kg.024.
16 Herodotus uses the old Persian form of the gentile name, Saranges; for consistency the Median form of the eparchy-name, Drangiana, is used throughout the text here, following the practice of the later Greek writers.
17 Kent, *op. cit.*, 144.
18 As in Strabo, XV, 724; cf. *TG*, 100.
19 D. Schlumberger, 'L'argent grec dans l'empire achéménide', in R. Curiel and D. Schlumberger, *Trésors monétaires d'Afghanistan*, 3–62.
20 J-P. Guépin, 'Greek coinage and Persian bimetallism', *Jaarboek voor Munt- en Penningkunde*, XLIX, 1962, 1–19.
21 Xenophon, *Oeconomicus*, IV, 2.
22 For example, S. P. Tolstov, *Auf den Spuren der altchoresmischen Kultur*, Berlin, 1953, 111.
23 A. T. Olmstead, *History of the Persian Empire*, 146.
24 Olmstead, *op. cit.*, 248.
25 J. Lasse, 'The irrigation system of Ulḫu', *Journal of Cuneiform Studies*, V, 1951, 21–32.
26 G. Caton-Thompson, 'Kharga Oasis', *Antiquity*, V, 1931, 221–6 and especially 224.
27 Xenophon, *Oeconomicus*, IV, 23.
28 M. N. Tod, *Greek historical inscriptions to the end of the fifth century*, Oxford, 1946, 12.
29 *Historia plantarum*, IV, 4, 2.
30 B. Laufer, *Sino-Iranica*, 539.
31 G. M. A. Richter, 'Silk in Greece', *American Journal of Archaeology*, XXXIII, 1929, 27–33.
32 *Historia animalium*, V, 19; 551 b 13.
33 Strabo, XV, i, 18.

34 Herodotus, VII, 66. For the Pactyes see H. W. Bailey, 'Kusanica' *BSOAS*, XIV, 1952, 430.

35 G. Posener, *La première domination perse en Egypte*, Cairo, 1936, 183; R. G. Kent, 'Old Persian Texts', *Journal of Near Eastern Studies*, II, 1943, 302–6, and especially 304.

36 S. I. Rudenko, *Kultura naselniya Gornogo Altaya v skifskoe vremya*, Moscow, 1953.

37 As in K. Jettmar, 'The Altai before the Turks', *The Museum of Far Eastern Antiquities, Stockholm: Bulletin*, XXIII, 1951, 182.

38 C. Trever, *Excavations in Northern Mongolia*, Leningrad, 1932.

39 B. V. Head, 'The earliest Graeco-Bactrian and Graeco-Indian coins', *NC*, 1906, Pl. I, 8; later references in J-P. Guépin, 'Leonine brows and the shadow of Pyrgoteles', *BABesch*, XXXIX, 1964, 129.

40 Arrian, *Anabasis*, IV, 10.

41 The ancient Greeks regarded the Hindu Kush as a branch of the Caucasus. The range was also known by its Prakrit name of Paropamisus.

42 The situation of the Rock is not exactly known. A similar mountain stronghold of Sogdiana, and no doubt one of many, was that of Mount Mugh in the Islamic period.

43 W. W. Tarn, *Alexander the Great*, II, 326, following Plutarch, *Alexander*, XLVII.

44 The Alexandropolis of Isidore of Charax, *Parthian stations*, 19, placed by Tarn (*TG*, 470) at Ghazni. However, the discovery of Greek inscriptions at Kandahar seems to strengthen the older identification with that site.

45 A recent discussion of Alexander's march in these regions based on local knowledge is by O. Caroe, *The Pathans*, 49–55.

46 In Diodorus, XVII, 99, 6, the mutineers are all said to have been massacred. But Curtius, IX, 7, 1–11, states that eventually they reached their homes.

47 The usual Greek designation of the provinces of the Iranian plateau, from Media eastwards. The phrase perhaps translates a Persian expression which is no longer attested, e.g., Diodorus, XIX, 14, 1; and in inscriptions of Seleucid date from Nihavend and Bisitun in Iran noticed by L. Robert, 'Inscriptions Séleucides de Phrygie et d'Iran', *Hellenica*, VII, 1949, 22–4; *Gnomon*, XXXV, 76.

48 Tarn, however, rejects the figure of 23,000 and believes that the true number of mutineers was only 3,000, *TG*, 72.

49 According to an inventory of 311/310 BC (IG²1492) she had dedicated to Athena Polias such typically Iranian gifts as a gold rhyton (drinking-horn) and torque; there seems to be no evidence that Roxana personally visited Athens.

50 Plutarch, *Alexander*, 62.

51 According to Strabo, XV, 689, some or all of Aria was ceded to Chandragupta and this was accepted by V. A. Smith, *Asoka*, 66; *contra* E. R. Bevan, *The House of Seleucus*, I, 296; *TG*, 100. Epigraphic confirmation is lacking and if the Mauryas had held Aria Seleucid communication with Bactria would have been broken.

52 But see W. W. Tarn, 'Two notes on Seleucid history', *Journal of Hellenic Studies*, LX, 1940, 89.

53 W. B. Henning, 'The Aramaic inscription of Asoka found at Lampaka', *BSOAS*, XIII, 1949, 80–8.

54 D. Schlumberger, L. Robert, et al., 'Une bilingue gréco-araméenne d'Asoka', *JA*, CCXLVI, 1958, 1–48.

55 D. Schlumberger, 'Une nouvelle inscription grecque d'Asoka', *CRAI*, 22 mai 1964.

56 W. W. Tarn, 'Two notes on Seleucid history', *Journal of Hellenic Studies*, LX, 1940, 84–94.

57 E. T. Newell, *Eastern Seleucid mints*, 231–6.

58 L. Robert, 'Inscription hellénistique d'Iran', *Hellenica*, XI-XII, 1960, 85–91.

59 Justin, XLI, ii, 3; 'Sermo his inter Scythicum Medicumque medius et utrimque mixtus'; cf. W. B. Henning, 'Mitteliranisch', *Handbuch der Orientalistik*, IV, Iranistik, erster Abschnitt, 93.

60 A lower chronology is preferred by J. Wolski, 'The decay of the Iranian empire of the Seleucids, and the chronology of Parthian beginnings', *Berytus*, XII, 1956–7, 35–52. The new Andragoras inscription weighs slightly against him.

61 A summary of the finds is given by A. Mongait, *Archaeology in the USSR*. The ivories are fully illustrated in M. E. Masson and G. A. Pugochenkova, *Parfianskie ritony Nisy*, Moscow, 1956, with introduction in French.

62 W. B. Henning, *op. cit.*, 27, 30; R. N. Frye, *The Heritage of Persia*, 148.

63 M. Sznycer, 'Nouveaux ostraca de Nisa', *Semitica*, XII, 1962, 105–26.

64 *The Christian Topography*, ed. E. O. Winstedt, Cambridge, 1909, 73–4.

65 A. K. Narain, *The Indo-Greeks*, claims to distinguish two portraits. The contrary opinion was expressed by E. T. Newell, *Eastern Seleucid mints*, 248.
66 For the surviving remains see B. Dagens, M. Le Berre, and D. Schlumberger, *Monuments préislamiques d'Afghanistan*, Paris, 1964, 69–75.
67 This paragraph is based on Polybius, X, 31.
68 *TG*.
69 A. K. Narain, *The Indo-Greeks*,
70 The standard coin-calatogues for this period are still P. Gardner, *A Catalogue of Indian coins in the British Museum. Greek and Scythic Kings of Bactria*, London, 1886, and R. B. Whitehead, *Catalogue of coins in the Punjab Museum, Lahore*, Oxford, 1914, vol. I, *Indo-Greek coins*.
71 Narain, *op. cit.*, 46 ff.
72 A. D. H. Bivar, 'The Bactrian treasure of Qunduz', *JNSI*, XVII, 1955, 37–52.
73 R. Curiel and G. Fussman, *Le Trésor monétaire de Qunduz* (Mémoires de la Délegation archéologique Française en Afghanistan XX), Paris, 1965.

Chapter 2

1 To be distinguished from the much later Apollodotus II, cf. D. W. MacDowall and N. G. Wilson, 'Apollodoti reges Indorum', *NC*, 1960, 221–8.
2 *Prologue*, XLI.
3 *Milindapañha*, tr. I. B. Horner, 1963; *The Questions of King Milinda*, tr. T. W. Rhys Davids, Oxford, 1890.
4 Narain, *op. cit.*, 42 and Pl. VI.
5 On the Chionites, XIV, 3, 1; on the European Huns, XXXI, 2, 1.
6 XI, 8, 2 (=p. C 511). The translation here follows the amendation of Vaillant, cf. G. Haloun, 'Zur Üe-tsi-Frage', *ZDMG*, XCI, 1937, 244, and reading *Sacaraucae* for *Sacaraulae*.
7 *TG*, 272, 294; *JNSI*, XVII, 1955, 43.
8 Justin, *Epitoma*, XLII, 1–2.
9 S. Konow, *Kharoshthi Inscriptions* (CII II, pt. i), Calcutta, 1929, 46–9. The interesting comments of A. H. Dani, 'Mathura Lion-Capital inscription (a palaeographical study)', *Journal of the Asiatic Society of Pakistan*, V, 1960, 128–47, regard the engrav-

ing of the inscription as of later date but do not weaken the conclusion that the document itself is of the first century BC.

10 Ptolemy, *Geography*, VII, 1, 55; *Periplus Maris Erythraei*, 38.
11 *Taxila*, I, 44–73.
12 Narain, *op. cit.*, 136.
13 G. K. Jenkins, 'Indo-Scythic mints', *JNSI*, XVII, 1955, 16.
14 Cf. S. Konow, *Epigraphia Indica*, XXI, 1932, 251; *JRAS*, 1932, 949; *Kharoshthi Inscriptions*, 71.
15 *Pompei Trogi Fragmenta*, ed. O. Seel, Leipzig, 1956, 179.
16 *TG*, 287, 533.
17 Haloun, *op. cit.*, 252.
18 D. Sinor, *Introduction à l'étude de l'Eurasie Centrale*, 233.
19 Cf. R. B. Whitehead, 'Notes on the Indo-Greeks', *NC*, 1940, 120–2.
20 *TG*, 508–10.
21 *Geography*, VI, 11, 6.
22 Extracts cited in S. Konow, *Kharoshthi Inscriptions*, lvi, lxii.
23 W. Wright, *Apocryphal Acts of the Apostles*, II, 146 ff.
24 Philostratus, *Life of Apollonius of Tyana*, II, xviii.
25 *Indica*, ed. Sachau, 207.
26 Bardesanes, *Le Livre des lois des pays*, tr. F. Nau, 41.
27 W. B. Henning, 'The Argi and the "Tokharians" ', *BSOAS*, IX, 1937, 564. A recent summary of opinions on 'Tokharian' is by W. Krause, 'Tocharisch', *Handbuch der Orientalistik*, Abt. I, Bd. IV: 3: Abschnitt, Leiden, 1955.
28 H. W. Bailey, 'Kusanica', *BSOAS*, XIV, 1952, 420; idem, 'Languages of the Saka', *Handbuch der Orientalistik*, Abt. I, Bd. IV: 1. Abschnitt, Leiden, 1958, 136.
29 S. Konow, 'On the nationality of the Kushanas', *ZDMG*, LXVIII, 1914, 99 ff.
30 Bailey, 'Languages of the Saka', 131.
31 G. Morgenstierne, *EI*, sv. 'Afghanistan'.
32 W. B. Henning, 'The Bactrian Inscription', *BSOAS*, XXIII, 1960, 47.
33 A. Maricq, 'La grande inscription de Kaniska', *JA*, 1958, 364.
34 W. E. van Wijk, 'On dates in the Kanishka Era', *Acta Orientalia* (Leiden), V, 1926, 168–70.
35 Cf. A. D. H. Bivar, 'The Kaniska dating from Surkh Kotal', *BSOAS*, XXVI, 1963, 498–502.
36 Found at Lou-lan in the Tarim Basin, cf. M. A. Stein, *Innermost Asia*, I, 241; Pl. XXX.

37 M. Wheeler, *Rome beyond the Imperial Frontiers*, London, 1954, 175.

38 J. Hackin et al., *Nouvelles recherches archéologiques à Begram*.

39 For Hariti see A. Foucher, *L'art gréco-bouddhique de Gandhara*, II, 130. For Ctesiphon see Dio Cassius, LXXI, 2, 4; Ammianus Marcellinus, XXIII, 6, 24.

40 A. G. Loundine and J. Ryckmans, *Museon*, LXXVII, 1964, 415.

41 M. A. Stein, 'Zoroastrian deities on Indo-Scythian coins', *Oriental and Babylonian Record*, August 1887, 88; recent observations by A. Maricq, 'La grande inscription de Kaniska', *JA*, 1958, 421–9.

42 See the Gurgan inscription noticed in note 58 to Chapter 1 above.

43 B. N. Mukherjee, 'Shah-ji-ki-Dheri casket inscription', *British Museum Quarterly*, XXVIII, 39–46.

44 T. Watters, *On Yuan Chwang*, 270–8; S. Frauwallner, 'Die buddhistischen Konzile', *ZDMG*, 1952, 250–6.

45 D. Schlumberger, 'Le temple de Surkh Kotal en Bactriane (III)', *JA*, 1955, 276.

46 B. A. Litvinsky, 'Arkheologiya Tadzhikistana za gody sovetskoy vlasti', *Sovetskaya Arkheologiya*, 1967, III, 118.

47 J. Brough, *The Gandhari Dharmapada*, London, 1962.

Chapter 3

1 T. Watters, *On Yuan Chwang*, I, 124.

2 Ed de Goeje, 819; T. Noeldeke, *Geschichte der Perser und Araber sur Zeit der Sasaniden*, Leiden, 1879, 15 ff.

3 E. Honigmann and A. Maricq, *Recherches sur les Res Gestae Divi Saporis*, Bruxelles, 1953, 11; 98–110.

4 E. Herzfeld, *Kushano-Sasanian coins* (Memoirs of the Archaeological Survey of India, XXXVIII), Calcutta, 1930.

5 A. D. H. Bivar, 'The Kushano-Sassanian coin series', *JNSI*, XVIII, 1956, 13–42.

6 *Scriptores Historiae Augustae*, Carus 8.

7 *XII Panegyrici Latini*, ed Baehrens, 288.

8 Cf. W. M. McGovern, *The early empires of Central Asia*, 307 ff.

9 W. B. Henning, 'The date of the Sogdian ancient letters', *BSOAS*, XII, 1948, 603.

10   By W. B. Henning in his discussion of the Pahlavi inscription, Persepolis, ii, in *Corpus Inscriptionum Iranicarum*, Pt. III, vol. II, Portfolio III, Introduction, where the date of the inscription is read as the 18th year of Shapur, instead of the 48th year, as in older editions.

11   XVI, 9, 4; XVII, 5, 1; XVIII, 6, 22.

12   *ZDMG*, XC, 1936, 17.

13   N. Fettich, *Le trouvaille de tombe princière hunnique à Szeged-Nagyszéksós* (Archaeologi Hungarica XXXII), Budapest, 1953, 105.

14   Cf. G. Frumkin, 'Archaeology in Soviet Central Asia: IV, Tadzhikistan', *Central Asian Review*, XIII, 1964, 176.

15   R. A. Miller, *Accounts of the Western Nations in the history of the Northern Chou dynasty*, 11–12.

16   Cf. R. Curiel, 'Le trésor de Tépé Maranjan', in R. Curiel and D. Schlumberger, *Trésors monétaires d'Afghanistan*, 103 ff.

17   W. M. McGovern, *The early empires of Central Asia*, 408.

18   K. Enoki, 'On the nationality of the Ephthalites', *Memoirs of the Research Department of the Toyo Bunko*, XVIII, 1959, 22, 25.

19   Procopius, *Wars*, I, 3.

20   His actual name was Istemi.

21   D. C. Sarcar, 'Three early medieval inscriptions', *Epigraphia Indica*, XXXV, 1963, 45–7.

22   V. Minorsky, 'The Turkish dialect of the Khalaj', *BSOAS*, X, 1940–2, 417–37.

23   R. Ghirshman, *Les Chionites-Hephthalites*.

24   See note 18 above.

25   Miller, *op. cit.*, 11–12.

26   O. M. Dalton, *The Treasure of the Oxus*, 3rd edn., London, 1964, 53, no. 201.

27   For the stirrup see A. D. H. Bivar, 'The stirrup and its origins', *Oriental Art*, n.s. I, 1953, 3–7.

28   A somewhat modified chronology was advocated by Lynn White, *Medieval technology and social change*, Oxford, 1962, 1–38. The discussion is stimulating but this chronology should not be followed in every detail.

29   The pioneer study was that of V. Thomsen, 'Inscriptions de l'Orkhon déchiffrées', *Mémoires de la Société Finno-Ugrienne*, V, 1896, 1–224. See now Giraud, *L'Empire des Turcs célestes*.

30   D. Sinor, *Introduction à l'étude de l'Eurasie Centrale*, 86–90.

31   J. R. Hamilton, *Les Ouïghours à l'époque des Cinq Dynasties*, 139.

32 E. Chavannes and P. Pelliot, 'Un traité Manichéen retrouvé en Chine', *Journal Asiatique*, 1913, 177.
33 Al-Biruni, *Al-athār al-bāqiya*, tr. Sachau, *The chronology of ancient nations*, 190.
34 W. B. Henning, 'The Book of Giants', *BSOAS*, XI, 1943–6, 52–74.
35 Chavannes and Pelliot, *op. cit.*, 194.
36 Ala-ad Din 'Ata-Malik Juvaini, the *Tarikh-i Jahān Gushā*, tr. J. A. Boyle, *The History of the World Conqueror*, Manchester, 1958, I, 54.

Chapter 4

1 F. C. Murgotten, *The origins of the Islamic state*, New York, 1924, II, 39; 139 ff.
2 J. Walker, 'Some new Arab-Sassanian coins', *NC*, 1952, 108 and Pl. IX, 3.
3 H. A. R. Gibb, *The Arab Conquest of Central Asia*, 66.
4 Mongait, *op. cit.*, 290.
5 Idem, 293.
6 Cf. E. G. Browne, *A literary history of Persia*, London, 1902, I, 247 ff.; W. Barthold, *Turkestan down to the Mongol invasion*, 199.
7 Ed. Malik al-Shu'ara Bahar, Tehran, 1314/1935, 156; 162. This recently discovered anonymous Persian text is of real importance for the early Muslim period and still awaits translation into a western language.
8 For the writing of Persian poetry by Hanzala of Badghis under the Tahirids see C. E. Wilson, 'The foundation of modern Persian', *BSOAS*, II, 1921–3, 218. However, the existence of Persian verse is sparsely attested before the time of the Saffarids. The *Tarikh-i Sistan*, 209, quotes a Persian poem recited in honour of Ya'qub b. al-Layth by the scribe Muhammad b. Wasif and claims that the use of Persian was then an innovation.
9 This anecdote from the *Jawami 'al-Hikayat* of 'Awfi (printed already by E. Thomas, *Essays on Indian antiquities*, I, London, 1858, 317) now receives confirmation from the *Tarikh-i Sistan*, 255.

10 Cf. J. Walker, *The coinage of the second Saffarid dynasty in Sistan*, New York, 1936. A narrative account of these later Saffarid rulers is now available in the Persian *Tarikh-i Sistan*.
11 Barthold, *op. cit.*, 242.
12 E. Denison Ross, 'A Qasida by Rudaki', *JRAS*, 1926, 213 ff.
13 The statement of Hamdullah Mustawfi Qazvini, *Tarikh-i Guzida*, tr. E. G. Browne and R. A. Nicholson, London, 1913, II, 78, that Alptigin reigned at Ghazni for 16 years is no doubt an error.
14 O. Pritsak, 'Die Karachaniden', *Der Islam*, XXX, 2–3, 1952, 21–2; idem, 'Von der Karluk zu den Karachaniden', *ZDMG*, CI, 1951, 270–300. Even Barthold changed his opinion as to the origin of the Qarakhanids. After once maintaining that they were Yaghmā, he subsequently adopted the view that they were of Qarluq origin. Cf. V. Minorsky, *Hudūd al-'Alam*, 280.
15 C. Brocklemann, 'Mahmud al-Kašghari über die Sprachen und die Stämme der Türken im II. Jahr.', *Körösi Csoma-Archivum*, I, 1921–5, 26–40.
16 Barthold, *op. cit.*, 255.
17 *Hudud al-'Alam*, tr. Minorsky, 110.
18 A. Maricq and G. Wiet, *Le minaret de Djam*, Paris 1959.
19 For the Qara-Khitay see K. A. Wittfogel and Fêng Chia-Shêng, *History of Chinese Society: Liao (907–1125)*, Philadelphia, 1949, 619–74.

Chapter 5

1 For the earliest records of Tibet see A. Herrmann, *Das Land der Seide und Tibet im Lichte der Antike*, Leipzig, 1938.
2 M. Herrmanns, *Die Nomaden nov Tibet*, Vienna, 1949.
3 J. N. Roerich, *The Animal Style among the nomads of northern Tibet*, Prague, 1930.
4 For the Bon religion see H. Hoffmann, 'Quellen zur Geschichte der tibetischen Bon-Religion', *Abhandlungen der Akademie der Wissenschaften und der Literatur in Mainz*, 1950.
5 These two princesses were later revered as incarnations of the Goddess Tara, the White and the Green Tara respectively. See A. Getty, *The Gods of Northern Buddhism*, 2nd edn., Oxford, 1928, 119–24, and G. Tucci, 'The Wives of Sron btsan sgam po', *Oriens Extremus*, 1962, 121–6.

6 The close connexion between Kashmiri and Tibetan Buddhism is discussed in J. N. and P. N. Ganhar, *Buddhism in Kashmir and Ladakh*, Delhi, 1956.

7 On Sino-Tibetan relations in this confused period see H. E. Richardson, *Ancient Historical Edicts at Lhasa*, London, 1952.

8 Plate 37 shows a Tantric disciple of Padmasambhava in traditional costume. In his right hand he holds the *vajra*, Indra's thunderbolt, symbolic of the Tantric method and in his left hand a dagger for subduing demons.

9 The political character of this conflict has been stressed by G. Tucci, *The Tombs of the Tibetan Kings*, Rome, 1950, 72.

10 G. Tucci, *Tibetan Painted Scrolls*, 2 vols., Rome, 1949, I, 7; II, 737-8.

11 G. Tucci, 'Rin c'en bzan po e la rinàscita del Buddhismo nel Tibet intorno all mille', *Indo-Tibetica*, II, Rome, 1933.

12 For the significance of the careers of Marpa and Milarepa the following works should be consulted: J. Bacot, 'La vie de Marpa le "traducteur",' *Buddhica*, Paris, 1937; B. Laufer, *Milaraspa. Tibetische Texte in Auswahl*, Hagen and Darmstadt, 1922; W. Y. Evans-Wentz, *Tibet's great Yogi Milarepa*, London, 1928; H. Hoffman, *Mi-la Ras-pa, Sieben Legenden*, Munich, 1950.

Chapter 6

1 No copy of the *Yasa* has survived and it can now only be partially reconstructed from contemporary references. See G. Vernadsky, 'The scope and contents of Chingis Khan's *Yasa*', *HJAS*, 1938; idem, 'Juwaini's version of Chingis Khan's *Yasa*', *Annales de l'Institut Kondakov*, 1940; C. Alinge, *Mongolische Gesetze*, Leipzig, 1934; and V. A. Riasonovsky, *Fundamental Principles of Mongol Law*; Tientsin, 1937 (reprinted at The Hague, 1965). The *Yasa* was probably assumed to confer special authority upon those who enforced it, which may account for its partial adoption far beyond the limits of the Mongol empire. See, e.g., A. N. Poliak, 'The influence of Chingiz-Khan's Yasa upon the general organization of the Mamluk State,' *BSOAS*, 1942.

2 For Prester John see C. R. Beazley, *The dawn of modern geography*, 3 vols., Oxford, 1897–1906; H. Yule, *Cathay and the*

way thither, 4 vols., London, 1913–16; J. K. Wright, *The geographical lore of the time of the Crusades*, New York, 1925; A. P. Newton, *Travel and travellers of the Middle Ages*, London, 1926; R. Hennig, *Terrae Incognitae*, 4 vols., Leiden, 1936–9; G. H. T. Kimble, *Geography in the Middle Ages*, London, 1938; V. Slessarev, *Prester John: the letter and the legend*, Minneapolis, 1959.

3 The women of Toghrïl's family were destined to play a great part in Chingizkhanid history. His niece Sorqoqtani married Tolui, Chingiz Khan's fourth son, and became the mother of Möngke, Qubilai and Hülegü. Hülegü's wife, Doquz Khatun, was a grand-daughter of Toghrïl and became the mother of the second Il-Khan of Iran, Abaqa (1265–81). Abaqa's son, Arghun (1284–91) married the niece of Doquz Khatun, Uruq Khatun, who became the mother of Uljaytu (1304–16). Karait influence at the Il-Khanid court continued into the reign of Abu Sa'id (1316–35).

4 Bartold, *op. cit.*, 404.

5 This strategy has been analysed in detail by O. Lattimore, 'The Geography of Chingis Khan', *The Geographical Journal*, 1963.

Chapter 7

1 The title *Il-Khan* was used of a khan ruling a particular *ulus* or fief as a subordinate of the *khaqan*. It was used in this sense by Hülegü and his descendants who until the reign of Ghazan (1295–1304) were punctilious in recognizing the suzerainty of the *khaqans* in Mongolia or China. See S. Lane-Poole, *The coins of the Mongols in the British Museum*, liv–lv. In recent times the title has been used in Iran by chieftains of the Qashqai and the Bakhtiari tribes who are not, of course, subordinate to any *khaqan*.

2 The definitive study of Mongol-Korean relations is W. E. Henthorn, *Korea: The Mongol Invasions*, Leiden, 1963.

3 H. Franke, 'Could the Mongol Emperors read and write Chinese?', *Asia Major*, 1953.

4 H. F. Schurmann, *Economic Structure of the Yüan Dynasty*, Cambridge, Mass., 1956, 4–6. For fourteenth-century experi-

ments with paper currency see H. Franke, *Geld und Wirtschaft in China unter der Mongolen-Herrschaft*, Leipzig, 1949; K. Jahn, 'Das iranische Papiergeld', *Archiv Orientalni*, 1938; W. J. Fischel, 'On the Iranian currency ALCHAV of the Mongol period', *JRAS*, 1939; M. Husain, *Tughluq Dynasty*, Calcutta, 1963, 185–92.

5   The Buddhism of the Il-Khans was not the Lamaism which spread later among the Mongols of Mongolia but a syncretic form of Mahayana. See B. Spuler, *Die Mongolen in Iran*, 180, and K. Jahn, 'Kamalashri—Rashid al-Din's "Life and Teaching of Buddha". A Source for the Buddhism of the Mongol Period', *CAJ*, 1956.

6   J. Kritzeck, 'Ibn-al-Ṭiqṭaqa and the fall of Baghdad', *The World of Islam*, ed. J. Kritzeck and R. Bayly, London, 1959, 167–8.

7   A. Waley, *The Travels of an Alchemist*, London, 1931, 67–8.

8   It has not been generally recognized that the early Il-Khans exercised suzerainty over Kashmir. See K. Jahn, 'A Note on Kashmir and the Mongols', *CAJ*, 1956.

9   D. N. Wilbur, *The architecture of Islamic Iran: The Il Khanid period*, Princeton, 1955. For the other arts see A. Upham Pope, *A Survey of Persian Art*, 6 vols., London, 1938–9.

10 For the Jalayarids see J. B. van Loon, *Ta'rīkh-i Shaikh Uwais'*, The Hague, 1954; C. Huart, 'Mémoire sur la fin de la dynastie des Ilékaniens', *JA*, 1876; H. L. Rabino, 'Coins of the Jalā'ir, Kara Ḳoyūnlū, Musha'sha', and Āḳ Ḳoyūnlū Dynasties, *NC*, 1950.

Chapter 8

1   C. Dawson, *The Mongol Mission*, 155.

2   P. Pelliot, *Notes sur l'histoire de la Horde d'Or*, Paris, 1950, 106.

3   J. A. Boyle, *The History of the World-Conquerors*, I, 267.

4   H. G. Raverty, *The Tabakat-i-Nasiri*, II, 1285–6.

5   F. A. Ballod (F. Balodis), *Privolzhskie Pompei*, Moscow, 1923; idem, 'Alt-Sarai und Neu-Sarai, die Hauptstädte der Goldenen Horde', *Latvijas Universitates Raksti* (Riga), XIII, 1926, 3–82.

6   A. N. Poliak, 'Le caractère colonial de l'Etat Mamelouk dans ses rapports avec la Horde d'Or', *Revue des études islamiques*, 1935, 231–48.

7   H. A. R. Gibb, *The travels of Ibn Battuta, AD 1325–54*, II, 473–4; 478. Cf. G. le Strange, *The geographical part of the Nuzhat-al-qulub*, London, 1919, 251–2.
8   Gibb, *op. cit.*, II, 515–16; 470–1. For Genoese relations with the Golden Horde see G. I. Bratianu, *Recherches sur le commerce génois dans la mer noire au XIIIe siècle*, Paris, 1929.
9   Presumably Jani Bek intended to retain Georgia and Azarbayjan. In A.H. 758/AD 1357 both he and Birdi minted coins in Qara-Aghach in south-eastern Georgia. D. M. Lang, *Studies in the numismatic history of Georgia in Transcaucasia*, New York, 1955, 75–6.
10 For the Russian *drang nach osten*, W. D. Wyman and C. B. Kroeber, *The Frontier in perspective*, Madison, Wis., 1957; R. J. Werner, *The urge to the sea: the course of Russian history*, Berkeley, Calif., 1942; R. H. Fisher, *The Russian fur trade*, 1550–1700, Berkeley, 1943; G. V. Lantzeff, *Siberia in the Seventeenth Century. A study of the colonial administration*, Berkeley, 1943.

Chapter 9

1   J. von Hammer-Purgstall, *Geschichte Wassaf's*, 141.
2   H. A. R. Gibb, *Ibn Battuta. Travels in Asia and Africa*, 1325–54, London, 1929, 174–5.
3   H. G. Raverty, *The Tabakat-i-Nasiri*, II, 1144–6.
4   E. Haenisch, *Die geheime Geschichte der Mongolen*, 136–7.
5   K. Jahn, *Ta'rīh-i-Mubārak-i-Gāzānī*, The Hague, 1957, 12–13; A. C. M. D'Ohsson, *Histoire des Mongols*, III, 430–1.
6   Wassaf, *op. cit.*, 153.
7   It has been assumed that Tarmashirin invaded India and E. Sarkisyanz, *Geschichte der orientalischen Volker Russlands bis 1917*, 117, states that in 1327 he reached Delhi. This is rejected by M. Husain, *Tughluq Dynasty*, 119–43. The role of the Mongols in Indian history has been somewhat neglected but see D. Pal, 'Ala-ud-din Khilji's Mongol Policy', *Islamic Culture*, 1947; K. Jahn, 'Zum Problem der mongolischen Eroberungen in Indien (13.–14. Jahrhundert)', *Akten des vierundzwanzigsten Internationalen Orientalisten-Kongresses*, Munich, 1957; K. Jahn, 'A Note on Kashmir and the Mongols', *CAJ*, 1956; A. Ahmad, 'Mongol pressure in an alien land', *CAJ*, 1961.

8 Babur and Mirza Muhammad Haydar Dughlat, both of whom must have been familiar with the genealogy of the Chaghatai khans, assert that he was a great-grandson. This is difficult to reconcile with the chronology.

9 A. S. Beveridge, *The Bābur-Nāma in English*, I, 160–1.

10 Abu Bakr's general, Mir Vali, is reputed to have conquered Gilgit and Baltistan. He is unlikely to have reached Ladakh. See L. Petech, *A study of the Chronicles of Ladakh*, Calcutta, 1939, 120.

11 The founder of a celebrated order of dervishes, Shaykh Ahmad Yasavi was born at Yasi and died there around 1166. Intensely venerated by the Central Asian Turks, his tomb (rebuilt by Timur) soon became an object of popular pilgrimage.

12 C. H. Payne, *Jahangir and the Jesuits, with an Account of the Travels of Benedict Goes, etc.*, London, 1930; G. Wessels, *Early Jesuit Travellers in Central Asia*, 1603–1721, The Hague, 1924.

Chapter 11

1 See V. V. Bartold, *Ulugh-Beg*, Leiden, 1963, 25.

2 J. Aubin, 'Comment Tamerlan prenait les villes', *Studia Islamica*, XIX, 1963.

3 For Iran in the fifteenth century see V. Minorsky, 'Le Perse au XVe siècle entre la Turquie et Venise', *Société des études iraniennes et de l'art persan*, XVIII, Paris, 1933; idem, 'La Perse au XVe siècle', *Serie Orientale Roma*, XVII, Roma, 1958; R. M. Savory, 'The Struggle for Supremacy in Persia after the death of Timur', *Der Islam*, 1964.

4 Beveridge, *op. cit.*, I, 258.

5 Idem, I, 300.

6 Idem, I, 283. For a detailed account of patronage by one particular Timurid ruler, Mirza Iskandar b. 'Umar Shaykh, see J. Aubin, 'Le mécénat timouride à Chiraz', *Studia Islamica*, VIII, 1957. The contribution of Ulugh Beg of Samarqand to astronomical studies is fully discussed in A. Sayili, *The Observatory in Islam*, Ankara, 1960, 259–89.

7 For two views of Muhammad Shaybani's last campaigns see N. Elias, 'An Apocryphal Inscription in Khorasan', *JRAS*, 1896, and H. Beveridge, 'Note on the Panjmana Inscription',

JRAS, 1896. For the Iranian side see G. Sarwar, *History of Shah Isma'il Safawi*, Aligarh, 1939.

8 N. Elias and E. Denison Ross, *A History of the Moghuls of Central Asia*, 261.

9 The standard work remains W. Erskine, *A History of India under the two first Sovereigns of the House of Taimur, Baber and Humayun*, 2 vols., London, 1854, supplemented by L. F. Rushbrook Williams, *An Empire Builder of the Sixteenth Century*, London, 1918, and R. C. Varma, 'The Great Mughal and Transoxiana', *Islamic Quarterly*, 1955.

10 J. Briggs, *History of the Rise of the Mahomedan Power in India till the year AD 1812*, 4 vols., Calcutta, 1908–10, II, 276. The relations between 'Abdullah and Akbar are still obscure. For the Indian side see Abu'l-Fazl, *Akbar-nameh*, tr. H. Beveridge, 3 vols., Calcutta, 1904, and R. C. Varma, 'Akbar and Abdullah Khan', *Islamic Culture*, 1947,

11 See R. C. Varma, 'Mughal Imperialism in Transoxiana', *Islamic Culture*, 1948; B. P. Saksena, *History of Shahjahan of Dihli*, Allahabad, 1962, 182–209.

Chapter 12

1 C. N. Seddon, *A Chronicle of the Early Safawīs, Being the Aḥsanu't-Tawārīkh of Ḥasan-i-Rūmlū*, 2 vols., Baroda, 1934, II, 134.

2 This period is described in detail in an unpublished Ph.D. thesis by M. B. Dickson, 'Shah Tahmāsb and the Uzbeks (the duel for Khurāsān with 'Ubayd Khān: 930–46:1524–40), Princeton, 1948.

3 Excellent bibliographies on artillery in the Ottoman Empire, Iran and India can be found in the *EI* under 'Barud' and 'Caldiran'. Central Asia is unfortunately omitted but the interested reader should consult Y. Pulatov and A. Mirkalikov, 'K istorii ognestrel'nogo oruzhiya v Srednei Azii', *Materialy po Istorii Uzbekistana*, Tashkent, 1963, and W. E. D. Allen, *Problems of Turkish Power in the Sixteenth Century*, London, 1963, 18.

4 'Abdul-Qadir Badauni, *Muntakhabut-al-Tawarikh*, tr. G. S. A. Ranking, W. H. Lowe and W. Haig, 3 vols., Calcutta, 1884–1925, III, 199; 210–11.

5 For examples of the work of the Bukhara School see N. V. D'yakonovoi, *Sredneaziatskie Miniatyury XVI–XVIII vv*, Moscow, 1964.
6 See L. I. Rempel', *Arkhitekturnyi ornament Uzbekistana*, Tashkent, 1961. For illustrations of some of the best buildings of the Uzbek period see *Istoricheskie Pamyatniki Islama v SSSR*, Tashkent, no date, and M. Hrbas and E. Knobloch, *The Art of Central Asia*, London, 1965.
7 See A. A. Semenov, 'Kulturnii uroven pervuikh Sheibanidov', *Sovetskoe Vostokovedenie*, 1956, III, 51–9, and A. Schimmel, 'Some notes on the cultural activity of the first Uzbek rulers', *Journal of the Pakistan Historical Society*, July 1960, 149–66.
8 A brief eye-witness account of Bukhara and its commerce during this period was written by an English merchant and adventurer, Anthony Jenkinson, who reached that city in 1558. See E. D. Morgan and C. H. Coote, *Early Voyages and Travels in Russia and Persia by Anthony Jenkinson and other Englishmen*, 2 vols., London, 1886, I, 87–90.

Chapter 13

1 Abu'l Ghazi Bahadur Khan, *Shajareh-ye Turk*, tr. Le Baron Desmaisons, II, 2.
2 For irrigation projects undertaken during the Uzbek period see A. J. Ahmad, 'Irrigation in relation to State Power in Middle Asia', *International Studies*, 1960.
3 This episode is described in detail from the Iranian point of view by L. Lockhart, *Nadir Shah*, London, 1938.
4 For anecdotes of Shah Murad see J. Malcolm, *History of Persia*, 2 vols., London, 1815, II, 241–61; A. Conolly, *Journey to the North of India, overland from England*, 2 vols., London, 1834, I, 158–63; A. Vambery, *History of Bokhara*, London, 1873, 348–62.
5 See 'The peoples of southern Turkmenistan and northern Khorasan in the 17th and 18th centuries', *CAR*, 1960, 264–72. This anonymous article does not, however, discuss the period of Shah Murad. Mir 'Abdul Karim Bukhari in his *Tarikh-i Bukhara*, tr. C. Schefer as *Histoire de l'Asie Centrale*, 142, states that 27,000 families were transported from Marv to

Bukhara. In 1813 the population of Marv was estimated at 3,000. See J. M. Kinneir, *A Geographical Memoir of the Persian Empire*, London, 1813, 179–80. For accounts of nineteenth-century Marv see C. Marvin, *Merv, Queen of the World; and the Scourge of the Man-Stealing Turcomans*, London, 1880; E. O'Donovan, *The Merv Oasis*, London, 1882.

6 For further details see J. Grover, *An Appeal to the British Nation on behalf of Colonel Stoddart and Captain Conolly, now in captivity in Bokhara*, London, J. Wolff, *Narrative of a Mission to Bokhara*, 2 vols., London, 1845; J. Grover, *The Bokhara Victims*, 2nd edn., London, 1845.

Chapter 17

1 For the study of the Mongols in China under Ming rule the works of H. Serruys are of seminal importance. These include: 'A Mongol Settlement in North China at the end of the 16th century', *CAJ*, 1958–9; 'Mongols ennobled during the early Ming', *HJAS*, 1959; and 'Sino-Mongol relatings during the Ming: Part I, The Mongols in China during the Hung-Wu period (1368–98)' and 'Part 2, The Tribute System and Diplomatic Missions (1400–1600)', *Mélanges chinois et bouddhiques*, 1959 and 1966.

2 W. Heissig, 'Zur Entstehungsgeschichte der mongolischen Kandjur-Redaktion der Ligdan Khan-Zeit (1628–29)', *SA*, and idem 'Beitrage zur Ubersetzungsgeschichte des mongolischen buddhistischen Kanons', *Abhandlungen der Akademie der Wissenschaften in Göttingen*, 1962.

3 Both have been translated into western European languages: C. R. Bawden, *The Mongol Chronicle Altan Tobči*, Wiesbaden, 1955; I. J. Schmidt, *Geschichte der Ost-Mongolen und ihres Fürstenhauses verfasst von Ssanang Ssetzen Chungtaidschi der Ordus*, St Petersburg, 1829. For the literary background see C. Ž. Žamcarano, *The Mongol Chronicles of the Seventeenth Century*, Wiesbaden, 1955; W. Heissig, *Die Familien- und Kirchengeschichtesschreibung der Mongolen*, 2 vols., Wiesbaden, 1959 and 1965, and idem, 'Mongolische Literatur', *Handbuch der Orientalistik*, Abt. I, Bd. V: 2. Abschmitt, Leiden, Cologne, 1964, 262–6.

4   P. Pelliot, 'Chrétiens d'Asie Centrale et d'extreme Orient', *TP*, 1914; H. Cordier, 'Le Christianisme en Chine et en Asie Centrale sous les Mongols', *TP*, 1917; P. Ratchnevsky, 'Die mongolischen Grosskhane und die buddhistische Kirche', *Asiatica. Festschrift Friedrich Weller*, Leipzig, 1954.

5   E. Obermiller, 'Tson-kha-pa le Pandit', *Mélanges chinois et bouddhiques*, 1935.

6   H. Serruys, *Genealogical Tables of the Descendants of Dayan-Qan*, The Hague, 1958, 109–10.

7   For legends of the Jebtsundamba Khutukhtus see C. R. Bawden, *The Jebtsundamba Khutukhtus of Urga*, Wiesbaden, 1961.

8   The different names applied to this people cause some confusion. Throughout this book the term 'Oirot' is used but 'Qalmuq', 'Kalmyk' and 'Jungar' are to be found in histories of Central Asia. The names 'Jungar' and 'Jungaria' are of Chinese origin and are almost certainly derived from the Mongol *'Jägün-Ghar'* ('left wing'). See P. Pelliot, *Notes critiques d'histoire kalmouke*, Paris, 1960, 3–8.

9   For a detailed study of one such relationship see D. M. Farquhar, 'Oirot-Chinese Tribute Relations 1408–46', *SA*.

10 Quoted in D. Pokotilov, *History of the Eastern Mongols during the Ming Dynasty from 1368 to 1634*, Chengtu, 1947, 136. This work should be read in conjunction with W. Franke, *Addenda and Corrigenda to Pokotilov's 'History of the Eastern Mongols during the Ming Dynasty'*, Chengtu, 1949.

11 E. F. Timkovsky, *Travels of the Russian mission through Mongolia to China, and Residence in Peking, in the years 1820–21*, 2 vols., London, 1827, I, 436.

12 C. D. Barkman, 'The return of the Torghuts from Russia to China', *Journal of Oriental Studies* (Hong Kong), 1955; Pelliot, *op. cit.*, 33–8.

13 J. K. Fairbank and S. Y. Têng, 'On the Ch'ing tributary system', *HJAS*, 1941, 158.

14 O. Lattimore, *Nationalism and Revolution in Mongolia*, 15–16.

15 G. M. Friters, *Outer Mongolia and Its International Position*, 156–7. Just prior to 1911 one Chinese firm in Mongolia collected annually as payment of interest 70,000 horses and half a million sheep. O. Lattimore, *Studies in Frontier History*, 279.

16 G. C. Binsteed, 'Mongolia', *China Year Book 1919–20*, ed. H. T. M. Bell and H. G. W. Woodhead, London, 1919, 582–6.

See also R. A. Rupen, 'The city of Urga in the Manchu period', *SA*, 162–3, for an account of the friction between the Lamas and Chinese merchants in Urga.

17 F. de Filippi, *An Account of Tibet. The Travels of Ippolite Desideri of Pistoia, S. J., 1712–27*, London, 1937; L. Petech, *I Missionari Italiani nel Tibet e nel Nepal*, 7 vols., Roma, 1952; G. Sandberg, *The Exploration of Tibet*, Calcutta, 1904; see also the bibliography in A. Lamb, *Britain and Chinese Central Asia*,

18 For an introduction to Tibetan art see A. B. Griswold, C. Kim and P. H. Pott, *Burma, Korea, Tibet*, London, 1964, and G. Tucci, *Tibet, Land of Snows*, London, 1967. See also A. K. Gordon, *The Iconography of Tibetan Lamaism*, New York, 1939; idem, *Tibetan Religious Art*, New York, 1957; G. Tucci, *Tibetan Painted Scrolls*, 3 vols., Roma, 1949.

19 Timkovsky, *op. cit.*, I, 115, 126. By the late nineteenth century Urga had become a major Buddhist centre and a rival to Lhasa as a training centre for lamas. This trend began when the Second Jebtsundamba Khutukhtu (1722–59) established a theological seminary in the Urga lamasery which thereafter drew theological students from all over Mongolia. R. A. Rupen, *op. cit.*, *SA.*, 160.

20 Père Armand David, for example, writing in 1866, took a very depressing view of Mongol education: 'The only learning these poor people have consists in knowing more or less the formulas of prayers in a language they do not understand'. H. M. Fox, *Abbé David's Diary*, Cambridge, Mass., 1949, 74.

21 Quoted in J. F. Baddeley, *Russia, Mongolia, China*, I, li–lii.

22 D. Carruthers, *Unknown Mongolia*, II, 362–4.

Chapter 18

1 S. Turner, *An account of an embassy to the court of the Teshoo Lama in Tibet*, London, 1800; C. R. Markham, *Narratives of the mission of G. Bogle to Tibet, and of the journey of T. Manning to Lhasa*, London, 1876; S. V. R. Cammann, *Trade through the Himalayas: the early British attempts to open Tibet*, Princeton, New Jersey, 1951.

2 P. L. Mehra, 'Tibet and Russian Intrigue', *RCAJ*, 1958; A. Lamb, 'Some Notes on Russian Intrigue in Tibet', *RCAJ*, 1959.

3 C. Bell, 'The Dalai Lama; Lhasa, 1921', *RCAJ*, 1924, 43.
4 H. E. Richardson, *Tibet and its history*, 183–223.
5 For an introduction to Tibetan concepts of nationalism see
   R. B. Ekvall, 'The Tibetan Self-Image', *PA*, 1960. For the period
   1951–9 see G. Ginsburgs and M. Mathos, 'Tibet's Administration in the Transition Period, 1951–4', and 'Tibet's Administration during the Interregnum', 1954–9, *PA*, 1959.

Chapter 19

1 O. Lattimore, *Studies in Frontier History*, 277.
2 R. A. Rupen, 'Mongolian Nationalism', *RCAJ*, 1958, 253–4.
3 For a brief account of the Mongols of Manchuria in the
   Manchukuo state see F. C. Jones, *Manchuria since 1931*,
   London, 1949, 60–8. The standard work is O. Lattimore, *The
   Mongols of Manchuria*, London, 1935, but see also W. Heissig,
   *Der mongolischen Kulturwandel in den Hsingan-Provinzen
   Mandschukuos*, Vienna/Peking, 1944. A number of penetrating
   contemporary articles in *PA* discuss developments in the
   Mongol world between the World Wars.
4 Quoted in G. M. Friters, *Outer Mongolia and Its International
   Position*, 66.
5 For the 1924 constitution see *China Year Book*, Tientsin, 1926
   and 1928.
6 An invaluable source for this period is Ma Ho-t'ien, *Chinese
   Agent in Mongolia*, Baltimore, 1949.
7 Quoted in Rupen, *op. cit.*, *RCAJ*, 1958, 165.
8 C. Bawden, 'Economic Advance in Mongolia', *The World
   Today*, June 1960, 259. For developments in the Mongolian
   People's Republic during the past two decades see R. A. Rupin,
   'Notes on Outer Mongolia since 1945', *PA*, 1955; idem, 'Outer
   Mongolia since 1955', *PA*, 1957; idem, 'Inside Outer Mongolia',
   Foreign Affairs, 1959; idem, 'Outer Mongolia, 1957–60', *PA*,
   1960; C. R. Bawden, 'Mongolian Review, October 1965',
   RCAJ, 1965, and idem, 'Mongolian Review, February 1967',
   RCAS, 1967. For the geographical background see E. M.
   Murzaev, *Die Mongolische Volksrepublik. Physisch-geographische
   Beschreibung'*, Gotha, 1954; E. Thiel, *Die Mongolei. Land,
   Volk und Wirtschaft der Mongolischen Volksrepublik*, München,

1958; H. J. Wiens, 'Geographical limitations to food production in the Mongolian People's Republic', *Annals of the Association of American Geographers*, 1951.

9 For an analysis of the 1940 constitution of the MPR see J. N. Hazard, 'The Constitution of the Mongol People's Republic and Soviet Influences', *PA*, 1948. Party membership has been estimated at three to four per cent of the population. R. A. Rupen, 'Inside Outer Mongolia', *Foreign Affairs*, 1959, 328.

10 Little material on Tannu-Tuva is available but see V. I. Dulov et al., *Istoriya Tuvy*, 2 vols., Moscow, 1964. Also O. Lattimore, 'Outer Mongolia and Urianghai', *China Year Book*, Shanghai, 1939; W. Ballis, 'Soviet Russia's Asiatic Frontier Technique: Tana Tuva', *PA*, 1941; W. Kolarz, *The Peoples of the Soviet Far East*, London, 1954; V. I. Dulov, *Sotsial'no-ekonomicheskaya istori Tuvy* (*XIX-nachalo XX v.*), Moscow, 1956. For travellers' impressions see D. Carruthers, *Unknown Mongolia*, and O. Manchen-Helfen, *Reise ins Asiatische Tuva*, Berlin, 1931. For more extensive reading consult V. I. Dulov *et al.*, *Bibliografiya Tuvinskoi Avtonomnoi Oblasti* (1774–1958 *vv.*), Moscow, 1959.

Selected Bibliography

The bibliography which follows is in no sense comprehensive and serious students of the area are advised to consult R. J. Kerner, *Northeastern Asia: a selected bibliography*, 2 vols., Berkeley, Calif., 1939, and D. Sinor, *Introduction à l'étude de l'Eurasie centrale*, Wiesbaden, 1963. The titles listed below consist of standard works together with those monographs and articles which the contributors consider to be of special interest. In general, titles of books given in the notes are not repeated in the bibliography and although the latter is arranged by chapters some books contain material relevant to more chapters than one.

Introduction

Bartold, V. V., *Die geographische und historische Erforschung des Orients mit besonderer Berücksichtigung der russischen Arbeiten*, Leipzig, 1913.
—— *Zwölf Vorlesungen über die Geschichte der Turken Mittelasiens*, Berlin, 1935.
—— *Histoire des Turcs d'Asie centrale*, Paris, 1945.
—— *Sochineniya*, 3 vols., Moscow, 1963–5.
—— *La découverte de l'Asie*, Paris, 1947.
Codrington, K. de B., 'A geographical introduction to the history of Central Asia', *The Geographical Journal*, 1944.
Franke, O., *Geschichte des chinesischen Reiches*, 5 vols., Berlin-Leipzig, 1930–52.
Grønbech, K., 'The Steppe Region in World History', *Acta Orientalia*, 3 parts, 1958, 1959, 1960.

Jochelson, W., *Peoples of Asiatic Russia*, New York, 1928.

Krader, L., *Peoples of Central Asia*, The Hague, 1963.

—— *Social organization of the Mongol-Turkic pastoral nomads*, The Hague, 1964.

Proceedings of the VIIIth Meeting of the Permanent International Altaistic Conference, 'The Horse in Ancient Altaic Civilization', *CAJ*, 1965.

Sarkisyanz, E., *Geschichte der orientalischen Völker Russlands bis 1917*, Munich, 1961.

Stein, M. A., 'Innermost Asia: its geography as a factor in history', *The Geographical Journal*, 1925.

Toynbee, A., *A study of history*, 12 vols., London, 1934–61.

Chapters 1–5

Original Sources. I. Texts

Sources for the history of pre-Islamic Central Asia are scattered and fragmentary. The principal passages in Greek and Latin authors are listed in W. W. Tarn, *The Greeks in Bactria and India*, 561. The early Muslim sources are discussed in W. Barthold, *Turkestan down to the Mongol Invasion*, 1–37. See also the following:

Bacot, J., Thomas, F. W., and Toussaint, C., *Documents de Touen-Houang relatifs à l'histoire du Tibet*, Paris, 1946.

Beal, S., *Buddhist records of the western world*, London, 1884.

Chavannes, E., *Documents sur les Tou-kiue (Turcs) occidentaux*, Paris, 1900.

—— 'Les Pays d'Occident d'après le Heou Han Chou', *TP*, ser. ii, VIII, 1907.

Dubs, H. H., *The History of the Former Han Dynasty by Pan Ku*, 3 vols., Baltimore, 1938–55.

Frye, R. N., *The history of Bukhara*, Cambridge, Mass., 1954.

Giles, H. A., *The travels of Fa-Hsien*, Cambridge, 1923.

Hirth, F., 'The story of Chang-Kien, China's pioneer in Western Asia', *Journal of the American Oriental Society*, 1917, 89–152.

Hitti, F. K. and Murgotten, F. C., *The origins of the Islamic state*, New York, 1916–24.

Liu Mau-Tsai, *Die chinesischen Nachrichten zur Geschichte der Ost-Türken (T'u Küe)*, 2 vols., Wiesbaden, 1958.

Miller, R. A., *Accounts of the Western Nations in the history of the Northern Chou dynasty*, Berkeley, Calif., 1959.

CENTRAL ASIA

Minorsky, V., *Hudud al-'Alam*, London, 1937.
Thomas, F. W., 'Tibetan documents concerning Chinese Turkistan', *JRAS*, 1930.
Watson, B., *Records of the grand historian of China*, 2 vols., New York, 1961.
Watters, T., *On Yuan Chwang's travels in India, A.D. 629–645*, London, 1904.
Wylie, A., 'Notes on the Western Regions', *Journal of the Anthropological Institute*, 1881 and 1882.

Original Sources. II. Archaeological Material
Ahrens, D., *Die römische grundlagen der Gandharakunst*, Munster, 1961.
Andrews, F. H., *Wall paintings from ancient shrines in Central Asia*, London, 1948.
Bussagli, M., *Central Asian Painting*, Geneva, 1961.
Curiel, R. and Fussman, G., 'Le Tresor monetaire de Qunduz', *MDAFA*, XX, Paris, 1965.
Dalton, O. M., *The Treasure of the Oxus*, 3rd edn., London, 1964.
Deydier, H., *Contribution à l'étude de l'art de Gandhara*, Paris, 1956.
Foucher, A., *L'art gréco-bouddhique de Gandhara*, 2 vols., Paris, 1905–22.
—— *La vieille route de l'Inde de Bactres à Taxila*, *MDAFA*, I, 2 vols., Paris, 1942–7.
Gray, B., *Buddhist cave paintings at Tun Huang*, London, 1959.
Hackin, J., *Nouvelles recherches archéologiques à Begram* (1939–1940), *MDAFA*, XI, 2 vols., Paris, 1954.
Ingholt, H. and Lyons, I., *Gandharan Art in Pakistan*, New York, 1957.
Konow, S., *Corpus Inscriptionum Indicarum:* Vol. II, Pt. 1, *Kharoshthi Inscriptions*, Calcutta, 1929.
Le Coq, A. von, *Chotscho*, Berlin, 1913.
—— *Die Buddhistische Spätantike in Mittelasien*, 6 vols., Berlin, 1922–4.
—— *Auf Hellas Spuren in Ostturkistan*, Berlin, 1926. (English translation: *Buried Treasures of Chinese Turkistan*, London, 1928.)
Maricq, A. and Wiet, G., *Le minaret de Djam*, *MDAFA*, XVI, Paris, 1959.
Marshall, J., *Taxila*, 3 vols., Cambridge, 1951.
Mongait, A., *Archaeology in the USSR*, London, 1959.
Pelliot, P., *Les grottes de Touen-houang*, Paris, 1922–4.

Stein, N. A., *Ancient Khotan*, Oxford, 1907.
—— *Ruins of Desert Cathay*, 2 vols., London, 1912.
—— *Serindia*, Oxford, 1921.
—— *Innermost Asia*, Oxford, 1928.
—— *On Ancient Central Asian Tracks*, London, 1933.
Tolstov, S. P., *Auf den Spuren der altchoresmische Kultur*, Berlin, 1953.

Original Sources. III. Coins
Curiel, R. and Schlumberger, D., *Trésors monétaires d'Afghanistan*, *MDAFA*, XIV, Paris, 1953.
Gardner, P., *Catalogue of Indian coins in the British Museum: Greek and Scythic kings of Bacrtia and India*, London, 1886.
Ghirshman, R., *Les Chionites-Hephthalites*, *MDAFA*, XIII, Cairo, 1948.
Haughton, H. L., *The H. L. Haughton Sale Catalogue*, Sotheby & Co., London, 30 April 1958.
Herzfeld, E. E., *Kushano-Sasanian coins* (*Memoirs of the Archaeological Survey of India XXXVIII*), Calcutta, 1930.
Sourdel, D., *Inventaire des monnaies musulmanes anciennes du Musée de Caboul*, Damascus, 1953.
Walker, J., *A catalogue of the Muhammadan coins in the British Museum*, 2 vols., London, 1941–56.
Whitehead, R. B., *Catalogue of the coins in the Punjab Museum, Lahore*, Vol. I, *Indo-Greek coins*, Oxford, 1914.

Secondary studies
Altheim, F., *Weltgeschichte Asiens in griechischen Zeitalter*, 2 vols., Tübingen, 1947–8.
Bacot, J., *Introduction à l'histoire du Tibet*, Paris, 1962.
Barthold, W., *Turkestan down to the Mongol Invasion*, 2nd edn., London, 1958.
Bataille, G., 'Notes sur le numismatique des Koushans et des Koushan-shahs sassanides', *Aréthuse*, 1928.
Bivar, A. D. H., 'The Bactrian Treasure of Qunduz', *JNSI*, XVII, 1955.
—— 'The Kaniska dating from Surkh Kotal', *BSOAS*, XXVI, 1963.
—— 'Seljūqid ziyarats of Sar-i Pul (Afghanistan)', *BSOAS*, 1966.
—— 'Indo-Bactrian problems', *NC*, 1965.

Bosworth, C. E., *The Ghaznavids*, Edinburgh, 1963.
—— 'Notes on the pre-Ghaznavid history of Eastern Afghanistan', *The Islamic Quarterly*, 1965.
Bosworth, C. E. and Clauson, C., 'Al-Xwarazmi on the peoples of Central Asia', *JRAS*, 1965.
Buchthal, H., 'The Western aspects of Gandhara sculpture', *PBA*, XXXI, 1945.
Clauson, C., 'Ak Beshim-Suyab', *JRAS*, 1961.
—— 'The Name Uyḡur', *JRAS*, 1963.
Debevoise, N. C., *A political history of Parthia*, Chicago, 1938.
Frye, R. N., *Bukhara. The Medieval Achievement*, Norman, Oklahoma, 1965.
—— 'The significance of Greek and Kushan archaeology in the history of Central Asia', *Journal of Asian History*, 1967.
Frye, R. N. and Sayili, A. M., 'Turks in the Middle East before the Seljuks', *Journal of the American Oriental Society*, LXIII, 1943.
Gabain, A. von, 'Steppe und Stadt in Leben der ältesten Turken', *Der Islam*, 1949.
—— 'Die Frühgeschichte der Uiguren, 607–745', *Nachrichten, Gesellschaft für Natur und Völkerkunde Ostasiens*, Hamburg, 1952.
—— *Das Uigurische Königreich von Chotscho*, Berlin, 1961.
Gibb, H. A. R., 'Chinese records of the Arabs in Central Asia', *BSOAS*, II, 1921–3.
—— 'The Arab invasion of Kashgar in 715', *BSOAS*, II, 1921–3.
—— *The Arab conquest of Central Asia*, London, 1923.
Giraud, R., *L'empire des Turcs célestes: les règnes d'Elterich, Qapghan et Bilgä, 680-734*, Paris, 1960.
Göbl, R., 'Die Munzpragung der Kušān von Vima Kadphases bis Bahram IV', in F. Altheim and R. Stiehl, *Finanzgeschichte der Spätantike*, Frankfurt am Main, 1957.
Grousset, R., *L'empire des steppes*, Paris, 1939.
Haloun, G., 'Zur Üe-tsi Frage', *ZDMG*, XCI, 1937.
Hamilton, J. R., *Les Ouighours a l'epoque des cinq dynasties (907-960)*, Paris, 1955.
Henning, W. B., 'The date of the Sogdian ancient letters', *BSOAS*, XII, 1948.
—— 'The Bactrian inscription', *BSOAS*, XXIII, 1960.
Hoffmann, H., *The Religion of Tibet*, London, 1961.
Jettmar, K., 'The Altai before the Turks', *Museum of Far Eastern Antiquities, Stockholm: Bulletin*, XIII, 1951.
Lamotte, E., *Histoire du bouddhisme indien*, Louvain, 1958.

Laufer, B., *Sino-Iranica*, Chicago, 1919.

Mackerras, C. P., 'Some Aspects of the history of the Uighur Empire (744–840)', unpublished M.Litt. thesis, Cambridge, 1964.

McGovern, W. M., *The early empires of Central Asia*, Chapel Hill, 1939.

Maenchen-Helfen, O., 'The Yueh-chih problem re-examined', *Journal of the American Oriental Society*, LXV, 1945.

Mélikoff, I., *Abū Muslim, le 'porte-hache' du Khorassan dans la tradition épique turco-iranienne*, Paris, 1962.

Minns, E. H., 'The art of the northern nomads', *PBA*, XXVIII, 1942.

Minorsky, V., 'Tamim ibn Bahr's journey to the Uyghurs', *BSOAS*, XII, 1948.

—— 'A Greek crossing on the Oxus', *BSOAS*, 1967.

Muir, W., *The Caliphate: its rise, decline and fall*, 4th edn., Cambridge, 1914.

Narain, A. K., *The Indo-Greeks*, Oxford, 1957.

Nazim, M., *The life and times of Sultan Mahmud of Ghazna*, Cambridge, 1931.

Phillips, E. D., *The Royal Hordes*, London, 1965.

Pritsak, O. I., 'Von dem Karluk zu den Karachaniden', *ZDMG*, CI, 1951.

—— "Stammesnamen und Titulaen der altaischen Völker', *Ural-Altaische Jahrbücher*, Weisbaden, 1952.

—— 'Die Karachaniden', *Der Islam*, XXXI, 1953.

Puech, H., *Le Manichéisme: son fondateur, sa doctrine*, Paris, 1949.

Pugliese Carratelli, G. and Garbini, G., *A bilingual Graeco-Aramaic edict by Aśoka*, Rome, 1964.

Rice, T. T., *The Scythians*, London, 1957.

Samolin, W., 'The historical ethnography of the Tarim basin before the Turks', *Palaeologia*, Isaka, 1955.

—— 'Ethnographic aspects of the Archaeology of the Tarim basin', *CAJ*, 1959.

—— *East Turkestan to the Twelfth Century*, The Hague, 1964.

Schlumberger, D., 'The excavations at Surkh Kotal and the problem of Hellenism in Bactria and India', *PBA*, XLVII, 1961.

Smith, V. A., *The early history of India*, 4th edn., Oxford, 1924.

Snellgrove, D. L., *Buddhist Himālaya*, Oxford, 1957.

Soper, A. C., 'The Roman style in Gandhara', *American Journal of Archaeology*, LV, 1951.

Spuler, B., *Iran in frühislamischer Zeit*, Wiesbaden, 1952.

Tarn, W. W., *The Greeks in Bactria and India*, 2nd edn., Cambridge, 1951.
Waddell, L. A., *The Buddhism of Tibet or Lamaism*, London, 1934.
Weil, G., *Geschichte der Chalifen*, Heidelberg/Stuttgart, 1846–62.
Wheeler, R. E. M., 'Romano-Buddhist art: an old problem restated', *Antiquity*, LXXXIX, March 1949.
Whitehead, R. B., 'Notes on Indo-Greek numismatics', *NC*, 1923.
—— 'Notes on the Indo-Greeks', *NC*, 3 parts, 1940, 1947, 1950.
Widengren, G., *Mani und der Manichäismus*, Stuttgart, 1961.
Yetts, W. P., 'The Horse, a Factor in early Chinese History', *Eurasia Septentrionalis Antiqua*, Helsinki, 1934.

Chapters 6–8

Original sources

Blake, R. P. and Frye, R. N., 'History of the Nation of the Archers (the Mongols) by Grigor of Akanč', *HJAS*, 1949.
Boyle, J. A., *The History of the World-Conqueror*, 2 vols., Manchester, 1958.
—— 'The journey of Het'um I, King of Little Armenia, to the court of the Great Khan Möngke', *CAJ*, IX, 1964.
Bretschneider, E., *Medieval Researches from Eastern Asiatic Sources*, 2 vols., London, 1888.
Dawson, H. C., *The Mongol Mission*, London, 1955.
Gibb, H. A. R., *The travels of Ibn Battuta, AD 1325–54*, 2 vols., Cambridge, 1958–62. (In course of publication.)
Haenisch, E., *Die geheime Geschichte der Mongolen*, Leipzig, 1948.
Hambis, L., *Le Chapitre CVII de Youan che*, Leiden, 1945.
—— *Le Chapitre CVIII de Youan che*, Leiden, 1954.
Hammer-Purgstall, J. von, *Geschichte Wassaf's*, Wien, 1956.
Mostaert, A. and Cleaves, F. W., 'Trois documents mongols des Archives secrètes vaticanes', *HJAS*, 1952.
—— *Les Lettres de 1289 et 1305 des ilkhan Arrun et Öljeitu a Philippe le Bel*, Cambridge, Mass., 1962.
Pelliot, P., *Histoire secrète des Mongols*, Paris, 1949.
Pelliot, P. and Hambis, L., *Histoire des campagnes de Gengis Khan*, Leiden, 1951.
Quatremère, E. M., *Histoire des Mongols de la Perse*, Paris, 1836.

Raverty, H. G., *The Tabakat-i-Nasiri*, 3 vols., London, 1881–9.
Waley, A., *The Travels of an Alchemist*, London, 1931.
Yule, H., *The book of Ser Marco Polo the Venetian*, 2 vols., 3rd edn., London, 1921.

Secondary studies
Altunian, G., *Die Mongolen und ihre Eroberungen in kaukasischen und kleinasiatischen landern im 13 Jahrhunderts*, Berlin, 1911.
Blochet, E., *Introduction à l'Histoire des Mongols de Fadl Allah Raschid ed-Din*, London, 1910.
Ch'en Yuan, *Western and Central Asians in China under the Mongols*, Los Angeles, 1966.
D'Ohsson, A. C. M., *Histoire des Mongols, depuis Tchinguiz-Khan jusqu' à Timour Bey ou Tamerlane*, 4 vols., 2nd edn., Amsterdam, 1852.
Dunlop, D. M., 'The Karaits of Eastern Asia', *BSOAS*, 1944.
Egami, N., 'Olon-Sume et la decouverte de l'eglise catolique romaine de Jean de Montecorvino', *JA*, 1952.
Gray, B., 'Art under the Mongol Dynasties of China and Persia', *Oriental Art*, 1955.
Grekov, B. and Iakoubovski, A., *La Horde d'Or*, Paris, 1939.
Grousset, R., *L'empire Mongol*, Paris, 1941.
—— *Le Conquérant du Monde*, Paris, 1944.
Haenisch, E., *Die Kulturpolitik des mongolischen Weltreichs*, Berlin, 1943.
Heyd, W., *Histoire du commerce du Levant au moyen-âge*, 2 vols., 2nd edn., Leipzig, 1936.
Howorth, H. H., *History of the Mongols, from the 9th to the 19th century*, 5 vols., London, 1876–1927.
Hung, W., 'The Transmission of the Book known as The Secret History of the Mongols', *HJAS*, 1951.
Kiselov, V. S., 'Drevnie goroda mongolii', *Sovetskaya Archeologiya*, 1957.
Krader, L., 'The Cultural and Historical Position of the Mongols', *Asia Major*, 1952.
—— 'Qan-Qayan and the Beginnings of Mongol Kingship', *CAJ*. 1955.
—— 'Feudalism and the Tatar Policy of the Middle Ages', *Comparative Studies in Society and History*, 1958.
Lane-Poole, S., *The coins of the Mongols in the British Museum*, London, 1881.

345

Lattimore, O., 'A ruined Nestorian city in Inner Mongolia', *The Geographic Journal*, 1934.

—— 'The Geography of Chingis Khan', *The Geographical Journal*, 1963.

Martin, H. D., *The Rise of Chingis Khan and his conquest of North China*, Baltimore, 1950.

Mostaert, A., 'A propos de quelques portraits d'empereurs mongols', *Asia Major*, 1927.

Olbricht, P., *Das Postwesen in China unter der Mongolenherrschaft im 13 und 14 Jahrhundert*, Wiesbaden, 1954.

Olschki, L., *Marco Polo's Asia*, Berkeley, Calif., 1960.

Pelliot, P., 'Chrétiens d'Asie Centrale et d'Extreme-Orient', *TP*, 1914.

—— *Notes on Marco Polo*, 2 vols., Paris, 1959–63. (In course of publication.)

Schurmann, H. F., 'Mongolian Tributary Practices of the Thirteenth Century', *HJAS*, 1956.

Spuler, B., *Die Goldene Horde. Die Mongolen in Russland 1223–1502*, Wiesbaden, 1965.

—— *Die Mongolenzeit*, Berlin, 1948.

—— *Die Mongolen in Iran*, Berlin, 1955.

—— *Les Mongols dans l'histoire*, Paris, 1961.

Vernadsky, G. V., *The Mongols and Russia*, New Haven, 1953.

Vladimirtsov, B. Y., *Gengis-Khan*, Paris, 1948.

—— *Le régime social des Mongols: le féodalisme nomade*, Paris, 1948.

Chapters 9–13

Original sources

Beveridge, A. S., *The Bābur-Nāma in English*, 2 vols., London, 1922.

Burnes, A., *Travels into Bokhara*, 3 vols., London, 1834.

Chekhovich, O. D., *Bukharskie Dokumenty XIV Veka*, Tashkent, 1965.

Desmaisons, Le Baron, *Histoire des Mogols et des Tartares*, St Petersburg, 1871–4.

Epifanovoi, L. M., *Mirza 'Abdul 'Azim Sami: Tarikh-i Salatin-i Mangitiyeh*, Moscow, 1962.

Elias, N. and Denison Ross, E., *A History of the Moghuls of Central Asia*, London, 1895.

Khanykov, N. V., *Bokhara: its Amir and its people*, London, 1845.

Kononov, A. M., *Rodoslovnaya Turkmen*, Moscow, 1958.

Le Strange, G., *Ruy Gonzalez de Clavijo. Narrative of the embassy to the court of Tamerlane at Samarcand, AD 1403–1406*, London, 1928.

Levchine, A. de, *Description des hordes et des steppes des Kirghiz-Kazaks*, Paris, 1840.

Michell, J. and R., *The Russians in Central Asia*, London, 1885.

Neumann, K. F., *Reisen des Johannes Schiltberger aus München in Europa, Asia und Afrika von 1394 bis 1427*, Munich, 1859.

Sanders, J. H., *Tamerlane or Timur the Great Amir*, London, 1936.

Schefer, C., *Histoire de l'Asie Centrale*, Paris, 1876.

—— *Relation de l'Ambassade au Kharezm*, Paris, 1879.

Scherzer, F., *Recueil d'itinéraires et de voyages dans l'Asie Centrale et l'extrême Orient*, Paris, 1878.

Semenov, A. A., *Mukhinkhanovskaya Istoriya*, Tashkent, 1957.

Senkowski, J., *Supplement à l'histoire générale des Huns, des Turks et des Mogols*, St Petersburg, 1824.

Vambery, A., *Die Scheibaniade*, Wien, 1885.

Secondary studies

Ahmad, A. J., 'Irrigation in relation to State Power in Middle Asia', *International Studies*, 1960.

Aubin, J., 'Comment Tamerlan prenait les villes', *Studia Islamica*, XIX, 1963.

Bartold, V. V., *Istoriya Kul'turnoy Zhizni Turkestana*, Leningrad, 1927.

—— *Istoriya Turkestana*, Tashkent, 1922.

—— *Four Studies on the history of Central Asia*, tr. into English by V. and M. Minorsky, 3 vols., Leiden, 1962–3.

Bellew, H. W., *The History of Kashgharia*, Calcutta, 1875.

Bouvat, L., 'Essai sur la Civilisation Timouride', *JA*, 1926.

Cohn-Weiner, E., *Turan. Islamische Baukunst in Mittelasien*, Berlin, 1930.

Dickson, M. B., 'Shah Tahmāsb and the Uzbeks (the duel for Khurāsān with 'Ubayd Khān: 930–46/1524–40)'. Unpublished Ph.D. thesis, Princeton, 1958.

Hartmann, M., *Der islamische Orient*, 3 vols., Berlin, 1899–1910.

Hill, D. and Grabar, O., *Islamic architecture and its decoration, AD 800–1500*, London, 1964.

Hinz, W., 'Quellenstudien zur Geschichte der Timuriden', *ZDMG*, 1936.

347

Holdsworth, M., *Turkestan in the Nineteenth Century*, London, 1959.

Ivanov, P. P., *Ocherki po istorii Srednei Azii*, Moscow, 1958.

Köprülü, M. F., *L'influence du Chamanisme turco-mongole sur les ordres mystiques Musulmans*, Istanbul, 1929.

Lane-Poole, S., *The Coinage of Buhkara*, London, 1882.

Majerczak, R., 'Renseignements historiques sur les Kazaks ou Kirghizes-Kazaks depuis la fondation de la Horde Kazake jusqu' à la fin du XIX siècle', *RMM*, 1921.

Nalivkine, V. P., *Histoire du Khanat de Khokand*, Paris, 1889.

Oliver, E. E., 'The Chaghatai Mughals', *JRAS*, 1888.

—— 'The Coins of the Chaghatai Mughals', *Journal of the Asiatic Society of Bengal*, 1891.

Roemer, H. R., 'Neuere Veröffentlichungen zur Geschichte Timurs und seiner Nachfolger', *CAJ*, 1956.

Savory, R. M., 'The struggle for supremacy in Iran after the death of Timur', *Der Islam*, 1964.

Shaw, R. B., 'The History of the Khojas of Eastern Turkestan', *Supplement to the Journal of the Asiatic Society of Bengal*, 1897.

Vambery, A., *Geschichte Bochara's*, Stuttgart, 1872.

Varma, R. C., 'Akbar and Abdullah Khān', *Islamic Culture*, 1947.

Vyatkin, M., *Ocherki po istorii Kazakhskoy SSR*, Leningrad, 1941.

Winner, T. G., *The Oral Art and Literature of the Kazakhs of Russian Central Asia*, Durham, North Carolina, 1958.

Zimine, L., 'Les exploits d'emîrzâdé 'Omar Cheikh, fils du Timour, à Kashghar, en Ferghana et en Mongolie', *RMM*, 1914'

Chapters 14 and 16

Allworth, E., *Central Asia. A Century of Russian Rule*, New York, 1967.

—— *Uzbek Literary Politics*, The Hague, 1964.

—— *Central Asian Publishing and the Rise of Nationalism*, New York, 1965.

Bacon, E. E., *Central Asians under Russian Rule*, Ithaca, N.Y., 1966.

Bennigsen, A. and Lemercier-Quelquejay, C., *The evolution of the Muslim nationalities of the USSR and their linguistic problems*, London, 1961.

—— Les Mouvements Nationaux chez les Musulmans de Russie. I. Le Sultangalievisme au Tatarstan, Paris, 1960; II. La Presse et les Mouvements Nationaux chez les Musulmans de Russie avant 1920, Paris, 1964.

—— Islam in the Soviet Union, London, 1967.

Caroe, O. K., Soviet Empire: The Turks of Central Asia and Stalinism, London, 1967.

Carrere d'Encausse, H., Réforme et Révolution chez les Musulmans de l'Empire Russe (Bukhara, 1867–1924), Paris, 1966.

Castagné, J., 'Le Bolchevisme et l'Islam', RMM, 1922.

Hostler, C. W., Turkism and the Soviets, London, 1957.

Kirimal, E., Der nationale Kampf der Krimtürken, Emsdetten, 1952.

Mende, G. von, Der nationale Kampf der Russlands Türken, Berlin, 1936.

Nove, A. and Newth, J. A., The Soviet Middle East, London, 1967.

Park, A. G., Bolshevism in Turkestan, 1917–1927, New York, 1957.

Pipes, R., The formation of the Soviet Union, Cambridge, 1954.

—— 'Muslims of Central Asia', Middle East Journal, 1955.

Sokol, E. D., The Revolt of 1916 in Russian Central Asia, Baltimore, 1953.

Spuler, B., 'Die Wolga-Tataren und Bashkiren unter russischer Herrschaft', Der Islam, 1949.

—— 'Mittelasien unter sowjetischer Herrschaft', Der Islam, 1964.

Wheeler, G., Racial Problems in Soviet Muslim Asia, London, 1960.

—— A Modern History of Soviet Central Asia, London, 1964.

—— The Peoples of the Soviet Union, London, 1966.

Zenkowsky, S. A., 'Kulturkampf in Pre-revolutionary Central Asia', The American Slavic and East European Review, 1955.

—— 'A Century of Tatar Revival', idem, 1958.

—— Pan-Turkism and Islam in Russia, Cambridge, Mass., 1960.

Chapter 15

Becker, S., Russia's Protectorates in Central Asia: Bukhara and Khiva, 1865–1924, Cambridge, Mass., 1968.

Capus, G., A Travers le Royaume de Tamarlan, Paris, 1892.

Curzon, G. N., Russia in Central Asia in 1889 and the Anglo-Russian Question, London, 1889.

Junge, R., *Das Problem der Europäisierung orientalischer Wirtschaft dargestellt an den Verhältnissen der Sozialwirtschaft von Russisch-Turkistan*, Weimar, 1915.

Khalfin, N. A., *Russia's Policy in Central Asia 1857–68*, London, 1964.

Krafft, H., *A Travers le Turkestan Russe*, Paris, 1902.

Krahmer, G., *Russland in Mittelasien*, Leipzig, 1898.

Lansdell, H., *Russian Central Asia*, 2 vols., London, 1885.

Macgahan, J. A., *Campaigning on the Oxus, and the Fall of Khiva*, New York, 1874.

Maksheev, A. I., *Istoricheskii Obzor Turkestana i Nastupatel'nogo Dvizheniia v Nego Russkikh*, St Petersburg, 1890.

Marvin, C. T., *The Eye-Witnesses' Account of the Disastrous Russian Campaign against the Akhal Tekke Turcomans*, London, 1880.

Middeldorf, A. T., *Einblick in das Farghana-Thal*, St Petersburg, 1881.

Moser, H., *A Travers l'Asie Centrale*, Paris, 1885.

Olufsen, O., *The Emir of Bokhara and his country*, Copenhagen, 1911.

Olzscha, R. and Cleinow, G., *Turkestan. Die politischhistorischen und wirtschaftlichen Probleme Zentralasiens*, Leipzig, 1942.

Pahlen, K. K., *Mission to Turkestan . . . 1908–09*, Oxford, 1964.

Pierce, R. A., *Russian Central Asia, 1867–1917: a selected bibliography*, Berkeley, Calif., 1953.

—— *Russian Central Asia, 1867–1917: A Study in Colonial Rule*, Berkeley, Calif., 1960.

Schwarz, F. von, *Turkestan, die Wiege der indogermanischen Völker. Nach funfzehnjahrigen Aufenthalt in Turkestan*, Freiburg in Breslau, 1900.

Schuyler, E., *Turkistan*, London, 1876.

Terent'ev, M. A., *Istoriia Zavoevaniia Srednei Azii*, 4 vols., St Petersburg, 1906.

Ulfalvy-Bourdon, M. de, *De Paris à Samarkand*, Paris, 1880.

Chapters 17–19

Ahmad, Z., 'China and Tibet, 1708–1959. A Resumé of Facts', *Chatham House Memoranda*, Oxford, 1960.

Aitchison, C. U., *Collection of Treaties, Engagements and Sanads, etc.*, 14 vols., Calcutta, 1929–31.

Baddeley, J. F., *Russia, Mongolia, China*, 2 vols., London, 1919.

Bawden, C. R., 'A joint petition of grievances submitted to the Ministry of Justice of autonomous Mongolia in 1919', *BSOAS*, 1967.

—— *The Mongol Chronicle Altan Tobči*, Wiesbaden, 1955.

Bell, C., *Tibet Past and Present*, Oxford, 1924.

—— *The Religion of Tibet*, Oxford, 1931.

—— *Portrait of the Dalai Lama*, London, 1946.

Bell, J., *A Journey from St Petersburg to Pekin, 1719–22*, Edinburgh, 1965.

Bleichsteiner, R., *Die gelbe Kirche*, Wien, 1937.

Cahen, G., *Histoire des relations de la Russie avec la Chine sous Pierre le Grande, 1689–1730*, Paris, 1912.

Carruthers, D., *Unknown Mongolia*, 2 vols., London, 1913.

Ch'en, Vincent, *Sino-Russian relations in the 17th Century*, The Hague, 1966.

Cheng, Chih-Yi, 'Bibliography of books and articles on Mongolia', *RCAJ*, 2 parts, 1950.

Cheng, Tien-Fong, *A History of Sino-Russian Relations*, Washington, 1957.

Cressey, G. B., 'Chinese colonization in Mongolia. A General Survey', *Pioneer Settlement*, American Geographical Society, Special Publication, No. 14, New York, 1932.

Ekvall, R. B., *Cultural relations on the Kansu-Tibetan border*, Chicago, 1939.

—— *Religious Observances in Tibet*, Chicago, 1964.

E-tu Zen Sun, 'Results of culture contact in two Mongol-Chinese communities', *SJA*, 1952.

Franke, W., *Addenda and corrigenda to Pokolitov's 'History of the Eastern Mongols during the Ming Dynasty'*, Chengtu, 1949.

Friters, G. M., 'The Prelude to Outer Mongolian Independence', *PA*, 1937.

—— 'The Development of Outer Mongolian Independence', *PA*, 1937.

—— *Outer Mongolia and its International Position*, Baltimore, 1949.

Ginsburgs, G. and Mathos, M., *Communist China and Tibet. The First Dozen Years*, The Hague, 1964.

Heissig, W., 'A Mongolian source to the Lamaist suppression of Shamanism in the 17th century', *Anthropos*, 2 parts, 1953.

Huth, G., *Geschichte des Buddhismus in der Mongolei*, 2 vols., Strassburg, 1892–6.

Korostovetz, I. J., *Von Cinggis Khan zur Sowjetrepublik*, Berlin, 1926.

Kozlov, P. K., *Mongoliya i Amdo i mertoyi gorod Chara-choto*, Moscow, 1923.

Krueger, J. R., *History of the Eastern Mongols to 1662 (the Erdeniyin Tobči of Segang Sechen)*, 2 vols., Bloomington, Indiana, 1964.

Lamb, A., *Britain and Chinese Central Asia: The Road to Lhasa, 1767 to 1905*, London, 1960.

—— *The China-Indian Border*, London, 1964.

—— *The McMahon Line: a study in the relations between India, China and Tibet, 1904 to 1914*, 2 vols., London, 1966.

Lattimore, O., 'Chinese colonization in Inner Mongolia: its history and present development', *Pioneer Settlement*, American Geographical Society, Special Publication, No. 14, New York, 1932.

—— *Inner Asian Frontiers of China*, New York, 1940.

—— *Nationalism and Revolution in Mongolia*, Leiden, 1955.

—— Studies in Frontier History, Paris, 1963.

—— *Nomads and Commissars*, New York, 1962.

—— 'Religion and Revolution in Mongolia', *Modern Asian Studies*, 1967.

Li, Tieh-Tseng, *Tibet: Today and Yesterday*, New York, 1960.

Michael, F., *The Origin of Manchu Rule in China*, Baltimore, 1942.

Miller, R. J., 'A Selective Survey of Literature on Mongolia', *The American Political Science Review*, 1952.

—— *Monasteries and culture change in Inner Mongolia*, Wiesbaden, 1959.

Moses, L. W., 'Soviet-Japanese confrontation in Outer Mongolia: The battle of Nomonhan-Khalkingol, *Journal of Asian History*, 1967.

Murphy, G. G. S., *Soviet Mongolia: a study of the oldest political satellite*, Berkeley and Los Angeles, 1966.

Pavlovsky, M. N., *Chinese-Russian Relations*, New York, 1949.

Pelliot P., *Huc and Gabet, Travels in Tartary, Thibet and China, 1844–1846*, 2 vols., London, 1928.

Petech, L., *China and Tibet in the early 18th century*, Leiden, 1950.

—— 'The Dalai-Lamas and Regents of Tibet: a chronological study', *TP*, 1959.

Pokotilov, D., *History of the Eastern Mongols during the Ming Dynasty from 1368 to 1634*, Chengtu, 1947.

Przhevalsky, N. M., *Mongolia, the Tangut country and the solitudes of northern Tibet*, 2 vols., London, 1876.

Richardson, H. E., *Tibet and its history*, London, 1962.

Rockhill, W. W., 'The Dalai Lamas of Lhasa and their relations with the Manchu Emperors of China, 1644–1908', *TP*, 1910.

Rubel, P. G., *The Kalmyk Mongols: A Study in Continuity and Change*, The Hague, 1967.

Rupen, R. A., 'The Buriat Intelligentsia', *The Far Eastern Quarterly*, 1956.

—— 'Mongolian Nationalism', *RCAJ*, 2 parts, 1958.

—— *Mongols of the Twentieth Century*, 2 vols., The Hague, 1964.

—— *The Mongolian People's Republic*, Stamford, Calif., 1966.

Schmidt, I. J., *Geschichte der Ost-Mongolen und ihres Fürstenhauses, von Ssanang Ssetsen Chungtaidschi der Ordus*, St Petersburg, 1829.

Schram, L. M. J., 'The Monguors of the Kansu-Tibetan frontier', *Transactions of the American Philosophical Society*, 3 parts, 1954, 1957, 1961.

Schulemann, G., *Geschichte der Dalai-Lamas*, Leipzig, 1958.

Shakabpa, T. W. D., *Tibet. A Political History*, New Haven, 1967.

Shen, T. L. and Liu, S. C., *Tibet and the Tibetans*, Stamford, Calif., 1953.

Sinha, N. C., *Tibet. Considerations on Inner Asian History*, Calcutta, 1967.

Stein, R. A., *La civilisation tibetaine*, Paris, 1962.

Tang, P. S. H., *Russian and Soviet policy in Manchuria and Outer Mongolia, 1911–1931*, Durham, North Carolina, 1959.

Teichman, E., *Travels of a Consular officer in Eastern Tibet, together with a history of the relations between China, Tibet and India*, Cambridge, 1922.

Tucci, G., *Tibet, Land of Snows*, London, 1967.

Wu, C., 'Who were the Oirats?', *Yenching Journal of Social Studies*, 1941.

Younghusband, F. E., *India and Tibet*, London, 1910.

Chapter 20

Ahmad, H. M., *Kampf um leese Räume: Turan-Turkestan-Tibet*, Leipzig, 1940.

Bales, W. I., *Tso tsungt'ang: soldier and statesman of old China*, Shanghai, 1937.

Bellew, H. W., *Kashmir and Kashghar*, London, 1875.

CENTRAL ASIA

Bosshard, W., 'Politics and trade in Central Asia', *RCAJ*, 1929.

Chu, W. J., 'Tso Tsung-t'ang's role in the recovery of Sinkiang', *Tsing Hua Journal of Chinese Studies*, Taipei, 1958.

Courant, M., *L'Asie Centrale au XVIIe at XVIIIe siècles: empire Kalmouk ou empire Mantchou?*, Lyons, 1912.

Dabbs, J. A., *History of the discovery and exploration of Chinese Turkestan*, The Hague, 1963.

Forsyth, T. D., *Autobiography and Reminiscences of Sir Douglas Forsyth*, edited by his daughter, London, 1887.

Heissig, W., *Das gelbe Vorfeld: Die Mobilisierung der chinesischen Aussenländer*, Berlin, 1941.

Hsü, I. C. Y., *The Ili Crisis: A Study of Sino-Russian Diplomacy, 1871 to 1881*, Oxford, 1965.

Imbault-Huart, C., *Recueil de documents sur l'Asie centrale*, Paris, 1881.

—— *Le pays da 'Hami ou Khamil*, Paris, 1892.

—— 'Récit officiel de la conquète du Turkestan par les Chinois (1758–1760)', *Bulletin de géographie historique et descriptive*, 1895.

Kiernan, V. G., 'Kashgar and the politics of Central Asia, 1868–1878', *Cambridge Historical Journal*, 1953–5.

Kuropatkin, A. N., *Kashgaria*, Calcutta, 1882.

Lattimore, O., *The Pivot of Asia*, Boston, 1950.

Lepage et Vissière, A., 'Soumission des tribus musulmanes du Turkestan par la China (1757–1760)', *RMM*, 1910.

Macartney, G., 'Eastern Turkestan: the Chinese as rulers over an alien race', *RCAJ*, 1909.

McLean, N. L. D., ' "The New Dominion" ', *RCAJ*, 1948.

Menon, K. P. S., *Delhi-Chungking, a travel diary*, Bombay, 1947.

Moseley, G., *A Sino-Soviet Cultural Frontier. The Ili Kazakh Autonomous Chou*, Cambridge, Mass., 1967.

Norins, M. R., *Gateway to Asia: Sinkiang, frontier of the Chinese Far West*, New York, 1944.

Shaw, R., *Visits to High Tartary, Yarkand and Kashghar*, London, 1871.

Skrine, C. P., *Chinese Central Asia*, London, 1926.

Teichman, E., *Journey to Turkestan*, London, 1937.

Trinkler, E., *Im Lande der Stürme*, Leipzig, 1930.

Whiting, A. S. and General Sheng Shih-ts'ai, *Sinkiang: pawn or pivot*, Michigan, 1958.

Wu, A. K., *Turkistan Tumult*, London, 1940.

354

Yang, R., 'Sinkiang under the administration of General Yang Tseng-hsin 1911–1928', *CAJ*, 1961.

Yuan, T., 'Yakub Beg (1820–1877) and the Moslem Rebellion in Chinese Turkestan', *CAJ*, 1961.

Yusurov, K., *Pereselenie Dungan na territoriyu Kirgizii i Kazakhstana*, Frunze, 1961.

Maps

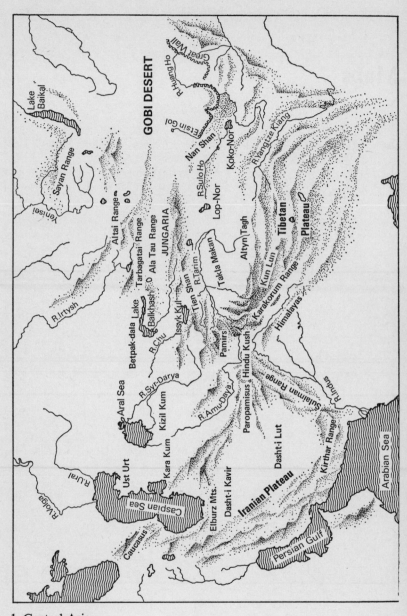

1 Central Asia.

358

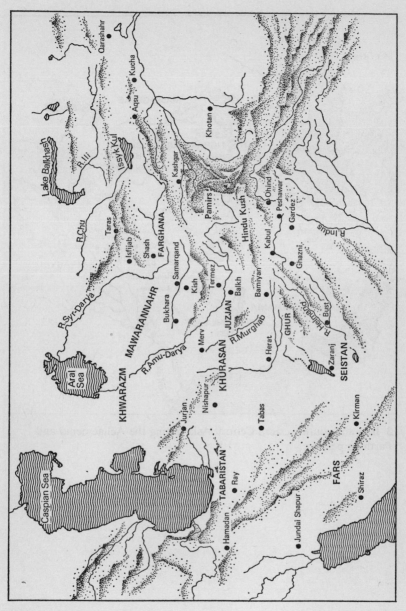

2 The expansion of Islam in Central Asia.

3 Iran and south-western Central Asia during the Achaemenid and Parthian periods.

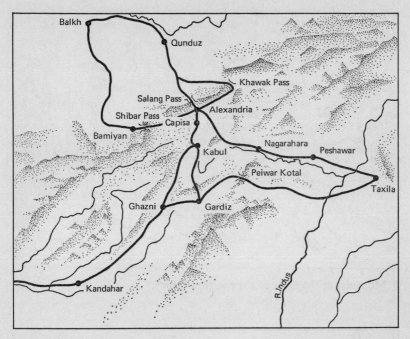

4 The Indo-Bactrian Greek kingdoms.

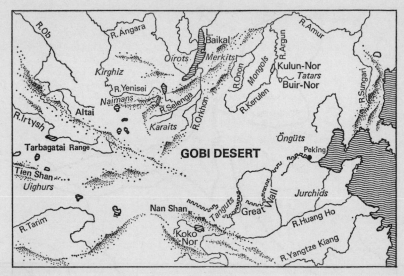

5 Mongolia at the close of the twelfth century.

6 The Chaghatai Khanate.

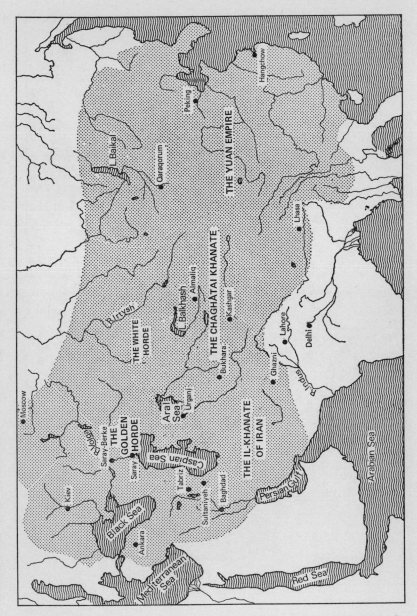

Map labels:

Hangchow
Peking
L. Baikal
Qaraqorum
THE YUAN EMPIRE
Lhasa
THE CHAGHATAI KHANATE
Almaliq
Irtysh
L. Balkhash
THE WHITE HORDE
Kashgar
Lahore
Delhi
Bukhara
Ghazni
Moscow
Indus
Aral Sea
Urganj
Volga
THE GOLDEN HORDE
Saray-Berke
THE IL-KHANATE OF IRAN
Caspian Sea
Arabian Sea
Saray
Kiev
Tabriz
Sultaniyeh
Baghdad
Persian Gulf
Black Sea
Ankara
Mediterranean Sea
Red Sea

7 The Mongol Empire of the Chingizkhanids during the second half of the thirteenth century.

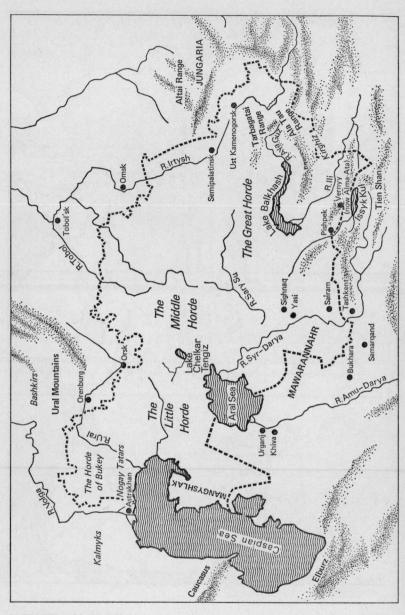

8 The Kazakh Hordes.

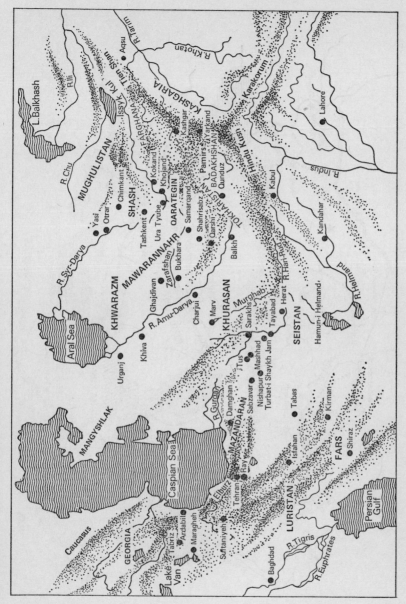

9 Mawarannahr, Khurasan and western Iran during the Timurid and Shaybanid periods.

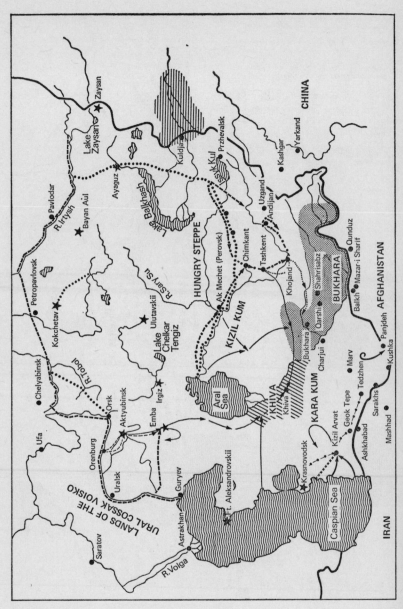

10 The Russian conquest of Central Asia.

366

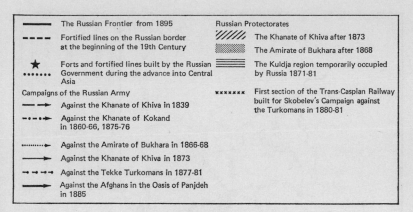

Key to Map 10.

■	Administrative Centres of Governor Generalships
■	Administrative Centres of Oblasts
●	Administrative Centres of Uzeds
\\\\\\\	Vassal States
─ ─ ─ ─	Governor Generalship of the Steppes and of Turkestan
─────	Oblast Divisions
⋯⋯⋯	Uzed Divisions

11 Russian Central Asia in 1917.

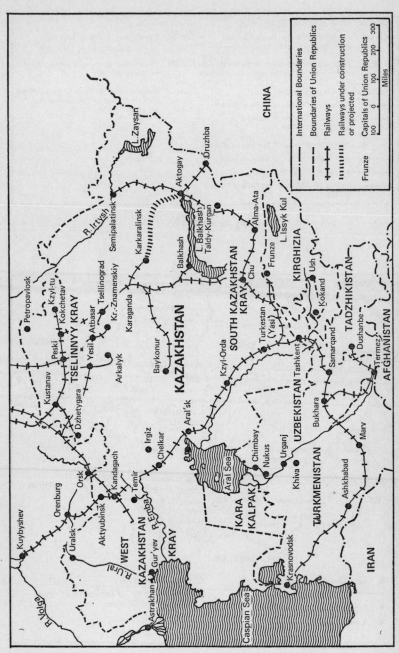

12 The Soviet Socialist Republics of Central Asia in 1964.

368

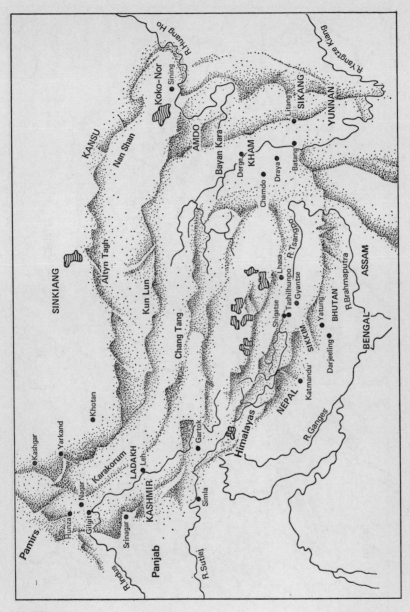

R.Huang Ho

R.Yangtze Kiang

Koko-Nor
Sining

KANSU

SIKANG

YUNNAN

Nan Shan

AMDO

Bayan Kara

KHAM

Litang

Derge

Chamdo

Draya

Batang

Altyn Tagh

Kun Lun

SINKIANG

Chang Tang

R.Tsangpo

Lhasa

Shigatse

Tashilhunpo

Gyantse

ASSAM

R.Brahmaputra

BHUTAN

SIKKIM

Yatung

Khotan

Himalayas

Darjeeling

NEPAL

Katmandu

BENGAL

Kashgar

Yarkand

Gartok

R.Ganges

Karakorum

LADAKH

Leh

Simla

Nagar

KASHMIR

Pamirs

Hunza

Gilgit

Srinagar

Panjab

R.Indus

R.Sutlej

13 Tibet.

369

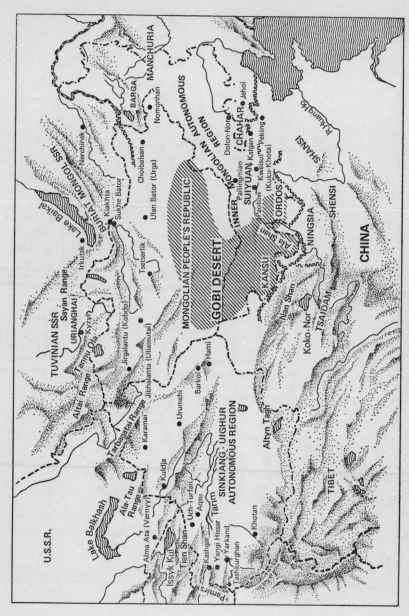

14. Mongolia and Sinkiang.

Index

Arrian, 27
Arsaces, 31, 32
Arsaces Theos, 43
Arsacid Dynasty, 31–2
Arslan, 126
Artabanus, 24
Artacoana, 27
Artaeus, 24
Artayntes, 25
Artyphius, 24
Asad b. 'Abdullah al-Qasri, 67
Asaf Jah (Nizam of Hyderabad), 110
Ashkhabad, 32, 217
Asii (Asiani), 39–40, 41
Asoka, 31, 33
Assassins (see Batinids), 103
Astarabad, 154, 164, 165, 166
Astrakhan, 8, 115, 120, 123, 124, 125, 144, 167, 187, 190–1, 192, 202, 208
Astrakhanids, 144, 167, 187
Athos, 23
Atisha, 85
Atossa, Queen, 24
Atsiz (Khwarazmshah), 76
Aulia-Ata (Dzhambul), 210
Aurangzeb (Mughul), 161, 177–8
Avars, 57, 58
Avidius Cassius, 47
Aya Guz river, 145–6
Aybak, 77
Ayuka Khan, 144
Azanes, 24
Azaq, 120, 123
Azarbayjan, 112, 113, 121, 123, 152, 154, 155, 181, 182, 183
Azeri language, 183
Azes I, 41, 46
Azes II, 43
Azilises, 31

Babur (Mughul), 134, 135, 155, 156, 157, 159–60, 171, 172, 180
Bactra, 3, 33
Bactria, 21, 22, 24, 27–37 passim, 39, 46, 49, 51, 54, 55, 56, 57
Badakhshan, 3, 6, 133, 136, 157, 161, 166, 176–7

Baghchesaray, 125, 194, 195
Baghdad, 7, 15, 69, 71, 103, 112, 151, 152
Baghlan, 42
Bahram II, 51, 52
Bahram IV, 55
Bahram 'Ali Khan, 181
Bahram Shah (Ghaznavid), 181
Bai, 135
Baian-Aul, 208
Baichu, 102
Baitursunov, 228, 229, 235
Bajaur, 29
Baku, 200, 239
al-Baladhuri, 63
Bal'ami, 72
Balasaghun, 73
Balkh, 5, 6, 47, 50, 52, 63, 64, 67, 71, 73, 96, 111, 128, 156, 157, 159, 161, 163, 164, 167, 176–7, 179–80
Baltistan, 136
Bamiyam, 48, 50, 73, 96
Banakat, 96
Baqi Muhammad (Janid), 167
Bardesanes, 44
Barga, 280
Barkyaruq (Seljuqid), 76
Barlas, 108, 132, 150
Barsaentes, 27
Baschich, General, 307
Bashghird, 73
Bashkirs, 144, 189, 234
Bashkiria, 147, 207
Basmachis, 206, 232, 236
Basmil, 73
Batang, 266; monastery, 273
Batinids, 103
Batu (Chingizkhanid), 100, 102, 103, 114–18, 121, 122, 124, 140
Batur (khungtayji), 144, 145, 253, 295
Batyrsha, 189
Batyr Srym Khan, 148
Bayan, 106, 107
Bayazid I (Ottoman), 152
Bayazid II (Ottoman), 158
Bayram Khan, 171, 184
Baysunqar (Timurid), 154

Begi Jan (Mangit), 180
Begram, 47
Behbudi, 230
Behistun, 21
Bekovich-Cherkasskii, Prince, 202, 214
Berke (Chingizkhanid), 103, 116–119, 122
Besnager pillar, 36
Bessus, 27
Bihzad, 156, 157, 171
Bilge, 59
Bilgetigin, 72
Bimaran casket, 49, 50
Birdi Bek (Chingizkhanid), 121
al-Biruni, 44, 61
Bishapur, 74
Bishbaliq, 128
Bishkent valley, 54
Bismil, 60
Bistam, 76, 164, 165
Bon religion, 79, 81–4
Boris Godunov, 125, 126
Borjigin, 89
Börte, 90
Bribsun, 80
Buddhism, 4, 9, 13, 31, 35, 39, 47, 48, 49, 60, 62, 79–85, 109, 128, 141, 144, 146, 252, 254, 289; *Milindapañha*, 35; Tibetan, 243, 244, 246–52, 259–62, 265, 280, 295, 297
Bughra Khan Harun (Qarakhanid), 74, 75
Bukey, 198, 199
Bukhara, 5, 6, 10, 64, 65, 71, 74, 96, 123, 127–33 *passim*, 137, 142, 143, 144, 157, 159, 162, 163, 166, 168–9, 172–87 *passim*, 203, 205, 206, 209, 210–11, 213, 218, 228, 294; People's Republic, 206, 232, 233–5
Bukholz, 202
Bulgar Khanate, 114
Buraq Khan (Chaghatai), 127, 130
Buriats, 279, 280, 281, 289
Burkhan, 311
Burunduk Khan, 142, 158
Bust, 70, 72

Bu-ston, 85
Buydash Khan, 143
Buzurg Khan, 300

Caldiran, 164–5
Calliope, 37
Callisthenes, 27
Cambyses, 21
Capisa, 20, 52
Carmania, 33
Caruq, 74
Carus, Emperor, 52
Caspian Gates, 26
Caspians, 22, 24
Cassander, 30
Castana, 45
Caucasus, 2, 19, 168, 203, 216, 225
Chagan-Nor, 131
Chaghatai (Chingizkhanid), 93, 100, 101, 103, 106, 110, 115, 127, 128–9
Chaghatai Khanate, 109, 112, 118, 119, 122, 127–39, 140, 141, 143, 145, 148, 149–52, 169, 245, 295
Chaghatai Turkish, 156, 162, 171, 184, 238–9
Chaghri Beg (Seljuqid), 75
Chahar province, 246, 252, 277, 283, 285
Chaman Huzuri, 22–3
Chamdo, 266
Chandragupta, 30, 31
Ch'ang-an, 80
Chang Chih-chung, General, 310–311
Ch'ang-chun, 111
Chang Hsueh-lang, 308
Changtreng monastery, 273
Chang Yung, General, 296
Chao Erh-Feng, General, 266, 267
Chao-hui, General, 298
Chapar (Chingizkhanid), 131
Charjui, 6–7, 179
Cherniaev, General M. G., 203, 209–10, 220
Chiang Kai-shek, 271, 307–8, 309, 310, 311
Chi'en-Han Shu, 39